HISTORY OF BROADCASTING: RADIO TO TELEVISION

HISTORY OF BROADCASTING: Radio to Television

Old Wires
and New Waves

The History of the
Telegraph, Telephone, and Wireless

By

Alvin F. Harlow

D. Appleton-Century Company
Incorporated
New York　　　　　　　　*London*
1936

Photographs from Houghton Mifflin Co.; Bell Telephone Laboratories and Radio Corporation of America.

SAMUEL F. B. MORSE

ALEXANDER GRAHAM BELL   GUGLIELMO MARCONI

Old Wires
And New Waves

Reprint Edition 1971 by Arno Press Inc.

© 1936, by Alvin F. Harlow
Reprinted by permission of Hawthorn Books, Inc.

Reprinted from a copy in The Newark Public Library

LC# 70-161145
ISBN 0-405-03566-7

HISTORY OF BROADCASTING: RADIO TO TELEVISION
ISBN for complete set: 0-405-03555-1
See last pages of this volume for titles.

Manufactured in the United States of America

Old Wires and New Waves

ALVIN F. HARLOW

ARNO PRESS and THE NEW YORK TIMES

New York • 1971

FOREWORD

THERE may be those who will think that a disproportionate amount of space is given in this book to the early history of the telegraph, as against the remarkable technical developments of the past quarter or half century. May it be suggested that the birth and infancy of ideas are intrinsically more noteworthy, more important, than their middle age? The centuries of groping for a method of quick communication, the one long century of man's striving to make electricity his servant, the pioneer days of the telegraph, when not only it but all America was simple and crude—these are to most folk to-day so exotic, the last-named phase is to the student so significant a picture of the youth of American society and the nation, that, in the judgment of the author, they should be dealt with in detail for the benefit of a generation which knows them not.

On the other hand, the rapid developments in telegraph, telephone, and wireless in recent days are described at length in newspapers and magazines as they appear; and they come so swiftly and we are so inured to them that the astounding invention of yesterday has to-day become a commonplace, and to-morrow is superseded by something still more miraculous. It is therefore scarcely worth while for so slowly built and so final a publication as a book to attempt chronicling all the minor details of recent progress in communication, especially since these matters become so complex and so abstruse that full explanation of their development and functioning would be too complicated for non-technically minded readers. Nevertheless, these modern developments have not been neglected, but are treated as fully as space limitations and the need for clarity seem to dictate.

As usual, I have leaned heavily in my research upon the

original documents and other materials in the collections of the New York Public Library and the New York Historical Society. The latter's Henry O'Rielly Collection is one of the most valuable telegraph sources in existence.

The great communications companies have all been very helpful. Through the good offices of Mr. William P. Banning, Assistant Vice-President of the American Telephone and Telegraph Company, I spent many hours in personally conducted tours through that company's three huge operating buildings in New York City, any one of which is worth a trip to New York to see; I was overwhelmed with pamphlets, reports, documents, magazine articles, and books; and any and all photographs I desired for illustrations were at my disposal. Mr. Langdon, the librarian; Miss Winburg, keeper of the photographs; Messrs. Fowler and Mills of the Bell Telephone Laboratories, Rood and Lea of the Long Lines Building; Carl and Sedgwick of the New York Telephone Company, all gave their assistance with the courtesy characteristic of the organization.

Mr. E. W. Goode, of the publicity department of the International Telephone and Telegraph Corporation, supplied all the data at his command, loaned books not to be found elsewhere, procured permission for me to see the company's operating rooms, gave me whatever photographs I desired, and searched the country over for older ones which were not in his files.

The Radio Corporation of America, through Messrs. Galvin, Wright, and Weaver, was also very helpful. I was conducted through its operating building and was supplied with photographs and technical information as needed. The Western Union Telegraph Company threw open its library and operating building to me, and the librarians were particularly helpful in looking up special items of information.

Mr. Norvin H. Green of New York, grandson of a famous Western Union president and great-grandson of Peter Cooper, has been an enthusiastic assistant all through my work—supplying books and papers, suggesting sources, loaning me old telegrams and envelopes for reproduction in this volume. At his

FOREWORD

request, his uncle, Mr. Erskine Hewitt, permitted me to examine a mass of correspondence of Peter Cooper and Abram S. Hewitt, regarding the Atlantic Cable and the American Telegraph Company.

Messrs. Frank E. Lawrance of Jersey City and George B. Sloane of New York also loaned rare old telegraph forms for the illustration of this book. Mr. Lawrance likewise contributed a number of private telegraph franking cards from his large collection. Albert Dressler of San Francisco was another such contributor, and gave me some valuable hints.

Among the many who gave assistance in one way and another were the Rochester Historical Society, Cornell University, Professor M. S. Munro of Tufts College, the National Museum at Washington, the United States Signal Corps, Mr. F. W. Crone of the New York Edison Company, Mr. Eugene P. King of Providence, Rhode Island, the Scott Stamp and Coin Company of New York, Dr. Lee de Forest of Los Angeles, the Museum of the City of New York and Miss May Davenport Seymour of that institution, the New York Chamber of Commerce, and Cunard White Star, Limited, of Liverpool, England.

Thanks are also due Messrs. Houghton Mifflin and Company, Charles Scribner's Sons, and Harper and Brothers for permission to use quotations and pictures from their publications.

CONTENTS

ix

CONTENTS

ILLUSTRATIONS

xi

ILLUSTRATIONS

ILLUSTRATIONS

xiii

ILLUSTRATIONS

CHAPTER I

THE CRAVING FOR INSTANTANEOUS COMMUNICATION

As when ... from out a town ... which foes are beleaguering ... at the setting of the sun, beacon fires blaze forth in close succession, and their flame darts on high for those who dwell about to behold, if haply they may come with ships and help them against their ruin.

HOMER, *Iliad.*

PICTURE to yourself a chilly spring night in the year 1183 B.C.—or it may have been the year 1260 or 1335; we cannot be certain because those early historians and epic poets were lamentably unhandy with dates. But after all, it was so long ago that a hundred years or so one way or another doesn't really matter.

Anyhow, it is a coolish spring night in Greece, more than a thousand years before the Christian era, and on the roof of King Agamemnon's palace at Mycenæ a watchman, according to the veracious dramatist, Æschylus, is grousing over his uncomfortable and monotonous job. For ten years the King has been over in Asia Minor, leading the Greek army in the unprofitable siege of Troy. At home, his wife, Clytemnestra, is amusing herself as wives are said sometimes to do when their husbands are absent. A bad lot, Clytemnestra; though it must be admitted that a woman whose husband has been away from home for ten years, waging a war to soothe the injured feelings of a friend whose silly wife had eloped with a young fribble on the enemy side—well, that lady undoubtedly has a legitimate grievance. Though she need not carry it as far as Clytemnestra did.

For several years past the Queen has kept the watchman on the roof of the palace at night, to catch a promised signal which

I

should announce the fall of Troy—a city more than two hundred and fifty miles distant in an air line, and much farther than that by the nearest travel route. How is the signal to come?

The watchman, while the palace below him sleeps, peevishly grumbles at the tedium of his task. "Couching on my elbows on the roofs of the Atreidæ like a dog," "drenched with dew," and suffering "fear instead of sleep," he implores of the Gods "a release from these toils."

Suddenly he springs to his feet and peers eagerly into the darkness. Far away to northward a spark of light, a tiny flame, has come into being. It flickers, wavers, increases in size; it is the expected signal fire. The watchman gives a shout of joy—largely on his own account, not his master's, we fancy. "Ho! Ho!" he cries, according to the dramatist, "I will give a signal distinctly to the wife of Agamemnon, that she, having arisen with all speed from her couch, may raise aloud a joyous shout in welcome to this beacon, if indeed the city of Ilion is taken, as the beacon light stands forth announcing; and I myself will dance a prelude."

This speech alone may be regarded as a sufficient answer to those D. Lit. Hums. who wonder why Greek plays are no longer performed save as a sort of literary votive rite. The subsequent dialogue supplies further proof. The watchman dashes down the stairs, and in a few moments the palace is in a joyous uproar. Lights flash in all the rooms, signal fires blaze outside and altars spring into flame. Of Queen Clytemnestra the chorus, more determinedly stupid than Conan Doyle's Dr. Watson, begs to know the meaning of the tumult; "Thou, daughter of Tyndarus, Queen Clytemnestra, what means this? What new event? What is it that thou hast heard?"

The Queen, with characteristic verbosity, reveals that Troy has fallen. The chorus are frankly skeptical. "Your words have escaped me, in consequence of my disbelief."

CLYT: I say that Troy is in the possession of the Achæans. Do I now speak clearly?
CHO: Joy steals over all my senses, calling forth the tear.

CLYT: Your eye gives token of your friendly sentiments....
CHO: And at what time hath the city been sacked?
CLYT: I tell thee that it was in the night that hath now brought forth this dawn.
CHO: And what messenger could come with such speed?

The Queen explains the remarkable system of signals which she and Agamemnon had arranged, ostensibly that she might rejoice in his victory and his imminent homecoming; in reality to give her opportunity to plan with her paramour for her husband's assassination, when he returns. A watchman stationed on Mount Ida, close by Troy, must have known for days that the fall of the city was near, and could look down into it and see it in flames on that last dreadful night of the siege. As soon as he was satisfied that the Greeks had won, he kindled a great bonfire of dry wood, whose flames leaped many yards into the air and were seen by the second watchman, who waited on the summit of a hill on the island of Lemnos, seventy miles to westward in the Ægean Sea.

From Lemnos the next point of land in the direction of the home palace was in Eubœa, nearly a hundred miles southwestward across the Ægean. But the curvature of the earth and the low elevation of the hills on both shores made it impossible to send a signal in that direction, so a clever detour was arranged— though the Queen does not explain all this as scientifically as we are doing.

Forty miles northwest from Lemnos is Mount Athos, a 6,350 foot peak on the Macedonian shore. To that point the signal was flashed, and from that great elevation a huge blaze could be seen over the earth's convexity by the next watchman, he on Mount Makistos, a hundred miles away to the southwest. Thence the signal was passed by shorter leaps, great piles of dry brush and scrub from the mountain sides bursting into flame on Mount Messapius, on the Crag of Cithæron, on Egiplanctus, until the final flame from the Arachnæan heights was seen by the watcher at Mycenæ.

From very early times mankind has yearned for some means

of instantaneous communication, primarily for purposes of war. In war it is highly desirable to know where the other party is and what he is doing, and to get an advantage of him, if possible. Polybius, noted Greek historian of the second century B.C., discussing fire beacons, then the best known method of signaling, remarks that it is "of the greatest service in warfare, because it is in war that the greatest advantage is derived from opportuneness, and this is best secured by fire signals." Therefore we have had from the dawn of history and doubtless before that, many kinds of signals—the great wooden wardrum and tom-tom of tropical savage peoples, whose booming sounds carry for miles over hill and jungle, the smoke column of the North American Indians, interrupted by flirts of a blanket or animal pelt, the horn blasts and signal fires from the hilltops by other peoples. Carrier pigeons, messengers with flaming torches were swift, but the signal flung through the air was swifter.

The antiquity of the fire beacon is attested by Homer in the *Iliad,* quoted at the beginning of this chapter. Sinon, according to legend, gave the signal by a beacon for the irruption of the men from the wooden horse into Troy.

The Greeks and Persians were early and extensive users of the signal fire. Herodotus mentions two instances; one, Book VII, during the invasion of Xerxes, when three Greek ships on outpost duty on the Magnesian coast, sight the vanguard of the Persian king's fleet, the news is sent to the Greek fleet at Artemisium by signal fires. A year later, Book IX, after Xerxes has decamped to Asia, he is taking it easy at Sardis, hoping to hear that his army under Mardonius has completed the Greek conquest. To bring him news of this, a line of beacons has been established "through the islands." The treatise, *De Mundo,* attributed to Aristotle, says that the dominions of the Great King, stretching from the Hellespont to India, have so complete a system of communication with the capitals, Susa and Ecbatana, by messengers and especially by beacon fires, that the king knows daily of any attempt at revolt or war. Xenophon

4

had a bitter taste of the Persian signal efficiency when, after his famous retreat, he tried to capture a wealthy Persian's castle near Pergamus, but found it stronger than he had expected. While he was battering at it, those inside summoned such powerful army help with their signal fires that Xenophon and his men were happy to save their skins by flight.

Diodorus Siculus, the Greek historian of the first century B.C., says, Book XIX, that Antigonus, "the One-Eyed," the general who took over a part of Alexander the Great's dominion after the latter's death, arranged a smoothly working system of messengers and beacons throughout his empire. The Talmud tells of a system of fire signals arranged by the Jews between Jerusalem and Babylonia: "One went to the top of the mountain and lighted them and waved the flame to and fro, up and down, until he could perceive his companion doing so on the second mountain, and so on to the third mountain. . . ." ". . . Blow the trumpet in Tekoa and set up a sign of fire in Bethaccarem," cries the prophet Jeremiah to the children of Benjamin, "for evil appeareth out of the north and great destruction." [1]

The historian Thucydides describes many fire signals used during the Peloponnesian War. In 429 B.C. when the Spartan confederacy made a night attack on Salamis, the warning was flashed to Athens by fire. In the following year when the 212 Plateans and Athenians succeeded in escaping by night from beleaguered Platea, the besiegers sent a beacon signal to Thebes when they discovered the heroic band climbing the wall, but the Plateans remaining inside the city were ready for this, and muddled the situation by lighting counter-signals to render those of the Spartan-Theban allies unintelligible. There was a difference in signaling the movement of enemies and friends, as Aristotle and others explain; the lights indicating an enemy were kept in motion, the contrary were stationary.

One evening in 427 when a Spartan fleet of 53 sail was lying off Sybota on the western shore of Greece, it was noti-

[1] Jeremiah VI, I.

5

fied by beacons from the island of Leucas just after nightfall
that a fleet of 60 Athenian triremes was stealing up the coast,
and so was ready to give them battle. The fire signal was employed at Torone to inform Brasidas, the Spartan general, who
was lying in wait near by, that certain gates of the town had
been left open by traitors, so that he might rush in and capture it. In the year 411, when 73 Spartan ships slipped away
from 67 Athenian vessels at Lesbos and made for Sestos,
Athenian lookouts sent the news ahead by fire. Undoubtedly
the use of beacons was common practice in those times.

Among the Romans one finds here and there references to
smoke and fire used for signaling. Livy, Book XXII, mentions
the system of watch-towers and signals in Spain for use against
the pirates. Plutarch, describing the state of the Mediterranean before Pompey's famous anti-pirate campaign, says that
the freebooters were well equipped with beacon towers. In the
works of ancient poets and dramatists—Sophocles, Aris-
tophanes, Pindar and others—are found many references to
beacon fires.

Such signals continued in use for more than twenty centuries after those primitive days. In Scott's *Lay of the Last
Minstrel,* the approach of the hated Southrons is announced by
lines of beacons leading from the border at the Cheviot Hills
and the River Tweed throughout Scotland:

> Till high Dunedin the blazes saw
> From Soltra and Dumpender Law;
> And Lothian heard the Regent's order
> That all should bowne them for the border.

Again in the same poem,

> On Penchryst glows a bale of fire,
> And three are kindling on Priesthaughswire.

Bale is an old word for bonfire or signal fire, which explains
an act of the Scottish Parliament passed in 1455, fixing the
signal code. One bale burned at a station was a signal that

the English were coming; two bales, that they were come; four bales side by side, they were in great force.

When the Spanish Armada approached England in Queen Elizabeth's time, the watchmen were ready, all around the coast. Macaulay thus describes that night when the great fleet was sighted:

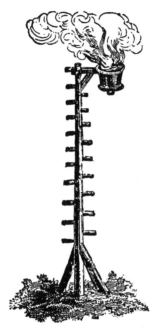

A SEVENTEENTH CENTURY
BEACON

From Eddystone to Berwick bound, from Lynn to Milford Bay,
That time of slumber was as bright and busy as the day.
For swift to east and swift to west the ghastly war-flame spread.
High on St. Michael's Mount it shone; it shone on Beachy Head.
Far on the deep the Spaniard saw, along each southern shire,
Cape beyond cape, in endless range, those twinkling points of fire.

The appended illustration is that of an English seventeenth-century beacon fixed on a post, with steps for climbing to place

7

fuel and light it. The beacon itself consisted of a wrought-iron basket, in which was usually burned a coil of rope smeared with tar. Undoubtedly a similar type fixed to a lighter, portable pole was used during the Peloponnesian War in the fifth century B.C. to give those signals in which the flame was moved to and fro or up and down.

One of the most curious of early telegraphs was the human voice. Diodorus Siculus says that the great Persian King Cyrus established lines of signal towers on high hilltops extending in several directions from his capital, and on these vantage points were men with leathern lungs who shouted messages in short, staccato sentences from one to another with great rapidity. Darius Hystaspes, a mighty successor of Cyrus, is also credited with using the vocal telegraph. Stentor, the noted Greek herald before Troy, roared the commander's orders to the besieging host with the voice of fifty men.

Julius Cæsar, while in Gaul in 53 B.C., hearing of some disorders in Rome and believing that he had the Gauls pretty well subdued, hastened back to the capital, leaving his army in winter quarters. But no sooner was his back turned than some Gallic chieftains began to conspire. The tribe of the Carnutes agreed to start an uprising if the other tribes would back them up. Under two daring chiefs, they rendezvoused near Orléans and massacred all the Romans there, including Cæsar's commissary of that department. The news spread throughout Gaul with lightning quickness. It is said to have traveled to the Arverni at Gergovia, in present-day Auvergne, about one hundred and sixty miles, between sunrise and the end of the first watch, 9 A.M. Men stationed in low towers or signal posts on hilltops shouted the news from one to another in a peculiar code of "sonorous monosyllables." This method of communication existed in some degree in Gaul until the Middle Ages. Remains of some of the towers could still be seen on hill-summits in France in recent years.

One hears of the people in Albania and Montenegro using this lung telegraph not so many years ago, and of the Kaffirs of South Africa doing a bit of it during their wars with the French and English in the latter part of the nineteenth century. Sir Samuel Moreland invented in 1670 the "Tuba Stentoro-phonica," an early megaphone, by means of which he conversed with jolly King Charles II at a distance of a mile and a half. Vague references seem to indicate that Alexander the Great had something of the sort three hundred years before Christ.

There is a knack of pitching the voice in the proper manner which causes it to carry great distances without apparent commensurate effort. Scott, in *Anne of Geierstein,* tells us that in Switzerland in the Middle Ages, even "The maidens will converse with each other in that manner, from cliff to cliff, through storm and tempest, were there a mile between"; while an Englishman who tried to shout across a gorge above the roar of a torrent could not be heard twenty yards away.

The inhabitants of the island of Gomera, in the Canaries, have a curious whistling language by which they converse from mountain to crag across the deep valleys and gorges of their rough little domain. With the aid of tongue, lips, teeth and fingers they make shrill whistles take the form of words. A traveler [2] tells how a woman, with her lips drawn tight across her teeth in a sort of death's head grin, made her whistle sound the word, "Pepe." The natives say, "Just whistle and speak the word at the same time"; easier said than done for a beginner. Conversations were held for this traveler, and the answers of the men on the opposite mountain showed that they understood every word. Various references show that this whistling language has been in use in Gomera for centuries.

How long ago did it occur to human beings that the glint of sunlight from a polished surface might be used as a signal? Many more centuries than we imagine. Herodotus tells of a signal flashed from Athens to Marathon by means of a burnished shield at the time, 480 B.C., when the Greeks were about to come to grips with Darius's army. Xenophon mentions

[2] Gest Very in *New York Times Magazine,* March 3, 1935.

one such signal given by Lysander before the Battle of Ægospotamos. King Demetrius of Macedonia is represented as giving the signal for battle at Salamis in Cyprus by displaying a gilded shield.

Henry Cornelius Agrippa, in a learned treatise published in Antwerp in the sixteenth century, seems to be describing the heliograph when he says that Pythagoras knew about it. The great Pharos or lighthouse at Alexandria, erected nearly three hundred years before Christ, is said by some to have had a reflecting mirror for signaling on the top of it, probably of burnished metal, for such was the material of ancient mirrors.

What method of signaling did the Emperor Tiberius use in his retreat in the island of Capri, from which he ruled Rome so ably for the last ten years of his life—what else than the heliograph? Tacitus pictures him, an old man of more than seventy, standing on a rocky point of the island, looking towards the hills on the mainland for news of the execution of the traitor Sejanus, which he had ordered, but which might prove fatal to himself. He had a ship ready and loaded with his treasure, on which to flee if Rome turned against him. But from the hill on shore the world flashed that all was well, and the old man turned and went back to his villa, to rule—partly by telegraph—for six years more.

The Moors in Algeria were using the heliograph as far back as the eleventh century A.D. But after ancient Rome, one hears nothing more of it in Europe for many hundreds of years.

The heliostat, a device by which a flash may be sent in any desired direction, regardless of the sun's motion, was invented by Willem Jakob van 's Gravesande (1688-1742), a Dutch physicist. The discovery of the art of making mirrors by silvering one side of a glass made greater distances possible with the heliograph. Early in the nineteenth century Johann K. F. Gauss, the German mathematician, discovered by experiments that the flash from a mirror one inch square could be seen 7 miles. With a much larger mirror the distance could be enormously increased. But little was done with the heliograph until the Morse dot-and-dash code was devised.

In 1861, the United States Coast Survey, testing a mirror equatorially mounted in the Lake Superior region, found that they could send signals as much as 90 miles. By 1890 the army, working from mountain peaks in Arizona, had been able to flash a message 215 miles. The British took it up, and added night signaling with an electric or calcium light, the dots and dashes being made by alternately exposing and masking the light. They employed the heliograph in the Afghan and Boer Wars, and it was also extensively used in the World War.

The invention of the rocket in the seventeenth century supplied another means of signaling much used by armies and navies until recent years. Thomas Moore in *Lalla Rookh* (1817), represents Hafed, his Persian fire-worshiper hero, as being called from his sweetheart's side by calcium lights and rockets:

> With sudden start he turned
> And pointed to the distant wave
> Where lights, like charnel meteors, burn'd
> Bluely, as o'er some seaman's grave
> And fiery darts, at intervals
> Flew up all sparkling from the main,
> As if each star that nightly falls
> Were shooting back to heav'n again.

"My signal lights! I must away...."

It was also in the middle seventeenth century that flags were first used for sending messages by the Duke of York, afterwards James II, in the English navy; though we have a right to suspect that not the dull-witted James but some unknown genius originated the idea.

Experimenters were busy as bees during that century, wrestling with the problem of gratifying mankind's desire to send a message through the air as quick as light. The invention of the telescope gave them many ideas. One Schottus proposed to spell out signs with huge letters at hilltop stations, while the next station watched the process through a telescope.

Another enthusiast named Kessler would adapt the system to the night by placing the letters, cut out of plank, one after another over the end of a cask, inside which a light was burning. In 1684, Dr. Robert Hooke suggested his improvement upon these ideas which will be discussed in the next chapter.

There have been other and curious instances of signaling; that line of cannon, for example, within hearing distance of each other from Buffalo to Albany and thence down the Hudson to New York, by which word was sent to New York in 1825 that Governor De Witt Clinton and his party had started from Buffalo through the Erie Canal in its grand opening celebration. The news traveled from Buffalo to New York in eighty minutes, and a "reply" thundered back in about the same time.

CHAPTER II

SEMAPHORE, OR VISUAL TELEGRAPHS

Then the wooden telegraph's long arm
Had just been taught to indicate alarm.

JOHN PIERPONT.

THOSE ancient fire signals were such a nuisance—you had to burn so many fires at once to let your allies know that sixteen enemy ships were coming up the coast, and so on —that an Arcadian Greek named Æneas Tacticus set himself to find something simpler. The device which he conceived must have cost him considerable mental travail, for it was rather more complicated than the old system, and unless perfectly handled, less dependable.

He proposed cylindrical earthen jars, four and one half feet high and one and a half feet in diameter, all precisely the same size, one to be placed at each signal station. In each there was to be a disk of cork, nearly fitting the jar, but small enough to slide up and down inside it. Set in the center of the disk was a light rod which protruded through the mouth of the jar. Spaces, three fingers wide, were marked off on the rod, each one marked with some message: "Enemy cavalry has passed the border"; "Light infantry ditto"; "Enemy retreating"; "Fleet coming to your assistance"; and so on, for the full length of the rod.

Next, small holes, all of exactly the same size, were drilled, one in the bottom of each jar, and corks fitted to them. The jars were now filled with water and the cork disks set afloat in them. When one station wished to give news to another, it set up the warning beacon which called that station. At the moment that the other station acknowledged the call by showing a

13

light, both operators pulled the stoppers from the bottoms of their jars, and the corks began to descend simultaneously. When the sender observed that the cork had sunk until the desired message was opposite the top of the jar, he displayed another light, and the receiver instantly stopped the outlet of his jar and noted the fact marked on·the rod, "Our army is retreating," or whatever it was.

This device required such hairline accuracy of handling that we have no assurance that it was ever used.

All these beacon systems were absolutely rigid; that is, the only messages they could send were a few which had been agreed upon beforehand. Two Greeks named Cleoxenus and Democlitus saw that what was needed was a system by which words could be spelled out through the air just as they were on paper. They made an attempt to create such a device, but bogged down on the job and the historian Polybius, who lived 204 to 125 B.C., took it over and put on the finishing touches. At least, that is Polybius's story. But no matter who did it, it contained the fundamental principle of the best systems of signaling which were developed in the centuries to come.

‹These Greek inventors divided the alphabet into five groups of letters, which were marked upon pieces of plank in regular sequence, thus:

A	Z	Λ	Π	Φ
B	H	M	P	X
Γ	Θ	N	Σ	Ψ
Δ	I	Ξ	T	Ω
E	K	O	Y	

Each signal station was to have a set of these boards. At each station there was also to be a fence closely built of plank, as

14

high as a man's head and several yards long. To announce the beginning of a message, the sender raised two torches, the observer responded with two. It was advisable, of course, to reduce the message to the fewest possible number of words. To spell out a word, the sender then raised torches at the left end of the fence to indicate the number of the plank, torches at the right to indicate the number of the letter on the plank. Supposing the name DARIUS ($\Delta A P E I O \Sigma$) is to be sent: D (Δ) is on the first plank and is the fourth letter. Hence raise one torch at the left and four at the right. A is the first letter on the first plank, so one torch is next raised on either side—and so on. After each letter was shown, the lights were to be veiled by lowering them behind the fence.

Again there is no record of this system's ever having been used. And there the matter of semaphore signaling rested for seventeen or eighteen hundred years.

One of the busiest minds of the seventeenth century was that of Dr. Robert Hooke (1635-1703). Every little while he bobbed up before a meeting of the Royal Society in London to read some paper or to report or perform some experiment in physics, mechanics or mathematics. About 1767, he toyed with the idea of telegraphing by means of symbols of some sort, to be displayed on high places and read through telescopes—for again that instrument was the inspiration.

The idea did not quite work itself out then; but sixteen years later, when the Turks laid siege to Vienna, and were finally beaten off only with the aid of Jan Sobieski of Poland, Dr. Hooke was fired again by the notion of devising some means by which a beleaguered city, for example, might communicate with its allies on the outside. He took up his telegraph once more, developed it, and made a report on it with drawings before the Royal Society in 1684. His device constitutes another and very important step in the direction of the semaphore telegraph.

Dr. Hooke's own drawings of his machine are reproduced herewith. His idea was to reduce the alphabet to simpler characters, and to have some symbols which would mean whole sentences. The two crescent-shaped pieces of wood or metal shown in the drawing were to be used in various ways as preliminary signals. When turned towards each other to form a

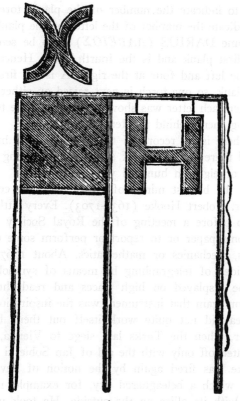

DR. HOOKE'S SEMAPHORE

letter **O** they meant, "I am ready to communicate." The next station answered by placing them back to back, thus,)(as in the picture, meaning, "I am ready to observe." A single curve with points facing towards the right, thus (meant, "I shall be ready presently"; with points towards the left) "I see plainly what you shew." A single one with points turned upward requested, "Shew the last again"; with points turned downward, "Go slower."

A mere right-angled symbol, shown in eight different positions, stood for eight letters of the alphabet. Dr. Hooke did not take time to work out a whole vocabulary. He was too busy, he said, which meant that his restless mind was too eager to pass on to something else. It was needless for him to devise all the symbols, anyhow, he thought:

... since, whensoever such a Way of Correspondence shall be put into Practice, those, and many more than I can think of at present will of themselves occur; so that I do not in the least doubt but that with a little Practice thereof, all Things may be made so convenient that the same Character may be seen at *Paris*, within a Minute after it hath been exposed at *London*, and the like in Proportion, for greater Distances.

Again the world was too slow in understanding to do anything with the idea, though a Frenchman, Guillaume Amontons, took it up a few years later with the French Academy of Sciences and improved Hooke's device; and so the matter rested for another century and more.

In 1763, the Liverpool (England) Town Commission placed a signal station at Bidston, on the Cheshire side of the Mersey estuary, where there was an outlook to sea, so that a vessel could be seen some hours before it reached port. Here more than seventy-five tall masts were erected in a long row, each representing some important Liverpool ship-owner, and on which his own house flag was hoisted when one of his vessels was sighted, homeward bound. The signal could be seen from the Merchants' Coffee House and other points of vantage in the city, and preparations were made for receiving the cargo.

Herman Melville, in his *Redburn,* published in 1849, recalls that the old church of St. Nicholas, on the water-front near Prince's Dock, Liverpool, helped to spread the news to wives, sweethearts and kinspeople of homeward-bound sailors. This church, dedicated to the patron saint of mariners, had a fine chime of bells. "Thirty or forty years ago," says Melville, "these bells were rung upon the arrival of every Liverpool ship from a foreign voyage." Then, as for many decades afterwards, the homecoming of a ship from foreign parts was one of the most important of events, not only to a seacoast city, but to its nation.

Later the Bidston masts were superseded by a semaphore, and in 1827, this was connected by a line of such telegraphs with the lookout station at Holyhead, seventy miles away, whence information of the vessel's approach could be obtained much earlier.

When Chappe's semaphore—the Chappes were three French brothers, discussed later—became famous in the closing years of the eighteenth century, Richard Lovell Edgeworth, a prominent Irish gentleman, well known in British social, sporting and governmental circles, declared that he had used a device of the sort more than a quarter century before. In his memoirs he tells how, in 1767, when a race between two famous horses was pending at Newmarket, Lord March, talking one night at Ranelagh to Sir Francis Delaval, expressed regret at being unable to attend the race, but said that by relays of express riders which he would place, he expected to hear the result at an early hour at the Turf Coffee House in London, "and I shall manage my bets accordingly."

Edgeworth, then a young man of twenty-three, was standing by, and asked when he expected to receive the news. "By 9 in the evening," said Milord. Edgeworth, who had read Dr. Hooke and others on the subject, said, "I can get it by 4 in the afternoon." March ridiculed the statement, whereupon Edgeworth offered to wager £500 that he could have the word by 5 P.M. Sir Francis Delaval, who knew Edgeworth as a clever scientific experimenter, looked into his face for encouragement, and then offered to lay another £500 on his side. Lord Eglintoun did the same, and a man named Shaftoe and some one else in the party took up their bets, which were all put into writing at the Turf Coffee House next day.

SEMAPHORE, OR VISUAL TELEGRAPHS

Edgeworth confided his scheme to Sir Francis alone, and they set up an experimental telegraph between Delaval's home in Hampstead and a house in Great Russell Street, Bloomsbury. What they needed was simplicity itself, for there were only two signals necessary, one for either horse. Naturally Edgeworth and his friends won their wagers. Perhaps it was the birth of his daughter about this time—in after years famous as the novelist, Maria Edgeworth—which diverted his mind from his telegraph, for he made no further effort to use or improve it until the Chappe semaphore became known.

Some time before the breaking out of the French Revolution, three brothers named Chappe, youths in their teens, were pupils in two French boarding schools—Claude, the eldest, at the Seminary d'Angers, while his brothers were in another school about half a league distant, but within sight of the seminary. It is asserted that the brothers had never read anything on the subject of signaling. Whether this be true or not, Claude devised what was really the first of the semaphores used for many years afterwards, and did it just for the fun of communicating with his brothers daily. It was at first an upright pole, with a movable arm attached to it. The brothers, no doubt conferring by letter, developed the idea further. Two more billets of wood were added to the ends of the main beam, and by setting these arms in various positions, they were able to work out 192 different signals. The school authorities permitted, perhaps encouraged them to erect their apparatus on the school grounds.

The young men believed that they had an idea which was destined to be of public service, and in 1791, some time after they had left their schools, they set up an experimental line in Paris. The populace, with typical mob intelligence, suspected treason to the Republic, overthrew the masts and burned them. A second attempt met the same fate, and the brothers narrowly escaped with their lives. But by this time the Revolutionary government had begun to see merit in the suggestion, and the Assembly voted 6,000 francs for a series of official tests. A line was set up and a committee of three members of the Assembly tested its operation. Their report, dated July 2, 1793, was favorable. It speaks of the sending of a *télégramme*—the first appearance, so far as known, of that word in a written or printed document. Claude Chappe wanted to call the instrument the *tachygraphe,* but was overruled.

The Assembly now took over the brothers' invention, and on August 4, 1793, ordered the construction of a line from Paris via Montmartre to Lille. M. Breguet, a famous watchmaker, aided the Chappes with the mechanism, and a prominent diplomat, familiar with cipher codes, helped to simplify the language so that a certain position of the wooden arms sometimes stood for a whole syllable, word or phrase.

ᚲ Half of Europe was making war at that time upon the bloodstained state which was trying to abolish the monarchistic form of government. The first telegram in history was creaked and clattered out by the waving arms of the machine on the hill of Montmartre on August 15, 1794. Fortunately for the prestige of the telegraph, it was a message of victory; it announced the capture of Quesnoy from the Austrians. A second message sent two weeks later regarding the taking of the town of Condé has erroneously been given first place by most historians. When the Convention replied to the victorious commander, "The Army of the North deserves the gratitude of the country," France was thrilled to its boundaries by the speed of the new communication.

Claude Chappe was made chief telegraph engineer of the Republic, with his brothers as his assistants. The Lille line was extended to Dunkirk in 1798 and to Brussels in 1803; and meanwhile other lines were building. In 1805, Napoleon, then Emperor, extended a line to Milan. After Claude Chappe's death that year, his brothers took over the management of the system. Under them the northern line was extended to Amsterdam, and other arteries were thrown out through Strasbourg to Mainz, to Calais, to Brest, while the Italian chain was extended to Venice and Mantua. At the end of the Napoleonic era, France had 1,112 miles of telegraphs, served by 224 stations. During the next twenty years many more extensions took place.

SEMAPHORE, OR VISUAL TELEGRAPHS

The accession to power of Louis Philippe in 1830 was disastrous to the Chappe brothers, for the Citizen King dismissed them and filled their places with friends of his own. He greatly extended the system, however, and by 1844, France had 533 stations and 5,000 kilometers of line. Through the country, a great number of semaphores were located on the stumpy Gothic church towers from which the spires had fallen ages before, or on which the projected spires had never been completed. Of course, every station must have a telescope with which to read the signals; those were halcyon days for the optical instrument makers.

In the early 1790's, the British army on the Continent did almost nothing in the way of signaling, orders and information being conveyed by messenger. During a campaign an observant British officer noticed near Menin in Flanders a distant windmill on a hill with two of its long arms broken off; and he observed that the two remaining arms changed their position now and then, such changes being quickly followed by movements of the French troops. He discussed his suspicions with a messmate, the Duke of York's chaplain, Rev. John Gamble, who had a flair for mechanics, and who now became deeply interested in the subject of signaling. When a drawing and alphabet of Chappe's telegraph were found on a French prisoner, they were taken at once to Gamble, who set to work to produce a better system. The Duke asked him to investigate and report on all known methods of signaling. The result, entitled, *Observations on Telegraphic Experiments,* was printed by the Duke early in 1795, and a copy sent to the Admiralty. Though the Admiralty had no telegraph then, a line of signal stations had been erected along the coast, whereby numbers of black balls hoisted in air could convey a few prearranged signals as to ship movements.

Gamble was encouraged to experiment with his telegraph ideas on the hills near Portsmouth, and there he worked out a machine entirely different from Chappe's. It was a vertical frame holding five shutters which could be opened or closed so as to make thirty-one changes. But when he laid his plan before the Admiralty, he was horrified to learn that another clergyman, Lord George Murray, a younger son of the Duke of Atholl, had barely preceded him with a six-shutter frame capable of sixty-three changes. The Admiralty accepted Murray's machine, awarded him £2,000 for the idea, and proceeded to build some lines along the coast.

Gamble now turned to another principle, and devised a signal with five rays which could be thrust out from a post by lazy tongs. It was much lighter than the cumbersome frame required for the shutters, and could be carried or even set up in an ordinary wagon. But though he tried again and again to obtain a hearing from the Admiralty, it refused to listen to him.

Thereafter for twenty years, whenever peace was made on the Continent, interest in telegraphs slackened in England, and was quickly revived again whenever Napoleon began to itch for another war. At one time our old friend R. L. Edgeworth is found superintending the building of a Government line between Dublin and Galway. In a telegraph line along the French coast the British, peering through their telescopes, noticed a modification of the Chappe system which struck their fancy, and a British officer named Thicknesse still further improved the device, his machines being used from 1808 onward in the Channel Islands. The name *semaphore,* formed from two Greek words and meaning loosely "signal displayer," was now born and bestowed on this form of signaling instrument. In 1811, the signal stations along the east coast of England were equipped with the new machines.

In 1814, when Napoleon was sent to Elba, telegraphs and signals were for the most part abandoned in England; but when the wily Corsican escaped from the island a few months later and France rose, cheering, to his standard, the Britons fell into a somewhat comical flurry of rehabilitating the systems. Admiral Sir Home Popham, an advocate of semaphores as against the shutter species, now worked out another improvement whereby the post upholding the arms could be revolved, thus making the signals readable from various directions. His telegraph soon replaced the shutter machines. There seems to have been little or no use in Europe of the system sometimes employed in early times in America, of spelling out words by hoisting black and white kegs on a rope attached to tall spars.

Among the other countries of Europe, Sweden was the quickest to adopt the semaphore, setting up an adaptation of the Chappe plan in 1795. In 1802, it was established in a modified form in Denmark. The Germans had a primitive and clumsy form in 1798, and comparatively little was done towards developing telegraphs in that country until long after the Napoleonic incubus was removed. In 1832, Prussia established a state line connecting Berlin with Magdeburg, Paderborn, Cologne, Coblentz and Treves, to which other lines were soon added. Herr Treutler of Berlin also developed a telegraph for railway use which combined the ideas of the semaphore and heliograph—the two movable arms each being furnished with a series of mirrors.

In Russia Nicholas I, who reigned from 1825 to 1855, saw great possibilities in the semaphore, and organized a telegraph system on a huge scale, connecting St. Petersburg with Warsaw, Moscow and other important cities. The instruments were set on stone towers of handsome appearance, high enough to overlook the tall pines of the dark Russian forests, and some five or six miles apart. The system cost many millions of rubles, and was well manned. The line from St. Petersburg through Warsaw to the German frontier required 220 stations staffed by six men each, or 1,320 operatives all told. The department heads and general administration staff numbered many more.

The chief weakness of the semaphore system, especially in regions such as the vicinity of London, was shown by a report that on 133 days during the fiscal year 1839 to 1840, the Admiralty was unable to communicate between its office and Chatham dockyard because of fog and smoke. On such days telegrams were carried by messenger to some near point to Chatham, and wigwagged from there.

23

OLD WIRES AND NEW WAVES

The semaphore was at first almost monopolized by the forces of war. It was with what seems at the present day almost unbelievable slowness that the French and then the English began to realize its commercial possibilities. The final removing of the Napoleonic blight in 1815 left men's minds free to promote the arts of peace, and the telegraph began to be known as an agency of commerce.

In the early 1840's, the India Mail was a matter of tremendous importance to England, and many minds were bent on the problem of rushing it to British shores at greater speed. In 1844 to 1845, for example, it was coming via the Red Sea, across the Suez Isthmus, then by ship through the Mediterranean to Marseilles, and from there hurried across France to Calais by horse diligence. The letters and papers were carried in sealed boxes; but accompanying these was a bag containing a digest of the news from India which a mounted messenger snatched at Marseilles and galloped to Calais, outstripping the diligence. A still more concise summary was taken from the bag at Marseilles and telegraphed to Calais, where a fast boat lay champing at the bit, waiting to rush it to British officialdom and the newspapers. The fly in the ointment was that French journalists "stole" the news from the telegraph en route, and were able to publish it from twelve hours to a day ahead of the London papers, which enraged the British editors almost to the point of apoplexy. "The insolent and conceited jealousy," fumed one of them, "which has marked the whole policy of France for some years past renders her people little deserving of the benefits conferred upon them by the selection of the present route for the conveyance of mails."

To Alexandre Dumas alone among the novelists of that age does the semaphore seem to have appealed as an element of romance. It appears several times in *The Count of Monte Cristo,* which was one of his few romances dealing with his own period. In that story a poorly paid telegraph tender on the line from Paris to Spain laments to a passing traveler, who

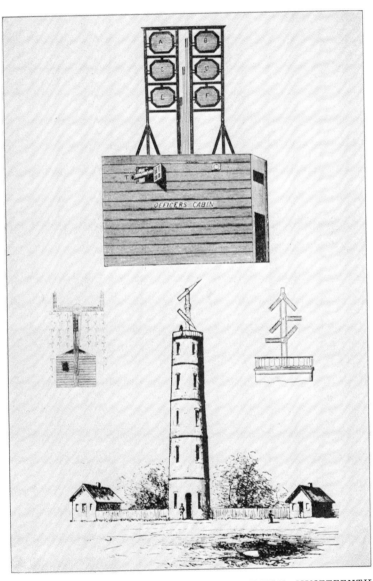

Top—BRITISH SHUTTER SEMAPHORE, EARLY NINETEENTH CENTURY. *Left*—GERMAN SEMAPHORE, 1798. *Right*—PRUSSIAN SEMAPHORE, 1832. *Bottom*—RUSSIAN SEMAPHORE, 1850

happens to be Edmond Dantes himself, that the dormice are eating his fruit. By pretending to suggest a remedy, Monte Cristo tricks the telegrapher into sending a masked message of great political importance and thus encompasses the ruin of one of his enemies. Later the Count himself is said to be visiting Paris to promote a new telegraph invention.

America was not long in noticing the development of the telegraph idea in Europe.'In those days when a blank, dead pall of silence fell behind every vessel, every traveler as soon as the port or home faded from view, and might not be lifted again for months or years, the news hoped for most eagerly of all was that of the sighting of a ship, one of the small, comparatively frail vessels of the times, whose venturing into the vast, impelled only by capricious winds, was a proof of the boundless daring of humankind. Thousands watched eagerly for its coming—wives, parents, sweethearts, kinsmen, friends to whom some one on board was important or to whom it might bring letters from the other side of the world, merchants for whom it brought goods or cash for cargoes already shipped, exporters and traders who anxiously awaited news of the foreign markets, bankers for whom it did business abroad and to whom the foreign money situation was important, journalists who could hardly wait to lay hands upon its news of other lands. This is why all the early telegraphs in America were erected on outlying points of land to report to near-by cities the approach of homecoming vessels, from one to several hours before they docked or cast anchor in the harbor.

In 1799, when the name of The Castle in Boston Harbor was changed to Fort Independence, the merchants of the city gave the commandant there three flags, with which he was to signal to shore the coming of a square-rigged ship, a brig or a schooner respectively. For years thereafter, in the shipping columns of Boston papers one saw such items as "Signal at the Fort for a Ship," "Brig below the Fort at Sunset," and so on, no effort being made to identify them. In later years, the merchants had a watchman stationed in the cupola or lantern of the old State House to watch for sails.[1]

On October 24, 1800, Jonathan Grout of Belchertown, Massachusetts, a Boston lawyer and Master of Arts of Dartmouth, procured a patent or charter for a line of semaphore telegraphs from Martha's Vineyard to Boston. "The Vineyard" was a good place for sighting not only coasting vessels, but those coming from the West Indies, South America or around Cape Horn. A year later Grout's line was not yet completed, for the Boston *Gazette* announced in October, 1801, that : "A line of telegraphs has been completed from the Vineyard to Cohasset. On October 21st, information of the arrival of the ship *Mercury* at the Vineyard from Sumatra was very expeditiously and correctly communicated, passing through eleven different stations. The line will be extended to Boston." Two or three weeks later the line was open to Dorchester Heights, and the *Gazette,* on November 13th, announced the arrival at the Vineyard of the sloop *Lucy* of Boston from Baltimore and the brig *Betty* of Portland from Demarara. "The above despatch information was communicated to this town through fourteen different telegraphs."

A few days later Grout announced through the *New England Palladium* that he had established a ninety-mile line of telegraphs to Martha's Vineyard, had a Boston office on Orange Street, "and is ready to convey correct intelligence reciprocally through said line." The fees, he added, were "rated according to a scale of reasonable proportions from $2.00 to $100. To know more of which please apply as above from 8 A.M. to 11 A.M. or from 6 to 8 P.M."

Sometimes the weather embarrassed Grout as it did all visual telegraphers, and at least once he apologized through the newspapers because a brig which had passed the Vineyard reached Boston before the news could be semaphored. To stimulate busi-

[1] William Upham Swan's interesting paper, "Early Visual Telegraphs in Massachusetts," in *Proceedings of the Boston Society for 1933,* from which much material in this chapter regarding the Boston telegraphs is drawn.

ness, he would now and then insert a tantalizing line in the papers, "The proprietor of the *Telegraph* has many items regarding ships," or "Intelligence is attained of divers vessels in distress at the Vineyard."

In 1804, he raised his rates. For the first news of the appearance of a schooner or sloop from domestic ports a subscriber paid $10; if the vessel came from Europe the fee was $18; or if from a far eastern or western port, $25. For brigs and scows from the same quarters, the fees were $15, $25 and $30, and for barks and ships, $20, $30 and $40 respectively. The rates seem pretty stiff to us, and evidently did to the public of that day, for Grout placed his affairs in a receiver's hands in 1807, and the last telegram was sent on April 24th of that year. Swan says that the course of Grout's pioneer line may still be traced by no less than seven eminences bearing the name of Telegraph Hill between Martha's Vineyard and Boston, all former sites of Grout's semaphores, and by Telegraph Street in Dorchester, leading to the old summit station.

In 1807, William Duane, editor of the *Aurora* of Philadelphia, was urging President Jefferson to study Europe's example and establish telegraph lines between the principal ports and the seat of Government. But the Government saw no reason for venturing farther into the matter of communication than the postal service. Five years later that busy soul, Christopher Colles, endeavored to interest New York and vicinity in a telegraph. Colles, then growing old, had been an early advocate of canals and a piped water supply for cities, and had seen both suggestions slowly being carried out. In July, 1812, he advertised in the New York papers that:

Mr. Colles, having completed his Telegraphs, informs the public that their Operations will be shown from the top of the Custom-House on Tuesdays, Thursdays and Saturdays, from 4 until 6 in the afternoon. Admittance, 50 cents.—The subscribers' tickets will be received.

A few days later, he published a long advertisement, declaring that he had

27

... with the assistance of God, the giver of all good things, been able to discover and invent two or three practical modes of executing this important object—the simplest of which exhibits figures, letters, words and sentences, by night or by day, either for the universal communication of unexpected intelligence, letter by letter, or by preconcerted sentences to any extent, for any event which may be expected and registered for that purpose.

Notwithstanding the "lamentable consideration" which he sadly admitted "that the utility of any improvement is not always a sufficient stimulation to insure success, and although the minds of intelligent persons are sometimes so obscured by prejudice or influenced by jealousy as to be invincible even by the most lucid arguments and incontestable facts," Colles nevertheless lectured at the Custom House on his device, and succeeded in getting sufficient financial backing to set up a semaphore on Sandy Hook, from which, via Coney Island, news of vessels sighted was relayed into New York.

The War of 1812 had just begun, and as it was principally a naval war, one marvels that the Government did not see the importance of placing semaphores along the coast to report war-ship movements. The State and City of New York had placed a signal station on Staten Island, which merely hoisted colored balls when ships were sighted; and there was consternation in the city one day in 1813 when four black balls and two white ones were raised, announcing four enemy ships of the line and two frigates outside of Sandy Hook. Perhaps the sight of the signal station reporting them, as undoubtedly seen from the decks of the squadron, was sufficient to deter them from entering the harbor.

In 1813 Colles published a pamphlet on his machine, one paragraph of which was headed:

CELERITY OF THE CORRESPONDENCE

As it has been found by experiment that 84 letters can be exhibited by this machine in five minutes, or 300 seconds, to the distance of one telegraphic station (averaged at ten miles), it follows that each letter can be exhibited at that distance in 3.57 seconds, and to a hundred miles in 35.7 seconds;—and by the same proportion, from Passamaquoddy to New-Orleans, a distance of 2600 miles, in 928.2 seconds, or 15 minutes, 28 seconds; and a communication of the length of the Lord's Prayer, in 36 minutes, 13 seconds—but say one hour. *Will not this be rapid enough?*

But notwithstanding his arguments and appeals, Colles's line never got farther than Sandy Hook, and was abandoned after a few years.

In 1821, a new line was built under the direction of Captain Samuel C. Reid, who had commanded the famous privateer, *General Armstrong,* during the War of 1812. The lookout who sighted the incoming vessels was on one of the hills of Staten Island. At a test on June 23, 1821, a boy at the Battery received messages with scarcely a mistake.

In 1824, Isaac Wright & Son and other merchants obtained from the Common Council a year's lease of the flagstaff at the Battery, where signals were received, they declaring that the telegraph was of great utility to merchants and ship-owners. Upon the completion of the Merchants' Exchange in Wall Street in May, 1827, the telegraph receiving station was placed on its roof, while at the other end of the line, it was extended to Sandy Hook.

In the latter '30's Stephen Holt's Hotel, corner of Water and Fulton Streets, became the receiving station, the semaphore and operator having a booth on its roof—for messages were often sent from owner to ship as the latter tacked in through the Ambrose Channel. Thus the line remained until Morse's invention eliminated it.

In San Francisco, Telegraph Hill still recalls the famous semaphore of Forty-niner days with its two black arms which pointed straight upward—like those of a man confronted by a highwayman's gun—when a "side-wheel steamer" was sighted; the most joyous moment of the month to the infant metropolis, and one which threw the whole city into an expectant bustle.

Captain Reid remarked that he had found from experiment that it was possible to send "orthographically" 400 words an hour. By orthographic he meant a condensation of part-time system. The spelling out of a word, a letter at a time, was too slow for the taste of most of the semaphorists. The Franklin Institute reported an early and primitive system in which the machine was so simple that it could attain only twelve positions. These were laid out to express figures and numbers as follows:

1	2	3	4	5	6	7	8	9	10	11	12
a	b	c	d	e	f	g	i	l	m	o	s
	p	k	t		v	j	y	r	n	u	z
		q	th		w						sh
		ch			wh						x

If, said the *Journal* of the Institute, signals were seen to read 4, 5—5, 10, 5, 10, 8—1, 12—9, 1, 10, 4, 5, 4—1, 4—2, 1, 9, 4, 8, 10, 11, 9, 5—6, 8, 4—1, 7, 11, 11, 11—10, 5, 10, the message, taking the letters in the upper line, would read "De ememi as landed ad Baldimole fid agooo mem." Here one must use one's intelligence. The message is already fairly clear with the exception of the eighth word. It is apparent that in some cases letters not from the first line, but the second or third line should be used; while in the eighth word, figures instead of letters should be chosen for the first two, giving us "17,000." The message therefore reads, "The enemy has landed at Baltimore with 17,000 men."

To improve on this, a machine was devised capable of more positions, and one simultaneously telescoped letters and words so that one position sometimes meant a word or phrase.

When Sir Home Popham was reforming the British semaphores about 1816, flag codes to spell out words were brought to a higher state of efficiency, and spelled-out messages now began to be sent from ships to shore and thence through the telegraph. Frederick Marryat, famous writer of sea stories, worked out a merchant marine code which was used by British ships for nearly forty years. In America, James M. Elford of Charleston, South Carolina, a native of England and a teacher of navigation, devised a marine signaling system, using seven blue and white flags, with which he compiled a vocabulary containing several thousand combinations. He also set up a harbor telegraph at Charleston which was used for many years to announce incoming ships.

Elford's flag signals soon began to be adopted by American vessels along the Atlantic coast. In Boston, Samuel Topliff, owner of the Exchange Coffee House, extended the range of the harbor signal system to a farther island, so that a vessel could be reported much sooner. John R. Parker, who had become Boston agent for Elford's flag system, set up in 1824 a semaphore telegraph to replace Topliff's black balls and extended it still farther out. The lighthouse keeper on Long Island, who was also Parker's operator, was annoyed by excursioning visitors, and announced through the *Columbian Centinel* in 1826, that:

There will not be any accomodations for Frolickers, as the keeper does not wish to make a tipling-shop of any house belonging to the United States Government. And that no liquors can be obtained, as his whole attention will be devoted to his duty to the Government and to the Marine Telegraph.

Parker, an indefatigable salesman, introduced the Elford flag system pretty thoroughly to American ships. On top of the masts of his harbor telegraph an indicator would first be hoisted which corresponded to the "Conversation Flag" in the Elford code, and which was used to start the message. Below were two other arms with which thousands of combinations were possible. The flag code was capable of making 8,000 signals, and Parker kept ship captains coming to his office to obtain the latest corrections and additions to it.

By this time, practically all American ships had been given numbers, and these numbers were known in all the leading American and English ports. When a ship captain approached a harbor or passed Holyhead on his way in towards Liverpool, he hoisted his number in signal flags. The captains all sent Parker their numbers, so that he had the most complete shipping list in America, and the most extensive signaling vocabulary, several editions of which were published. A lecturer before the Boston Marine Society in 1833, alluding to Parker's system, said:

> It must be evident, even to the most common observer, that no means of conveying intelligence can ever be devised that shall exceed or even equal the rapidity of the Telegraph; for with the exception of the scarcely perceptible relay at each station, its rapidity may be compared with that of light itself.

In 1837, a memorial was presented to the Twenty-fourth Congress, praying for the construction of a telegraph line from New York to New Orleans. The House, before acting, asked the Secretary of the Treasury to report upon the propriety of establishing a system of telegraphs for the United States. The Secretary in turn sent a circular letter to naval and revenue officers and to a few prominent scientists, asking for their opinions as to the best system, distances between stations, the rapidity with which messages could be sent, the possibilities at night and in foggy weather, and so on.

Many of the replies were not illuminating, and showed little knowledge of the subject. Captain Reid of New York found here a golden opportunity to voice a grievance. He said the telegraph built in 1821 to Staten Island was intended to be completed to Sandy Hook, but was not because the Merchants' Exchange showed no disposition to aid him.

Captain Hunter of Baltimore estimated that with a well-managed telegraph, news could be sent from New Orleans to Washington in one hour, or about ten minutes to the hundred miles. He thought Sir Home Popham's system the best—two or more arms near the top of a mast, so moved by ropes as to be capable of a complete revolution. Stations eight miles apart could be built, he said, for about three hundred dollars each. The distance between Boston and Washington, for example, would require about fifty-six such stations, which could be operated at a cost of, say, $18,000 a year.

SEMAPHORE, OR VISUAL TELEGRAPHS

Among the replies was a protest from a New York college professor named Samuel F. B. Morse, who told the Secretary in effect that it would be unwise to spend a lot of money on visual telegraphs, which would be out of commission at night and in bad weather, and would soon be obsolete, anyhow; for he, Morse, had under way a system of telegraphing by electricity which could be used at any time and in any weather and would sweep the semaphore out of existence. He so impressed some of the Congressmen with the possibilities of his device that governmental interest in visual telegraphs quickly died out.

But meanwhile other semaphore lines had been built. There was one between New York and Philadelphia, passing through Mount Holly, which worked for a few years, mostly for the benefit of market operators. When the Morse telegraph forced it out of business, the Philadelphia *Public Ledger,* announcing on January 7, 1846, the sale of its equipment, remarked that it had "no doubt done good service to its owners":

Intelligence was conveyed from one city to another in about ten minutes, by elevating boards on a pole in a particular way.... At night, lamps of different colors were used. The whole concern has been sold for about $3,000. It was a great affair when first established, and many mysterious movements in the Philadelphia stock and produce market were laid at the door of the speculators who worked the telegraph. No doubt the speculators paid them well. But though a good thing at first, it has been superseded by a better. Morse's electro-magnetic telegraph has prostrated all rivals.

In 1844, the year when Morse sent his first message, Parker, shrewdly foreseeing the triumph of electricity, sold his Boston line and retired. New ship telegraph promoters came into the field, however. In 1845, Henry J. Rogers, then superintendent of the United States Magnetic Telegraph at Baltimore, and Furman Black obtained a patent on a new system of marine flag and semaphore signals, to be used in connection with the new electric telegraph. Their grandiose scheme included stations or observatories all along the coast, from which the positions of vessels, especially those in distress, would be signaled and the news scattered by wire. Storm or news schooners and life-boats would be maintained by the company at various points. These visionary proposals never proceeded very far towards realization. Semaphore telegraphs continued in operation in Algeria until 1860. An occasional isolated one still continued waving its arms at scattered points on the world's seacoasts until very recent years. But to-day the so-called semaphores which swing sedately up and down over railway tracks or wink red and green eyes at night in mute warning or release to locomotive engineers are practically the only reminders left of the "telegraph" developed by the Chappes and others a century and a half ago.

The visual telegraphs did indeed perform good and useful service in their day. To an earlier generation, they typified the ultimate in speed, even as radio and the airplane do to us. Long before electricity had been put to work in communications, crack stage-coaches were being named "Telegraph," as a hint at high velocity. Did not Mr. Pickwick and his friends, in the year 1827, according to their chronicler, ride down on the Muggleton Telegraph to that famous Christmas house-party at Dingley Dell?

CHAPTER III

GROPING TOWARDS THE ELECTRIC TELEGRAPH

Soon, like Orion's belt of fire,
Its broad electric arm shall hold
With all a monarch's strong desire
The world and all its varied fold.

E. J. O'REILLY.

THE discovery of lodestone, or magnetic iron ore, was
another event which set men's imaginations to working,
centuries ago. Giambattista della Porta, an Italian natural
philosopher, commenting upon "the wonders of the magnet," in
his book, *Magia Naturalis,* published in 1569, said, "I do not
fear that with a long absent friend, even though he is confined
by prison walls, we can communicate what we wish by means of
two compass needles circumscribed with an alphabet."

Nearly fifty years later, Faminianus Strada of Rome, in his
Prolusiones Academicæ, published 1617, repeated the suggestion, but this time described it as an accomplished fact. As Addison paraphrases Strada, there was "a certain loadstone which
had such a virtue in it that if it touched two several needles,
when one of the needles so touched began to move, the other,
though at never so great a distance, moved at the same time and
in the same manner." The two friends each had one of these
needles set on a pivot in the middle of a dial plate having the
letters of the alphabet around its circumference. When one
friend turned his needle so that it pointed to a letter, the other
needle, a thousand miles away, did the same: "By this means
they talked together across a whole continent, and conveyed
their thoughts to one another in an instant over cities or mountains, seas or deserts." [1]

---

[1] *The Spectator,* No. 241, December 6, 1711.

OLD WIRES AND NEW WAVES

This yarn of Strada's is often cited in awe-stricken tones by modern writers as a prediction of the telegraph. Nearly all of them overlook della Porta's prediction, decades earlier, and the fact that Strada admitted getting his idea from a screed of Cardinal Pietro Bembo's (secretary to Pope Leo X) who died in 1547, and therefore preceded Porta, too, in the suggestion. To be honest, however, it must be admitted that the thing is no more than a coincidence, an accidental coupling of man's longing for quick communication with his semi-superstitious awe of the magnet.

The idea took hold strongly of the imagination of the seventeenth century, and several other amateur scientists who were the best the age afforded, repeated it in various forms. Even long afterwards, in 1744, Mark Akenside sang, in *Pleasures of the Imagination;*

> Two faithful needles—from the informing touch
> Of the same parent stone, together drew
> Its mystic virtue;—
> And though disjoined by kingdoms—though the main
> Rolled its broad surge betwixt—and different stars
> Beheld their wakeful motions—yet preserved
> Their former friendship and remembered still
> The alliance of their birth.

That ardent experimenter, Sir Thomas Browne, actually had two dials fashioned, magnetized two needles, and carefully tested the theory, but found to his disappointment that when he moved one needle, the other paid no attention whatsoever. "That it continued motionless," says Dr. Johnson in his life of Browne, "will be easily believed; and most men would have been content to believe it without the labour of so hopeless an experiment." But Browne, he adds, "appears to have been willing to pay labour for truth." The Doctor forgot or was not aware that in Browne's day the knowledge of magnetism was still in its swaddling clothes.

But slowly men were groping, groping through the murk of ignorance towards the light; and now we begin to discover, at intervals of several years, real suggestions of the telegraph. Electricity had been discovered, and in 1729 an English gentleman, Stephen Gray, sent a spark and excited an electroscope through 293 feet of wire suspended by silk threads. He continued improving his apparatus and lengthening his line until in August, 1730, he sent the impulse through 886 feet of wire. He described the experiment in a letter to the Secretary of the Royal Society of London, dated February 8, 1731. But clearly he was thinking only of the conductivity of electricity and the capacity of metal to carry it; there was as yet no thought of communication.

The Leyden jar was discovered in 1745, and several experimenters during the succeeding year received such shocks from it that some of them well-nigh lost their interest in science. One Boze, on the contrary, wished to die by the current so that the account of his death might be spread upon the Memoirs of the French Academy. News of the discovery spread over Europe and excited great wonder. Amateur electricians went about, gratifying public curiosity at so much per shock. Many of us can remember when the same thing was being done by fakirs at county fairs and elsewhere not so many decades ago, when the shocks were supposed to be good for what ailed you.

The first advance was in the matter of distance. Daniel Gralath, early in 1746, was first to extend the field of the shock, which he did by discharging a battery of three jars through a circle of twenty persons with linked hands. A month or so later Joseph Franz, at Vienna, discharged a jar through 1,500 feet of iron, and next a man sent a charge through 30 ells of insulated wire (the ell in divers countries varies in length from 22¼ to 47 inches, so make your own guess), laid along the bank of the River Pleisse, whose water formed the return half of the circuit.

The Abbé Nollet, a famous clerical scientist of the period, in the same year sent a Leyden jar shock through a chain of 180 of the Royal Guards in Paris, and shortly afterwards demonstrated on a grander scale in a Carthusian monastery. By placing lengths of iron wire between the hands of every two of the monks, he formed a circuit a little more than a mile in length. At the discharge of the jars, the brethren all leaped simultaneously into the air in undignified fashion, and then laughed heartily at the spectacle they had created.

Progress was rapid that year. Lemonnier of Paris next sent a shock through 12,780 feet of wire lying on the ground. At this, Watson of England was spurred to new tests under the sponsorship of a committee of the Royal Society. In July, 1747, a wire was carried across the Thames on Westminster Bridge; one end of it touched a Leyden jar, the other end was held by a man on the opposite shore, who grasped in his other hand an iron rod, which he dipped into the water. Another man stood near the jar, holding in one hand a wire communicating with the exterior coating of the jar, and in the other an iron rod. On dipping the rod into the water and thus completing a circuit, a shock was felt by both men, but most strongly by the man near the jar, because some of the current escaped into the stone of the bridge. Later Watson learned that the shock would pass through earth as well as water, and what seemed to be fairly dry earth, at that.

In 1748, Benjamin Franklin sent inpulses in similar manner across the Schuylkill River, and De Luc some months later across Lake Geneva. Franklin, in a letter to his friend Peter Collinson of London early that summer, said:

Chagrined a little that we have hitherto been able to produce nothing in this way of use to mankind, and the hot weather coming on, when electrical experiments are not so agreeable, 'tis proposed to put an end to them for this season, somewhat humorously, in a party of pleasure on the banks of the Skuylkill. Spirits at the same time are to be fired by a spark sent from side to side through the river . . . a turkey is to be killed for our dinner by the electrical shock, and roasted by the electrical jack, before a fire kindled by the electrified bottle, when the healths of all the famous electricians in England, Holland, France and Germany are to be drank in electrified bumpers, under the discharge of guns from an electrical battery.

GROPING TOWARDS THE ELECTRIC TELEGRAPH

At last, in 1753, we came to the first authenticated suggestion of communication by electricity; and the name of the seer who proposed it will probably remain forever an uncertainty. A letter written at Renfrew, Scotland, on February 1, 1753, signed merely "C.M." and published in the *Scots Magazine* of Edinburgh, under the caption, "An Expeditious Method of Conveying Intelligence," proposed the stringing between two distant points of as many insulated wires as there are letters in the alphabet, through which "electrical discharges should separately exhibit themselves by the diverging balls of an electroscope, or the striking of a bell by the attraction of a charged ball."

An investigation as to the identity of this unknown genius was started by "Inquirendo" in *Notes and Queries* in 1853, and for seven years the subject was discussed. Sir David Brewster, writing in *The Engineer* (London, Dec. 24, 1858) expressed his firm belief that the writer was Charles Marshall of Paisley, who was remembered by his fellow townsmen as a man "who could light a room with coal reek, and make lightning write and speak upon the wall"; which sounds as if he had been one of the earliest experimenters, not only with electricity but with illuminating gas. But another investigator wrote two years later that he had learned positively from Marshall's son that Marshall was not the man, but instead, one Charles Morrison, of Renfrew.

Joseph Bozolus, a Jesuit and lecturer on natural philosophy in the college at Rome, was next to suggest an electric telegraph. This must have been prior to 1767, for his idea is described in a Latin poem, *Electricorum,* by Josephus Marianus Parthenius, published that year. Father Bozolus's plan was that of two wires laid underground between two stations. At one station, the inner coating of a Leyden jar or charged plate was connected to one wire, the outer coating to the other. The discharge through the wires would produce a spark between the contiguous ends of the wires at the other station. An alphabet of such sparks could, he thought, be devised without much difficulty. But nobody did it.

OLD WIRES AND NEW WAVES

(As this chapter is growing continually more technical, any lay reader who chooses may skip the rest of it and be none the worse off, save that he will miss seeing the slow but steady progress towards success; he will not learn how much spade work was done, indeed, how near to being practical the telegraph became before Morse or Wheatstone even took up the subject.)

The first telegraph instrument of which there is any record was that of Georges Louis Le Sage, set up at Geneva in 1774. His line consisted of twenty-four insulated wires for the letters of the alphabet (i, j and u, v each being represented by a single wire), each wire ending in an electroscope, duly lettered, where a ball of pith became nervous when its key at the other end of the wire was pressed. The receiving operator, watching the little bobbing balls, spelled out the words. Le Sage said in a letter written in 1782 that the notion of corresponding by means of electricity had been contemplated by him for thirty or thirty-five years. His first thought of it must therefore have been nearly coincidental with that of the unknown Scotch genius.

In 1787, Lomond in Paris is reported to have operated one of those pith-ball telegraphs with a single brass wire extending from one room to another at some distance. Arthur Young, an English traveler, saw it at work. Madame Lomond went to the instrument in the other room, Young wrote a short sentence on paper, Lomond manipulated the machine a while, and lo! Madame came in with the sentence correctly written out in her own hand. Young thought that she identified the letters by the motions of the ball.

In 1794, Reizen of Geneva rigged up a queer device of thirty-six wires, connected at the receiving station with strips of tin foil pasted on glass, and representing the letters of the alphabet and the ten digits. The flash of a spark at breaks in these strips spelled the message. But it was evident that these systems which required a wire for each letter and figure were not the final answer to the problem.

In 1795, Tiberius Cavallo experimented in England with a wire 250 feet long, insulated by successive coatings of pitch,

THE FIRST TELEGRAPH—LESAGE'S, GENEVA, 1774

GROPING TOWARDS THE ELECTRIC TELEGRAPH

linen strips, woolen cloth and oil painting, and announced vaguely that "by sending a number of sparks at different intervals of time, according to a settled plan, any sort of intelligence might be conveyed instantaneously." But the idea was evidently beyond his capacity to make practical.

We are totally in the dark as to what sort of telegraph D. F. Salva set up in Spain a little later, and through which messages were sent to a hitherto unheard-of distance. The Madrid *Gazette*, on November 25, 1796, tells how the Prince of the Peace, having heard of Salva's telegraph and of a paper which he had read on it before the Academy of Sciences, went to see it, and being "delighted with the promptness and facility with which it worked," he presented it before King Charles IV and the court, operating it himself. Later the Infanta Don Antonio had a Salva telegraph constructed "of great extent and on a large scale, by which the young prince was informed at night of news in which he was much interested." He also entertained Salva at court. The explorer Humboldt declares that a telegraph was built under this plan between Madrid and Aranjuez, a distance of twenty-six miles. But why do we never hear more of it?

In 1816, Francis Ronalds demonstrated a telegraph at his home in Hammersmith, England. He had suspended by silk strands eight miles of wire on his lawn. An electrical machine or a small Leyden jar supplied the power. The sending of the message depended upon two clocks at each end of the wire, synchronized to beat as nearly the time as possible. On each clock, on the axle which ordinarily turns the second hand, a dial with letters and figures around its circumference was fixed in place on the hand. Of course, it turned as fast as the hand would have done. In front of it and covering it was a stationary plate of similar size, with an aperture through which one of the letters or figures could be seen. At the instant when the desired letter passed the aperture, the inventor charged the wire and a pith ball electrometer at the other end moved. The letter passing the aperture at that moment was written down by the receiver, and thus the word was spelled.

This is the earliest authentic example of a dial telegraph or of a letter indicator employing but a single wire. Forty years later this idea was developed by David E. Hughes, a Kentuckian, into a fast and accurate letter-printing telegraph which was one of the most successful among the early machines of communication. Another type of dial telegraph was invented by Professor Charles Wheatstone of England, in which the lettered dial was revolved by successive impulses of the electric current nudging a ratchet wheel on its axis—the desired letter or figure being halted as long as necessary. This idea in turn was made the basis of the excellent letter-printing telegraph invented by Royal E. House of Vermont in 1846—nearly ten years before Hughes's machine appeared. In the strange cycle of human events, both these machines have become in a sense, distant spiritual ancestors of the up-to-the-minute automatic printing telegraph of to-day.

In 1828, Harrison Gray Dyar invented a chemical telegraph wherein the electric current, causing an acid reaction, made red marks on a roll of blue litmus paper involved by hand. Dyar ran his single wire several times around the race track on Long Island, a distance of several miles, supporting it by glass insulators fixed on trees and poles, and making zigzags in it for a more strenuous test. Those who saw its trials testified that the marks were distinct and satisfactory. Dyar induced a man named Brown, of Providence, to invest a little money in the device and go into partnership with him, and they employed one Connell of New York to raise additional capital with which to carry the wire to Philadelphia. They thought themselves on the road to success; but suddenly Connell brought suit against them for $20,000 for services rendered, "hoping to extort a share in the project from them." Failing in this, he had the partners arrested, charging them with conspiracy to carry on secret communication between the two cities for speculative purposes; "and thus," says Dyar, "effectually put an end to the enterprise without the formality of judicial trial on this novel accusation."

GROPING TOWARDS THE ELECTRIC TELEGRAPH

Professor C. A. Steinheil, great European electrical authority, says: "All these experiments put it beyond a doubt that frictional electricity may be employed for giving signals at any distances, and that when these signals are properly contrived, they offer convenient means of telegraphic intercourse."

The discovery of galvanism by Galvani, and then the introduction of the galvanic battery by Volta at the beginning of the nineteenth century opened the way for several other kinds of telegraphs. These were all of the electro-chemical or decomposing type. Dr. Samuel T. von Soemmering of Munich appears to have been the first to use Volta's invention for this purpose in 1807-8. He used the energy of a powerful Voltaic pile for the decomposition of water. Again he had the incubus of thirty-five wires, each ending in a gold pin or electrode immersed in its individual test-tube of water, bearing each its own letter or numeral. A flash of the current through any wire caused bubbles of oxygen to appear in that particular test-tube; and thus slowly and clumsily, words were formed. Soemmering began working through 724 feet of wire, and gradually increased the distance to 10,000 feet. His device was intricate and inconvenient, yet the inventor persisted for years in believing that it was practical.

In 1816, Dr. John Redman Coxe of Philadelphia, Professor of Chemistry in the University of Pennsylvania, suggested telegraphy either by the decomposition of water, (he had evidently never heard of Soemmering's apparatus), or of metallic salts. Not until twenty-seven years later was his second suggestion utilized by a Scotsman named Robert Smith; though Smith had probably never heard of Coxe. In Smith's machine, the alphabet and digits cast in iron type were at the receiving station, connected with the sending station each by a separate wire. A band of paper damp with a solution of ferro-cyanide of potassium was moved by machinery under the receiving instrument, and an impulse sent through any individual wire caused the impression of a blue letter on the band. Two or three years later Smith reduced his device to a single circuit of two wires, and impressed marks of different lengths on cloth to represent the letters and figures.

In 1846, Alexander Bain of Edinburgh obtained an English patent on a galvano-chemical telegraph which closely resembled that of Smith, with some ingenious improvements. This was introduced into the United States and widely used for a time. Twenty years later, Wheatstone improved it into an automatic telegraph. Morse in 1849 also obtained a patent on a galvano-chemical telegraph somewhat like Smith's—this several years after his electro-magnetic telegraph invention.

Gian Domenico Romagnosi of Trent, about 1800, discovered that if a galvanic-charged wire be held just above or just below a magnetic needle and parallel with it, the needle will be deflected to westward or eastward respectively. Two decades later, Professors Hans C. Oersted of Copenhagen and J. S. C. Schweigger of Halle developed therefrom the galvanometer, or instrument for measuring the galvanic current. This suggested a new mode of telegraphy. Ampère in 1820 affirmed the possibility of deflecting a magnetic needle through a wire at a great distance from the pile or battery, and said that the idea was suggested to him by Laplace. The telegraph which he proposed, however, did not differ greatly from that of Lesage, constructed nearly half a century before.

The first to make a practical development of Ampère's suggestion was a Russian, Baron Paul Ludovitch Schilling, of Cronstadt. Schilling was attached to the Russian embassy at Munich when Soemmering's telegraph was shown at the Academy of Sciences there, and he was greatly intrigued by it. Early in 1812, he was trying to insulate a cord so that the galvanic current could be carried through earth or water. He was hoping to perfect a telegraph for the use of the Russian army before the threatened invasion of his country by Napoleon that year, and if he had succeeded, events might have borne even harder upon the Corsican invader than they did. But it was not so to be, though Schilling succeeded in exploding powder by a

44

wire laid through the River Neva near St. Petersburg that autumn.

It was not until 1823 that he reduced his telegraph to working form. His signals were produced by five galvanometer needles, each provided with its own galvanic circuit. By giving the needles positive and negative motions, and combining two or more of these motions into a single signal, he was able to contrive a code reproducing the alphabet and numerals. He exhibited a working model to the Czar Alexander I in 1824 or 1825. This was in reality the first electro-magnetic telegraph. Later Schilling reduced his five needles to one needle and a multiplier, and by a more intricate combination of movements produced all the letters and numerals. The Emperor remained keenly interested in his device and visited the inventor's home in 1830 to inspect it. In 1835, Schilling exhibited it to a congress of German physicists at Bonn, and later, assisted by two of them, operated it with wires swung across the streets and housetops of Vienna. He preferred aërial to underground or underwater lines; but in 1837, he ordered from a Russian rope factory the necessary length of insulated cable for connecting St. Petersburg with the fortress of Cronstadt through the Gulf of Finland. His death occurred within a few months, however, and put an end to the enterprise, for there was no one to carry on after him.

Many scientists in Germany and England in 1829-30 were unaware of his success, for one inventor in each country produced an electro-magnetic telegraph after the suggestion of Ampère, though both had the incumbrance of a wire for every letter.

In 1820, Dominique Francis Arago of Paris discovered that with the galvanic instruments of Oersted and Schweigger he could develop greatly the magnetic power in bars of iron and steel, and give them permanent magnetism. William Sturgeon of Woolwich carried his experiment a step further, and in 1824 produced a true electro-magnet, with its intermittent control of an armature. It was of soft iron, of the now typical horseshoe

45

shape, coated with a non-conducting resinous varnish, and with a copper wire wound in a loose coil directly around its limbs. By touching the ends of this wire to the poles of a single galvanic pair of moderate size he created a temporary magnet that would sustain several pounds' weight. On breaking the circuit, it immediately lost its power.

Two methods of signaling were suggested by this device. In one the determined oscillations of the magnetic bar, in the other of the armature, by means of intermitted currents, might be arranged to indicate letters and figures. Hence the two types of electro-magnetic telegraph—the magnetic needle system and the magnetic armature system.

We now come to Joseph Henry, one of America's most famous explorers in this field. Henry was born of Scotch ancestry in Albany, New York, in 1797. In his early 'teens, while staying with an uncle in a small village near Albany, he chased a rabbit through a hole in the foundation of a church, and creeping up through a break in the floor he discovered a small library. He became fascinated with the books, especially those on science, and the course of his life was determined. At fifteen he was apprenticed to a watchmaker in Albany. He began attending a night-school, and later entered Albany Academy, paying his way by teaching a country school and tutoring in the city. Science was his chief interest, but his notion as to the particular branch that would be his varied from time to time. At first he rather favored medicine, but when he was sent out at the age of twenty-eight to survey a State road, he became enamored of engineering, and thought that his life work. In the following year, however, he was offered the position of professor of mathematics in Albany Academy, and accepted it. Though the work was arduous, he found time to do much experimenting in physics, and especially in electricity, in which he had become deeply interested.

In 1828, at the age of thirty-one, he first exhibited at the Albany Academy his electro-magnet wound with copper wire, which had been insulated by covering it with silk thread. "To him belongs the credit for inventing the magnetic 'spool' or

46

'bobbin,' that form of coil since universally employed for every application of electro-magnetism." [2] In 1830, he bent a piece of iron 20 inches long into a horseshoe magnet and lifted 750 pounds with it. Then he bent a bar 30 inches long, and it lifted 2,300 pounds—eight times more than any magnet hitherto known in Europe could cope with. "Professor Henry," remarked Sturgeon, a contemporary scientist, "has been enabled to produce a magnetic force which totally eclipses every other in the whole annals of magnetism; and no parallel is to be found since the miraculous suspension of the celebrated oriental impostor in his iron coffin."

"Henry," says Taylor, "was the absolute *creator* of the intensity magnet."

In 1831, he suspended around the walls of a large class-room in the Academy a mile of copper wire, interposed in a circuit between a battery and an "intensity" magnet. At each excitation of the magnet, a rod which had been in contact with a limb of the soft iron core was repelled from it, and its other end struck a bell. Henry explained to his classes that signaling might be done in this way, but that was as far as he went with it. He did not formulate a code of language, nor attempt to develop an actual telegraph instrument; yet his simple circuit and bell had elements which no previous telegraph had had, and which were destined to be essential to the telegraph of the future. It is therefore claimed by those who think that Henry's contribution to the science has been underrated that it was he and not Morse who "invented" the telegraph.

His biographer, Taylor, points out that this experimental apparatus "involved three significant and important novelties":

1. It was the first electro-magnetic telegraph employing an intensity magnet capable of being excited at very great distances from a suitable "intensity" battery.

[2] So says William B. Taylor in *An Historical Sketch of Joseph Henry's Contribution to the Electro-Magnetic Telegraph*, published by the Smithsonian Institution in 1879, a book which has been largely drawn upon in the preparation of this chapter.

2. It was the first electro-magnetic telegraph employing the armature as the signaling device; or employing the *attractive* power of the intermittent magnet, as distinguished from the *directive* action of the galvanic circuit. That is to say, it was, strictly speaking, the first *magnetic telegraph*.

3. It was the first *acoustic* electro-magnetic telegraph. One practical inconvenience of the needle system was found to be the perfect silence of its indications; and hence, in almost every case a call-alarm was required to draw attention to its messages.

How different would have been the estimate of Henry's labors (and especially the *practical* estimation of subsequent patentees) if the modest discoverer and inventor had been worldly-wise enough to secure an early patent on these three indisputably original and most pregnant features of telegraphy—to contest which no rival has ever appeared.

In the decades immediately following, hundreds of patents were granted for improvements upon or modifications of the electro-magnetic telegraph, all of them dependent upon Henry's original invention.

In 1832, Henry was called to the chair of natural philosophy in the College of New Jersey at Princeton, later to be developed into a famous university. Here he conceived a new form of galvanic battery and made his most powerful magnet. He also strung a wire between two buildings on the campus and did some more signaling. He describes it in a letter to a friend on the college faculty, Professor Samuel B. Dod, written after Professor Henry had gone to the Smithsonian Institution:

I think that the first actual line of telegraph using the earth as a conductor was made in the beginning of 1836. A wire was extended across the front campus of the college grounds, from the upper story of the Library Building to Philosophical Hall on the opposite side, the ends terminating in two wells. Through this wire signals were sent from time to time from my house to my laboratory. The electro-magnetic telegraph was first invented by me in Albany in 1830. Professor Morse, according to his statements, conceived the idea of an electro-magnetic telegraph in his voyage across the ocean in 1832, but did not until some years afterward—1837—attempt to carry his ideas into practice....

At the time of making my original experiments on electro-magnetism in Albany, I was urged by a friend to take out a patent, both for its application to machinery and to the telegraph, but this I declined, on the ground that I considered it incompatible with the dignity of science to confine the benefits which might be derived from it to the exclusive use of any individual. In this, perhaps, I was too fastidious.

In briefly stating my claims to the invention of the electro-magnetic telegraph, I may say that I was the first to bring the electro-magnet into the condition necessary to its use in telegraphy, and also to point out its application to the telegraph and to illustrate this by constructing a working telegraph, and had I taken out a patent for my labors at that time, Mr. Morse could have had no ground on which to found his claim for a patent to his invention. To Mr. Morse, however, great credit is due for his alphabet, and in bringing telegraphy to practical use.

Notwithstanding Henry's afterthought that perhaps he had been "too fastidious" in his feeling that "a discoverer's position and attitude are lowered by courting self-aggrandizement from scientific truth," he could never change it, but maintained this high unselfishness throughout life and died a comparatively poor man.

In his Princeton telegraph, the signals were conveyed by taps of a bell, as before.

James Smithson, illegitimate son of the first Duke of Northumberland, dying in 1829, left to the United States a fund to set up "An Establishment for the Increase and Diffusion of Knowledge Among Men." The Smithsonian Institution was not actually set going until 1846, at which time Joseph Henry was chosen to be its first Secretary—which really meant Director. Commenting upon his appointment, Sir David Brewster, Scottish physicist and President of the British Association for the Advancement of Science, said: "On the shoulders of young Henry has fallen the mantle of Franklin." "Young" Henry was fifty at the time. It was after his going to the Smithsonian that the controversy with Morse arose, which we shall discuss later. Henry remained at the helm of the Institution until his death in 1878.

In 1833, ten years after Schilling's experimental telegraph

had been exhibited, Charles Friedrich Gauss and William Edward Weber constructed a galvanometer telegraph of a single circuit connecting the Cabinet of Natural Philosophy in Göttingen with the Observatory, about a mile and a half distant. The two wires were carried over the housetops of the city, upheld by insulators. In the receiving station, a needle alternately attracted and repelled caused slight deflections to right and left of a small mirror suspended by a silk thread—the alphabet being represented by differing combinations of right and left movements. These tiny tremors were watched from a distance of ten or twelve feet through a telescope. This may have been the first reflecting galvanometer; an instrument which Sir William Thomson later developed, and with which he made the first ocean telegraphs possible.

Gauss, who was too deeply engrossed with other research to spend much time on the telegraph, asked his friend, Professor C. A. Steinheil of Munich, to carry his and Weber's invention further towards practicability. Steinheil, after some experimentation, set up a galvanometer telegraph between Munich and Bogenhausen—about two miles—employed greater power and added new features. The magnetic bars, alternately attracted and repelled, struck two bells of different tones instead of one, thus making letters and figures easier to express. Not only that, but to the adjacent ends of the two bars, the inventor fastened fountain pens, which, on a roll of paper moved by clockwork, made dots capable of representing an alphabet. Although Dyar in America had attempted a chemical register in 1828, this machine of Steinheil's seems to be the earliest automatic, recording, electro-magnet telegraph which was actually practical.

A few months later Steinheil discovered that the earth might be used as one-half of the connecting chain, and therefore reduced his two wires to one. He modestly gave credit to his predecessors. "To Gauss and Weber," said he, "is due the merit of having, in 1833, actually constructed the first simplified, galvano-magnetic telegraph." Of his own he said, "I by no means look on the arrangement I have selected as complete;

but as it answers the purpose I had in view, it may be well to abide by it until some simpler arrangement is contrived."

The Bavarian Government built many miles of telegraph under Steinheil's system for its own use. But with the unselfishness of the true scientist (what a contrast with some others who have furthered communication!), when a "simpler arrangement" of the receiving instrument was brought to his attention some years later, he was the first to express public recognition of its worth, and to urge upon the Bavarian Government the abandonment of that part of his own excellent system which had been improved upon.

Contemporaneously with Steinheil's work, Professor John Frederic Daniell, a noted English chemical philosopher, developed a new galvanic battery with a steadiness and continuity of action far beyond anything previously known. Time and again in the story of the Civil War telegraphs and at other times during several decades, one reads of instruments being operated with a Daniell battery—though the name is usually spelled Daniels or in any other way than the right one.

Next we encounter the man who, in England, is hailed to this day as the inventor of the electric telegraph. Beginning life as a musical instrument manufacturer, Charles Wheatstone while yet a young man began studying the laws of sound, and in the early 1830's became intrigued with electricity. It may be remarked in passing that he was also the inventor, in 1838, of the stereoscope, a little entertainer which used to lie on thousands of Victorian parlor tables in America, as well as elsewhere, each with its collection of views of world scenery, statuary, and a few comic and sentimental subjects.

In 1834, Wheatstone undertook—with an ingenious revolving mirror which he had devised, capable of measuring the millionth of a second—to detect the velocity of electricity passing through half a mile of copper wire; and then through four miles of wire. That year he was appointed Professor of Experimental Philosophy in King's College, in London.

In 1836, he completed a telegraph with five needles, which

could present thirty signs. At about that time William Fothergill Cooke, another Englishman who was working on a telegraph and had produced one with three indicating needles on three circuits of six wires, heard of Wheatstone. Cooke had recently visited Germany, where a Heidelberg professor had told him something of the progress of telegraphy on the Continent. One report has it that the professor described Schilling's instrument to him, another is that Cooke had never heard of Schilling. Anyhow, he was fired with a desire to invent a telegraph of his own. He heard of Wheatstone's progress, they compared notes and decided to consolidate ideas and apply for a joint patent.

They strung an experimental wire a mile and a quarter long between Euston Square and Camden Town which worked with partial success early in 1837. Documentary evidence too lengthy to reproduce here shows that Wheatstone received advice and assistance from Joseph Henry when the latter visited his laboratory in London in April, 1837. The machine on which the inventor-partners obtained their patent in July of that year was often called a chronometric telegraph. At each station, sending and receiving, there must be cylinders revolving synchronously and arrested simultaneously as desired by a magnetic armature, somewhat after the general idea of Ronald's synchronous clock dials of twenty years before. In this telegraph, says Taylor, "Henry's intensity magnet was used, but no acknowledgment of the fact was ever made by the inventors."

In 1839, Wheatstone completed a greatly improved dial telegraph, comprising an escapement and index operated by the stop-motion of an armature. The transmission principle of this machine was used by Royal E. House, an American, in his printing telegraph, perfected in 1846, just as the synchronous clock-movements of the earlier Cooke and Wheatstone system were used by David E. Hughes, another American, in his printing telegraph of 1855.

Soon the inevitable dispute arose between Cooke and Wheatstone as to which deserved the greater measure of credit for the "invention" of the telegraph. It seems likely that, as in the

GROPING TOWARDS THE ELECTRIC TELEGRAPH

case of Morse and Henry in America, the controversy was egged on by the partisans of each. They issued rejoinders to each other from time to time, though Cooke, who was angriest, seems to have done the major part of the pamphleteering and castigation. Impartial scientists were called upon to adjudicate the matter, and in April, 1841, Sir I. M. Brunel and Professor Daniell, after long investigation, drew up a statement which read in part:

Whilst Mr. Cooke is entitled to stand alone, as the gentleman to whom this country is indebted for having practically introduced and carried out the electric telegraph as a useful undertaking, promising to be of national importance, Professor Wheatstone is acknowledged as the scientific man, whose profound and successful researches had already prepared the public to receive it as a project capable of practical application. It is to the united labors of two gentlemen so well qualified for mutual assistance that we must attribute the rapid progress which this important invention has made during the five years since they have been associated.

This statement was acknowledged by Cooke and the good-natured Wheatstone to be correct; but it applies only to the first patent in which they were associated; not to the dial telegraph of 1839, for which Wheatstone is given the bulk of the credit by most authorities. Professor Daniell considered his and Brunel's statement as making no assertion whatsoever as to the originality of the invention on either side—although to the present writer, it certainly appears strongly to favor Cooke as the original genius.

England evidently regarded Wheatstone as the master mind of the partnership, and to this day Englishmen are firmly convinced that he was the inventor of the telegraph, "The popular infatuation in England," says Taylor, "as to the originality and priority of the Cooke and Wheatstone telegraph is probably quite equal to that prevalent in America as to the superior claims of the Morse telegraph." French scientists in 1840, were also declaring that Wheatstone had been the first to invent means of transmitting signals under water. The English Vice-Admiral

53

Smyth in 1850, backed Wheatstone as "undoubtedly the first contriver of the electric telegraph in the form which made it available for popular use"; adding, "of his submarine telegraph he showed me plans and publicly explained the details upwards of eighteen years ago" (this would have been in 1832 or earlier). De la Rive in 1858, also gave Wheatstone credit for inventing a "practical" telegraph instrument.

This leaning towards Wheatstone by press, public and others naturally irked Cooke almost beyond endurance, and he continued battling over the question as long as he lived. In 1854, he published a book on the controversy entitled, *The Electric Telegraph; Was It Invented by Professor Wheatstone?* And thirty years after their first patent had been issued, Cooke's son brought out a volume, *Invention of the Electric Telegraph: The Charge Against Sir Charles Wheatstone of Tampering with the Press.*

For Wheatstone had by this time been knighted. He completed, in 1867, an automatic instrument which increased the speed of telegraphy, but was not equal to some designed in America. His military telegraph was used by all the principal armies of Europe. He appears to have been on the whole a modest sort of person. When the British Society of Arts awarded its fourth gold medal to him and Cooke, he acknowledged the honor, but did not call for his medal. It is practically impossible at the present day to decide whether he or Cooke deserves the greater honor.

Another man whom some believe to have been outrageously neglected in the story of the telegraph is Edward Davy. Born in Devonshire, Davy was a dispensing chemist in youth, but before he had reached thirty, he became interested in electricity. In 1836 to 1837 a needle telegraph of his design was on exhibition in London. Fahie, a telegraph historian, insists that

He had a clearer grasp of the requirements and capabilities of electric telegraphy than Cooke and Wheatstone themselves; and had he known how to promote it, to get hold of the right men, had his idea been taken up by capitalists, he would have successfully competed with Cooke and Wheatstone for a share of the profits and honors.[3]

Davy's idea was that of a number of insulated copper wires connecting, say, London with Liverpool, each wire with a small brass ball at each end. An electric spark applied to the ball at the London end would be drawn from the connecting ball in Liverpool for the same duration of time. With the numerous changes and combinations possible with six wires, he thought the alphabet and digits might be easily represented. In fact, he envisioned a code whereby whole sentences might be flashed at once. In March, 1837, he became alarmed by rumors that Wheatstone was engaged upon a telegraph, and to secure priority, he hastened to lodge a caveat, and at the same time deposited with the Secretary of the Society of Arts a sealed description of his telegraph as it then stood.

He now added the relay, or as he called it, the "electrical renewer," which was later found to be absolutely essential to the success of an electric telegraph. Said he:

It occurred to me that the smallest motion (to a hair's breadth) of the needle would suffice to bring into contact two metallic surfaces so as to establish a new circuit, dependent on a local battery; and so on, ad infinitum. . . . In Cooke and Wheatstone's first patent there is . . . not a word about any renewer or relay as applicable to general electric telegraphy.

Nor did Morse have at first any inkling as to the necessity of a relay. When in March, 1837, Cooke and Wheatstone applied for their first patent, Davy entered an opposition, giving the Solicitor-General a full description of his apparatus. That jurist decided that the two systems were different, and allowed both patents to be granted, "although time has since shown," says Davy, "that they contained some of the clearest identities."

He had now also invented a chemical or recording telegraph. In connection with these devices he planned a dial for railway

³ J. J. Fahie. *A History of Electric Telegraphy to the Year 1837* (London, 1884).

stations, on which hands or pointers would indicate the momentary location of all principal trains passing over the line. As a train passed a milestone, its hand would move forward one notch and a tiny bell would ring. A waiting passenger could thus trace with fascinated eyes the approach of his own train, and if it was still many miles away, he could with an easy mind step out for a bite of lunch or attend to some neglected matter. The idea sounds delightfully useful.

Through some unaccountable oversight, Davy neglected to mention this dial arrangement in his patent applications, and Wheatstone obtained a patent on a similar one in 1840.

At one time Davy had several English railroads interested almost to the point of adopting his inventions, "and had he stood his ground but six months longer," says Fahie, "things would undoubtedly have gone hard with Cooke and Wheatstone." But just at this time a private matter came up which seemed to necessitate a trip to Australia. He sailed in 1839, and never returned to England. In Australia he became absorbed in other matters and gave up the thought of pushing his telegraph. "A magnificent failure," says Fahie.

In the 1830's and '40's new telegraphs sprang up like weeds everywhere. In one and the same year with the Cooke-Wheatstone patent, 1837, Professor Stratingh of the University of Groningen, M. Amyot of France and William Alexander of Edinburgh produced appliances. Alexander's had a board on which were thirty characters in white enamel on a black ground —the twenty-six letters, a comma, period, asterisk and semicolon. Eash character had behind it a magnet attached to a movable piece of metal which veiled the character, so that at first glance at the board you saw only the black surface. The operator had a sort of piano keyboard with thirty keys. On striking the desired key, the magnet at the other end moved its little plate aside and you saw the letter. The receiving operator, watching this process, wrote down the words.

Mungo Ponton of Edinburgh saw Alexander's machine and made some improvements in it; but neither his machine nor

TELEGRAPH INVENTORS

C. A. STEINHEIL   JOSEPH HENRY
S. F. B. MORSE (ABOUT 1870)
ALFRED VAIL   SIR CHARLES WHEATSTONE

any of the other three just mentioned nor that of Professor Luigi Magrini of Venice, which resembled Cooke and Wheatstone's five-needle or hatchment telegraph of 1837, ever made any stir in the world.

Inventors continued toying with the subject, however, and dozens of devices, many of them differing but slightly from older ones, appeared in the next few years. One of the most curious was that of David McCallum—also British—and was christened by him the Globotype. In this curious machine the electric impulse released small colored balls or marbles at the receiving station, which rolled down a slot to form words in a trough below. One white ball represented the letter A; two, B; three, C; four, D. Then he began with the blue balls. E was one blue; F was two blues; G, three; H, four; I was a white and a blue; K, a blue and a white; L, white, blue, white; M, blue, white, blue and so on. Z was three whites and one blue; & was three blues and one white.

But stay! There must be black balls, too; one between every two letters, for example; two blacks meant the end of a word; three, a change to or from numerals, and four, the end of the message.

The inventor, in a pamphlet, published in 1856, pointed out the disadvantages of all other systems; among them, the fact that in the United States alone, £500 was expended in a year on pencils by operators of the Morse Telegraph! Moreover, pencils required constant sharpening, the slightest wabble in clicking the Morse instrument caused mistakes in receiving, and if your pencil point broke in the middle of a message, there you were! But the world refused to listen to these common-sense arguments.

CHAPTER IV

AN ARTIST TURNS INVENTOR

Canst thou send lightnings, that they may go, and say unto thee,
Here we are? JOB, XXXVIII, 35.

ON OCTOBER 2, 1832, the packet ship *Sully*—small, but comparing favorably in size with other vessels of her day —lay rocking gently beside her pier at Havre. In the saloon sat an American painter named Samuel Finley Breese Morse, writing an embarkation letter to his friend, James Fenimore Cooper. He expected to sail in a few hours.

But the wind decreed otherwise, and as the *Sully* must depend upon sails for her locomotion, Mr. Morse still had his letter open three days later. "Here I am yet," he added on the 5th, "wind-bound, with a tremendous southwester directly in our teeth. Yesterday the *Formosa* arrived and brought papers, etc. to the 10th September. . . . " Next day the wind changed, and in the evening he wrote, October 6, 7 o'clock. "We are getting under way. Good-by."

Morse was now forty-one years old, and life so far had been somewhat disappointing to him. True, he had received a medal some years before from a fine arts society for his first essay at sculpture, "The Dying Gladiator," and he had been elected first President of the National Academy of Design upon its organization in 1826, holding that position for sixteen years. But in the matter of financial reward, Art had been a stingy mistress. There were as yet no millionaires to be painted in young America, little decoration of public buildings, and artistic taste was still undeveloped. As a consequence, commissions were few and prices low, and a picture ventured upon any subject of the artist's own choosing was hard to sell.

AN ARTIST TURNS INVENTOR

Morse had been in Europe for three years, 1829 to 1832, doing some painting and some vagabonding about, forgetting his worries in the artistic or congenial atmosphere which he found in England, France and Italy, and the pleasant living in picturesque scenes at low cost.

Returning on the *Sully* were—among others—Mr. Rives, the American minister to France and his family, and a certain Dr. Charles T. Jackson of Boston. At the dinner table one day, Dr. Jackson was discoursing upon electro-magnetism, then an almost unknown subject to most people. Jackson was describing the electric circuit, and saying that the presence of the current could be detected in any part of the line by breaking the circuit. According to Edward Lind Morse, biographer of his father:

Morse was naturally much interested, and it was then that the inspiration, which had lain dormant in his brain for many years, suddenly came to him, and he said: "If the presence of electricity can be made visible in any part of the circuit, I see no reason why intelligence may not be transmitted instantaneously by electricity."

The company was not startled by this remark; they soon turned to other subjects and thought no more of it. Little did they realize that this exclamation of Morse's was to mark an epoch in civilization; that it was the germ of one of the greatest inventions of any age....

Little does Edward Morse seem to realize—or if he does, he conceals it—that men for the better part of a century past had been toiling over that very problem, and that several instruments had already been put together which did convey intelligence "instantaneously," though in a crude way. Morse's suggestion was by no means new or profound. Furthermore, if Dr. Jackson was discoursing at all learnedly of the progress of electro-magnetism in Europe, it seems odd that he did not mention the telegraphs of Ronalds, Soemmering, Schilling and others, which were the finest developments of electricity then extant.

Dr. Jackson's story is that Morse knew nothing about electricity, while he, Jackson, was perfectly familiar with it, having made it a study since childhood; and that he gave Morse much information on the subject. The Morse cohorts retort that Morse had studied a bit of physics (including electricity) at Yale under Professor Silliman. That must have been rather elementary, but undoubtedly the pupil had absorbed more of it than one is apt to suspect.

Edward Morse says that the idea had "taken root" in his father's brain and obsessed him:

> He withdrew from the cabin and paced the deck, revolving in his mind the various means by which the object sought could be attained. Soon his ideas were so far focussed that he sought to give them expression on paper, and he drew from his pocket one of the little sketch-books which he always carried with him and rapidly jotted down in sketches and words the ideas as they rushed from his brain.

On pages of the note-book appear drawings of wound and unwound magnets, insulated wires and other devices, showing some familiarity with such things. When partisan controversy arose in after years, there were scoffers who found it difficult to believe that a painter who had never devoted much time to anything but his art should have had sufficient knowledge of electrical appliances to make these drawings and plan a telegraph. One of the drawings, showing a magnet wound with wire, indicates, says Edward L. Morse, that his father was familiar with the discoveries of Arago, Davy and Sturgeon in electro-magnetism. But long before this book was brought to public notice, Dr. Jackson had made a deposition regarding his aid to Morse, in the course of which he said that Morse knew nothing whatsoever about magnets, that he, Jackson, made sketches of them, *which Morse copied into his note-book*. In view of the ignorance which Morse later displayed regarding magnets and batteries, Jackson's statement seems the most plausible and likely explanation of those pages in Morse's little book. Any man who understood magnets would not have needed to make sketches of them for his own guidance.

That Jackson gave this information does not, however, prove that he had any part in the invention of the telegraph.

One finds it hard to reconcile the assertion that Morse was

AN ARTIST TURNS INVENTOR

familiar with the work of Arago, Davy and Sturgeon in electricity with his "honestly supposing," as he says he did, that he was "the first person that ever put the words 'electric telegraph' together." It seems inexplicable that (as he wrote to Professor Sears C. Walker in 1848) he could have been "utterly ignorant that the idea of an electric telegraph of any kind whatever had been conceived by any other person." And yet so palpably ignorant was he of some fundamental facts then known about electricity that one is disposed to accept this disclaimer as true.

E. L. Morse says that, "This original sketch book was burned in a mysterious fire which, some years later, during one of the many telegraph suits, destroyed many valuable papers. Fortunately, however, a certified copy had wisely been made, and this copy is now in the National Museum in Washington." Certain opponents and Henry partisans were disposed to hint that the mere disappearance of that original book, leaving only a handmade wraith of itself behind, looked quite as bad for one side as another.

On one page of the note-book there is even the alleged embryo of the famous dot-and-dash alphabet, though here it is merely a series of dots and spaces, representing the ten numerals. This page was offered as confuting the claim, made long afterwards, that not Morse, but Alfred Vail originated the so-called Morse code. On another page there was a suggestion that these signs be imprinted by chemical decomposition on a strip of paper passing over rollers—as in some previous telegraphs, though we have Morse's assurance that he had never heard of them.

He frankly admitted five years later that he and Jackson had agreed to experiment together on the problem, but they never did. When lawsuits and controversy arose, and some were denying that Morse had thought of a telegraph as far back as 1832, he sought corroboration from some of his fellow-passengers on the *Sully*. One of them, J. Francis Fisher, a prominent attorney of Philadelphia, readily testified that "During the voyage the subject of an electric telegraph was one of frequent conversation. Mr. Morse was most constant in pursuing it, and *alone* the one who seemed disposed to reduce it to a practical test, and I recollect that for this purpose he devised a system of signs for letters, to be indicated and marked by ... strokes or shocks of the galvanic current. ... I did not suppose that any other person on the ship claimed any merit in the invention, or was in fact, interested to pursue it to maturity, as Mr. Morse seemed to be, nor have I been able since to recall any fact or circumstance to justify the claim of any person other than Mr. Morse to the invention."

Some other passengers, including Mr. Rives, the minister to France, gave similar evidence, and Captain Pell, commander of the *Sully*, testified under oath that when he saw Morse's working instrument in 1837, he recognized it as containing principles which Morse had expounded to him during the voyage; and he added that just before landing, Mr. Morse had said to him, "Captain, should you hear of the telegraph one of these days as the wonder of the world, remember the discovery was made on board the good ship *Sully*."

After more than a month on the water, the "good ship *Sully*" tacked into the harbor of New York on November 15, 1832, and Morse was met at the dock by his brothers, Richard and Sidney. Richard later testified that:

Hardly had the usual greetings passed between us ... before he informed us that he had made during his voyage an important invention, which had occupied almost all his attention on shipboard —one that would astonish the world and of the success of which he was perfectly sanguine. ... He took from his pocket and showed us from his sketch-book, in which he had drawn them, the kind of characters he proposed to use. These were dots and spaces representing the ten digits or numerals, and in the book were sketched other parts of his electro-magnetic machinery and apparatus. ...

Sidney remembered that "he was full of the subject of the telegraph during the walk from the ship, and for some days afterwards could scarcely speak about anything else." Sidney also mentions the "cogged or saw-toothed type," the object of which was to close and break the circuit, so as to print the dots and dashes. He stayed for quite a while at Richard's home, and there tried to cast some of the type in a primitive way, melting the lead on a shovel in the open fireplace. His sister-in-law even fifteen or twenty years afterwards remembered with annoyance how he had spilled molten lead on her drugget and on the seat of a rush-bottomed chair.

But he had little time to spend on invention. Necessity's whip was scourging him; there must be money earned somehow for the needs of his motherless children and himself. His brothers were generously financing him for the moment, but that could not go on indefinitely. He turned to his easel and palette again, and for nearly three years little or nothing more was done with the telegraph. There is pathos in a circular letter which he wrote to several prominent members of Congress in 1834, saying that he had heard that the four panels still blank in the Rotunda of the National Capitol were soon to be filled with pictures, and "I should esteem it a great honor to be selected as one of the artists." He points to his twenty years of study, seven of them in Europe, and humbly begs for "favorable recommendation."

But largely because of the belief of John Quincy Adams, then a member of Congress, that there were no American painters capable of doing such work in the best style, and particularly because of a scathing anonymous retort to this opinion in a New York newspaper, erroneously ascribed to Morse, the inventor was eliminated from the competition. This was a heavy blow to him, and he never afterwards did much painting; but it had the effect of turning his attention more intensively to his telegraph again.

In 1835, he was appointed Professor of Literature of the Arts of Design in the University of the City of New York. His salary was distressingly small, for the university was just getting under way and its budget was limited. He was given spacious quarters in the still unfinished building of the university on the east side of Washington Square (for which, however, he paid $325 a year rent, later $400). Here he could live and have not only his painting studio, but a laboratory and workshop for tinkering.

Now, relieved of the necessity for pot-boiler art, he could give some time again to his cherished invention. The first apparatus which he put together was set in one of the light wooden frames over which canvas is stretched for a painting. As will be seen by the picture of it, the message was to be recorded on a strip of paper passing over rollers, by a pencil point fixed in the lower end of a wooden pendulum. A small iron bar at the center of this pendulum acted as armature for the Sturgeon electro-magnet fastened at the right of the frame. A single galvanic cup supplied power, and the circuit including the electromagnet was closed and opened by means of a lever ending in a wire fork which dipped into the two mercury thimbles connected with the positive and negative poles of the battery.

In the sending instrument appeared the saw-tooth type which Morse had cast with his own hands. His original idea was to make type which stood only for the ten numerals. These numbers, by a vocabulary which he was working out, were, in certain combinations, to stand for whole syllables. Thus in the short message which he sent around a room on wire in September, 1837, the figures 215 represented the three syllables of the word "successful." Morse's first idea was that the telegraph should be the property of the Government, and so imbued was he with European governmental practices that he thought all messages should be kept secret by cipher. But the dictionary necessary to such a system must be so appallingly voluminous that Morse finally abandoned the scheme, and in 1838 made type instead for each letter of the alphabet.

To send that word "successful," you picked out the type for 2, 1 and 5, from a case just as a printer would, and set it in a printer's composing stick. Its appearance is shown on the opposite page. On the bottom of the composing stick a series of sharp points were fixed; and when you turned a crank, a strip of carpet binding passing over two rollers caught these points and pulled the stick forward. The free end of the circuit-lever

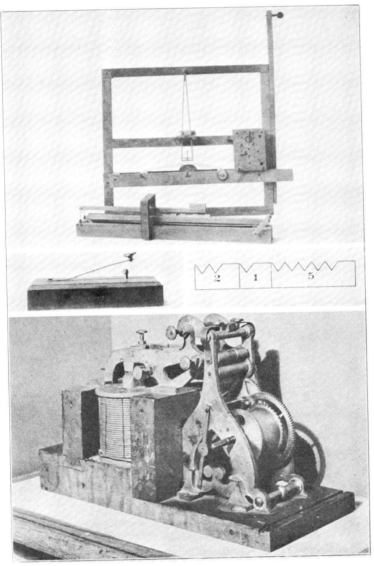

Upper photographs from National Museum; lower from Cornell University

Top—MORSE'S FIRST INSTRUMENT, 1837. *Left*—THE FIRST TELEGRAPH KEY. *Right*—SAWTOOTH TYPE. *Bottom*—THE WASHINGTON-BALTIMORE INSTRUMENT, 1844

rested on the type and dragged over it as it moved. As it fell into the notches and rose again over the points, it opened and closed the electric circuit. In the receiving instrument, the pencil point which rested lightly on the strip of paper would simply record a straight line along the strip as long as the pendulum was at rest. But at each momentary attraction of its armature by the magnet (caused by completion of the circuit as a tooth passed under the lever), the pendulum moved to one side; and thus was produced a zigzag line, with longer laterals whenever the circuit remained open or closed for a time.

In answer to the charge that Alfred Vail designed the alphabet after he began helping Morse, it is pointed out that the zigzag line made by the pencil really shows the first form of the dot and dash system. In the number illustrated here, the lower points of the saw-tooth represent the dots. The figure 6 was represented by a dot and a dash; 7 by two dots and a dash, and so on.

"Early in 1836," said Morse sixteen years later, "I procured forty feet of wire, and putting it in the circuit, I found that my battery of one cup was not sufficient to work the instrument." ("Fifty or a hundred cups," says Taylor, "would have been equally insufficient; a fact which he ignores.") As Professor Henry says in his letter—already mentioned—to Professor Dod, "He [Morse] found himself so little acquainted with the subject of electricity that he could not make his simple machine operate through the distance of a few yards." [1]

Not knowing what to do, Morse called upon a colleague, Professor Leonard D. Gale, Professor of Chemistry in the University, for advice. Gale knew at once that a battery of many cups was necessary; that Morse's one large battery should be divided into a number of smaller ones of the same total capacity to make it a battery of intensity. Accordingly he submitted a multiple cup battery. There was another defect in Morse's machine, said Gale, namely, that:

[1] Letter now in the Treasure Room, Princeton University Library.

OLD WIRES AND NEW WAVES

The coil of wire around the poles of the electro-magnet consisted of but a few turns only, while to give the greatest projectile power, the number of turns should be increased from tens to hundreds, as shown by Professor Henry in his paper published in the *American Journal of Science* in 1831.... After substituting the battery of twenty cups for that of a single cup, we added some hundred or more turns to the coil of wire around the poles of the magnet and sent a message through 200 feet of conductors; then through 1,000 feet; and then through ten miles of wire arranged on reels in my own lecture room in the New York University in the presence of friends. All these experiments were repeated with the original Morse machine, modified as stated.

Dr. Gale wrote the above for the composite memorial volume to Morse compiled and published by order of Congress in 1875, after the inventor's death. Here we enter the curious maze of contradictions and mysteries surrounding the birth of the telegraph. In one of the patent suits in 1851, Dr. Gale testified that he first saw Morse's telegraph in January, 1836—which coincides with all other chronologies. He was asked whether the machine was complete when he first saw it. "It was in perfect order," he replied, "when I first saw it." The next question was, "Could said Morse successfully operate his telegraph prior to your communicating to him scientific intelligence?" To which the Doctor replied, "The said Morse could have successfully operated his telegraph, and did so operate it, prior to my communicating any scientific intelligence."

If these answers of his were correct, how could he have explained his words, written after Morse's death, telling how Morse failed to operate his instrument until Gale had substituted a new battery and an improved magnet? And where was the need for Morse's calling upon him for help in setting the thing going? What strange inconsistencies in the human animal! Dr. Gale would no doubt have hotly resented any suggestion that he was not a truthful man. But when, on the stand in 1851, he was a witness for Morse, it is only charitable to suppose that he had been so coached and drenched with argument as to the rightfulness of Morse's side that he involuntarily remembered

66

things as the Morse attorneys wanted him to remember them. William B. Taylor remarks:

> The practical improvements introduced by Professor Gale into the arrangement devised by Professor Morse appeared to the latter so obviously mere matters of degree that he felt confident (after they were shown) that he would himself have effected them by simple trial or experimentation; and he does not appear ever to have realized that any scientific principle was involved in the difference. But had he increased separately either the number of his galvanic elements or the number of coils upon his magnet, he would equally have failed to accomplish the desired result. The chance that he would have *combined* these increments may be estimated as very low, when we consider that much wiser and more scientific heads had failed entirely to attain such purpose and arrangement.

"Up to the autumn of 1837," says Morse, "my telegraph apparatus existed in so crude a form that I felt reluctance to have it seen." On September 2nd of that year, some English scientists and others, including Alfred Vail, son of Judge Stephen Vail, proprietor of the Speedwell Iron Works at Morristown, New Jersey, witnessed a test in the cabinet of New York University through 1,700 feet of wire strung around the walls. This test was so successful that young Vail was pleased with the thought of having a hand in the enterprise, and agreed to experiment and manufacture parts at the iron works on a basis of partnership. His father and brother were also persuaded to advance money for the furthering of the work.

It was about a month after this test that Professor Morse filed in the United States Patent Office a caveat—signed October 3, 1837—stating that "the machinery for a full practical display of his new invention is not yet completed, and he therefore prays protection of his right till he shall have matured the machinery." He said that he had "invented a new method of transmitting and recording intelligence by electro-magnetism." Among the items which he claimed as original and wished to patent were "a system of signs by which numbers and consequently words and sentences are signified," a dictionary or vocabulary, a set of type and cases, a port rule for regulating the type movements, a register which recorded the signs permanently, and modes of insulating the wires. It is regarded as significant b᷐ his critics that most of these features were discarded or greatly changed soon after Vail had begun working with him, and that not one of them remained as a part of the telegraph system twenty-five years later.

The Secretary of the Treasury in March of that year had issued the circular letter already mentioned, asking the advice of prominent men as to the possible establishment of a Government telegraph. Although little seems to have been known about Morse or his work, even for years afterwards, he received a copy of the letter, and promptly wrote to the Secretary that he was working on an electric telegraph. Thereafter he kept the Secretary apprised of his progress—informing him in November, for example, of their sending through 10 miles of wire. Upon returning from a visit to the iron-works at Morristown, he had written back to Vail:

I arrived just in time to see the experiment Professor Gale was making with the entire ten miles.... The result now is that with a little addition of wire to the coils of the small magnet which I had all along used, the power was as great apparently through ten as through three miles. This result has surprised us all (yet there is no mistake) and as I conceive, settles the matter;

which proves again that he did not realize that the additional winding of the magnet was the salvation of his telegraph.

Meanwhile, Morse had been having a brush with his old fellow-shipmate, Dr. Jackson. In August, while on a visit to Boston, Morse, full of naïve enthusiasm, called at Jackson's office to tell him of the progress of his project, but finding the Doctor out, had written him a letter. Evidently he never dreamed that Jackson would claim a share of the credit for the invention. In his reply Jackson expressed himself as "rejoiced" to learn that the instrument was a success, and added, "I have seen several notices of it in the newspapers, but observe that my name is not connected with the discovery." He supposed that it was "an accidental inadvertency" of the editors; they did not know that the telegraph was "our mutual discovery." He hoped Morse would correct this error.

The astonished Morse replied temperately, rejecting any thought of Jackson's collaboration; reminding the Doctor that Morse had asked him to name some substance easily decomposed by electricity, and Jackson had suggested glauber salts upon a paper which had been first colored with turmeric. They had agreed to experiment together upon the idea for a chemical telegraph, but never did so. Morse in his letter deftly casts the blame upon Jackson for this failure to coöperate. "Your neglect retarded my invention," he charges, "and compelled me, after five years' delay, to consider the result of that experiment a failure, and consequently to devise another mode of applying my apparatus—a mode entirely original with me." This sentence refutes Morse's claim that the idea of the electric telegraph originated with him on the *Sully* in 1832; but probably Morse wrote it just as a "throwoff" on Jackson, failing, in his naïve way, to realize all the implications in it. Apparently, neither he nor Jackson had heard of Dr. Coxe's suggestion of a chemical telegraph more than sixteen years before their meeting, nor of Dyar's successful experiment with one in 1828.

Jackson's letters to Morse were so specious and hollow in their pretensions that one is left with little belief in his claim to a share in the actual invention. He says with a foggy pretense at profound knowledge of the subject:

There are many ways of marking at any distance required.... In the application of the Electro-Magnet, I had proposed to mark an actual type, having a packet of 24 wires for conductors to the several magnets, each of which moved a letter pressed with great power. I have several other applications of Electro-Magnetism that I shall soon bring to bear on the useful arts. Nothing but the urgency of my present avocations could have prevented me from making public exhibitions in the lecture-room of my new applications. I have drawings of several instruments, and hope next winter to make public trials of the experiments, and shall not publish anything until the work is done and perfected.

This paragraph has "bluff" written all over it. The fact that, so far as can be ascertained, he never published, exhibited nor invented anything eliminates Jackson as a serious contender for honors in the telegraph.

Judge Vail had advanced a little money to Morse upon the urging of Alfred, but he was still skeptical, irritated by the jeers of his neighbors and worried by the slowness of progress and the anxious demeanor of Morse and his son. He would have ceased aiding the enterprise had it not been for proof that they gave him. The two partners had avoided him for some time, but finally invited him to come to the workshop on January 6, 1838, and witness the machine in operation. By this time a change had been made in it. The recording pendulum, instead of swinging to and fro and marking a zigzag line, now had an up and down movement, so that it marked actual dots and dashes on the paper.

The Judge came to the shop at Morristown along with several others. He wrote on a slip of paper—taking care that Morse did not see it—a sentence which he had decided upon at random, "A patient winner is no loser." He handed this to his son at the transmitting instrument, saying, "If you can send this and Professor Morse can read it at the other end, I shall be convinced."

Alfred, with an eye on the sentence, slowly picked out type from the case and set it in the composing stick. He placed the stick on the machine and turned the crank. Morse, at the other end of the wire, wrote busily; finally he arose and came to the group with the sentence correctly written on a sheet of paper. The Judge at once became such an enthusiastic partizan that he wanted to rush off to Washington at once and urge upon Congress the establishment of a Government line. But Morse and Alfred were not yet quite ready for that.

Many years afterwards Morse paid a high tribute to the Vail family. "It is to their joint liberality," said he, "but especially to the attention and skill and faith in the final success of the enterprise maintained by Alfred Vail that is due the success of my endeavors to bring the Telegraph at that time creditably before the public." At one time Morse was ill in the Vail home, and Mrs. Vail, Alfred's mother, nursed him as tenderly as if he had been her own son.

In a letter written February 15, 1838, to Francis O. J. Smith (here a sinister name enters our history), Chairman of the Committee on Commerce in the National House of Representatives, Morse remarks, "It is proper that I should here state that the patent right is now jointly owned in unequal shares by myself, Professor Gale of New York City University and Messrs. Alfred and George Vail." The patent was not actually issued until a date more than two years later.

Changes in the system now took place rapidly. On January 24th, only eighteen days after the test before Judge Vail, a demonstration was given at New York University, at which, for the first time, new saw-tooth type marked the letters of the alphabet, instead of numbers, in dots and dashes, and actually spelled out words. The New York *Journal of Commerce* announced that Morse could now send twenty words a minute as against only ten by his former numeral-and-dictionary system. But a little later that year the type was discarded entirely for the familiar key which telegraphers pounded for so many decades afterwards. Dr. Gale's own statement is that:

After a few weeks of trial, he (Morse) laid the types and the port-rule aside, and substituted therefor a key and key-board called the "correspondent" with which the telegrapher broke and closed the circuit between his own and a distant station where his message is to be recorded.

Gale here seems to give credit to Morse for the new device; but these changes came rapidly after Alfred Vail's association with him, and many people were firm in the belief that Vail was solely responsible for them. William B. Taylor declares that concurring testimony shows that:

The new recording instrument built for Morse during October, November and December, 1837, by Vail was entirely Vail's own design, without suggestions from Morse ... its arrangement for

71

discontinuous marking was specially contrived by its maker for an alphabet exclusively designed by himself; which he abstained from publicly claiming, owing to a delicate sense of obligation incurred by his contract with Professor Morse....

That Morse had no conception on October 3, 1837, of the form of instrument contemplated by Vail is clearly shown by his autographed "caveat" of that date, and his letter to Vail October 24th, announcing the completion of the numbered dictionary (in which he wrote, "We can now talk or write anything by numbers") is equally conclusive evidence that at this later date he was still unconscious of any alphabetic improvement.

Moses S. Beach, editor and proprietor of the New York *Sun*, said in an editorial headed "Honor to whom honor is due," published September 25, 1858:

Alfred Vail entered into these experiments with his whole soul, and to him is Professor Morse indebted quite as much as to his own wit, for his ultimate triumph. He it was who invented the far-famed alphabet; and he too was the inventor of the instrument which bears Morse's name. But whatever he did or contrived went cheerfully to the great end.

Twenty years later Beach wrote to Taylor that he was at the time acquainted with both Morse and Vail, and that "My impression is that the article was at the time approved for its exact statement—*never controverted.*"

Dr. William P. Vail, uncle of Alfred Vail, writing in *Hours at Home,* in 1869, claimed the honor of the alphabet and the final instrument for his nephew. "All this is well understood," he said, "and for the most part is written down, and the record some day in the near future must find its place in history." But unfortunately this hidden proof has not, so far, come to light.

Neither the statement by Beach nor by William P. Vail, comments Taylor, both published in Morse's lifetime, were contradicted by him.

Frederick Brent Read, in his book, *Up to the Heights of Fame and Fortune,* published in 1873, says that "Alfred Vail first produced in the new instrument the first available *Morse* machine.... The new machine was Vail's, not Morse's."

72

From Samuel I. Prime's "Life of Morse"

MORSE IN HIS WORKSHOP, BUILDING HIS FIRST
INSTRUMENT

AN ARTIST TURNS INVENTOR

In a speech delivered at a banquet given in his honor in New York in 1869, Morse said of his invention, "It found a friend in Mr. Alfred Vail of New Jersey, who, with his father and brother, furnished the means to give the child a decent dress." Read comments indignantly:

It would have been more magnanimous if in the last days of the aged savant, he had stated the precise facts, and given Alfred Vail the full credit to which he was justly entitled.... He makes no allusion to Alfred Vail which would lead any one to suspect that he was anything but a skilled mechanic—that Vail had ever done anything beyond putting into form the conception of Morse's brain.

Morse too often showed this unwillingness to give proper credit to those who had aided him; thereby supplying ammunition to his critics and confirming the belief of many that he had merely profited by ideas supplied by others.

Vail himself chafed somewhat under this conception of him as a mere subordinate during his association with Morse. Writing to his brother George on one occasion, he said: "Professor Morse has received a letter from Mr. Patterson, inviting us to exhibit at Philadelphia, and has answered it, but has said nothing to *me* about his intentions. He is altogether inclined to operate in his own name, so much so that he has had printed five hundred blank invitations in his own name at your expense." And again to George a few months later: "In regard to Professor M. calling me his '*assistant*,' this is also settled, and he has said as much as to apologize for using the term."

It seems evident that it was Vail who, after much experimentation with pencils, fountain pens and inked roulettes for marking purposes, finally discarded all and substituted a blunt steel stylus, playing over a groove in the roller over which the strip of paper passed, thus indenting the dots and dashes clearly in the paper. In a memorandum attached to the original model of this improvement, Vail wrote, "I have not asserted publicly my right as first and sole inventor, because I have wished to preserve the peaceful unity of the invention and because I could not, according to my contract with Professor Morse, get a patent for it."

On the other hand, Alfred Vail in his book,[2] a brief early history of the telegraph, made no claim to authorship of the dot and dash alphabet, but gives the credit to Morse. In a letter to Morse, he speaks of it as "your system of marking, lines and dots, which you have patented." Nor did he in any of his numerous letters and diaries, which were examined after his death, make any claim to have originated the alphabet nor any essential parts of the new Morse instrument. He wrote a letter to Morse on March 19, 1838, while he was making, so it is claimed, some of his greatest contributions to the invention, in which he exclaims, "I feel, Professor Morse, that if I am ever worth anything, it will be wholly attributable to your kindness. I now should have no *earthly* prospect of happiness and domestic bliss had it not been for what you have done. For which I shall ever remember with the liveliest emotions of gratitude, whether it is eventually successful or not." Whether this gush of emotion may not have been inspired by some other occasion than the telegraph, we cannot say now.

Vail did away with the old clumsy saw-tooth type in the original instrument by inventing the spring circuit-closer, the clicking key which the calloused fingers of operators have pounded, even unto this day. This he elaborated into the form in which it was evermore used. After the first line was in operation, he continued making contributions to the science—a reduction in the number of battery cups, better magnets, a register, reel, pen-key, the substitution of the galvanometer for the receiving magnet. Whether his abstention from publicly claiming any credit said to be rightfully due him was just another manifestation of his delicate and scrupulous faithfulness to his agreement with Morse is another question which cannot now be resolved.

[2] *Description of the American Electro-Magnetic Telegraph, now in operation between the Cities of Washington and Baltimore* (Washington, 1845).

AN ARTIST TURNS INVENTOR

Undoubtedly he made a large contribution in the way of ideas to the system. Franklin Leonard Pope, writing in the *Century Magazine* in April, 1888, says of the telegraph:

Prior to 1837 it embodied the work of Morse and of Henry alone. From 1837 to 1844 it was a combination of the inventions of Morse, Henry and Vail; but ... the elements contributed by Morse have gradually fallen into desuetude, so that the essential telegraph today, and the universal telegraph of the future comprises solely the work of Joseph Henry and Alfred Vail.

Even before Morse's first line was erected, Vail had invented and operated a clever printing telegraph; but he did not even patent it. He honestly thought that the simplicity of the so-called Morse system gave it an advantage, and furthermore, he felt prohibited by his contract with Morse from marketing any ideas of his own. Only a few years later he had the bitterness of seeing the printed telegraphs of House and Hughes patented, put on the market and extensively used.

From Washington Vail wrote petulantly to Morse in September, 1848, "I shall in a few months leave Washington for New Jersey, family, kit and all, and bid adieu to the subject of the telegraph for some more profitable business." He explained to his brother George that: "The reason why I must give up remaining here is that I am wearing myself out in the telegraph, for the interest of the patentees, without compensation, and the care and study is accumulating every day."

It seems evident that the promoters were "freezing" him out of the business. Vail at times was a bit difficult, but that constitutes no reason why this should have been done. Had they, as modern magnates would have done, given him a laboratory and a modest salary, the improvement which he might have worked in communication is incalculable. But instead, as he wrote acridly to Amos Kendall, manager for the Morse interest, in 1852:

I am told that the Telegraph Companies will never again give to the Patentees an office. ... I took hold of the Telegraph in its infancy, and when the world was laughing at it and the Inventor —by mismanagement or misfortune, I have the smallest mite in the concern and am prohibited from holding any lucrative office in it, because I in its early developments hazarded it my assistance. Even some little portions of the telegraph which I invented have never been publicly awarded to me....

Vail died in 1859, in actual poverty, while all others who had a hand in creating and promoting the telegraph were prospering. At a meeting of the Magnetic Telegraph Company directors shortly afterwards, resolutions of respect were proposed, and Kendall, in seconding them, said:

If justice be done, the name of Alfred Vail will forever stand associated with that of Samuel F. B. Morse in the history of the invention and introduction into public use of the Electro-Magnetic Telegraph.... Mr. Vail was one of the most honest and scrupulously conscientious men it has ever been my fortune to meet.

CHAPTER V

THE FIRST MESSAGES

Lo, the golden age is come!
  Light has broken o'er the world.
Let the cannon-mouth be dumb,
  Let the battle-flag be furled.
God hath sent me to the nations
  To unite them, that each man
Of all future generations
  May be cosmopolitan.

American Telegraph Magazine, 1852

IMMEDIATELY after the New York demonstration of their new and improved instrument on January 24, 1838, Morse and Vail escorted it to Washington for exhibition to officials and lawmakers, in the hope of procuring a Congressional appropriation. En route they paused at Philadelphia to display it to the admiring eyes of a committee of the Franklin Institute, who expressed themselves as "much pleased." They remarked (which may have been news to Morse) that "the idea of using electricity for telegraphic purposes has presented itself to several individuals, and it may be difficult to settle among them the question of originality." But neither they nor Morse and his aides seem to have heard that Gauss and Weber and Steinheil were using bare wires for their telegraphs, insulating only at the points of support. In America it was still the belief that the wires must be covered—kept away from rain and snow. Morse's were wound with cotton thread, then painted thickly with a gum-elastic varnish, and as a final precaution, they were to be enclosed in a leaden tube.

In February, the instrument was shown in Washington to Congressmen and Government functionaries, and a memorial was handed to Congress by Morse, asking for an appropriation to defray the cost of an experimental line between two cities. The paper was referred to the Committee on Commerce, which in April reported favorably through its chairman, Francis O. J. Smith, and recommended an appropriation of $30,000, to be spent under the direction of the Secretary of the Treasury. A bill was prepared, but did not pass at that session, nor for five years afterwards. One of those financial panics by which human beings periodically manifest their incapacity for affairs had taken place in 1837, and the nation was so much debilitated by it that Congress was reluctant to spend money on wild experiments. Moreover, there were still many people in America— some of them in high places, too—who thought of a telegraph as did Dr. Birkbeck of the Mechanics' Institute in England, who remarked to Edward Davy in 1837, that "The electric telegraph, if successful, would be an unmixed evil to society; would be used only by stock jobbers and speculators—and that the present Post-Office was all that public utility required."

In April, Morse also presented his application for a patent; and therein one finds several additions to and changes from the caveat of the preceding autumn; the new alphabetic type, for example, the marking of dots and dashes instead of the zigzag line, the relay (also called the registering magnet, the local circuit, the repeater, and so on) by which the current is reinforced or renewed. Morse says that the idea of the relay, one of the most important features of the telegraph, came to him early in 1835.

Though Congress did not act on the bill at that session, Congressman Smith regarded the matter as only temporarily deferred, and believed so strongly in the invention that he wanted a share in it. As Taliaferro P. Shaffner, an early telegraph builder says, in a style worthy his own name: "The hidden power of the crudely formed agencies employed by the Professor were seen and appreciated by Mr. Smith's searching perceptions, and their sublimities and subtleties seemed to challenge his admiration and aid. He felt the awe of a divinity's wisdom and presence." In other words, Smith offered to go with Morse to Europe that spring, paying his own way, to aid in obtaining foreign patents, on condition that he be admitted to partnership in the concern. Morse, never a good judge of men, agreed to the arrangement, and thereby stored up much future trouble for himself. Smith, a Portland, Maine, lawyer, as well as editor and proprietor of the *Maine Farmer*, came to be still more noted for his lack of scruple.

In order to give Smith an interest, Gale and the Vails must yield a half of theirs—for Morse did not intend decreasing his own holding. The new deal therefore left Morse with his undiminished half, Smith with one-quarter, Gale and the Vails with one-eighth each.

Morse and Smith sailed from New York on May 16th. The money for Morse's expenses was doubtless supplied by the Vails. He asked the Patent Office to defer issuing his patent until he returned to America. England was their first stopping place, and there they failed to obtain a patent, largely because of the opposition of Wheatstone and Cooke. After the exaction of heavy fees, the Attorney-General ruled against Morse "on an unquestionable judicial quibble." Notwithstanding their dog-in-the-manger policy, both Wheatstone and Cooke had the nerve, eighteen months later, to write letters to Morse, begging him to aid them in obtaining an American patent; which he refused to do. In refreshing contrast to the British procedure, the Englishmen, to their own surprise, were granted an American patent on June 10, 1840, ten days before the issuing of Morse's patent, applied for more than two years earlier.

Morse had little better success in France; for though, after long blowing of hot and cold by the French authorities, a nominal patent was granted, it was rendered worthless by some of those ingeniously negative legal conditions in which the French are particularly apt, especially when dealing with a foreigner. But one kindly Gaul, M. Amyot, recent inventor of an unsuccessful telegraph, was generous enough to aid Morse in an effort to place his system in Russia. Baron de Meyendorff, a

Russian nobleman, had tried to introduce Amyot's telegraph there, and now undertook to do the same for Morse's, but in vain. Colonel Komaroff, writing in the *Annales Telegraphiques* in 1861, says, "Emperor Nicholas saw in it only an instrument of subversion"; and by ukase it was forbidden during his reign to give the public any information regarding the apparatus, not even translations of articles from foreign journals being permitted.

Morse returned to America in very low spirits in the spring of 1839; Smith had long preceded him. Jackson was still clamorous, and finally brought suit against Morse, but was decisively defeated when the matter came into court. Smith, Vail and Gale had all been hit by the depression, and in saving their own concerns had suffered a slackening of interest in the telegraph, so that its progress was but little advanced. Morse wrote to Smith, complaining of his disappointment "in finding nothing done in Congress.... I had hoped to find on my return some funds ready for prosecuting the enterprise.... I return with not a farthing in my pocket, and have to borrow even for my meals"; not to mention a "debt of rent" which must be cleared up. The University was in a low state financially, and he feared he might have to leave it.

Within a month after his return, he asked if he might call upon Professor Henry at Princeton, "In the absence of Dr. Gale, who had gone south," for some scientific advice. The latter replied cordially, and Morse spent an afternoon and evening with him, receiving all the information that Henry had to give on the subject of electricity. Henry was one of those selfless, ideal scientists who care not who receives the glory and emoluments for a discovery or invention, so long as science is advanced thereby. At this time it had not occurred to Henry to claim his bell-ringing device as a telegraphic invention. Then and for years afterwards he was ready to give Morse every possible aid in attaining his end. Henry was an explorer, a discoverer rather than an inventor. He was interested in pure, abstract science for its own sake, not in devising practical and marketable apparatus. Not until he was drawn into controversy several years later, and Morse and his attorneys had made ungracious, even malevolent attacks upon him did the gentle scholar, embittered by the ingratitude and misrepresentation, begin to speak of his own simple device as a telegraph and to regret that he had not asked for a patent on it.

Now began for Morse the darkest years of his life. His professorship had faded out. Gale had gone to a southern college, Alfred Vail was in Philadelphia and Smith seemed to be doing little to further the telegraph measure in Congress. Morse worked for a time at promoting the new invention of his French friend Daguerre for making pictures of any object automatically on a sensitized plate by means of sunlight; then he opened a small studio and taught painting and drawing. He was shabby and threadbare, sometimes did not even have the price of a meal in his pockets. Once when a pupil who owed him $50 promised to pay next week, Morse retorted sadly, "Next week! I shall be dead by that time!" "Dead, sir!" repeated the startled student. "Yes, of starvation." "Would $10 be of any service?" asked the youth. "It would save my life, that's all," replied Morse.

He wrote long and frequent letters to his partners, telling of his difficulties, not blaming them harshly, but urging assistance in any way possible. His patent was granted in 1840, but Wheatstone, as already mentioned, had received one ten days earlier. Wheatstone had money to spend in promotion, and business men were beginning to listen to his sales talk. Then, as now, the foreign idea, whether in science, literature or art, had more glamour for America than the one conceived at home. Moreover, another man named Gonon had actually been permitted to erect a semaphore telegraph on the Capitol building, and a slow-witted Congress was regarding the clumsy thing seriously, in half a mind to spend some money on it.

In all his spare time—and he had much of it—Morse was tinkering with his invention. He developed a more powerful battery. He was enormously cheered when Joseph Henry, after a visit to his little laboratory, wrote him on February 24, 1842, a commendatory letter whose final paragraph read:

About the same time with yourself Professor Wheatstone of London, and Dr. Steinheil of Germany, produced plans of the electro-magnetic telegraph, but these differ as much from yours as the nature of the common principle would well permit; and unless some essential improvements have lately been made in these European plans, I should prefer the one invented by yourself.

With my best wishes for your success, I remain, with much esteem, etc.

Morse's biographer, Prime, says that "This was the most encouraging communication Professor Morse received during the dark ages between 1839 and 1843." Morse also heard of Henry's saying to a friend that "without exception it (Morse's telegraph) was the most beautiful and ingenious instrument he had ever seen." Morse now wrote dozens of letters to Congressmen, repeating this praise of Henry's, "a high authority" on this subject, and begging for action. He had hoped for something that year, but it was a bitter disappointment when Congressman Boardman wrote him in August: "The Treasury and the Government are both bankrupt, and that foolish Tyler has vetoed the tariff bill; the House is in bad humor, and nothing of the kind you propose could be done."

Morse was well-nigh crushed by this blow, but soon revived and fought on. In October, he attempted a demonstration of his telegraph in New York City. He had laboriously covered two miles of wire with a gooey mixture of pitch, tar and rubber, and on one moonlit night he employed a man with a yawl to row him from the Battery to Governor's Island, while he paid out the wire over the stern—impressing a few loungers on the Battery with the belief that he was laying a "trot-line" for fish. Next morning the New York *Herald* announced editorially that a demonstration of Morse's Electro-magnetic Telegraph would be given that day between the hours of twelve and one at Castle Garden. Eccentric Editor Bennett was sufficiently impressed with the device to utter a noteworthy prophecy: "It is destined to work a complete revolution in the mode of transmitting intelligence throughout the civilized world."

A huddle of curious folk assembled at Castle Garden that day to witness the test of under-water telegraphy. Professor Gale, recently returned from the South, was at the other end of the wire on Governor's Island. Morse sat down at his instrument, and had succeeded in exchanging two or three signals with Gale when the wire suddenly died. Looking out of a window, Morse promptly guessed the reason. There were three or four vessels anchored between the Battery and the island, and one of them had just lifted its anchor, bringing the cable up with it. The surprised sailors, not knowing what the queer, gummy thing was, cut it to see what was inside, then flung the ends into the water and went on their way. The spectators around the doleful inventor, thinking they had been hoaxed, jeered and departed.

In December, however, the experiment was repeated across a canal at Washington, and was successful. Morse, now terribly pinched for money, appealed to Alfred Vail's brother George, but without success as he, too, was hard up. The inventor had by this time enlisted the physical aid of another scientist, Dr. James C. Fisher, and they jointly discovered that two or more currents could be passed simultaneously through one wire—though they did not develop this into actual duplex telegraphy. Fisher, who knew several members of Congress, was a good booster, and aided considerably in that way. As the year 1842 drew to a close, Morse had more and more prominent men, both in and out of Congress, working in his behalf. He strung a wire between two committee rooms in the Capitol at Washington, and those who could be induced to look and listen were much impressed by the performance. But even many of these remained utterly oblivious to the possibilities of the telegraph as a mode of communication, or else, like the Russian Czar, thought it dangerous.

But as the year 1843 dawned, it gave promise of being a brighter period for the weary but still hopeful dreamer. His bill, still calling for a $30,000 appropriation, was before the House of Representatives again, though with many corn-fed members still incredulous or fearful of it. Morse was there, watching and lobbying. His letters to his brother Sidney give evidence of the long strain which he was enduring with remarkable fortitude. On January 6th, he wrote that he had vainly hoped to see the measure brought up that day. "Everything looks favorable," he wrote, "but I do not suffer myself to be sanguine, for I do not know what may be doing secretly against it. I shall believe it passed when the signature of the President is affixèd to it, and not before."

The opening sentences of his letters to Sidney for weeks thereafter are significant:

Jan. 16th: I snatch the moments of waiting for company in the Committee Room of Commerce to write a few lines. Patience is a virtue much needed here....

Jan. 20th: My Patience is still tried in waiting for the action of Congress on my bill....

Jan. 25: I am still *waiting, waiting*....

Jan. 30: I am still kept in suspense which is growing more and more tantalizing and painful....

Feb. 21: I think the clouds begin to break away and a little sunlight begins to cheer me....

On that day some of the "showoffs" in the House, led by Cave Johnson of Tennessee, indulged in a rodeo of rustic wit at the expense of the telegraph. The report of it in the pages of the *Congressional Globe* was of course thickly peppered with those interpolations of "(laughter)" so dear to the legislator's soul. We quote from it:

Mr. Cave Johnson wished to have a word to say upon the bill. As the present Congress had done much to encourage science, he did not wish to see the science of mesmerism overlooked. He therefore proposed that one half of the appropriation be given to Mr. Fisk, to enable him to carry on experiments, as well as Professor Morse.

Mr. Houston thought that Millerism should also be included in the benefits of the appropriation.

Mr. Stanly said he should have no objection to the appropriation for mesmeric experiments, provided the gentleman from Tennessee (Mr. Cave Johnson) was the subject. (A laugh.)

Mr. Cave Johnson said he should have no objection, provided the gentleman from North Carolina (Mr. Stanly) was the operator. (Great laughter.)

Several gentlemen called for the reading of the amendment and it was read by the Clerk, as follows:

Provided, That one half of the said sum shall be appropriated for trying mesmeric experiments under the direction of the Secretary of the Treasury.

Mr. S. Mason rose to a question of order. He maintained that the amendment was not *bona fide,* and that such amendments were calculated to injure the character of the House. He appealed to the chair to rule the amendment out of order.

The Chairman said it was not for him to judge of the motives of members in offering amendments, and he could not, therefore, undertake to pronounce the amendment not *bona fide.* Objections raised to it on the ground that it was not sufficiently analogous in character to the bill under consideration, but, in the opinion of the Chair, it would require a scientific analysis to determine how far the magnetism of mesmerism was analogous to that to be employed in telegraphs. (Laughter.) He therefore ruled the amendment in order.

Poor Morse, lurking uneasily in the balcony, must have found it difficult to join in the (Great laughter)!

The mesmeric amendment was lost, and two days later the bill squeezed through the House by a vote of 89 to 83. "I have no desire to vaunt my exertions," wrote Morse, "but I can truly say that I have never passed so trying a period as the last two months." But there was still greater tension to come. The Senate had yet to act, and only eight days of the session remained. Morse heard that some of the opposition members of the House were working hard to bring about an adverse vote in the Senate. Every day his spare, worn figure, like an uneasy ghost, haunted the gallery and the lobbies, helpless to do anything save listen or buttonhole a Senator now and then between times.

In a letter written many years later, he tells a pretty story of the last day of the session, March 3rd, when there were 140 bills to be acted upon before his could be reached. According to custom, President Tyler sat in a room in the Capitol, signing bills as fast as they were ground out of the mill. Morse watched all day, so the story goes, and after dark in the evening went home thoroughly discouraged, having been assured by Senators that his could not possibly be reached before midnight, which would end the session of Congress. He made his arrangements to leave Washington next day. But as he was eating his breakfast on the following morning, a servant announced a young lady caller. He found her to be Miss Annie Ellsworth, daughter of his old friend and college classmate, the Commissioner of Patents.

"I have come to congratulate you," she exclaimed.

"Indeed, for what?"

"On the passage of your bill."

Morse insisted that she was mistaken.

"It is you that are mistaken," she replied. "Father was there at the adjournment at midnight, and saw the President put his name to your bill, and I asked father if I might come and tell you. Am I the first to tell you?"

Morse says that the news was so unexpected that he could not speak for several moments. At last he said: "Yes, Annie, you are the first, and now I am going to make you a promise; the first dispatch on the completed line from Washington to Baltimore shall be yours."

The Senate journal flatly contradicts this story, showing that Morse's bill was passed early on the morning of the 3rd, promptly laid before the President and reported back to the Senate as signed several hours before adjournment. We are all aware that legislators in their final sessions sometimes play curious tricks with the clock, but this discrepancy seems a little difficult to explain away.

Morse in his reported speech to Miss Ellsworth takes it for granted that Washington and Baltimore will be the termini of the experimental line, though this was not settled with the

86

Secretary of the Treasury until later. The Secretary also approved Gale, Fisher and Vail as assistants in the undertaking. To Vail, Morse wrote peremptorily, "You will not fail, with your brother and if possible, your father, to be in New York on Tuesday the 21st, to meet the proprietors of the Telegraph." Undoubtedly he meant, "to meet with the other proprietors," for Vail was one of them. Vail readily agreed to "devote my whole time and attention to the business so as to secure a favorable result," his chief part being the making of the instruments. "Three dollars per diem," he modestly specified, "with traveling expenses, I shall deem a satisfactory salary."

When Morse first described his telegraph to the Secretary of the Treasury in 1837, he contemplated aërial wires. "Stout spars of some thirty feet in height," he wrote, "well planted in the ground and placed about 350 feet apart, would be required, along the tops of which the circuit might be stretched." But later suggestions that it would be impossible to maintain a line in air against storms, falling boughs and human malice or mischief finally convinced him that the line must be subterranean. The notion also prevailed that the wires must be shut away from the air—which a few years later was declared to be a valuable auxiliary in the carrying of the current. Some of Wheatstone's lines in England had been laid underground, and Morse had not yet heard that they didn't work very well. European countries tried for years afterwards to bury their wires—in some cases laying iron wires in a bed of bitumen or asphalt and covering them with the same; but even after the discovery of gutta-percha as a covering, they had very indifferent success.

Morse and Fisher now filed a caveat on "a mode of filling lead pipe with wire." Fisher's job was to superintend the manufacture of the wire, its insulation and insertion in the leaden tubes. Gale's scientific knowledge was to be used wherever needed; and he quickly brought it into play by objecting to underground wires encased in lead. Lead in acid soils, he said, is apt to corrode and let water in; and furthermore, any tiny hole left in the soldering will admit water and destroy the insulation. But Morse overruled him.

Smith, as his part of the work, undertook to get a good contract for digging the 44-mile trench from Washington to Baltimore in which the wires were to be laid. Advertisements asking for bids on lead piping were published, and among the replies was this one from Morris, Tasker & Morris, who, as may be guessed from the text, were located in Philadelphia:

Thy advertisements for about one hundred and twenty miles of ½ in. lead tube, for Electro Magnetic Telegraphic purposes, has induced us to forward thee some samples of Iron Tube for thy inspection. The quantity required and the terms of payment are the inducement to offer it to thee at the exceeding low price here stated, which thou wilt please keep *to thyself undivulged to other person*....

During the first few weeks, everything moved smoothly. Morse wrote regular and meticulous reports of expenditures to the Secretary of the Treasury. He was anxious to make a good impression by keeping costs as low as possible. In the covering of the wire with thread, he was able to make some changes which cut the cost from the first estimate of $1,010 to a trifle over $500, and this he very happily reported. Fancy his annoyance when Smith made a contract for the ditching at a figure much above the estimate given to the Government. "There are plenty of applicants here," he wrote to Smith, "who will do it for much less, and one even said he thought for one half." It did not occur to Morse that Smith might have included a slice of graft for himself in the contract price. But a bright and clarifying light is soon cast upon the subject.

Ezra Cornell—and here we introduce one of the stalwart early figures of the telegraph—was a six-foot, lank, York-State Yankee, who began life as a carpenter and moved when young to Ithaca, where there are souvenirs of him yet. The panic of 1837 threw him out of a job, and he bought the sales rights for a patent plow for the States of Maine and Georgia. As a walker, Cornell was remarkable even in an age when the purpose of the human foot was better understood than it is now. To sell his plow he walked most of the way to Maine and pretty well all over the State, then walked to Georgia, covered that commonwealth largely on foot and walked back.

On his first trip to Maine he had naturally sought the acquaintance of F. O. J. Smith, proprietor of that influential agricultural journal, the *Maine Farmer*. On his second trip down East, he entered Smith's office in Portland and found the editor on his knees, drawing a crude diagram with chalk on the floor, whilst a plow manufacturer stood by, looking on and grinning broadly. Smith welcomed Cornell as a godsend and said he was trying to explain to the manufacturer his idea of a ditching plow which would cut a trench two feet deep, throwing the earth on either side, whence it might be brushed back again with some sort of scraper after Professor Morse's lead pipe was laid in the trench. "I have taken the contract," said Smith, "to lay the pipe at $100 a mile, and I must have some kind of a machine to enable me to do the work at any such price."

Cornell was much intrigued by the problem, and was not long in reaching an unexpected solution. He proposed and made rough drawings of a knife-like plow which cut a mere slit through the earth. The leaden cable to be rolled on a drum mounted on the beam, and as the share clove the earth, the tube, unreeling from the drum, passed down behind the share and was laid in the bottom of the slit, the earth falling back immediately and closing the gash. Morse came all the way up to Maine to see a trial of the machine, and to him and Smith its working seemed almost like magic.

Smith wanted not only the plow, but its inventor, too. He asked Cornell to superintend the laying of the wire between Washington and Baltimore. This meant giving up his plow business, but Cornell's shrewd perception did not hesitate long over that: "A little reflection convinced me that the telegraph was to become a grand enterprise, and this seemed a particularly advantageous opportunity for me to identify myself with it."

And thus, at thirty-six, lean Ezra took the path towards fame and fortune, and Cornell University was assured of being.

And now ensued more trouble for the harassed Morse. The best place to lay the wire seemed to be between the two tracks of the Baltimore & Ohio Railroad, that offering a level grade. Permission was obtained from the railroad, and work began, starting from Baltimore. At first, a team of spirited horses were used to pull the wire-laying machine, but the animals were so disquieted by the occasional passing of trains—and no wonder!—that Cornell substituted a team of eight mules whose nerves must have been very steady, indeed. They laid from a half mile to a mile of pipe daily.

At that time Morse was using a double circuit to work his telegraph, and so four copper wires were placed in the pipe. To insulate them from each other, these were covered with cotton yarn, each wire in one of four different colors—black, red, green and yellow—so that it could be identified at the terminus and properly attached to the instruments. The wrapped wire was next coated with shellac. Lead ingots were cold-rolled into cable size, the four wires being drawn into it through a hollow mandrel during the rolling process.

Vail was superintending the soldering of the lengths of pipe together as they were laid in the trench. Cornell says that he suspected the "integrity" of the pipe and asked Vail how searching his tests were, but "Vail was uncommunicative." Cornell next asked Avery, who was in charge of the batteries, whether it would not be well to make tests by attaching the wires in every possible combination to the battery and galvanometer, but Avery would offer no suggestion to Vail, who "appeared very jealous of any interference, and had already intimated to Mr. Avery that he should confine himself to his own duties."

Cornell then suggested to Avery that they make a secret test of the wires, and they stole out and did so at midnight, proving to their own satisfaction that the insulation was faulty, and that current was passing from one wire to another. Cornell urged Avery to report this to Morse, "but he dared not do so," and so Cornell went on with his work and kept his own counsel. Not until about nine miles of the pipe had been laid would Vail admit that anything was wrong. One afternoon Morse, pale and troubled, stepped off the train at the Relay House, near which they were working, walked along the track to Cornell and drew him aside, so that the workmen might not hear him.

"Mr. Cornell," said he, "can you contrive to stop this work for a few days in some manner, so the papers will not know it has been purposely interrupted? I want to make some experiments before any more pipe is laid."

Cornell was not unprepared for such a request, and quickly evolved an expedient:

I stepped back to the machine and said, "Hurrah, boys, whip up your mules, we must lay another length of pipe before we quit to-night." The teamsters cracked their whips and the animals started at a lively pace, as I grasped the handles of the plow, and watching an opportunity, I canted it over so as to catch into a point of rock, breaking the machine into a complete wreck.

The following morning's newspapers in Baltimore contained accounts of the "accident," and said that work would be delayed for a few days until repairs could be made. Morse and Fisher next decided to try a hot process, drawing the wire in the hollow mandrel through molten lead; but this, too, was a failure, because the heat charred the yarn covering of the wire, and so ruined the insulation.

Morse was almost in despair. By this time he and Smith had quarreled violently. For the first time, Morse had come face to face with what we now call graft, and did not at first recognize it. Smith had told Morse that he had made an advantageous contract for the lead pipe, whereby a thousand-dollar profit accrued, which he would split with Morse. That the latter was so simple-minded as not to realize what this meant will seem well-nigh incredible to-day, yet he wrote of it to his brother with naïve enthusiasm. The more practical Sidney wrote back, "Are you sure this is right? Will it be considered so if it is made public?"

91

OLD WIRES AND NEW WAVES

Your remark led me to think of the matter [Morse admitted in reply], and I determined at once that, since there was a doubt, I would not touch it for myself, but credit it to the Government, and I accordingly credited it as so much saved to the Government from the contract.

And now, will you believe it! the man who would have persuaded me that all was right in that matter, turns upon me and accuses me to the Secretary as dealing in bad faith to the Government, citing this very transaction in proof. But providentially, my friend Ellsworth, and also a clerk in the Treasury Department, are witnesses that the sum was credited to the Government before any difficulties arose on the part of Smith.

The enterprise was now in a precarious position. It was December; nine months had passed since the appropriation was made. Nearly $23,000 had been spent, and between $7,000 and $8,000 remained. Salaries were eating into it—$2,500 a year for Morse, $1,500 each for Gale and Fisher, and for Vail about a thousand dollars. Of the small balance remaining, Smith claimed $4,000 in satisfaction of his contract for laying the pipe the full 44 miles, whether it was actually laid or not, as he stood ready to lay it according to plan. He had by this time decided that the whole affair was a failure, and he was going to get what he could out of it, regardless of the others.

Morse was so angry at Fisher for failing to test the pipe as it was being made that he dismissed him. He wrote one of his bitterest letters to his brother about this time:

The trenching is stopped in consequence of this among other reasons, and has brought the contractor upon me for damages (that is, upon the Government). Mr. Smith is the contractor, and where I expected to find a *friend,* I find a FIEND. The word is not too strong, as I may one day show you. I have been compelled to dismiss Fisher, and have received a very insolent letter from him in reply. The lead-pipe contract will be litigated, and Smith has written a letter full of the bitterest malignity against me to the Secretary of the Treasury. He seems perfectly reckless, and acts like a madman. . . .

It seemed to all concerned that it would now be impossible to build the line without another appropriation from Congress

92

of at least $25,000. There might be some economy effected if the wire could be saved by removing it from the lead covering: Vail said this couldn't be done without melting the lead, but Cornell believed that he could peel the lead off; and Morse being convinced, Cornell was appointed a Government assistant, and began work on the job in the basement of the Patent Office.

Desirous of better knowledge of his new vocation, Cornell decided to spend the winter evenings in study of it. He asked the Patent Office for a list of books on electricity and telegraphs, and Commissioner Ellsworth gave him an order, permitting him to take them from the Patent Office library. But when he applied for them, he found them all "out":

> Repeated applications only served to obtain the same response, and further inquiry led to the discovery that Mr. Vail had drawn these books the very day of my interview with the Commissioner. Finally, becoming satisfied that he was keeping the works to prevent my examination of them, I explained the circumstances to Mr. Smith, who thereupon introduced me to the Librarian of Congress, from whom I had no difficulty in obtaining the desired books.

If Cornell's surmises are true, his experience throws a new and interesting side-light on Vail's character.

"Fisher I have dismissed for unfaithfulness; Dr. Gale has resigned from ill-health; Smith has become a malignant enemy, and only Vail remains true to his post," wrote Morse in January, 1844. As with other men, Morse was slow to realize or acknowledge what a valuable helper he had in Cornell—one whose name was destined to stand high in the annals of telegraphy. The latter's reading convinced him that they had been having the same trouble as had Cooke and Wheatstone, who finally put their wires on poles. Vail's reading brought him and Morse to the same sad conclusion, and one day Morse said to Cornell that he might change his plans for the wiring. "Light was breaking in an important quarter," mused Ezra. While he continued removing lead from the wire, he made no move to rewind the wire, having a scheme of his own in mind. This was to separate the wires from each other, attaching each to a pole by its own glass insulator—the plan which has been pursued ever since, and so obvious and common sense an idea that it is amazing that it did not occur to everybody.

Vail, however, was still obsessed with the idea of insulating each wire, fastening them all in a bunch to each pole, and Morse, agreeing with him, started to New York to have the fixtures made. But on the way he stopped at Princeton to see "my old friend, Professor Henry," to tell him of the failure of the ground wire and the new plan. But when he explained Vail's notion of making a cable of the wire, Henry shook his head.

"It will not do," said he. "You will meet the same difficulty you had in the pipes."

Morse then spoke of Cornell's suggestion, of which Henry approved, and it was so ordered. Cornell's first insulators for the wire were very primitive. A square notch was cut in the cross-arm, just wide enough to contain a small square of thick glass. The wire passed over this, being wrapped in cotton and saturated with shellac. Another square of glass was laid on the wire, and a wooden cover nailed over the glass "to keep off the weather" and hold the glass in place.

Pestered meanwhile by Smith's suit over the ditching contract, Morse made a counter-claim for seven months' salary during the European trip of 1839-40, when Smith suddenly returned home and left Morse to work alone. "If he goes forward with his claim," Morse wrote, "(he) is a ruined man in reputation, but he may sink the Telegraph also in his passion."

John W. Kirk, in an article in *Scribner's Magazine*, [1] says that in 1843 he was in Washington, keeping an eye on some stage-coach mail contracts on which he was bidding. One day Second Assistant Postmaster-General John A. Bryan said to him angrily, "There is an abominable scheme to ruin me." He explained that his superiors, in order, as he believed, "to implicate him in a foolish transaction," had put into his hands the handling of the $30,000 appropriation made for Morse. Bryan,

[1] "The First News Message by Telegraph," *Scribner's Magazine*, May, 1892, p. 652.

like many others, was convinced that the experiments would prove Morse crazy, or at least, impractical. He asked Kirk to help him keep an eye on the inventor and see that he did some actual work for the money drawn.

Kirk remembered to have seen Morse waylaying Congressmen during the previous winter, they dodging the "crank" whenever possible. Kirk went often to see him thereafter. "He had taken possession of a little room in the Capitol, and day after day, as I watched the careworn, spare and anxious man working in the midst of his curious apparatus, I learned to have sympathy with his sincerity and perseverance." But he still doubted that there was any value in the inventor's work.

Towards the end of April, 1844, the wires had been erected for five miles in the direction of Baltimore, and Morse summoned a Congressional committee to see the line work. "Now, gentlemen," said he, "what shall we send over the wire? Pick out your own message, and I will show you how simple the whole thing is, and how it accomplishes everything I claim."

One of the legislators proposed the message, "Mr. Brown of Indiana is here." Morse clicked away at his instrument, and by way of the circuit it came back again and was imprinted on the paper of the receiving machine. But the Congressmen, as Morse ought to have known, unable to read the dots and dashes on the fillet of paper, derived nothing from the test save an impression of trickery. "That's what I call pretty thin," whispered one of them to Kirk. "It won't do," said another. "That doesn't prove anything."

It now occurred to the promoters that some real publicity could be gained by reporting in Washington the names of the nominees in the Whig national convention, which was to meet at Baltimore on May 1st. The poles had been set as far as Annapolis Junction, twenty-two miles from Washington, and wires were now hastily strung on them. Morse about this time reports finding that he could use the earth for a return circuit, and that the ground and one wire worked with better effect than two wires.

OLD WIRES AND NEW WAVES

On the last day of April Morse sent an anxious letter to Vail, who was to telegraph the news from Annapolis Junction as soon as the train reached there from Baltimore, bringing the names of the nominees, which a friend was to send by one of the train crew. Morse cautioned Vail about his sending—spacing the letters better and so on; "and do not be out of hearing of your bell."

Political conventions then did not waste several days in oratory, committee meetings and platform making before reaching the nominations. It was expected that the whole thing would be over and the candidates nominated on the first day. Crowds swarmed around the Baltimore & Ohio station in Washington and lined the tracks for a hundred yards, waiting for trains to arrive, bringing the latest gossip from the convention. They could be seen from the window of the room in the Capitol where Morse had his office.

Kirk describes that room: "On a shelf across the window was the strange machine with its paper tape and the crank by which the weight was wound up, to revolve the rollers through which the tape moved when the message was being received. At the other end of the room were shelves, on which were the pots and jars of the primitive battery." The wires ran along the floor with narrow strips of scantling on either side for protection, and loose plank laid over all to walk on. Morse was "very quietly dressed, his coat muffled about his throat and his long hair tumbled about his forehead. He appeared to be nervous and apprehensive." Kirk claimed to have noticed no interest or anxiety as to whether the test would succeed. Morse, on the other hand, asserted that his room was "thronged" that day.

Passengers on the train which left Baltimore after the nominations but before the convention adjourned, saw a novel sight at Annapolis Junction. Alongside the track was a rough platform laid on a crib of railroad ties; on the platform a table with a queer-looking little machine on it; a young man—some one heard that he was a Mr. Vail of New Jersey—sitting beside the table, reading from a bit of paper which had been handed to

TELEGRAPH PROMOTERS

AMOS KENDALL   HIRAM SIBLEY

HENRY O'RIELLY

F. O. J. SMITH   EZRA CORNELL

him from the train and wiggling a sort of lever on the machine with his forefinger. Two wires led from the instrument up to a near-by pole about twenty feet high, thence to another such pole, and so on as far as the eye could reach in a long row towards Washington. None of the open-mouthed passengers on the cars had ever seen anything like this before.

When the leisurely train, stopping for several minutes at every tiny station, finally rumbled into Washington an hour and four minutes later, passengers were astounded to find many Washingtonians aware that Henry Clay had been nominated for President and Theodore Frelinghuysen for Vice-President, having heard the news an hour ago, though many of them did not believe it. Morse had the names scribbled on slips of paper and men handed them out sparingly on the street and at the railway station, also announcing the names orally. Many hearers said, "You're quizzing us! It's easy for you to guess that Clay would be the Presidential nominee, but who in the devil is Frelinghuysen?" Morse proudly wrote to his brother that the message had been sent and an acknowledgment returned to Vail in two minutes and one second.

The fact that the first news dispatch in American history had been sent that afternoon passed unnoticed by the newspapers of Washington and Baltimore. Editors of those days were sometimes among the last to hear a piece of news, and often did not recognize one when they saw it. The Washington *Daily Globe,* published late in the evening, said, "The newspapers in Baltimore with which we exchange failed to arrive here to-night, but we have been permitted to look over the Baltimore Patriot of this afternoon, which enables us to state from recollection all that is important"; and then followed the names of the nominees.

Next day, however, Morse had so many visitors that he wrote to Vail:

There is great excitement about the Telegraph.... Get from the passengers on the cars from Baltimore or elsewhere, all the news you can and transmit. A good way of exciting wonder will be to tell the passengers to give you some short sentences to send me; let them note time and call at the Capitol to verify the time I received it. ... Your message to-day that "the passengers in the cars gave three cheers for Henry Clay" excited the highest wonder in the passenger who gave it to you to send when he found it verified at the Capitol.

But Vail must have been having his troubles with Morse, for on that same day he wrote to his wife, "Morse changes oftener than the wind, and seems to be exceedingly childish sometimes." The harassed inventor was having fits of melancholy and distraction. "It is as much as I can do to keep Morse from being sick," wrote Vail at another time, "and don't seem to know sometimes how to operate his own instrument." On May 6th he noted in his diary: "Prof. M. is again low spirited—Prof. M.'s plan is to desist, let the Patent expire, and then, if Government uses it and remunerates him, he will not see Prof. Gale and myself want. This he told me in the Capitol this a. m."

But these moments of depression quickly passed and they did not "desist." On May 11th he wrote to Vail:

I shall have a great crowd to-day and wish all things to go off well. Many M.C.s will be present, perhaps Mr. Clay. Give me the news by the cars. When the cars come along, try and get a newspaper, from Philadelphia or New York and give items of intelligence. The arrival of the cars at the Junction begins to excite here the greatest interest.

On May 14th, Vail notes, "Telegraphed from the Relay House. All worked well." One week later the wires were entering Baltimore. Their stringing on poles had been so inexpensive that there was still enough money left to pay Morse's and Vail's salaries for the balance of the year.

And now came the great opportunity for publicity, and plans were laid for the formal opening of the completed line on May 24, 1844. In accordance with his promise to Miss Ellsworth, Morse asked her to choose the words of the first message. She and her mother conferred, and turned to the Bible for inspiration. Their choice fell upon the final phrase of the twenty-third

98

verse of the twenty-third chapter of Numbers, "What hath God wrought!" The profoundly pious Morse, who had a mystic's belief that he was a divinely chosen instrument for the furtherance of communication, was deeply impressed by the significance of the line.

For the auspicious ceremony, the wires had been carried into the Supreme Court room in the Capitol, and there around Morse gathered a comparatively small group of Congressmen, judges and Government officials. It was impressed upon them that Vail, at his instrument in the Mount Clare station of the Baltimore & Ohio Railroad in Baltimore, did not know what message was to be sent. Morse ticked off the words, Vail received them without an error and quickly flashed them back. Morse then asked Vail to "Stop a few minutes." Those around him were offering congratulations, waiting to shake his hand. Morse asked them to suggest messages. Those grouped around Vail did the same, and during the next few minutes these were some of the sendings:

From Morse: "Have you any news?" "No." "Mr. Seaton's respects to you." "My respects to him." "What is your time?" "Nine o'clock, twenty-eight minutes." "What weather have you?" "Cloudy." "Separate your words more." "Buchanan stock said to be rising." "I have a great crowd at my window." "Van Buren cannon in front, with foxtail on it."

The strip of paper on which the message was indented at Washington was claimed by Representative, afterwards Governor, Seymour of Connecticut, because Annie Ellsworth was a native of his State—and was deposited in the Atheneum or Museum at Hartford.

CHAPTER VI

THE INFANT TELEGRAPH

No more we'll trust the carrier dove
Or iron steed or lagging gale,
But call the lightnings from above
To spread the news and tell the tale.

ANONYMOUS, 1847

A CONTINUED strange insensibility on the part of press and public to the possibilities of the telegraph is apparent for long after the formal opening of the first line. The Baltimore *Patriot* on the following day, May 25th, made a magnificent gesture by directing Vail to send a message to Washington, reading, "Ask a reporter to send a dispatch to the Baltimore Patriot at two o'clock P. M." Within a minute's time the eager Morse replied, "It will be attended to."

The *Patriot* that evening pridefully reports what seems to have been the first use of the telegraph by a newspaper:

Two o'clock p.m.—The dispatch has arrived, and is as follows:—
One o'clock—There has just been made a motion in the House to go into the Committee of the Whole on the Oregon question. Rejected, ayes 79, noes 86.
Half past one—The House is now engaged on private bills.
Quarter to two—Mr. Atherton is now speaking in the Senate. Mr. S—— will not be in Baltimore to-night.
So that we are thus enabled to give our readers information from Washington up to two o'clock. This is indeed the annihilation of space.

But not for months afterwards did the *Patriot* ask for any more of this news service.

Next day, the 26th, the Democratic National Convention met, also in Baltimore; it seemed as if both parties were in a kindly

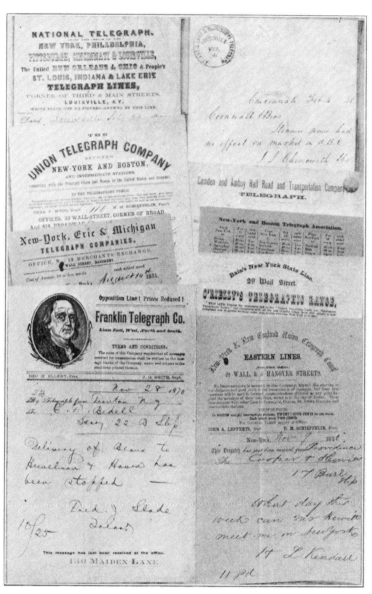

Atlantic, Lake & Mississippi from Frank E. Lawrance; others from Norvin H. Green

TELEGRAMS, 1848 TO 1870

conspiracy that year to boost Professor Morse's invention. The Democrats had a longer and more difficult job than the Whigs. On the 27th, the Washington *Madisonian* had a brief dispatch from the convention, over which was printed for the first time the heading, "Telegraphic News." The Washington *Globe* on that day carried the important item, "By a Telegraph which is in operation between this city and Baltimore, we learn that the convention reassembled at four o'clock p. m." In the same issue is a "Postscript from the Telegraph at nine o'clock P.M."

Vail waited for hours at his instrument, ready to send the names of the nominees as soon as they were voted in. Van Buren had an early lead for the Presidential honor, but could not control the necessary votes, and finally a dark horse, James K. Polk of Tennessee, dashed by him and captured a majority. There were skeptics in Washington who would not believe Morse's announcement of this until it was confirmed by mail and word of mouth.

The name of Silas Wright of New York for Vice-President soon followed that of Polk. But the convention was thrown into astonishment and tumult ten minutes later when a message was handed the chairman announcing that Senator Wright, quickly notified in the Capitol building by Morse, had declined to run. The majority of the delegates positively refused to believe in any such necromancy, all the more nonsensical because it suggested that a man would refuse the Democratic nomination for the Vice-Presidency. The convention was temporarily halted, and a committee went to Washington by rail to see Wright in person, returning with the dumbfounding news that the report of his declination was true. The convention voted to plead with him, and now believed so thoroughly in the telegraph that the pleading was done by wire. In Baltimore a committee sat solemnly around Vail, in Washington Senator Wright sat beside Morse, all others being excluded. After Wright had stated his reasons for refusing and declared that his declination was positive and final, the convention gave way.

By this time there was great interest in Washington over the magic of the wire, and a crowd, consisting mostly of members of Congress, stood on the Capitol lawn below the windows of Morse's instrument room, eagerly awaiting news. When he was able to report that Dallas had been named to replace Wright, the audience gave him three cheers, the Professor took several bows, and then a self-appointed chairman presented a resolution which was voted unanimously:

Resolved: That the thanks of this meeting be and they are hereby tendered to Professor Morse for the promptitude with which he has reported, via his electro-magnetic telegraph, the proceedings of the Baltimore political convention; and that we consider this invention as worthy the countenance and support of the Government.

On the 28th, the *National Intelligencer* headed an item from Baltimore, "By the Magnetic Telegraph," explaining that it was "politely furnished by Professor Morse," commenting editorially: "The working of this wonderful result of human ingenuity, acting upon developments in science excited universal admiration in this city yesterday."

"I begin to fear now the effects of public favor," wrote Morse, "lest it should kindle that pride of heart and self-sufficiency which dwells in my own as well as in others' breasts, and which, alas! is so ready to be inflamed by the slightest spark of praise." Many who had ridiculed him in years past now hastened to curry favor or to make humble acknowledgment of their error. "Sir, I give in," said Cave Johnson. "It is an astonishing invention."

It is during the Democratic convention that we find evidence of the approach of that wholesale abbreviation and telescoping of words which later became the rule in news dispatches by telegraph. Morse writes to Vail:

Condense your language more, leave out "the" whenever you can. . . . The beginnings of a long common word will generally be sufficient—if not, I can easily ask you to repeat the whole, for example, "Butler made communication in favor of majority rule"— "Butler made com in fav of maj"—"rule" or similar words are unnecessary to repeat when the subject has been considered.

THE INFANT TELEGRAPH

F. O. J. Smith was now in a distressing predicament. He was tremendously impressed by the performance of the telegraph, and if it was destined to be a financial success, he wanted to be in on the ground floor, yea, even to control it. But would it be a money-maker? Morse had chosen Amos Kendall, a Massachusetts man who had been Postmaster-General under Jackson, as his agent, or in other words, promoter; and Gale and Vail had also placed their affairs in Kendall's hands. Smith preferred to retain the management of his own share; nevertheless, he desired to placate Morse. He began pondering ways of withdrawing from his lawsuit without loss of face. He worked out a telegraph code, by which sentences and phrases might be condensed to a single word, and published it in July, 1844, writing for it a lengthy introduction, dripping with saccharine praise for Morse. He asserted, in a noteworthy example of scrambled metaphor, that "the names of Franklin and Morse are destined to glide down the declivity of time together," that illustrious toboggan race continuing "until the hand of history shall become palsied, and whatever pertains to humanity shall be lost in the general dissolution of matter." When he submitted the proof of this to Morse, the latter replied coolly that he would prefer to have the dedication "much curtailed and less laudatory."

A thick fog of ignorance as to the nature of the telegraph still overlay many minds. A prominent Government functionary asked, "How large a bundle can be sent over the wires? Can't the United States mails be sent on them?" A wag hung a pair of old boots over a wire in the outskirts of Washington one night, and explained to passers-by nex' day (some of them believing), that the shockingly dirty condition of the boots was due to their having come so fast from Baltimore. A woman near whose house the wires passed, glaring at them with hands on hips, said, "Now I s'pose a person can't spank a brat without it bein' known all over creation."

Others were beginning to discover real uses for the wires. Just as the Democratic convention was closing a note was handed to Morse which read, "As a rumor is prevalent here this morning that Mr. Eugene Boyle (son of Mr. John Boyle of this place) was shot at Baltimore last evening, Professor Morse will confer a great favor upon the family by making inquiry by means of his Electro-Magnetic Telegraph if such is the fact." Instructions for finding Mr. Boyle were given, Vail sent out a messenger, and in a few minutes was able to report that the rumor was unfounded.

A man in Baltimore, given a check upon a Washington bank, asked Morse by telegraph to ascertain whether the drawer of the check had any funds in that bank and was quickly assured. A thief escaping from Washington by rail, was pursued by the telegraph and arrested as he stepped off the train in Baltimore. Two or three or more incidents of this sort which occurred during the next few years led editors to decide that crime would soon be almost eliminated, as it would be practically impossible for a criminal to escape the long arm of the "lightning."

Morse recounted these incidents with much pride in his report to the Treasury on June 3rd, adding its political services in the statement that the telegraph, "In the few days of its infancy," had "already casually shown its usefulness in the relief in various ways of the anxieties of thousands." He reported that after the settlement of all outstanding accounts, about $3,500 of the Congressional appropriation remained, which could be used for running expenses. In conclusion, he pointed out that "The proprietors respectfully suggest that it is an engine of power, for good or for evil, which all opinions seem to concur in desiring to have subject to the control of the Government, rather than have it in the hands of private individuals and associations." He therefore suggested that the proprietors would be willing either to sell it outright to the Government or build the line to New York under contract for the Government. No figure was mentioned in either case.

The price to be paid if Uncle Sam made an outright purchase was a much debated subject. Morse's good friend Ellsworth, Commissioner' of Patents, made a generous suggestion; he thought the Government should be permitted to buy the line from Washington to Baltimore at the rate of $50 per mile! In August, Vail wrote to Morse that he would not accept less than $50,000 for his one-eighth share. Morse had already said that he would be satisfied with $110,000 for his interest. Later the whole concern was offered to the Government for $100,000. But by this time, Congress, thrilled by the thought of grabbing some more land in the southwest, was working up a rage against Mexico, as Morse wrote in January, 1845, "Texas drives everything else into a corner," and science had to take a holiday. Europe was showing interest in the Morse telegraph, especially France and Russia. Morse was an honored guest at an elaborate dinner at the Russian ambassador's table, and began longing to rush over to Europe again and dispose of patent rights.

In September, 1844, the Washington terminus was moved from the Capitol to the second story of the city post-office building. Morse being eager to get away, a new operator, Henry J. Rogers, was broken in and took over the office at Baltimore, Vail coming to Washington. Morse never thereafter manipulated the telegraph key. He tried it in the following January, but found himself much out of practice.

For nearly a year, the telegraph was free for the public to use, but its operators found time hanging heavy on their hands. In November, Vail and a Baltimorean named John Wills played a game of checkers by telegraph, Rogers sending for Wills. This became a popular stunt for a time. Then three chess-players in Baltimore challenged any three members of the Washington Chess Club, and this match was played by wire. Forty and fifty years later, chess games by telegraph were still something of a fad. Around Christmas time Vail wrote that he and Rogers were busy reporting the doings of Congress for the Baltimore *Patriot*.

Smith had decided to try the experiment of organizing a New England corporation to build a line between New York and Boston. Morse supplied apparatus to exhibit in Boston, and in the summer of '44 Ezra Cornell strung a line from School

Street over the roof of the City Hall to Sudbury Street. To pay running expenses, an admission fee of twenty-five cents to the operating-room was charged, which seems a poor way to promote a company. Cornell reported much interest, but, although Morse himself went up and assisted him for a time, nobody seemed willing to buy any stock. The patentees thought it was all that pestiferous Dr. Jackson's fault, and he certainly did plenty of adverse talking and sneering while the exhibition was on.

Cornell was then moved to New York, and he and O. S. Wood, another new pupil of the Morse key, tried to promote a line between New York and Philadelphia. They succeeded in stringing a wire for several blocks over the roofs of houses, but only after paying Professor Silliman a $50 fee for a written opinion, assuring the householders of its safety. An office was opened at each end of the line. Again a twenty-five cent admission fee was charged, and few paid it—not enough to cover expenses. Cornell and Wood slept on chairs in the offices, and once the former was saved from going breakfastless by the finding of a shilling on Broadway. The rooms looked poverty-stricken and were not calculated to attract investors.

Even the marvelous achievements of the Baltimore-Washington line could not persuade the smart capitalists of Gotham. "Each feared to be the first fool." Jacob Little, the first of the great Wall Street plungers, who made and lost about three fortunes in his lifetime, told the promoters that the telegraph was a "chimera." "Mr. Little," said either Cornell or Wood to him, "before you cease to exist, the telegraph lines will cover the country like a network, and will become the great opposition to the United States mails." "Nonsense, nonsense!" exclaimed Little. "No, I will not invest any money in them. Look at the poles and wires! They are not safe; the boys in the streets can destroy them as easily as they would a kite-string. No, sir; I will give you a hundred dollars as a gift towards building a line, but I won't invest a dollar." Fifteen years later he remarked ruefully that he could have owned most of the telegraph wires in the country had he been wise enough to take over a controlling interest in that first little $15,000 line. By way of contrast, the keeper of a little beanery on Nassau Street, where you could enjoy a plate of chicken pie for ten cents, was the first man in New York to invest, and he could put up only $200. When the company was finally organized, not much of the money had come from New York.

John P. Monroe, a successful railroad-building contractor, had talked largely in 1842 of organizing a company for Morse, to build a line from New York to Washington, but he soon faded out of the picture. On the eve of Polk's inauguration, Congress adjourned with no action taken on the telegraph; but Kendall and Smith had already the organization of their New York-Philadelphia company pretty well under way. Being up-and-coming promoters of the modern type, they started out by watering the stock. Shares were $50 each, but every original subscriber received another share as a bonus; in other words, there was a "ground floor." The patent owners received another $30,000 for their rights, making the total capital stock $60,000. F. O. J. Smith, in addition to his interest as a patentee, was the largest cash subscriber, taking $2,750 worth. Corcoran & Riggs, the Washington bankers, B. B. French and two others each bought $1,000 worth. Ezra Cornell wrote his name down for $500, though it must have pinched him considerably to pay for it, and even Henry Rogers, the operator, bought a modest $100 worth.

Meanwhile, on April 1, 1845, the original line became a commercial one under the ægis of the Postmaster-General; which meant that instead of getting its messages sent free, the public now had to pay for them. The employees took the Government service oath, and here for a brief time, the telegraph in America was a part of the Post-Office Department, as it is to this day in England and some other countries.

The Postmaster-General fixed a charge of one cent for every four characters; that is, if you sent one eight-letter word, it would cost you two cents. On the first day of operation, a man from Virginia who was in Washington, trying to get a remunerative but not too onerous job under the new administration came into the telegraph office and said he wanted to see the machine work. There were no telegrams passing over the line at the time—in fact, there hadn't been a thing doing all day— and the operator replied that it could not be shown free of charge. The Virginian was aggrieved; as an American citizen and taxpayer, he thought he had a right to see a Government machine in operation. Surely there could be no harm in just showing him how it worked! The operator cited his oath of office. The visitor might send his name to Baltimore and back at four letters for a cent; or he might ask Baltimore about the weather or the time. The stranger said he had no change in his pocket, and continued wrangling with the clerk. The latter finally said, "If the Postmaster-General orders me to show the machine gratis, I will gladly do it; but not until then." The Virginian claimed to be an old friend of the P.M.G., and threatened the operator with his displeasure. The operator told him to go ahead and do his worst. After an hour's debate, the man departed in high irritation.

On April 2nd and 3rd, there was not a message sent. On the 4th, the office-seeker appeared again, and once more began teasing the clerk for a free exhibition. "Have you got the permission of the Postmaster-General for me to show it to you?" asked the employee. The man admitted that he hadn't. Another long discussion ensued, and finally the insistent one capitulated, but declared that he had only a $20-bill and one cent in his pocket. What could the office do about that?

"Well, I can give you one cent's worth of telegraphing," replied the operator. The man, after more garrulity, agreed to this. The operator called Baltimore and clicked off "4," which in the simple code they were then using meant, "What time is it?" Baltimore replied "1," meaning one o'clock.

"Two characters," said the clerk, sarcastically. "Only half a cent, if you have the change." The man hadn't, but paid over his penny and left, apparently satisfied. Thus the receipts of the telegraph for the first four days were one cent. On the 5th of April there was a great rush of business, and the two offices took in, all told, 12½ cents. The 6th was Sunday. On the 7th, 60 cents clattered into the tills; on the 8th, $1.32; on the 9th, $1.04. It was a curious fact that the merchants sent more telegrams after fees were charged than when service was free. The receipts for the whole month of April, however, were only $21.23.

By October, only $413 had been collected, while operating expenses had been $3,925. This led the Postmaster-General (now Cave Johnson, destined to have many early contacts with the telegraph) to reply officially to the patentees: "That the operation of the telegraph between Washington and Baltimore has not satisfied me that under any rate of postage that could be adopted, its revenues could be made equal to its expenditures." Nevertheless, he remarked in his annual report, there were reasons why it should not be left in the hands of individuals. He feared that much business formerly done by mail would now be done by telegraph, and the Government would thereby lose heavily in revenue. Let individuals do such part of the business of the Government as they might find profitable, and the Government would presently be left to do only that which was unprofitable.

Furthermore, the telegraph might become the most potent instrumentality the world has ever known to rob the many for the benefit of the few. "If permitted to be thus held, the public can have no security that it will not be wielded for their injury rather than their benefit. . . . Its value in all commercial transactions to individuals having the control of it cannot be estimated." It ought not, therefore, be left in private hands, uncontrolled by law. Forty and fifty years later, during the Jay Gould period, these remarks were quoted as prophetic.

There were editors, too, who were alarmed over the possible perversion or suppression of news by the telegraph. The New York *Express* feared that "Stock gambling, bread gambling or political gambling of the most frightful kind may be carried on secretly by it, and successfully, too, often in the hands of adroit men, whose fortunes might be made by single operations." The curious thing is that all this has since taken place, and the public conscience has grown quite accustomed to it. As with other things, what was scandalous in 1845, has now become a commonplace, a legitimate business transaction, by the moral standards of the twentieth century.

Henry Clay also saw danger in letting private interests "monopolize intelligence"—meaning news. "I think such an engine should be exclusively under the control of the Government," said he. But there were many in opposition. H. B. Ely, a prominent citizen of Rochester, New York, wrote to his friend, Henry O'Rielly, telegraph promoter, that "there would be as much propriety (and more) in the Government controuling all the Rail Roads and all the Steam power and all the Cotton Gins, as that they should controul this patent." He and many others, particularly in the South, were alarmed at the centralization of power and influence inherent in such control. What would they have thought of the New Deal of 1933?

Congress, however, was now too excited over the coming conflict which it was promoting with Mexico to wrestle with such constructive matters as the telegraph. So it just appropriated $8,000 to keep the line going for a few months and let it rest at that.

Vail had written a small book, a history of the telegraph, in which Morse was considered to have a share. With the inevitable vanity of fledgling authors, they could not see how it could fail to be a best seller. It was agreed that Morse should have one-fourth of the profits. During the summer of 1845, Vail notified Morse that the printing had so far cost $600, and asked for a check for $150 as Morse's quarter of the expenses. Morse was now seized with a fear that the publishing of the pictures and diagrams of apparatus in the book would enable Europe to steal his invention; but he offered to give up all interest in the pamphlet if Vail would give up his interest in the foreign rights to the telegraph. This Vail refused to do, nor would he stop the printing of the book. Cuts and descriptions of Morse's instruments were already being published in scientific magazines, and Europe could glean all the information she wanted therefrom.

It would have been better for Vail had he accepted Morse's proposal, for the book brought some small profit, whereas Morse never realized anything of consequence from the use of his telegraph in foreign countries, although he went to Europe in 1845 and did his best to uphold his interests. Several countries used no other system than his, and in Great Britain it was competing on nearly even terms with the Cooke-Wheatstone instruments.

The new organization, the Magnetic Telegraph Company, began building its line from Philadelphia to New York in the fall of 1845. Vail came from Washington to assist in the job. The wires started in a strangely contrary direction, northwestward from the Quaker City, as if uncertain of the location of New York. The fact is that the company was unable to get a concession along the railroads' rights of way, save at exorbitant rates, and so followed wagon roads and planned to cross the Delaware above Trenton, where the river was narrower and not so great a problem. It is said that Kendall, while Postmaster-General, had been so exacting with the railroads in the matter of mails that they held a grudge against him, and now proceeded to get even.

The wires were strung to Norristown, fourteen miles, by early November, and so great was public curiosity that an operator was installed at the latter place and the line opened. The offices at both places were crowded all day long with gaping spectators, to whom every move of the operator had something of magic in it. The *Dollar Newspaper* of Philadelphia remarked that the telegraph was "transmitting intelligence with a velocity infinitely more rapid than thought"—which was not highly complimentary to the brains of the day. The reporter then chronicled one of its astonishing achievements:

A remark and reply quite amusing to a number of persons in attendance to witness the operations, were made just before tea in the evening. Mr. Vail, at this station, communicated to his Norristown correspondent, the operator at that end of the line, that he was "going to supper." "So am I," came back the ready response, with as little interval of time as if they were speaking face to face in the same room; and the audience left, evidently delighted at the wonderful facility of communication attained by this extraordinary power.

Through that winter the line was pushed forward, past Dolyestown and Somerville, reaching Newark in January, 1846. Kendall informed the public in a card that the line ended there because it could not cross the Hudson; but that messages would be sent between that place and New York by messenger six times a day. The Newark office was in the county court-house. It was soon decided, however, that this arrangement should be bettered, so the line was extended up the Jersey side to Fort Lee and a lead pipe, enclosing a wire covered with cotton and saturated with pitch, a device of Ezra Cornell's, was laid across the river. On the Manhattan shore, an office was opened in "Minnie's Land," the home of Audubon, the naturalist, a land wire leading from there to the city, then some 10 miles distant. A lottery man, one of the best customers, used carrier pigeons between Fort Lee and the city.

Cornell's cable was, unhappily, a failure. An extension was therefore strung from Newark to Jersey City, and for a time, telegrams were carried across the river in rowboats by youthful messengers who presently inaugurated a racket of their own by having a wooden stamp cut, reading "25 cents due," with which they marked envelops and collected pocket-money for some time before being discovered. Ice presently stopped their skiffs, and then they traveled by steam ferry.

Those infant telegraph lines had troubles undreamed-of to-day. From experience with fence posts, the early builders knew that cedar, black locust and chestnut were the best woods for poles; but their ideas on wire and insulation were deplorable. All-copper wire was used at first, as it was believed that iron wire would not carry the current properly; but when the first sleet storm blew out of the North, forty miles of that soft wire between New York and Philadelphia went down.

Again on April 15th, Kendall wrote to O'Rielly that:

The job from Jersey City to Newark was a botched affair; posts and masts badly set, and the glass caps put on without any cement. Now the elements have conspired against us. The wind has blown a gale all this week, making it difficult to work at the masts, and whirling off some dozen of the glass caps, throwing our wire across the R.R. track, where it is broken to pieces and then carried off by foot passengers.

An ingenious mechanic who tried to increase the tensile strength of the wire was a bit eccentric, and the repairers broke the line frequently, to annoy him! Talk about rugged individualism! Iron wire was now strung by the Magnetic and found to work fairly well. But the glass insulation—mere bureau-drawer knobs, small and hard to keep on the pins, as Kendall points out —these were favorite targets for huntsmen and stone-throwing boys, as indeed they have been even into our time. For some time after the line was constructed, people living near it did not know what it was, and would cut out pieces of wire for their own use without compunction. During the first five months of operation, the line was out of commission for thirty-six whole days.

Meanwhile, other companies were being hastily created, and were shooting lines out from New York and Philadelphia in various directions—all their grants from the patentees during 1845 and most of '46 being conditioned upon the possibility that the Government might yet take over the whole business. F. O. J. Smith organized the New York and Boston Magnetic, financing it with his own money and that of a few friends. His wires left New York over the route of Governor Lovelace's seventeenth-century post, and later, the first stage-coach; running up the Bowery and Third Avenue, along the Post Road to New Haven, thence via Hartford, Springfield and Worcester to Boston. Smith at first was convinced that insulation was unnecessary—a mere whim of those unpractical fellows, the electricians. He was somewhat like the English preacher-electrician, Highton, who wanted to lay a naked wire for telegraphy across the Atlantic. Smith made a concession, however, to the fad when his line was built: "I put my wires up," he wrote to O'Rielly, "in both a more useful, and in milder latitudes, a cheaper form. I use no glass cap nor cross-bar, but only blocks saturated thoroughly with tar and resin, and also a tin cover and saturated cloth." The woes of the operator who tried to maintain service over such a line, especially on rainy days, may be imagined by any present-day electrician.

A line between Boston and Lowell was completed before that to New York, and on February 21, 1846, the Lowell office was opened, under the management of the first woman operator in history—Miss Sarah G. Bagley. Those who are under the delusion that women never held any salaried jobs until the typewriter came into general use in the nineties, should read telegraph history (not to mention other data). Female telegraphers were common before the Civil War.

John Butterfield, successful stage-line owner in central New York, later expressman and, in 1858, founder of the Overland Mail line to California, went down to Washington in 1844 to check up on some mail contracts, and became interested in the first primitive telegraph line then building. Theodore S. Faxton, another York State stage-coach promoter, followed hard after him. Then he and Butterfield and a third man put their heads together, and decided to connect the Great Lakes by wire with the Atlantic seaboard. In June, 1845, Butterfield closed a contract with Kendall, whereby he and his associates procured the right to build a telegraph line from Springfield, Massachusetts—connecting there with Smith's New York and Boston line—through Albany and Utica to Buffalo. The proposed eastern terminus was soon changed from Springfield to New York City.

The promoters promptly took in two more expressmen, Crawford Livingston and Henry Wells (first President of the American Express Company and one of the founders of Wells, Fargo & Company). The company was first organized in July, 1845.

The five promoters appointed themselves trustees, and then appointed the trustees as contractors to build the line at a neat margin of profit—a smart piece of business which proves that our great-grandfathers weren't as slow as some folks think they were. By way of promotion, they first opened a line from downtown Utica to the fair grounds, and as a sample feat, charged burghers and peasants 6¼ cents for sending their names over the wire. When regular business began, you could send a 25-word message for 25 cents, while a 12-word answer to it cost 12½ cents. The rate decreased until at 50 words and more it was only a quarter of a cent per word.

On his way back from Washington with the contract in his pocket, Butterfield encountered on the night boat from New York to Albany, that eccentric, likeable human dynamo, Henry O'Rielly, and told him of his plan. O'Rielly's restless soul at once became excited over the thought of building a great telegraph network from the seaboard to the Mississippi River. Ideas born in his brain were already lusty and crying for action at birth. Within a week he had called upon Kendall and procured from him the famous O'Rielly contract, the most important concession given out by the patentees during 1845, and the one which brought the most trouble and contention down upon everybody's head. With the ink still wet upon it, O'Rielly dashed back to Rochester to raise capital—for he had little of his own —to begin building the first section of his line westward from Philadelphia to Pittsburgh.

That same summer Henry J. Rogers, the operator at Washington, organized the Baltimore and Offing Telegraph Company, which ran a line from Baltimore to North Point, on the outer bay, and reported the approach of vessels. Their charges "For reporting vessels within the range of the telescope at North Point" were, for ship or bark, $1.50; for brig $1; for schooner 50 cents. Rogers had a gorgeous vision—never realized—of extending his service all up and down the Atlantic coast, with operators every few miles to watch passing vessels through telescopes and report their whereabouts, and also trusty lifeboats and crews, with which they might rush out through the billows and rescue sailors in distress.

The New York and Offing Telegraph, launched in 1845, built a line from the city to Coney Island, which was rather for news purposes than for the mercantile interest, and will be mentioned later.

During that busy year of 1845, when the new-born telegraph business in America was growing with weed-like rapidity and often with no more than weed-like stability, men's minds fluttered in a curious and to us amusing muddlement of hopes and fears as to what the new force would mean to them and their businesses. Some railroad men, for example, feared that with communication so easy, people would travel less. When the Magnetic Telegraph Company prepared to extend its line from Philadelphia to Baltimore, it sought a right of way along the tracks of the Philadelphia, Wilmington and Baltimore Railroad. The railroad company craved to possess some interest in the telegraph *if* it was going to be a success; so it stipulated that it must have a year's option on one-third of the stock in the Magnetic Company, either to buy or to dispose of the right to buy to some one else. Also:

> Should the Rail Road Company find the system of Telegraphic communication to be a serious injury to their Road in depriving them of passenger travel, they reserve the privilege of requiring the Telegraph Company to remove the posts, wires and fixtures from their Road within twelve months after notice shall have been given.

Some predictions uttered then were quite as silly as many being made in our own time as to our social, industrial and political future. But there were some editors who foresaw rather shrewdly certain effects of the telegraph. The *National Police Gazette* surmised that it would be a leading agent in overthrowing the old cumbersome system of State and private paper moneys—all inflated, all discounted everywhere—and setting up more firmly a national currency; but it went a little too far for the imagination of the period:

THE INFANT TELEGRAPH

The system of domestic exchanges will be almost annihilated. The precious metals and bank notes have no other use as commercial agents but as signs of value, and if the transmission of equal guarantees can be achieved with the speed of light between far distant climes, why, gold and silver may stay at home for mere local purposes, or be laid aside in flower pots and old stockings. The lightning will have taken up their task, and the whole active capital of the country will be ringing its changes upon these magic cords. We are on the eve of a great commercial and financial revolution. No man can at present measure its results or even make a tolerable guess at what it may achieve.

The New York *Express* said in June, 1846:

The power of the States will be broken up in some degree by this intensity and rapidity of communication, and the Union will be solidified at the expense of the State sovereignties. We shall become more and more one people, thinking more alike, acting more alike and having more one impulse.

Never were more truly prophetic words uttered. The greatest factor in destroying our old community self-government—and likewise our individuality, if you please—has been the increase in the facility of communication. Now that the telephone and the ether wave have been added, with each succeeding year, our dialects and folk customs fade away, we become more standardized, we lose more of our local autonomy and become more and more the puppets of a great central government, great newspaper chains, great propaganda agencies which shape minds through wire and air, cramming them into narrow, mass-produced molds.

The spinning of the great wire web gathered impetus in 1846-47 as the public conviction grew that the Government would not take over the Morse patent. Perhaps the news that the Magnetic's receipts were much smaller than expected had something to do with Congressional skittishness. On July 1, 1846, the Magnetic's treasurer could report only $516 profit for the preceding three months. The total receipts for that year were $4,228.77. But had Uncle Sam decided to take over the lines even in that year or the next, before the public had been educated to use them, there would have been some grievously disappointed promoters.

On December 1, 1846, Vail and Rogers leased the Washington-Baltimore line from the Government and ran it until April 16, 1847, by which time Congress had definitely decided to shun the hazards of the telegraph business, and the Magnetic added the pioneer line to its system. In Europe the various governments, one after another, were assuming control of the telegraph as an adjunct of their post-office departments, and so they have remained to the present day. Our governmental avoidance of further extension into the realm of business was in accordance with the best American tradition of the period; and—except for extraordinary measures during war times—it has continued, with but slight change, to be national policy until our definite swing towards radicalism began in 1932.

The Government thus abandoned to private enterprise what came in later years to be one of the most enormous of monopolies. But the politicians thereby lost a happy hunting ground, whose potential richness in graft, jobbery, patronage, nepotism, franking and all the other delectable flora and fauna of politics was beyond human imagination to conceive.

CHAPTER VII

O'RIELLY, EMPIRE BUILDER AND FIGHTER

Then hurry along the wire, boys, the sooner we get through
To New Orleans, the sooner we will have a chance to blow.
For there's no stopping this O'Rielly; it may happen very soon
He'll get the notion in his head to telegraph the moon.

LINE BUILDERS' SONG, 1848

ENTER another of the most colorful figures in early telegraph history; a man, however, now almost forgotten.
Henry O'Rielly—it was a characteristic whimsy of his own to
alter the spelling of his name from the ancient patronymic,
O'Reilly—was born in Ireland in 1806 and brought to this
country by his parents at the age of ten. With but little schooling,
he was apprenticed to a printer, but later released and went to
work in a newspaper office, where he was writing articles at the
age of seventeen. When the *Daily Advertiser* was established
at Rochester in 1826, the twenty-year-old Irish firebrand was
chosen as editor. He promptly became involved in the Anti-
Masonic row then raging in the State, and was arrested for libel,
but never tried. He wrote a history of Rochester in 1838. He
had been serving as Postmaster of the town for several years
when, fired by visions of the future of telegraph, he decided to
cover the Middle West with wires.

Kendall, who had been his old superior as Postmaster-General,
was quite ready to sign the ambitious contract with him. The
whole telegraph business was such a mushroom, harum-scarum
affair then that no dream was considered too fanciful. That
contract on June 13th provided for the extension of the wires
over a vaster field than any which promoters had yet dared to
contemplate. By its terms O'Reilly "undertakes to use his best

119

endeavors to raise capital for the construction of *a line* of Morse's Telegraph" to connect with the Magnetic at Philadelphia and run "thence through Harrisburg and other intermediate towns to Pittsburg, and thence through Wheeling and Cincinnati, and such other towns as the said O'Rielly and his associates may elect, to St. Louis, and also to the principal towns on the lakes." Which lakes? With charming nonchalance, the contract did not say. What a loophole, nay, what a wagon-gate for honest lawyers!

The patentees were to have one-fourth of the stock in the project in exchange for their grant. It was further stipulated:

Nor shall anything herein be construed to prevent an extension of a line by the patentees from Buffalo to connect with the lake towns at Erie; nor to prevent the construction of a line from New Orleans to connect the western towns directly with that city; but such lines shall not be used to connect any western cities or towns with each other which may have been already connected by said O'Rielly.

O'Rielly within six months from the date of the contract, must build his line from Philadelphia to Harrisburg and have funds in hand for its extension to Pittsburgh, else the contract would be considered forfeited—unless it could be proven that he had not been able to obtain a right of way along public roads; in which case, "the conditional annulment shall take effect at the end of six months after such permission shall be given or refused."

And the party of the second part shall convey said patent right *on any line* beyond Pittsburgh *to any point of* commercial magnitude, when the necessary capital for the construction of the same shall have been subscribed, within the period contemplated by this agreement.

By this loosely drawn contract, with its many loopholes for evasion and misunderstanding, Kendall had in mind midwestern territory with a great wire system under one company—though the contract did not specify this. O'Rielly at once called together some friends in Rochester, and succeeded in raising sufficient

120

money for the building of the line between Harrisburg and Lancaster, forty miles. From Rochester to assist in the prosecution of the work he brought two men later noted in telegraph annals—James D Reid, who had been his post-office assistant and later bookkeeper in a newspaper office where Anson Stager, the other man, began as "devil." Stager, who as telegraph czar, became a brigadier-general during the Civil War, wrote anxious letters to O'Rielly, discussing the proper touch on the telegraph key and so on, but presently, after a little practice, became operator at Lancaster.

O'Rielly was blissfully ignorant of electricity, but in that particular was little worse off than many other men who were rushing into the business. Hearing that Morse, some years earlier, had sent faint signals across a canal at Washington by immersing a copper plate attached to a wire in the water on each margin of the stream, O'Rielly tried this at the crossing of the Susquehanna and other rivers, but found that it would not do for sending messages; so he must either get a right of way along a bridge or erect high masts on each side of the stream.

The building of the line was begun at Lancaster in September, 1845. Reid, who published a telegraph history in 1886, thus reports the innocence of those early builders:

The poles were small and had pins resembling chair rungs inserted through an auger hole near the top, to bear the wires, which were to be wrapped around either end, and for which purpose a shallow groove had been worked near either extremity. If there is beauty in simplicity, it was surely here. As to insulation, it was a long word few of us understood. Vail's pamphlet came to our relief, and it was faithfully studied. In it we were directed to dip cotten cloth in beeswax, as a method of securing good insulation.

The waxed cloth was of course to be wrapped around the ends of the pins before the wire was applied. The woes of the operators who tried to send signals over such a wire can be only faintly imagined by the layman. Some of the notions about insulation then seem almost incredible now. Smith's have already been recited. One company used a mere rubber washer, with sad results. Amos Kendall evolved an idea that if a slit were sawed diagonally downward in the side of a pole and the wire slipped into it with a piece of "rubber cloth" around it, the flaps of the cloth being tied back with twine around the pole, all would be well. Fortunately, this was never tried. Even Cornell was seized with the urge to do something bizarre, and developed an insulator shaped like a small iron plug hat, filled with brimstone in which was fixed a double hook. This was set as in position on a man's head, and the wires were hung in the hooks. Reid attributed the ruin of at least one company to this alleged insulator.

In 1846, by the way, O'Rielly—by that time an "expert"—built by contract for the Magnetic Telegraph Company its extension from Philadelphia to Baltimore; total cost, $14,000. By way of insulation against rain and all other detriments, it was specified that the wires must be coated with tar! The first man assigned to the task gave out at Wilmington and Reid was assigned to his place. Says Reid:

I took the bucket and the sponge and lathered the electric road to the Susquehanna. There O'Rielly made a bonfire of my saturated garments. It was a sad business. All the tavern keepers on that road long remembered the man with the tar bucket. At the town of North East they would not give me a bed. As I sat one night on the end of an empty cider barrel in the bar-room of a small tavern, bewailing my fragrant condition and anxiously trying the cleansing qualities of sweet oil, the two plump daughters of the hostess passed me with signs of unmistakable horror. From another room came the exclamation: "Oh, mother, how that man stinks!" How sweet, thought I, is the Saxon language on the lips of a North East maiden!

O'Rielly had scarcely gotten started with his own company when he encountered opposition, some of it stealthy, from other promoters. In his files, one finds a letter written by Henry Wells from the Livingston & Wells express office in Buffalo on July 5th, less than a month after O'Rielly signed his contract. In it, Wells tells O'Rielly of a great scheme for a telegraph line between Philadelphia and Cincinnati, which he is graciously going to let O'Rielly in on. On the top of this letter O'Rielly has penciled the acrid comment, "Judas, in the end, and soon." At the bottom he wrote, "This movement of Wells proved fallacious. All the information he got from me was *only used* [by Livingston & Wells] *to forestall my efforts to get up lines in opposition*. But this game did not succeed well with them."

But though Livingston & Wells did not build their Cincinnati line, they deftly helped to make it very difficult for O'Rielly to raise capital in the cities of western New York, where he was best known. He was having other troubles, too—physical ones.

The line was completed from Harrisburg to Lancaster on November 24th. A handbill issued at the time set forth the following interesting picture:

The Telegraph to be opened at all reasonable hours to all persons according to the priority of their visits. No person except a public officer on business of urgent public interest (such as the prevention of crime and the detection of criminals) being allowed the use of the Telegraph more than ten minutes at a time when others are waiting.

Dispatches not exceeding fifteen words, including address and signature, sent for twelve and a half cents. Newspaper editors half this rate, and a larger reduction when much intelligence is sent.

Visitors desirous of seeing the operation of the Telegraph between Harrisburg and Lancaster, may have their names sent and returned, 72 miles, for six and one-fourth cents.

Pamphlets describing the Telegraph fully, with plates, twelve and a half cents.

The reduced rate to newspapers proves O'Rielly to have been one of the shrewdest of the telegraph promoters of his day, the only one who realized the growing power of the press and the advisability of giving reduced prices for quantity. He thereby won the staunch support of editors and publishers, who stood by him loyally during the conflict with the patentees which followed.

But his feeble little line had been open only a few days when a blizzard swept over it with heavy snow, and the tightly drawn copper wire contracted and broke in scores of places. The offices were closed, and the line was not opened again until January 6th, following. Meanwhile, on December 13th, the deadline was passed; a seventy-mile gap between Lancaster and Philadelphia was unbridged and no money in hand to build to Pittsburgh. The contract was automatically voided, and Smith loudly proclaimed the fact, but Kendall, knowing that poor O'Rielly had done his best, was disposed to be lenient, and no official notice of breach of contract was served upon him.

When the line was opened again, although the offices were crowded with curious folk, gaping at instruments and operators, it was two days before the first message was sent. The report of the Harrisburg manager for the week ending February 7th, is illuminating. His total receipts had been $8.50. He lists each day, with the price of each telegram, most of which brought in only $6\frac{1}{4}$ cents, and from that up to 25 cents. On Tuesday there were 23 telegrams, with total receipts of $1.87½; a big day. On Friday there were only five, with receipts of 50 cents.

"You will observe," says the agent, "that the receipts some days are much smaller than others. I cannot account for it in any way than that the office being so far from the business part of the town; and in inclement weather the walking bad; nothing but necessity will induce persons to patronize it." The connection with Lancaster ceased Saturday evening at 6 o'clock; why, he didn't know, but possibly the fact that it had been snowing and raining all day had something to do with it, and this robbed them of some additional telegrams. The expenses for the week were—candles and salt, 37½ cents; nitric acid, 85 cents; total, $1.22½.

Not much nutriment here for a promoter. But just as folk were beginning to learn the uses of the current, along came another norther, and again the wires were shattered to bits. The tribulations brought on the early builders by that soft copper wire were beyond our conception. After one storm in 1847, the Magnetic's line between Philadelphia and Wilmington, 27 miles, was broken in 17 places. But the prize hard-luck

124

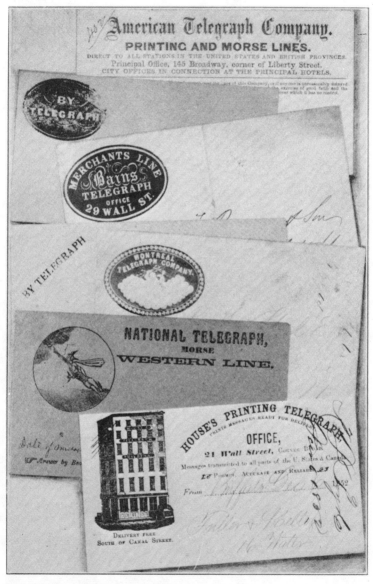

From the collection of Frank E. Lawrance

ENVELOPES IN WHICH TELEGRAMS WERE DELIVERED,
1850 TO 1860

story was that of the New York and Boston, with 170 breaks overnight in a stretch of 30 miles.

That second cataclysm looked as if it might be O'Rielly's death-blow; but he was more resilient than that. His few employees, all with salaries far in arrears, struggled through the snowdrifts, gathering up and stripping from the poles every scrap of wire, which was then sold as junk copper, and with the money a few bills and salaries were paid. O'Rielly was in desperate straits that winter. One finds in his files, duns and notices of notes protested. A man who was begging for payment for poles said, "I have been sued by everyone from whom I bought poles, and had to pay costs. . . . " O'Rielly is found pleading with Rochester merchants for more time on his grocery and clothing bills, begging credit for a ton of coal for his home.

Kendall was holding Smith off, saying, "Give him a chance." The Magnetic even gave O'Rielly an opportunity to earn a bit of change by building their new line from Philadelphia to Baltimore. He spent the spring of '46 on the job, and at its close, was publicly thanked and congratulated by Morse on his success in "connecting the Hudson and the Potomac by links of lightning." This was good publicity for O'Rielly, and aided him in selling stock in Philadelphia and Pittsburgh for his westward line. When a Quaker capitalist subscribed for $5,000 worth, the ice was broken, and he soon had money enough to rebuild the Harrisburg-Lancaster line—which had been idle all spring and summer—to bring it into Philadelphia and extend in the other direction to Pittsburgh. When his line reached Philadelphia in September, Kendall wrote a congratulatory letter to him, which, however, had a sting in it—a frank warning of an Ethiop in the woodpile, a condition which might always be expected, as long as F. O. J. Smith lived:

It is of much more importance to you to secure your main line to Cincinnati, Louisville, etc., than to be extending your views to Nashville or Erie. The same mail which brought your letter brought me two from Cincinnati, stating that the funds can now be had there to build a line to Pittsburgh, probably as soon as you reach that place; and as your privilege is understood to be forfeited, they ask to be made a separate company. I presume Mr. Case is the chief agent in this movement, and he is brother-in-law to Mr. Smith.... Mr. Smith says your privilege is forfeited—that you have not the means to build the line.... My views and wishes, however, are not changed.

Within three months, however, his views had changed; he had gone over to the opposition.

From Harrisburg the new extension ran southwestward along the railroad to Chambersburg, then followed the road which is now the Lincoln Highway to Pittsburgh. Pure copper wire was now being discarded by the companies and iron wire substituted. O'Rielly adopted a three-strand wire made by Hugh Downing of Philadelphia, which was supposed to be a very superior article. The fallacy of many of those early ideas could be discovered only by trial and error—mostly error. When this wire broke (as even it sometimes did), the three strands would sprawl wildly, sometimes get entangled in the wheels of trains if alongside a railroad track, or tear holes in the thin roofs of passenger cars. A single wire replaced it within a few years.

The line to Pittsburgh was declared open on December 29, 1846. Two days before that a faithful rustic friend and helper had written a letter which gives such a quaint picture of the flimsiness of a telegraph line of the period that it must be reproduced:

Mechencsburg December 27th, 1846

Mr H O Riely Sir a Cording to your Request the first obstruction is ¾ Mile east of Shelesburg a pine lim Paterson Run East of Lukencrick on Cove mountain at the Short Curve wire against a tree Say 12 miles East of McConesltown ½ mile fithe East wire soe slack that it is tied up to a Chesnut tree Mr. Brucks Contracted with a man in Landon to fix it but he had not don it I urged him on and told him that it must be don for fere of wagons Catche it Mr Ashway promised me that he wood get that hand that Mr. Brucks had imployed to tend to it if posebl at the big Cut east of Chambersburg wire off a pole but the bank is high nothing will interfaer tell your hand Come a Long they are a few poles Lening a little but the lines Stand Except these few places first rate Much

126

better then aney body Could have Expecte.... I was this Day at Susquahane bridge and Saw the wire in full Streck a Cross the Susquahanah and joined to gathe it was taking aCross the old bridge the fire in shures Company wood not allow them to Cross the new bridge nothing more at present but remain yours

HENRY HUMMEL

Those slack wires and tree contacts may have been in that selfsame condition when the line opened, two days later. But on the day of dedication, Adjutant-General Bowman sent the

From Shaffner's Telegraph Manual

A LINEMAN OF 1855

first telegrams, to President Polk and the Governor of Pennsylvania, and messages of congratulation to O'Rielly somehow trickled through. And a few days later John Hite wrote from Stoystown that "A trea has fallen on the wire on Alleghany and broke a post and thrown the wire of for a mile in lenth." Luckily an obscure genius named Smith invented the lineman's

127

climbers about this time, and repairs thereafter were just a little less difficult.

By the time the Pittsburgh office was opened, its promoter was officially an outlaw. Kendall had gone over to the opposition, and he and Smith, in behalf of the patentees, issued a manifesto fiercely denouncing O'Rielly. They forbade all artisans to construct machinery or lines for him, warned operators against working his instruments, forbade all orthodox telegraph lines to connect with his, warned capitalists against aiding him with money, and threatened all persons who aided him in any way with prosecution.

O'Rielly, somewhat intoxicated by the hero worship of Pittsburgh, was little daunted by this anathema, and went ahead with his preparations to push into the midwest as if no trouble threatened him. A handbill issued at the time announces that "The Pittsburgh Telegraphery" pays attention not only to business, but to comfort and elegance. It must have been rather spacious, for there were:

APARTMENT I, an Enclosure designed exclusively for LADIES, and for Gentlemen accompanying them; APARTMENT II, an Enclosure designed exclusively for Gentlemen of the Press, Resident in Pittsburgh, or visiting the City; APARTMENT III, Designed exclusively for Persons Writing or Receiving Despatches by Telegraph.

It was pointed out that:

GENTLEMEN visiting the room merely as SPECTATORS are assigned ample space, and respectfully requested to OBSERVE THE RULES, as the most PERFECT ORDER is desirable for the convenience of the Public, as well as for the Telegraphers.

For some time little was done to restrain O'Rielly. Morse, inclined to be peaceful and patient, was now the only brake on the patentees—by which one means Smith. That cold, greedy, unscrupulous plotter was determined to break O'Rielly and seize a large share of the middle western field for himself. Morse held Smith back as long as he could. An attempt at an injunction against O'Rielly in the United States District Court at Philadelphia was stopped, and there was great rejoicing in the O'Rielly camp and in Pittsburgh. The Morse patentees were now mentioned only with execrations. James D. Reid, in a letter to O'Rielly, thanking him for a gift of stock in his company, said:

I have done you no service to warrant it. I have often wept the live-long night that I was drawing from your meagre stores the weekly stipend of life.... We will name our first boy after you.... Mr. Morse and his associates have rolled themselves in filth and must abide their own stench. I am sick of the bare mention of them. The low personality of their manifesto has sunk them in public estimation immeasurably.

But how one's opinions change! The same man thirty years later wrote rhapsodically of "The beauty of Mr. Morse's character, the versatility of his intellect, the sweetness of the life of a man modest as he was great."

Kendall, weary of wrangling with Smith about O'Rielly, now consented to the latter's building competing lines from Buffalo to Chicago and other northern points in opposition to the fiery Irishman; and any battle promptly became uglier when Smith entered it. General Moorhead, an associate of O'Rielly, said in later years, "I believe we could have compromised with Mr. Kendall at any time had the contract by which the settlement was placed in the hands of Smith not existed."

O'Rielly now sent agents out and went himself to seek stock subscriptions in his contemplated territory. The argument was, "If this town will buy so many thousand dollars' worth of stock, we will bring the telegraph through here. Otherwise, it may go elsewhere." A letter from the editor of the Columbus, Ohio, *Cultivator* tells O'Rielly that he fears there is little chance to sell stock among the citizens of that place. "They are not an enterprising people, like the citizens of Rochester. Then, too, there is not much business done here of a kind that will be much benefited by the use of the telegraph.... Not so with Cincinnati —there must be your main chance for subscriptions."

Nevertheless, O'Rielly found some loose money in Columbus.

His first two new companies were the Pittsburgh, Cincinnati & Louisville, and the Lake Erie Telegraph Company, the latter to connect Pittsburgh with the southern rim of the lake named. With the promoter's brother, John O'Rielly, as chief builder, construction was driven forward rapidly. From Smith, O'Rielly had learned the trick of building the line himself and charging up to the stockholders a handsome profit on the construction.

The Cincinnati line followed the Ohio River to Steubenville and Wheeling, then the National Road via Zanesville, Columbus and Dayton to Cincinnati, thence down the northern bank of the Ohio to Louisville, Kentucky. The two lines reached Cleveland and Cincinnati almost simultaneously, late in August, 1847. The Cincinnati *Daily Commercial* of August 31st, under the heading, "The Lightning Line," said:

Our readers were no doubt astonished yesterday to find Cleveland news up to 12½ and 1 A.M. in the *Commercial* of the same morning. Such, however, is the fact. Under our telegraphic head we gave yesterday news from Cleveland, Pittsburgh, New York, Philadelphia, etc., up to 1 o'clock A.M. We attended the telegraph office at this late hour of the night, and found Mr. O'Rielly and his assistants busy in taking down notes from these distant points, received by the Lightning Line. We got our dispatch and hurried to the Commercial office ... and a little before 3 o'clock, our steam cylinder power press was striking off sheets at the rate of thirty-three per minute....

Will the reader pause a moment and think of what we have stated above? Is it not wonderful? Does it not astonish us all? The press, steam and the lightning line—what a combination!

Here is seen in action one of the early functions of the telegraph—that of gathering and selling brief news items; which not only brought in some revenue, but was good publicity for the service. But news gathering was a thorny path to travel. Hard upon the heels of the puff from Cincinnati came an apoplectic outburst from the *Ohio State Journal* of Columbus, whose editor protested that news he received was identical with that sent to Cincinnati the day before. Fancy his feelings, upon receiving a copy of the Cincinnati *Gazette* of the previous day, to read in it news which had just been delivered to him by the telegraph not ten minutes ago. Said he:

THERE IS MOST FOUL PLAY, such as renders the Telegraph a COMMON NUISANCE to all but the *favored* portions of the State; and the State should at once abandon it to the *exclusive support* of those to whom are extended its exclusive benefits. Nay, more—the Telegraphs should be presented by the Grand Juries as *instruments of fraud* and *abated* by our courts.

O'Rielly's lines all through the Middle West were hastily and flimsily constructed, sometimes by back roads through sparsely settled areas when better rights of way could not be cheaply procured. The poles were such as could be found on adjacent land—pine, hickory, beech, oak—any kind of oak, whether black, red, water oak or what not, and all with the bark left on, which caused rapid decay.

For some time the wires stopped on the north bank of the Ohio opposite Louisville, and telegrams had to be rowed across. The editors there thought it was because the city had not subscribed for enough O'Rielly stock. But it was partly because the builders were having trouble in crossing the broad river. High masts were erected on the two shores and on Towhead Island in midstream, and the wire crossed the river in two jumps. At first they tried twisting three Number 18 wires together, but this made a cable so heavy that they could not raise it to the tops of the masts. Next they tried fine piano wire, but that broke too easily. A twist of medium weight wire finally proved fairly serviceable, though not entirely dependable, as the Louisville *Courier* found to its sorrow.

On December 7, 1847, President Polk's message would be read to Congress. There would be much in it about the current war with Mexico, the seizure of the Pacific Coast and other important matters, and the *Courier* had arranged to receive it by telegraph—"one of the most magnificent enterprises ever attempted by the newspaper press." It "will require the incessant labor for sixteen or eighteen hours of the most skilful operators to telegraph it through; and the regular charge for

131

telegraphing is eight cents for every word from Philadelphia to Louisville." But alas, the *Courier* did not succeed in publishing the message until the 9th, a day late:

> But for a series of accidents that may never occur again, we could have had the entire message in type yesterday evening. Nearly four hours were lost yesterday by the breaking of the wire across the river. This delay threw the telegraphing into the night, and the fog was so heavy and the night so dark that all attempts to cross the river failed until nearly daylight yesterday morning.

Many people came from a distance to Louisville to get the message. Several farmers came into town through the cold rain and remained all night, in order to read it at the earliest possible moment.

O'Rielly's new Ohio & Mississippi Telegraph line was building at the time from New Albany, across the river from Louisville, towards St. Louis, Missouri. The wires had reached Vincennes on November 26th, and the editors of the Vincennes *Gazette* had telegraphed their "respects" to the editors of the Cincinnati *Gazette*, "by O'Rielly's irresistible lightning line," together with Wabash River steamboat news and a weather report. Four days later the St. Louis *Republican* said:

> To-day we publish accounts which, at the time their reception here, were only two and a half days from New York; this, too, when, after travelling on a streak of lightning to Vincennes, they were subjected to the inconvenience of being put into CAVE JOHNSON'S slow line and lagging along a route of a hundred and eighty miles.

Cave Johnson's line was of course the United States mail. There was then no railroad into St. Louis. A few days later, when the time for the President's message grew near, the *Republican* made arrangements with the Eastman stage line to run a special fast coach from Vincennes to St. Louis. The senior editor himself went to Vincennes to get the copy. His coach left Vincennes just after 8 A.M., and with rain falling in torrents all the way, rocking, pitching, sloshing through mud over "roads excessively bad," it reached Belleville, Illinois, 155 miles, in twenty-four hours and ten minutes. Two hours later the battered and bespattered editor was delivered at his office door with the precious document.

One editor was a bit shocked to find upon later checking some three hundred errors in his copy of the message, but admitted that the strain on the operators was probably too great for accuracy.

When the wire was approaching St. Louis in December, the *Daily Union* of that city said:

By the middle of next week, the telegraph wires will be stretched across the river.... All the efforts of FOG SMITH and Company to arrest the progress of this enterprise have failed. The public have now an interest in the matter which requires that we should state more fully than we have done before, the trickery and deception they have used.

"Fogsmithery" was thereafter a cant word among O'Rielly partizans as meaning any sort of chicanery.

St. Louis was reached on December 22nd, and editors announced two days later that "the first streak of lightning passed through the wires yesterday."

Even before that date O'Rielly's salesmen were in northern Illinois, canvassing for the Illinois & Mississippi Telegraph Company. Leaving St. Louis, this line crossed the Mississippi just above the city, and passing through Alton, Springfield and Peoria, reached Chicago and Milwaukee. An office was established wherever a specified sum of money—whatever it was thought the community would stand—was subscribed for stock. Olney, an O'Rielly agent, stepping ashore for only half an hour at Rock Island while a steamboat lay there, promised an office there if the town would buy $3,500 worth of the nicely engraved certificates, and Davenport, across the river, $2,500 worth. Rock Island citizens quickly scurried about and raised their quota, but learned that Davenport wouldn't put up a cent. The Rock Island *Advertiser* was peevish because Olney hadn't

stayed longer; believed that if he had visited Davenport and
let loose his eloquence upon it, the matter could have been
arranged. However, Rock Island was soon granted a branch
line of telegraph, as were also Hannibal, Quincy, Keokuk, Burlington and Dubuque.

Through the summer and autumn of 1848 exultant editors
in these little cities were recording day by day the approach of
the "lightning." Peoria's Fourth of July celebration was made
perfect by the opening of the telegraph office. The *Register*
announced that it would be open on the Fourth "for the gratifi-
cation of the Ladies of the city, who will find the gentlemanly
Superintendent, Mr. R. Chadwick, in attendance to describe
the apparatus."

The columns of brief news items by telegraph in the papers
of those days were headed variously, "The First Streak," "By
Lightning," "Latest News by Lightning," "Magnetic Dispatches," "Telegraphic Flashes," "Off the Iron Wire," and so
on. Many midwestern papers subheaded the column, "By
O'Rielly's Lightning Line." The lettering of the heading often
had a background of clouds with zigzag lightning flashing
through them.

After the custom of the day, O'Rielly charged the stockholders of the Illinois and Mississippi company $300 a mile
for the construction of the line, and double the cost of erecting
masts for river crossings at St. Louis, Hannibal, Keokuk and
half a dozen other places. Of the $89,950 rapidly collected on
stock subscriptions, $75,660 was turned over to O'Rielly for
construction costs. And this for a hastily built line, with bark
posts of all sorts of wood, of differing heights, set at irregular
intervals and with poor insulation, through a wilder country
than any yet encountered—where, when there were great flights
of wild pigeons, they sometimes perched on the wires in such
numbers that they broke them down. But the editors were so
delighted at getting telegraphic news that they were almost all
for O'Rielly; and truth to tell, he really desired lines that were
well constructed; but he was not a thorough man, he had no

technical knowledge and haste was the paramount consideration with him—he wanted the mid-West tied up in his network before the Morse patentees could reach it.

Those river crossings were a vexatious problem for years. O'Rielly had many large streams to negotiate; the Ohio at Wheeling and Louisville, for example, the Mississippi at at least four places, and when he was building his lines from St. Louis to Nashville and from Louisville to New Orleans, Louisiana, there were the lower Ohio, the Cumberland, the Tennessee and others. Remember that there were no bridges over these streams then. Even had there been, they would doubtless have been of wooden construction, and the owners and insurance companies, as we have already seen, would have been afraid of the telegraph wires. Even when permitted to cross by a bridge, there were drawbacks. The bridge across the Susquehanna at Havre de Grace, Maryland, over which the Magnetic Company's Philadelphia-Baltimore line passed, had a draw span in it, and when the draw was opened to let a boat through, telegraph service was cut off.

The wires must be swung high enough above a river to clear the steamboat chimneys, and the only solution was that of very tall masts. At the crossing of the Mississippi near St. Louis a shot-tower 185 feet high on the Missouri shore held that end of the wire; from there it swung 2,200 feet across the steamboat channel to a mast equally tall on Bloody Island, then across another arm to a 160-foot mast on the Illinois shore. To cross the Mississippi at Cape Girardeau there must be a single span of 2,980 feet. On the Illinois shore there was a 215-foot mast, and on the opposite shore a 205-foot stick on a hill 110 feet high, making a total elevation of 315 feet. To span the Ohio near Paducah, there must be two stretches of wire, 2,400 feet and 3,720 feet in length respectively, with an island between them. The mast on the Kentucky shore was 307 feet high and stood on a 32-foot bank. It was made of five great spars with ends overlapping, bound together with iron bands and then wound with wire. It was guyed with several lines of the linked rod known as hog-chain. At the Tennessee River crossing near Paducah, a 90-foot tree standing on a 120-foot bank was utilized as one of the masts.

From Shaffner's Telegraph Manual
CARRYING A WIRE ACROSS A RIVER BY HIGH MASTS, 1848

Every little while, communication ceased during a storm, and then news would come that one of the big masts had been blown down, stopping all telegraphic news for days or weeks thereafter. The Burlington, Iowa, *Hawk-Eye* announced gloomily, late in August, 1848, that:

The mast which was blown down at Warsaw some five or six weeks since had just been reconstructed when the storm last week snapped the one opposite, at Alexandria, in two and brought it to the ground. Our citizens have waited with commendable patience for a lightning communication with St. Louis and the East. It is hoped that the mast will be up to-day.

136

It is related that the mast on the Iowa shore at Keokuk stood near the cabin of a crusty old pioneer who was much annoyed by the humming of the wire. One night during a high wind, the noise became insufferable to him; he sprang out of bed, seized his ax, and after an hour or more of hard chopping, laid the mast low.[1] You see, people weren't aaccustomed to calling upon Government or other agencies for help or redress in those days; such small chores as the abating of nuisances, they performed for themselves.

From Shaffner's Telegraph Manual

MAKING A CABLE FOR A RIVER CROSSING ON THE SPOT, 1850

To overcome these difficulties, desperate efforts were made to create a submarine cable which could be laid across the rivers. The newly discovered gutta-percha did pretty well in tidal waters such as the Hudson at New York, but in the swifter rivers of the interior, sand and gravel, driven against it by the current, quickly wore it off the wire. To protect the gutta-percha, Shaffner, one of the early builders, covered it with

---

[1] "Telegraph Pioneering," by Ben Hur Wilson, in *The Palimpsest* (State Historical Society of Iowa), November, 1925.

three layers of the cotton cloth known as osnaburg saturated with tar. To hold the cloth in place, he laid six wires around the cable laterally, and lashed them fast with a binding of wire every twenty inches. This worked tolerably well, but frequently failed; so presently he learned to do the final lashing with wire wound spirally, about an inch apart. This work was done with primitive apparatus on the river bank, as shown in the accompanying picture. Still later on, lead coverings for the wires were devised.

Smith had beaten O'Rielly into Chicago with his wire. When the "Irish Aztec," as Smith called him, started driving westward from Pittsburgh, the Yankee promoter was thoroughly alarmed. "I wish the Devil had kept O'Rielly under his special keeping and out of our way," he wrote to Kendall. In addition to pondering legal traps for him, Smith resolved to build new lines to connect the Morse wires at Buffalo with Chicago and the Northwest. He sent Ezra Cornell and two brothers named Swift (one of whom later became a celebrated astronomer) to Chicago to solicit stock subscriptions. As usual, lank Ezra was on his own; there were to be no salaries for any of the trio and no expense money was supplied. They just had to get along as best they could. They reached Chicago in July, 1847, with only a few silver coins jingling in their pockets.

To get some expense money, it was decided that one of the Swifts should deliver some lectures on electricity. They could find no empty hall, and the only theater was tenanted by a minstrel troupe. They were finally granted the use of the courthouse for a month, and induced the *Tribune* to print some handbills on credit. They exhibited the telegraph in action, they promised to drown a rat in the presence of the audience, and restore it to life by galvanism, to exhibit and explode guncotton, to let anybody in the audience don the Magnetic Slippers, to put a silver dollar into water, and give it to anybody who could take it out, all this in addition to Mr. Swift's lecture on the marvels of electricity.

They packed the court-room several times at 25 cents single

admission or 37½ cents for couples, children half price, and took in enough money to pay all their expenses and buy each a much-needed suit of clothes. Cornell in particular was looking much too seedy to be an effective stock salesman. Their campaign was not a great success, only a few hundred dollars being subscribed; but Smith, with the aid of Livingston & Wells, the expressmen, John J. Speed, Jr., and others, nevertheless, financed the Erie & Michigan Telegraph Company, which rapidly built a line from Buffalo around Lake Erie to Detroit, and thence to Chicago. It strung a wire between Chicago and Milwaukee before the line arrived from the East, completing it on January 15, 1848. The first communication over the eastern wire was achieved in the following April.

Late in 1847, O'Rielly had organized the Ohio, Indiana and Illinois Telegraph Company, to connect his Pittsburgh-Cincinnati line at Dayton, via Indianapolis with Chicago. Because of slow stock subscribing, this line did not reach Indianapolis until the following May, and Chicago in the early part of 1849. Farmers along the right of way sold poles to the company, with bark on, at ten cents apiece, and not only cut and distributed them where needed for that price, but helped to set them up. The insulation was, as usual, disastrous. A new glazed earthenware insulator was tried, and the glazing was so thin that the wire quickly sawed through it, letting rain soak the porous mass, so that the "mud balls," as they were called, did quite as much harm as good.

From its main line the company threw out branches through Logansport and Fort Wayne, Indiana, to Toledo, Ohio; from Cincinnati to Piqua, Ohio, from Crawfordsville via Terre Haute to Evansville, Indiana, and from Indianapolis to Madison, Indiana. Smith's line from the East was giving such poor service that the Milwaukee *Sentinel and Gazette* said in May, 1849, "All the men, boys and devils in our office curse the very name of Telegraph," and urged O'Rielly to extend his wire to Milwaukee, which he did a little later.

O'Rielly's lines suffered much from vandalism in Indiana,

139

and almost as much in Ohio. In Indiana not only were wires severed, but poles were felled. In Ohio it was a favorite trick to cut wires and leave them trailing across a road, where vehicles ran over them. Once the line between Fort Wayne and Toledo was out of commission for a week before repair men found the break, about eighty miles east of the former city; a pole had been cut down, and two or three hundred yards of wire were gone. The Fort Wayne operator attributed much of the antagonism to the absence from his post of Mr. Rainey, "the gentlemanly Toledo operator." "During his absence," said the Fort Wayne *Times,* with the delightful frankness of the period, "his place is occasionally occupied, when the line works for a short time, by some vulgar, filthy blackguard who is evidently out of his element. He must belong to the lowest doggery and brothel in Toledo, for the language he uses could be picked up nowhere else."

The ill-fated Ohio, Indiana and Illinois was ahead of its time. Much of its territory was still in a pioneer condition, thinly settled and poor, and the people were temperamentally not yet ready for the telegraph. Within two or three years, Ezra Cornell was able to pick up large blocks of O. I. & I. stock at $2.00 per share. By the middle '50's most of its mileage had either fallen into ruin or been taken over by the Morse lines.

Interesting bits culled from mid-western newspapers as O'Rielly's wires overspread that region, picture some popular conceptions of the telegraph. The Zanesville *Tri-Weekly Courier,* for example, reported that when the hub of a rapidly moving wagon struck a telegraph pole in that city, the horse was thrown to the ground by the electric shock. A few days later, however, the editor had decided that the shock had been physical rather than electrical.

Lightning still interfered annoyingly with the operations of the primitive lines. "Occasional flashes of lightning," said a Peoria editor one June day, "prevented the communication by telegraph between this city and St. Louis up to the time of our going to press"; and therefore he had no Eastern news. Nevertheless, the suggestion was gravely passed around that after the country had been covered with a network of wires, nothing more would be struck by lightning—save perhaps an occasional operator—and from that, the dream grew to the point of predicting that there probably wouldn't be any more thunderstorms!

But it was the newspapers in the cultured East which began whispering the rumor that the telegraph might be responsible for the spread of the great cholera epidemic of 1849. As against this, another school of savants believed that electricity was destined to drive out cholera. A so-called electrical machine was devised, which was supposed to indicate the presence of electricity in the atmosphere. It was watched for several days, and when traces of electricity were noted, there was rejoicing, for now it was believed that the dreaded epidemic would fade away. "The connexion between electricity and epidemic diseases seems to be fully established," wrote an editor, "and we hope that any of our scientific men who have been observing the condition of the atmosphere will make known the results of their experiments."

A doctor of medicine sent this questionnaire to telegraph superintendents:

1. How have the telegraph lines under your control worked before and during the prevalence of Cholera Asiatica?
2. If any disturbances, what are they, and when greatest? Before or during the epidemic?
3. Are these disturbances most in day or night?

As telegraph history of those days was simply one long catalogue of "disturbances" of various kinds, the harassed superintendents must have found it difficult to give any enlightening answers.

CHAPTER VIII

THE ERA OF LITIGATION

The steed called Lightning (says the Fates)
Is owned in the United States.
'Twas Franklin's hand that caught the horse;
'Twas harnessed by Professor Morse.
By Smith and Kendall injured—vilely,
But driven westward by O'Rielly.

POPULAR DOGGEREL, 1848

S TORM clouds began to gather about the telegraph before it
had lighted its second birthday candle. The patentees not
only fell out with O'Rielly and earned the odium of their public
by bad service, but by 1847 were menaced by new inventions.
Scientists in several lands were and had been for some time
toiling earnestly on telegraphic machinery which, it was hoped,
would automatically print the message as received, in clear,
legible type. In America, Vail had produced a beautiful machine, as already related, but did not patent it. In England,
Wheatstone had patented his dial printing machine in 1838.
Following him, Froment and Breguet in France and Siemens in
Germany worked out systems.

In America, the first printing telegraph was patented by
Royal E. House, a citizen of Vermont, in 1846. Though containing some highly original features, it employed Wheatstone's
dial, rotated step by step by successive impulses of the current
on an electro-magnet, the necessary letter or figure being stopped
as long as desired. It printed its message in fine, readable type—
all capitals, of course—on a strip of paper; the type slightly
larger and the paper a little wider than that which the telegraph
machines use to-day. But the strip was not gummed then and
pasted on a telegraph blank, as is the custom now. At the end

of your telegram, it was simply cut off, folded up, put into an envelope and delivered to you. If the telegram was a long one, the strip might be a yard or two in length. They look queer to us now, for not a few of those old telegrams are still in existence, mostly in the hands of philatelists, for whom this sort of collecting is a branch of their fad.

House quickly procured patents in England and other European countries, and some lines over there were equipped with his system. The Morse patentees opposed the granting of an American patent to him, but were overruled.

The next to introduce a new system to America was Alexander Bain, a Scotch scientist, who applied for a patent on a chemical telegraph in June, 1848. He had patented it in England a year and a half before, and it was being used there to a limited extent. In his receiving device, the electric current, acting through a fixed metal stylus on a paper ribbon wet with a solution of potassium prussiate, produced a series of blue marks by decomposition of the mineral salts. The sending was at first accomplished with the ordinary Morse key; then Bain tried a perforated paper ribbon through the holes in which electric impulses intermittently flowed—a device probably originated by Wheatstone. To this day, in the offices of those great telegraph companies which send messages across the ocean by cable and air, you may see typewriters punching holes in a strip of paper, which then proceeds to send messages in the ninety-year-old way, though the receiving is not the same.

The chemical features of Bain's telegraph, as explained in Chapter III, were really a development from that of another Scot, Robert Smith. But his machinery included not only a sending key like Morse's, but a relay magnet similar to his, while the alphabet of signs representing the letters differed in only a few small particulars from Morse's. "It is God's truth and within man's reach to demonstrate," exclaimed F. O. J. Smith, passionately, "that Bain has not introduced into the Telegraph one original conception of any denomination."

But if Bain's chemical telegraph was not highly original, he seems to have been, as far as we can ascertain, the first to send facsimiles of script by telegraph, and to do it by means of a cylinder, moving just like those in the machines which send pictures by wire and wave to-day. The New York *Commercial Advertiser* gave this fine scientific description of his new device in 1848:

> The system is based upon *electro-chemistry*, and the process is as simple as eating. The person in Albany who wishes to communicate to a friend in New York writes what he wishes with a gummy substance upon prepared paper. This is placed upon a cylinder, and at once transmitted to the other extremity. What the operation is, we do not fully comprehend; but the gummy substance and the prepared paper has everything to do with it.

In other words, the script was written with an insulating ink; one variety which was tried was made of sealing wax dissolved in spirits of wine. The paper bearing the writing was wrapped around a copper cylinder which not only revolved rapidly, but had a gradual lateral movement—that is, endwise; an idea which is fundamental in the sending of pictures by telegraph to-day. The moving cylinder passed under the point of a copper stylus through which an electric current flowed save when it crossed a line written with the insulating ink; the current was then momentarily broken.

At the other end of the wire was a copper cylinder moving in perfect synchronization with the sending one. Wrapped around it was a sheet of paper dipped in a solution of potassium prussiate or ferrocyanide, while playing over it was a stylus through which the current came. With the current flowing through the stylus, the solution decomposed, producing a blue mark on the paper; but when broken from the other end, it left the paper white. The writing was thus reproduced in white, on a background of fine blue lines.

Smith had had his own troubles in quantity with his New York and Boston Magnetic Company. Due to the use of soft copper wire, to Smith's perverse notion that he knew more about electricity than the electricians and to his contempt for insulation, he was compelled to report at the end of the first year's business that the wires had not worked half of the time. His line was a favorite butt for the jeers of such editors as that of *Vox Populi* at Lowell—"The Magnetic Telegraph is at the present time in status quo, and is likely to remain so for some time. What an everlasting humbug this affair is!" Miss Bagley, the woman operator there, had little to do for a long time because the public neither understood nor trusted the new gadget. As late as August, 1846, Dr. Colton, a local scientist, attracted much attention by giving an exhibition of it in a hall, with himself on the rostrum and Miss Bagley in the balcony at the other end of a wire. As proof of its performance, those in the audience were asked to write messages which Colton sent to Miss Bagley, who read them aloud. No feat of legerdemain to-day seems any more marvelous than did this to some of those auditors.

After one storm, there were 170 breaks in one 30-mile stretch between New York and Boston. The poles were too far apart, the soft wires stretched and swung against each other, and when they broke, they sometimes became entangled with the trains whose track they followed, at one time causing the death of one man and the serious injury of another. Smith, in his report of 1848, used the railroad as the scapegoat, though it was in no way to blame, and said telegraph lines should never follow railroad tracks. He also declared that it had been found "utterly impracticable" to keep the wires apart. But when galvanized iron wires were introduced, and the poles set closer together, this statement was refuted.

So antagonistic did public sentiment become that the Connecticut Legislature repealed its telegraph protective law, and instead, passed one laying heavy responsibility upon the telegraph company for public safety and the rights of property owners along the route. No one would buy stock to aid in extending the lines, and Smith had to do that largely with his own funds, so that he became the heavily dominant power in the New England lines. There was much breaking of insulators and cutting of wires in this territory. The Boston *Traveler* in 1847, told of a party of railroad laborers riding on a hand-car between Worcester and Newton, who discovered "two or three men" on the brink of a deep cut, trying to break a telegraph wire by twisting it with a stick. The *Traveler* called them "rogues in broadcloth, perhaps speculators in breadstuffs"; but it is quite as likely that some animus against Smith or the telegraph com-

FIVE DOLLARS REWARD!

The Proprietors of the Boston, Salem & Newburyport
MAGNETIC TELEGRAPH,

Having been subjected to great expense and inconvenience, in consequence of the frequent interruptions of their business, occasioned by the breaking of caps, and other injuries wantonly committed on the same, therefore,

The above Reward will be paid to any person
who will furnish such information as will enable me to prosecute and convict any person or persons who may be detected in wantonly or maliciously injuring any of the wires, glass caps, or other fixtures of the said Telegraph, by *throwing of stones or otherwise*; and all persons who have been guilty of so doing, are hereby cautioned against a repetition of the offence, as they will, in case of detection, be prosecuted to the utmost extent of the law.

PARENTS would do well to caution their Boys, in re-
lation to this matter, as most of the injury is believed to have been caused by them, without any consideration of the consequences.

C. H. HUDSON, *Superintendent.*

Newburyport, August 1st, 1848.

From American Telephone and Telegraph Co.

POSTER OF 1848, WARNING AGAINST BREAKING OF GLASS
INSULATORS

pany was the impelling force. The men fled into the woods when the laborers leaped from the hand-car, leaving a horse and chaise tethered to a tree near by. The workmen lay in wait, and after a time a "genteelly dressed man" appeared, walking along the road. He was asked whether the horse and vehicle were his property. He answered "No," and hurried away. After a time the laborers gave up waiting and went on their way. Next morning the horse and rig had disappeared.

It was Smith's own personal order to the New York & Boston Company's employees late in 1847 which banned the handling of any telegram destined to or coming from the O'Rielly lines—a high-handed proceeding which of course would be impossible at the present time. Some time later he announced this policy through the newspapers, stating that the company would refuse "messages for or from the lines established by Henry O'Reilly and associates between Philadelphia, Pittsburgh, Louisville and Cincinnati." Naturally this brought an outburst of fury from midwestern editors, and even those in New England did not withhold their pens. The Louisville *Courier,* speaking of "the work of slander and defamation so industriously pursued by F. O. J. Smith," said that he had "played the blackguard in a style that shows a long and familiar acquaintance with the art. We present him this to-day, with the compliments of the season." The New York, Albany & Buffalo line collaborated with the Boston line by refusing O'Rielly messages, whereupon the Rochester *Daily American* exclaimed that "This is as bad as robbing hen roosts. . . . The arbitrary meanness of Professor Morse, 'Fog' Smith and Company ought to be rebuked in a manner that will be felt."

It may be said before proceeding further that Smith did not find it practicable to continue this ban long. But this was only one of many things which now led O'Rielly to throw caution and consideration to the winds. He considered that he had been so badly treated by the Morse clique that he was released from moral obligation to them. The terms of his contract with them forbade his building lines south of the Ohio River, but he had become gripped with a longing to connect his midwestern network with New Orleans and intervening cities. He no longer felt any squeamishness about violating that clause, but he was in some concern as to his legal jeopardy in case he did so and used Morse instruments.

Two of his employees, however, Ed Barnes and Samuel K.

Zook, offered to remove that care from his shoulders by inventing a new instrument. The one which they produced and which they cristened the Columbian was the most absurd imitation and infringement of the Morse system that supposedly sane men ever tried to "get away with." It is due to O'Rielly to say that he was so ignorant of mechanisms that he probably did not know how bad a cheat this was. The two young men who produced it were probably also under the influence of the roistering, happy-go-lucky, help-yourself spirit which had characterized O'Rielly's enterprises, and under other circumstances would not have attempted it. One of them, Zook, showed his mettle in later years by rising to a brigadier-generalship in the Union Army during the Civil War, and dying bravely in the bloody wheat-field at Gettysburg.

during his Postmaster-generalship, had been so impressed by
Morse wires had already reached New Orleans. Kendall, the volume of mail carried by his horse post to New Orleans that he regarded that region as one of the most important of all for the patentees to consider. Accordingly, a company was organized in 1846, and in November a contract for the construction of the line was given to John J. Haley, of New York, the Nassau Street pie-maker who was an early investor in Magnetic stock, and by a singular coincidence, also a cousin of F. O. J. Smith. As Mr. Haley knew nothing about telegraph construction, he turned the actual supervision over to an expert, young Charles S. Bulkeley, whose entire experience consisted of a few months' service as clerk and operator in the New York office of the Magnetic. Kendall did his bit for chaos by specifying that there were not to be more than twenty poles per mile! His idea was to diminish the horrors of bad insulation by decreasing the number of points of contact.

Bulkeley learned so much from that first job that he later became a famous telegraph builder. But this first product of his 'prentice hand was frequently out of commission, and its service was slow. Charleston sent its first message over the wire on St. Valentine's Day, 1848, but soon began to complain of it.

From there the work progressed more rapidly through Montgomery and Mobile, and New Orleans was in touch with New York late in July.

The Charleston *Mercury* remarked on one occasion in 1849, that during the past nineteen days there had been only one day when the telegraph was in working order and messages were received on time. Both Charleston and Washington papers charged "gross mismanagement." The Charleston *Courier* added "fraud and villany somewhere on the line," and cited the instance of a telegram costing $8 which was eight days in traveling from Washington to New Orleans, whereas the mail went through in seven days. In answer to the *Courier's* complaint, B. B. French, President of the company, wrote on May 27, 1848:

> Your complaints are just. Indeed, I may say, under all the circumstances, you are merciful. I am troubled, vexed and made almost sick at heart by the want of care and attention to business which exists *somewhere* on the line; and to add to my vexations, I have thus far, with all the energy I could use, found it impossible to ascertain the point where the difficulty lies.
>
> I am now responsible to the public and to the stockholders for the proper organization of the line and for its working; and by the blessing of God, I am determined it *shall* work better than it has been working, or be discontinued altogether—it is now a disgrace to the telegraphic system.

If another so frank and humble a confession as this can be found elsewhere in business history, we should like to see it.

It is evident, however, that Mr. French did not succeed in correcting conditions, for the New Orleans *Commercial Times* charged in January, 1849, that bribery prevailed on the line, adding that the President had admitted to the editor having discovered that messages from New Orleans destined to Washington and New York had been sidetracked at Charleston, and Charleston messages sent over the single wire ahead of them. Remember, that with only one or two wires to a line and no multiplex telegraphy, messages must just limp along from point to point, becoming more or less garbled as they were telegraphed over and over again, and frequently delayed by way messages which had gotten on the wire ahead of them.

The New Orleans *Daily Crescent,* speaking of "that sink of iniquity, the telegraph," charged that the *Picayune* had been favored by the company and hinted at bribery. It added, with regard to the telegraph company, that: "The managers and stockholders have begun to quarrel among themselves, and the old maxim about rogues falling out, etc., finds here its appropriate application.'"

One of the sorest spots in the early history of the telegraph, when only one or seldom more than two wires worked feebly and intermittently between important cities, was this matter of precedence. As an instance of the complaints constantly occurring, the New York *Sun* charged in 1846, that its messages were sidetracked at Boston to favor others. Two of its Boston correspondents "prove that they were first at the office. . . . The operator was seen to displace our communication to send one for two persons named Keith and Norton; and being remonstrated with, he replaced it, keeping Norton's before him. Our agent of course supposed that his dispatch had gone on, according to the rules of the office." But the *Sun's* man at Springfield "proves that Norton's dispatch was delivered there first and ours was detained an hour." Correspondents at Albany and Hartford also proved priority, but their messages were shelved in favor of others.

Another editor inquired:

Do the persons engaged in the management of the Magnetic Telegraph intend granting a monopoly of the wires to any one paper? . . . If money is the word, other papers could afford to pay as well as "Madame Restell's Organ"—and some we know could outbid it if the benefits of the great scientific contrivance are to be put up at auction.

The *Monroe Democrat* of Rochester, New York, drew a graphic picture of a telegraph day in 1848:

In the morning, two or three of the most important stations, such as New York, Albany and Buffalo, have exclusive possession of

THE ERA OF LITIGATION

the wires till their business is completed. If that takes half the day or all day, well and good, so far as they are concerned. The moment the favored points have been served, there is a general scramble among the operators for the wires, and the boy that is successful in getting possession keeps hold of them so long as he chooses, by cutting off all communication with those beyond him on the line. ... Many times when the telegraph has been announced as "broken down" at the West, the rupture has been nothing more than the cutting off of the current at Syracuse, Utica or some other place. As soon as the lucky man gets through and lets the current loose, the struggle for the wires is repeated. This fight frequently takes place a dozen times a day; and very often, with the needless conversation that follows, consumes more time than would suffice to do the legitimate business of the concern.

The editor mentioned a telegram on highly important business sent from Rochester to Troy one morning at 8 o'clock. An answer was placed in the Troy office within an hour, but did not reach Rochester until the following morning, "solely because the operator could not get his turn at the wires":

The operator here, knowing the importance of the communication, attempted a dozen times during the day to get possession of the line to speak to Troy, but was unsuccessful each time. Late in the afternoon no communication could be had with the East at all, and the line was announced as "broke," but it was repaired suddenly about the time of the evening report for the press. Immediately after the reception of this report, the operator made another drive at the wires, but was forced to give way to the operator at Utica, who wished to send some trifling *private* messages for the President of the company. Before these were finished Troy had gone to bed.

The comic stories of these battles for precedence would fill volumes. Two brokers dashed into the Magnetic office in New York side by side one day, scribbled messages, each so determined to beat the other that his scrawl was barely legible, and then ran a dead heat to the receiving counter, each shouting, "I was first"! There the one with the louder voice struck down the hand of the other and called him a liar. At that, the other led with his right to the jaw, and in a moment there they were, at it ding-dong. The manager called a husky battery man, who threw them both out. On the sidewalk their wrath turned against the telegraph company, they apologized to each other and went across the street for a drink. Presently they returned to the office, feeling much more kindly towards the company and the world in general, and were informed that their messages had been sent to Philadelphia and answers just received; whereupon they invited the whole staff out for a drink; and although the report does not specify further, we should not be surprised to learn that the invitation was accepted.

O'Rielly's dash for New Orleans started from Louisville late in 1847, with his brother John and two other men in charge of construction, and pushed forward so rapidly that on March 7, 1848, the line was open to Nashville. So hasty had been the building, however, that one of the first incidents in the line's history was a two weeks' hiatus due to breaks in the wire and bad insulation. The earthen insulators—"mud balls"—were here used again and with disastrous results.

From Nashville the wire was hurried towards Tuscumbia, but was halted by a violent legal assault by the Morse cohorts. The Morse patentees of course asked for an injunction against the "Columbian" instrument devised by O'Rielly's faithful henchmen, and O'Rielly in his ignorance, welcomed the opportunity to fight. In order to have other strings to his bow, however, he had acquired the right to use House's machine on his lines if he so desired, and he procured a similar agreement from Bain even before the inventor had gotten his American patent.

Kendall, scribbling many letters to the papers, claimed that the Morse patent embraced any and all combinations of machinery moved by electro-magnetism, "which may be used to imprint signals upon paper or other material, or to produce sounds in any desired manner, for the purpose of telegraphic communication." In other words, he insisted upon an absolute monopoly. In one of his open letters, he said:

The House humbug has been constantly thrown in the way of Morse's Telegraph ever since we commenced building it in 1845.

THE ERA OF LITIGATION

It has found new patrons in Henry O'Rielly and Hugh Downing, the former of whom had denounced it to me by letter as a mere *bother,* and the latter also, by letter a year ago, offered to sell it bodily to the proprietors of Morse's patent *for the express purpose of securing to them a monopoly of telegraphing;* and now they are the greatest enemies of monopoly in the wide world.

Greeley in the New York *Tribune* made a scathing attack upon Smith—then in Albany, lobbying against a bill for free competition in telegraphs which was before the Legislature— and

Amos Kendall, annoying Kentucky with his twaddle through the Louisville *Journal.* Age and avarice go together, and here we have the sickening spectacle of a couple of the pharisees of Democracy, one an Ex-Member of Congress, the other an Ex-Postmaster-General, holding on to a monopoly most injurious to the press and the public with the grip of a dying miser to his money-bags.

The trial over the Columbian instrument which came on in the United States Court at Frankfort, Kentucky, in September, 1848, was referred to by the press as "the lightning lawsuit." Editors for the most part were vociferous for O'Rielly and against "Fogsmithery," which had come to be a cant word for any sort of crookedness. They shuddered at bits of evidence which were produced, such as the holding over of Morse's patent—" 'Professor' Morse, as he calls himself," sneered the Oshkosh *True Democrat*—from 1838 to 1840 because of his absence from this country; in this they saw a fraudulent sub-dating. Our law then specified that if an inventor patented his device in foreign countries, his American patent, though procured later, must be considered as bearing the date of the earliest foreign patent. The presiding judge in this trial, Monroe, pointed out that as Morse had received his French patent in 1838, his American right must bear the same date; whereby he lost two years in the life of it by this suit, its expiration falling in 1852 instead of 1854. Editors were also shocked to learn that Smith's secret agreement with Morse dated from 1838, and therefore, they were partners all the time that Smith was working for the telegraph in Congress. The Louisville *Courier* and other O'Rielly partisans flatly asserted that not Morse, but Dr. Jackson was the real inventor of the telegraph.

O'Rielly was beaten in this suit, Judge Monroe granting a permanent injunction against his using the Columbian machine —which was a just decision, it being a palpable infringement. But Monroe went too far by ruling that Morse had the *exclusive* right to the use of electro-magnetism for telegraphic purposes; which, if sustained, would have eliminated House and all others. This brought forth the cry of monopoly. The Richmond *Whig* led the way in declaring that "no man has a right to patent thunder and lightning." "Shall the telegraph be republican and free," demanded Greeley, "or an agent of aristocratic despotism—shall it be American or shall it be Russian?" The New York *Sun* declared that, "The Telegraph system in this country is nothing but an odious monopoly, and must be broken up," and announced that it was going to build a line of its own from Boston through New York to Washington. It would cost $125,000 and be ready within three months. But it never materialized.

O'Rielly promptly appealed the case to the Supreme Court. As the injunction against him applied only to Kentucky, he moved his Louisville office to Jeffersonville, just across the river in Indiana, closed all his way offices in Kentucky and sent only through business across the State. But Judge Monroe had an answer to this; he ordered the United States Marshal to destroy the O'Rielly line, poles and wire, all the way across Kentucky.

At that, many editors boiled over. The Boston *Chronotype* charged that Monroe owed his elevation to the bench to Kendall. The Albany *Knickerbocker* said:

The judge who could make such a decision must be either a superannuated old ignoramus, an ass clothed in ermine, or a hired and paid agent of Fog Smith, Kendall & Co. The persecutors of Mr. O'Rielly have never yet dared to bring their cause before a middle or an Eastern state jury. They hope to obtain a verdict against him by taking it to a magistrate in some unenlightened part of the country, who knows about as much in relation to the subject as a horse knows how to handle a jack plane. Mr. O'Rielly is too universally respected and has made too many friends on the lines to be put down as easily as his opponents think. The day has gone by when Fog Smith and other like cattle could accomplish their ends and put down all opposition with a nod from the block they carry on their shoulders as substitutes for heads.

A new stench was let loose when it was discovered that Dr. Gale, one of the Morse patentees, had for some time been holding a job in the Patent Office. But Gale hastened to announce that he had sold his share to Morse shortly after he accepted the position. Next it was found that Charles G. Page, head of the Patent Office, had subscribed for a block of Magnetic stock. In some confusion, Mr. Page now canceled his subscription, explaining that he had never paid anything on it, anyhow.

For a time in the winter of 1848-49, O'Rielly was forced to send telegrams between Louisville and Nashville over the new wire of the New Orleans & Ohio, the Morse company which had hastily built a line down the Ohio River from Pittsburgh to Louisville and thence via Nashville towards New Orleans. Meanwhile, O'Rielly was aiding Bain in his fight to obtain a patent. The latter had made application in June, 1848, but found that Morse had antedated him by several months with an application for a patent on an allegedly original chemical telegraph. Bain then pointed out that he had gotten an English patent on his machine on December 11, 1846, and under our law, his American patent should bear that date, therefore automatically eliminating Morse's chemical device. Bain's patent was ordered granted early in 1849, at the time when Chief Justice Taney of the Supreme Court was pronouncing the opinion, on O'Rielly's appeal, that Morse had claimed more than he invented; that his patent must be confined to the method or process invented by him, and could not be extended to other methods or processes not invented by him; and that, as he had claimed too much, he could recover no costs in the suit. By such exaggerated claims, said the Chief Justice, "He prevents others from attempting to improve upon the manner and process which he has described in his specification, and may deter the public from using it." Nevertheless, the injunction against the Columbian instrument was justifiable and must stand.

That illegitimate child having been thus put to death (though not painlessly), O'Rielly equipped his New Orleans line with Bain instruments and began business again, Judge Monroe consenting. Nevertheless, O'Rielly vainly memorialized Congress in an effort to have Monroe removed from the bench. Mrs. George D. Prentice, wife of the distinguished editor of the Louisville *Courier,* wrote an ode in salutation to O'Rielly and his brother:

TO THE O'RIELLYS

Ye are the mighty harbingers of good,
  The instruments of blessing to your race.
Ye bind men in electric brotherhood,
  And bring remotest cities face to face.
From mast to mast your well-trained lightning dashes,
As leap from cloud to cloud heaven's own red flashes.
  They think to quell your energies by law,
  They seek injunctions in each town and city;
  They hope your fiery bolts, their hearts that awe,
    To stop by aid of Blackstone, Coke or Chitty.
Alas, poor fools!—they're doomed to find their error—
First let their writs arrest Heaven's bolts of terror.

Nevertheless, the year 1848 marked the turn in O'Rielly's fortunes. By April, 1849, his southern line was open only as far as Baton Rouge, and messages were carried between that place and New Orleans by steamboat. The wire reached New Orleans in July. The whole line was cheaply constructed and frequently broke down. Long stretches through the Mississippi forests were attached to pine trees instead of poles, and gum exuding from the trees sometimes reached the wires and grounded the current. Below Baton Rouge the poles were set along the levees, and when spring floods came and tore crevasses therein, down went the wires.

There was human opposition, too. The belief grew up in the deep South that the operators of the "Underground Railroad" used the telegraph in smuggling runaway Negroes northward— which notion caused much cutting of wires. A Hard-Shell Baptist preacher in southern Kentucky proved to be another menace. "See thar, my bruthren!" he cried out to his hearers one day during a disastrous drought. "Out along the road thar, a set of ongodly men have dared to interfere with the Almighty's lightnings, and what, my bruthren, is the upshot of it? They have robbed the air of its electricity, the rains are hendered, and ther ain't been a good crop sence the wire was put up, and what's more, I don't believe ther ever will be." The result was that the congregation went forth from the church, stirred up their neighbors, and collectively cut down several miles of poles and carried off the wires.

In the summer of 1849, a Federal judge in Tennessee granted an injunction against O'Rielly, which gave him trouble for some time. Musing upon the fact that he had beaten an attempt to enjoin him in Ohio, the editor of the Oshkosh *True Democrat* remarked that "These things of courts, decisions, etc., are necessary, but they work most outlandish sometimes."

The Morse line from Pittsburgh to New Orleans was just about as badly constructed as O'Rielly's, but it provided opposition which hurt him seriously. More opposition was supplied by a connecting line strung from Nashville to St. Louis. Taliaferro P. Shaffner, a noted telegraph character of the period, built these lines, and then in 1849, threw one across Missouri from St. Louis to St. Joseph, a town which was just then a favorite outfitting and starting point for covered wagon Argonauts with eager eyes fixed on the golden glow in the West which was California.

It was in 1848, that O'Rielly decided to invade the East and fight the Morse companies on their own ground with the Bain instrument. Tests of it showed that over a short circuit, where no static charge interfered, as high as a thousand words a minute could be sent by it. This was alarming to the Morse concerns, already highly unpopular because of their poor service and arbitrary methods. The New Haven *Palladium* was saying of Smith's New England company that, "The experiment is being tried of how much imposition our citizens will bear without resisting." The Rochester *Daily Advertiser* fumed thus:

The Telegraph is and has been a kind of "infernal machine," which compels the press to submit to its exorbitant demands, and whether we get regular reports or not, pockets our cash with the impunity of a highwayman. We should be glad if we were well rid of the whole concern. The true way to bring the company to a sense of their duty is to construct a parallel line with HOUSE's Machines, and then induce our business men to patronize that line exclusively. If HOUSE's instrument cannot be used, the community will be compelled, for the purpose of self-protection, to *dodge* MORSE's patent in some way, no matter how, and get a rival line with the instruments now in use. Sooner or later, there will be double lines everywhere, and then we would advise the old monopoly to take down their wires. The stock will be a drug in the market.

The *Advertiser* thought there were some operators on the line who would better be cutting cord wood or driving stages. The New York *Express* said it had foreseen for some time that the Morse companies were bound to bring new inventions into the field. Suggesting basic faults, it mentioned incompetence, carelessness and sometimes knavery, and concluded, "But whatever may be the cause, the result has been the *great unpopularity* of the Telegraph."

O'Rielly enlisted the interest of Marshall Lefferts of New York, a prominent iron merchant and importer of galvanized wire, who helped to promote two companies and became president of each. In 1848-49 these two were building lines under O'Rielly's supervision, one from New York via Albany to Buffalo (with branches to Watertown, Ogdensburg and other points), the other, the New York & New England Telegraph Company, between New York and Boston—from which a wire was even pushed up to Portland, Maine. A third line was opened between New York and Washington in 1850.

O'Rielly launched his Boston line in a characteristic way by offering to send all messages free on the first day. Naturally, the offices were jammed all that day with those who wanted to get in on the free lunch. But sad to relate, the wires were perverse, worked badly, and most of the messages had to be forwarded by mail!

The most harebrained aspect of O'Rielly's New England invasion is found in the fact that a second line had already been constructed between New York and Boston, this to use the House Printing system. Hugh Downing of Philadelphia had taken up House's machine in 1847, and had first strung his New England wire, and then, early in 1848, organized the New York & Washington Printing Telegraph Company, which built, however, only from New York to Philadelphia.

The Morse patentees meanwhile were carrying on a campaign of vituperation against House. It was even charged that he was an Englishman—which, to some infantile American minds of that day and even of this, was and is one of the worst things that can be said about a man. While the line was building to Boston, House urged the patentees to sue him, and when they delayed doing so, he published a card in the newspapers, touching upon

allusions made to the English Patent granted for my Letter-Printing Telegraph as an *original invention,* when MORSE'S Telegraph was refused an English Patent for its *want of originality....* My assailants, NOT DARING to submit their pretensions and their calumnies to the ordeal of the UNITED STATES COURTS, are welcome to all the capital they can now manufacture from their falsehoods about my nationality....

To this, Smith said publicly, "Neither Mr. Kendall nor myself call in question the validity of House's patent"—which was in direct contradiction to recent threats of prosecution for infringement, and was belied very shortly afterwards when Morse suits were filed against Downing and House.

While the House Boston line was building, Smith publicly announced that he would bet $1,000 that his 2,500-pound Durham bull could carry a message from Boston to New York faster than House's telegraph. He thought this such a good joke that he wrote Kendall that it would cause the House folly to be laughed off the map. He was too bovine in his mentality, too nearly a blood brother to his bull, still too unaware of the general detestation of him to foresee the probability that such a gibe from him would merely give House some desirable publicity. Downing came back smartly by offering to wager $10,000 in six different bets that House's machine could beat Morse's by anywhere from a minute to an hour in sending a thousand words between Boston and New York. But as both parties were bluffing, no money ever changed hands.

As a recompense for the privilege of running a line along the streets of New York, Downing and House agreed to connect the various fire stations with wire and apparatus, to give free and perpetual service for communicating alarms from these stations to the City Hall, where the alarm bell was rung and to instruct firemen and bell-ringers in the use of the instruments.

The House line reared the tallest masts yet seen at New York to carry its wires across the Hudson. That river had been the bane of the telegraphers' existence ever since the Magnetic line first reached its shores in 1845. Submarine wires across it were tried again and again, but either their insulation failed or anchors brought them up and broke them. The Magnetic erected fairly tall poles on the opposite cliffs of Fort Lee and Fort Washington, but as the stretch of wire between was about a mile, they could not prevent it from sagging so low that it interfered with the masts of passing vessels. They rigged pulleys on both poles so that the wire could be lowered into the water when a vessel approached, and let the craft pass over it; but this was a nuisance. Finally the Magnetic carried its wires up to West Point, where the river is narrow, and crossed it there.

The House company erected on the heights of Fort Washington, on the Manhattan shore, a mast whose tip was 400 feet above the river. Opposite this, on the Fort Lee summit, was a still taller spar whose top was said to be 750 feet above low water, though this smacks of exaggeration. Between these tall masts two steel wires were strung.

The Bain company announced in 1850 that its line to Washington had been laid under water across the Hudson. But the usual difficulties were encountered, and in the following year an advertisement announced that, "the wires are now suspended above the North River from lofty spars 310 feet high." Until very recent years a large iron ring soldered into the rocky ledges of Fort Washington marked the anchorage of a guy wire of one of those huge masts.

When O'Rielly's New York-Buffalo wire was nearing Albany, the Morse line reduced its rate for supplying news to Albany papers to $5 per week; Buffalo editors thereafter paid only $4. But, "We will not use you a cent's worth if we can help it, Sir Old Monopoly," said the Albany *Messenger*, "for that real man of the people, O'Rielly, is coming."

But even with two or three lines in operation between these principal cities of the East, one could not always be sure of service. On July 20, 1850, the Buffalo papers had not a word of what went on in Washington the day before, because a storm kept the wires from working. The O'Rielly wire was working indifferently as far as Albany, and the "old or Morse line" to Troy. Even as late as a December day in 1852, the New York *Express* remarked that, "The heavy rain storm which has prevailed since ten o'clock last evening has nearly or quite stopped the operations of most of the telegraph lines to-day." Some lines were working intermittently, some only part way, some not at all. It is remarkable to find that at that late date the *American Telegraph Magazine* still thought glass a poor insulator, and insisted that there was nothing better than wood covered with shellac.

One of the aggravations of the period was that if a telegram came by the House or Bain line to New York and found its connecting line to Boston out of commission, the Smith line would refuse to carry it the rest of the way, and it would have to be sent by mail. The numerous independent companies which were springing up hither and yonder were a great vexation to all concerned. A telegram might have to go through the hands of three or four of them before reaching its destination. If it failed to arrive or was greatly delayed, the sender demanded the return of his money from the first transmitting company, even though that company might have done its part faithfully and well.

With so many parallel lines between principal cities, a general rate war was inevitable. Telegrams could now be sent between New York and Boston for twenty cents. The volume of business was large, but none of the companies made any great profit. Nevertheless, the Bain-Lefferts-O'Rielly New York and New England Company somehow succeeded in paying a 7 per cent dividend for 1850. At a dinner given to President Lefferts in celebration of this triumph, he was presented with a handsome service of silver, supposedly by the directors and the New York Associated Press, at which, according to the newspapers, he was surprised and overwhelmed. "Surprise, indeed!" jeers O'Rielly in a private memorandum. "It 'surprised' some other people to learn that the whole thing was got up by Lefferts himself. I was 'taken' for $100 by his agent, Rogers."

All this time the inevitable war of briefs and depositions and judgments was increasing in impetus and violence, its battles becoming more frequent and deadly. These litigations developed an unprecedented enmity among scientists. Probably no other inventions in history have brought about as much legal embroilment, bitterness, venom, backbiting, slander, perjury and other chicanery and dissension as have those of communication—the telegraph, the telephone and, in but slightly milder degree—radio.

Suits over the House system were brought by the Morse patentees against Downing and associates, the Bain system was even more violently attacked, and later Henry J. Rogers who had developed an "improvement" on the Bain machine was likewise sued. When Bain planned to bring his family from

THE ERA OF LITIGATION

Scotland to America in 1849, the Louisville *Courier* witheringly remarked that, "He may be restrained from doing so by the fear that Amos Kendall will claim his wife and children as inventions of Professor Morse, or perhaps of Amos Kendall." Morse, on the other hand, plaintively sighed that some people thought he had no right to claim his invention because he had not discovered electricity, nor the copper from which his wires were made, nor the brass of his instruments nor the glass of his insulators.

It should be said in justice to Morse that he strongly disapproved of the methods of Smith, and was much grieved by the insistence of opposition papers upon regarding him as of the same stripe as Smith, one of the same breed. "I wish nothing short of entire separation from that unprincipled man if it can possibly be accomplished," he wrote to Kendall. "I can suffer his frauds upon myself with comparative forbearance, but my indignation boils when I am made, *nolens volens,* a *particeps criminis* in his frauds upon others. I will not endure it if I must suffer the loss of all the property I hold in the world." But the entanglement of their interests was too complete to permit him to escape. He and Vail brought suit against Smith in an effort to force a separation, but in vain; after years of judicial seesawing, Smith won it.

The long series of legal battles began with the one already mentioned, against O'Rielly at Frankfort. In that case, the old enemy, Dr. Jackson, appeared as an O'Rielly witness, and modestly admitted himself to be the true inventor of the telegraph. One of the most unfortunate phases of this warfare was the resulting estrangement between Morse and Henry, with subsequent injudicious public statements by each, overdrawn and erroneous because of the anger of the utterers, but flagrantly so in the case of Morse.

In 1845, Henry's feelings had been wounded when Vail's little book appeared, making no mention of Henry's bell-ringing, of his intensity magnet or, in fact, of anything that he did to make Morse's success possible. His name was not even mentioned. Hearing of his displeasure, Morse prepared a letter of apology and offer of retraction, which Vail signed. Henry was in too petulant a mood even to answer the letter; which the patentees regarded as so discourteous that it is offered by Morse's son in his biography of his father as a sort of extenuation of Morse's unjustifiable attack on Henry ten years later.

Professor Sears C. Walker, the astronomer, in a deposition given in another telegraph case, that of B. B. French *et al.* against Henry J. Rogers *et al.*, recorded his recollection of a meeting in his office in January, 1848, between Henry, Morse, and Gale, with himself present. During that interview, said Walker, he became convinced that Henry was the sole discoverer of the law:

> ...on which the 'intensity' magnet depends for its power of sending the galvanic current through a long circuit. He was also convinced that Morse had encountered the same difficulty that others had met in trying to force the galvanic current through a long line. His own research had not overcome this obstacle, and he overcame it only by constructing a magnet on the principle invented by Professor Henry, and described by him in Silliman's *Journal*—his attention being directed to it by Dr. Gale.

Immediately after this interview, Morse, with generous and highly creditable frankness, wrote to Professor Walker:

> The allusion you make to the helix of a soft iron magnet prepared after the manner first pointed out by Professor Henry, gives me an opportunity of which I gladly avail myself, to say that I think justice has not hitherto been done to Professor Henry, either in Europe or this country, for the discovery of a scientific fact which, in its bearing on telegraphs, whether of the magnetic needle or electro-magnetic order, is of the greatest importance.... Thus was opened the way for fresh efforts in devising a practical electric telegraph; and Baron Schilling in 1832 and Professors Gauss and Weber in 1833, had ample opportunity to learn of Henry's discovery and avail themselves of it, before they constructed their needle telegraphs.... To Professor Henry is unquestionably due the honor of the discovery of a fact in science which proves the practicability of exciting magnetism through a long coil or at a distance, either to deflect a needle or magnetize soft iron....

From American Telephone and Telegraph Co.

WHAT SLEET DOES TO TELEPHONE AND TELEGRAPH WIRES

Here Morse did Henry more than justice; for Schilling's experiments were earlier than Henry's discovery, and Gauss and Weber, in their earlier experiments, did not avail themselves of Henry's discovery. This glimpse of Morse at his best shows us a much finer man than the one who, several years later, completely reversed himself and declared that no credit whatsoever was due Henry for any part of the Morse instrument.

Henry, in his depositions in the telegraph trials, said that in this meeting in Walker's office, Gale had told how he was called in by Morse and found the latter unable to produce effects at a distance; that he (Gale) then told Morse of Henry's paper in Silliman's *Journal,* which Morse had not seen; that they followed Henry's plan, and found success. To this statement of Gale's, Henry continued, Morse made no reply.

As already related in Chapter IV, Gale, when on the stand in one of these telegraph trials, contradicted this testimony of Henry's, and said that when he was called in by Morse, he found the latter's instrument in perfect order and ready for use. And then, in the Morse memorial volume published in 1875, he reverses himself and confirms Henry! Morse, in his depositions, denied that Gale had made any such statements in this Walker interview, and said that Gale had no recollection of them. Henry added another proof of the fallibility of human memory by thinking that this historic interview took place in his own office instead of Walker's.

Henry's sensitive soul shrank from taking part in these public controversies, and he could be induced to testify only when forced by subpoena. Salmon P. Chase (later Chief Justice of the Supreme Court), one of the attorneys in the trials, wrote in later years that not one of Henry's statements was volunteered; all were drawn from him by questions, either verbal or written; and that "nothing in his testimony or his manner of testifying suggested to me the idea that he was animated by any desire to arrogate undue merit to himself or detract from the just claims of Professor Morse."

OLD WIRES AND NEW WAVES

In that first O'Rielly suit, Henry deposed that the battery used by Morse was not invented by Morse; that Steinheil used the metallic conductors before Morse's invention, and that the latter was advised to adopt them; that the ground circuit was used by Steinheil and others before Morse; that he, Henry, saw a local circuit in use by Professor Wheatstone in 1837; that Wheatstone used the motive power of electro-magnetism to record in the early part of April, 1837; that the combination of two or more circuits was known and used by Wheatstone and Henry; that the thing patented by Morse in his first claim in this patent was previously known and used by Henry, Davy and Wheatstone.

He was called again in the suit against the Bain instrument in Boston in September, 1849, and yet once more in the suit of Smith vs. Downing and associates over the House telegraph in 1850. In these cases he declared that in 1832, nothing remained to be *discovered* to reduce the proposition of the electromagnetic telegraph to practice. He himself had shown that mechanical effects could be produced at a distance and had designed the sort of battery and coil around the magnet to be used for such a purpose. Lest it seem that he was arrogating too much credit to himself, he drew a distinction between *discovery* and *invention*. Discovery, he said, relates to the development of new facts; invention to the application of these or other facts to practical purposes. Admitting the correctness of his logic, it must also be conceded that a considerable amount of inventing remained to be done to make a practical telegraph after Henry had developed his magnet.

One of his statements which seemed to irritate Morse as much as anything else was his categorical assertion that the House machine was not an infringement upon Morse's patent.

All of the editors in the country were ranged upon one side or the other in these quarrels—there were practically no non-partisans then—and their utterances added fuel to the flame. Donald Mann, editor of the short-lived *American Telegraph Magazine,* wrote in 1852 of a "great defect in Vail's book—

166

a defect which, considering that Mr. Vail is a partner of Professor Morse, appears in a particularly unfortunate light, namely, the total omission to narrate in proper manner the extraordinary electric discoveries of Professor Henry, on which the Morse system is essentially founded"; though Mann refused to believe that "this inexcusable omission could have been sanctioned by Professor Morse."

Magnified and distorted constructions placed upon Henry's statement by partisans of both sides further embittered Morse, and he began, as early as 1852, preparing a "defense"—incited and aided, so it is said, by Tal P. Shaffner. That busybody had turned from telegraph building and management to editing and writing about the business. His *Telegraph Companion* was another short-lived magazine which lasted but little more than a year in 1854-55. When there was no news, Shaffner knew, like the modern yellow journalist, how to create it by stirring up controversy. Upon his return from a trip to Europe in 1854, he wrote in his magazine that while he was in England, Wheatstone spoke to him of Morse as a "lucky robber" of that which was due Professor Henry. He found not only Wheatstone but others in Europe thinking that Morse had been clever enough to steer clear of legal fraud, and therefore lucky enough to escape adverse decisions on mere technical grounds, although he had actually defrauded Henry.

Shaffner wrote Morse on December 27th, of that year, telling him that the use of his telegraph was spreading over Europe; that the needle system was being used in France and England, but that in Germany, Prussia, Austria, Belgium, Russia and the Scandinavian countries, Morse's system was the only one in successful use; although he was deriving little or nothing from any of these countries in the way of remuneration for the privilege. Shaffner said, however, that he was pained to hear "a few in high scientific position asserting that Prof. Joseph Henry was the true inventor of your system, for, say they, you obtained all you knew of the invention from his writings and in conversation with him." This, Shaffner thought, had been caused by the widespread publication of Henry's depositions in Europe: "Many persons have been led to believe that it is to Professor Henry that the world is indebted for your Telegraph, and that you have in some way wronged him out of it." He quoted from the *London Mechanics' Magazine,* which asserted that the world was more indebted to Professor Henry than to any other living man for the telegraph, "and he has neither received the public credit nor honor which are justly his due; much less any remuneration for his invaluable discoveries. He was the first man in the world who moved machinery by an Electro-Magnet; and he is the inventor of the Electro-Magnet to do this—and without this, Morse's Telegraph would yet be in oblivion."

Morse replied sorrowfully that Shaffner's letter acquainted him with facts of which he was unaware; that "the absolutely groundless pretensions to any participation in my invention set up by or for Professor Joseph Henry, on the ground of his depositions in the Telegraph suits, has produced and is still producing, impressions unfavorable to my personal character in Europe."

The outcome of all this was the publication in 1855 of Morse's 90-page pamphlet—which had been long in the brewing—entitled, *A Defense against the Injurious Deductions Drawn from the Deposition of Professor Joseph Henry.* Its utterance was the greatest mistake, the most unlovely act of Morse's lifetime. Had it not been for Shaffner and other unwise friends, the document might not have issued from the press. Its title was fair enough, but instead of being a defense against the injurious deductions from Henry's testimony, it was for the most part an attack upon the testimony itself and upon Henry.

In the light of what we know about the history of the telegraph, Morse's utterances in this document sound like those of a man who has completely lost his balance. He repudiates entirely all his earlier acknowledgments to Henry, and starts off by stating two premises which it was logically impossible for him to carry out:

First, I shall certainly show that I have not only manifested every disposition to give due credit to Professor Henry, but, under the hasty impression that he deserved credit for discoveries in science bearing upon the telegraph, I did actually give him a degree of credit not only beyond what he had received at the time from the scientific world, but a degree of credit to which subsequent research has proven him to be not entitled.

Secondly, I shall show that I am not indebted to him for any discovery in science bearing upon the telegraph; and that all discoveries of principles having this bearing were made, not by Professor Henry, but by others, and prior to any experiments of Professor Henry in the science of electro-magnetism.

Here he is trying to contradict clear and well-established historical facts. "It is charitable," says William B. Taylor, "not to impugn the writer's candor." As the Board of Regents of the Smithsonian Institution said in an indignant reply to the attack in 1857, Morse's pamphlet is:

... simply an assault upon Professor Henry; an attempt to disparage his character; to deprive him of his honors as a scientific discoverer; to impeach his credibility as a witness, and his integrity as a man. It is a disingenuous piece of sophistical argument, such as an unscrupulous advocate might employ to pervert the truth, misrepresent the facts and misinterpret the language in which the facts belonging to the other side of the case are stated.

Mr. Morse charges that the deposition of Professor Henry contains imputations against his (Morse's) personal character, which it does not, assumes it as a duty to expose the utter non-reliability of Professor Henry's testimony; that testimony being supported by the most competent authorities, and by the history of scientific discovery....

Taylor says:

With that strong "subjectivity" (perhaps essential to the success both of the artist and the artisan) which characterized him, Professor Morse always believed his invention to have been practically full-fledged at birth, or rather, at its conception; and quite unconscious of the slow and small advances derived from gathered experience or external suggestion, failed seemingly to realize how completely his earlier methods were discarded and displaced by later improvements.

In his pamphlet Morse makes no acknowledgment to Gale—he does not even mention Gale; which may account for the fact that in his latter years, Gale repudiated his testimony in the telegraph trials and went back to his original statements as to the unworkability of Morse's instrument when he was called in for advice. Morse thus appears to us as a man in many ways highly admirable, yet with grave faults. He did devise a method of conveying intelligence by wire different from any that had been conceived before, and it was the first really practical one achieved in America. He was fundamentally an honest man, and probably arrived at his success as honestly as do most inventors. But he was too much inclined to belittle contributions of others to his success, and he was too prone to berate and vilify other scientists upon slight provocation, and in the heat of controversy to remember things as he wanted to remember them.

As the suits progressed, the Bain companies saw the hand upon the wall, and one by one they effected peaceable amalgamations with the competing Morse companies so that their own stockholders might salvage something of their investment. The Washington line thus emerged in 1850, the New York-Buffalo line in 1851 and the New York-Boston line in '52—the last-named combination, known as the New York & New England Union Telegraph Company, becoming one of the best of the existing lines.

All this was of course as bitter fruit in Henry O'Rielly's mouth. The period of litigation finally broke his never-too-stable power. After 1848 his curve was steadily downward. His misfortunes were many. To injunctions, bad insulation and other troubles was added the yellow fever epidemic which swept the far South in 1849 and almost caused a cessation of business south of Memphis. Then came the big sleet storm of the winter following, which editors called the greatest disaster that ever befell the telegraph in a single night. Not only O'Rielly's but the Morse lines in southern Indiana and Illinois, all of Kentucky, Tennessee, northern Alabama and Mississippi as far south as Jackson, were ruined—wires swept from the poles, hundreds of poles felled, while in the forests, falling boughs added to the tangle. For about a month, telegraph service was cut off from most of the area, while all hands toiled to repair the damage. The Morse lines were better able to stand the shock than O'Rielly's; some of his lines never recovered from the blow.

In those primitive days, by the way, when linemen and repair crews often worked far from their base of supplies, they did not always have enough wire to piece the gaps, and had to use their wits. Once a lineman bought some joints of stove-pipe at a country store, fastened them together and bridged the gap with them. Another, lacking about a foot of wire, spliced his climbers into the breach until more wire could be brought.

Morse lines were built paralleling most of O'Rielly's flimsy wires in the Middle West and South. Two or three of his own lines practically disintegrated and were eventually gathered in, almost at junk prices, by the opposition; others were developed by other men into powerful agencies of communication. After 1853, O'Rielly was no more than a minor figure in the telegraph world. His name appears occasionally in some promotion or attempted promotion for five or six years thereafter, then vanishes from that category. In the last quarter-century of his life he was for ten years employed in the New York Custom House, and spent much time in fighting for public rights, as secretary, for example, of the National Anti-Monopoly Cheap Freight Railway League and in other movements. He died on August 17, 1886. During his brief promotion period, he built 8,000 miles of telegraph lines, and gave hundreds of American communities their first telegraph service; but to-day, scarcely one in a million Americans has ever heard his name.

CHAPTER IX

THE RISE OF THE ASSOCIATED PRESS

Little birds sit on the slender lines
   And the news of the world runs under their feet;
How value rises and how declines,
   How kings with their armies in battle meet
And all the while, 'mid the soundless signs,
   They chirp their gossipings, foolish-sweet.
MRS. ADELINA D. T. WHITNEY

A T THE beginning of the nineteenth century, there was no organized system, no great effort made to collect news. If citizens didn't report local happenings to the editor, they might never be mentioned in the paper. The first selling of news began in Boston a few years later by two men named Topliff and Blake. The latter prowled about the harbor in a rowboat, boarding incoming vessels and collecting European items and market reports which he and Topliff sold to newspapers.

By 1827, New York papers were combining to get ship news. When Hale and Hallock, new owners of the *Journal of Commerce,* began in 1828 to send a yacht twenty or thirty miles beyond Sandy Hook to meet expected vessels, the news association angrily expelled them as sneaks. For a time Hale and Hallock had a semaphore telegraph station on the lower bay. They ran a pony express to Philadelphia with eight changes of horses, and later extended it to Washington. J. Watson Webb of the *Courier and Enquirer* and James Gordon Bennett of the *Herald* carried on a lively war with them. Bennett, in the 1840's, had horse expresses both to Boston and Washington, and carrier-pigeons brought the Governor's annual message and other political news to him from Albany, so that he could print it ahead of all competitors. For these reasons, Bennett did not at first favor the telegraph; he saw in it an agency for destroying the advantage which he had so carefully built up. When it was established, however, the dour Scot accepted it as inevitable and even came to favor it. William M. Swain, proprietor of the Philadelphia *Public Ledger,* was another vigorous newsman, one who ran a horse express to bring Washington political gossip hot off the wires at Baltimore to his paper, and still more important, the latest news from the Mexican War zone.

There were many editors who at first did not comprehend the fact that the telegraph was potentially the greatest aid to their business that ever came into being. Some of them even vaguely feared that it would be detrimental to their profession. Of course, not one of them had the faintest notion of the revolution which it was destined to work with them, of the future almost complete dependence of the newspaper upon it.

The association of New York newspapers, which had come to be known as the New York Associated Press, was the first agency to use the telegraph in an expert way. It was interested in promoting the New York and Offing Electro-Magnetic Telegraph Company, which ran a wire down to Coney Island in 1845, and had news boats going out daily to board incoming vessels and to report wrecks. On a day in 1846, the papers reported that their line "withstood the recent storm without a break":

But the gale was too severe for their news boats to make their usual cruises at sea, consequently no disaster could be reported by that means beyond the distance reached with their telescope. Had the Offing lines of telegraph been constructed along the coast of New Jersey, many of the disasters which occurred on Saturday night would have been reported from hour to hour as they occurred, and relief could have been sent, which ... might have preserved many of the human beings who have perished.

But they had their moments of triumph, as is indicated by a New York newspaper headline of 1846:

OLD WIRES AND NEW WAVES

Arrival of the
GREAT WESTERN!
In Advance of all our Contemporaries
by the
NEW YORK AND OFFING TELEGRAPH
Eleven Days Later
Triumph of the Corn Bill
The King of France Shot at Again on the 16th

As the news boats were open yawls rowed by the reporters, the job naturally became a pretty difficult one in rough weather. By 1847, the Associated Press was using pigeons, as a better means than the telegraph. They had an agent stationed at Sandy Hook lighthouse, and pigeons whose home cote was in New York were taken down to him every day or two. With several pigeons in his yawl, he rowed alongside vessels coming from Europe, and the news—by previous arrangement, written on very thin paper—was tossed over to him in a water-tight can. He affixed one small sheet of the flimsy to each bird's leg, and it carried the news to New York, whence it was flashed to Boston, Philadelphia, New Orleans and other cities, often before the vessel had left quarantine.

But the telegraph was scarcely out of its swaddling clothes before conflict arose between it and the press. One of the first complaints was against the high cost of getting news by telegraph. The Lancaster, Pennsylvania, *American* gave the rough side of its tongue to both O'Rielly and the State Legislature on January 17, 1846, in this satirical item:

Telegraphic Correspondence—Late from Harrisburg
EXPRESSLY FOR THE *AMERICAN*
We this morning lay before our readers the *proceedings of the Legislature* up to the hour of going to press—by means of the Telegraph now in successful operation between this city and Harrisburg. In reply to our inquiry of
"What have the Legislature done to-day?" we received in answer, *quick as thought*—

"I will inquire."

After a lapse of about *three minutes*—while a messenger ran to the Capital and back, we received in reply—

"*Nothing* of any consequence."

"As *usual*," said someone present. And we are sorry to admit that a large portion of the people are willing to believe that at the close of the session, the same may in truth be said of their proceedings.

For this information we were charged fifty cents—the office is open at all hours of the day, and for the same price, any person can be gratified to the same extent.

As this indicates, the telegraph companies themselves were, in the beginning, news agencies. Operator-managers were expected to ascertain facts when requested, and even to gather and send out news of events in their own towns important enough to interest the rest of the country. Naturally, such items often did not reach the wires, because of the preoccupation of the operator. When this duty was found to be too arduous for operators, some of the telegraph companies took on news reporters in the larger cities. Presidents' and Governors' messages were sent by the companies to any newspaper able to pay for the service.

In the East in 1846-47, the publishers began to coöperate; several papers in a town would band together and receive one dispatch for all. The Magnetic Telegraph, still swinish with the first enthusiasm of monopoly, struck back at them by charging full price for one dispatch and 50 per cent for each additional newspaper using it. This struck the editors as unfair and oppressive. "Suppose we charged 50 per cent extra," said one, "for every neighbor whom a subscriber allowed to read his newspaper"—a widespread practice in those days. On Smith's New York and Boston line, 200 miles long, the rate was fifty cents for ten words, and no reduction for news messages; in fact, he began penalizing still more heavily, as the New York *Tribune* testified in 1848:

If this office was to receive a message by telegraph—and the telegraph bill was instantly paid at the full regular rate of two cents a word—Messrs. Smith and Kendall, in case we gave a copy of this PAID-for message to the *Sun,* and then to the *Herald,* a third to the *True Sun* and a fourth to the *Express,* would demand OTHER FOUR CENTS A WORD, or say half price over again, from these papers for no additional service at all, and if they refused to pay, would say, "There is no line but ours, and if you do not pay us over and over again for the use of the message which *The Tribune* has already paid us in full at our regular prices, we will instantly stop sending your messages until you pay us six cents a word for what we charge other people only two."

The associated New York newspapers next tried the use of ciphers. The telegraph companies' news agents themselves had already begun using codes in sending market quotations. Their first amateur idea in compiling a code was to compress bits of a whole phrase into one word; the result being that they produced some of the most staggering words ever seen in print, such as caserovingedsable, hoveesness, rehairoringed, rehoeing-edableness, preveeror and retackmentativeness. The distracted editor of the Pittsburgh *Gazette* burst out in protest to them in 1849, against such polysyllabic atrocities, made worse by crabbed writing and the inevitable errors of the operators who frequently lost their way in the alphabetical jungle:

These Hottentish cyphers must be abolished, both for our own safety and reputation, your credit and the general good. Webster has good saxon enough to answer every purpose; he asks nothing for his patent, and we will supply dictionaries to all who need them.

That watchful demon, Fog Smith, didn't propose to let a parcel of slick New York newspapermen get around him with this cipher racket; so after some pondering, he issued a decree to the effect that five letters constitute the average English word; therefore, all the letters in a newspaper telegram were to be divided by five, and thus the true number of words ascertained, and charged for!

This floored the New York newspaper lads only momentarily. It really was a blessing in disguise, for they thereupon sat down and produced a real code, with no word in it containing more than five letters. They had it printed in a book of about seventy-five pages at considerable cost. What was Smith's retort to this? Why, he issued a new ukase to the effect that a recheck indicated that the average word is only three letters in length, and therefore, all the letters in a news telegram would now be divided by three, and charged for accordingly.

The newspapers endured this briefly until the House and Bain telegraph lines were completed between New York and Boston, and then they were able to thumb their noses at Smith.

From the very start, messages by O'Rielly's wire could be sent from Pittsburgh to Louisville, more than twice the distance from New York and Boston, at 50 cents for 10 words; from Pittsburgh to Philadelphia or Cincinnati, 40 cents. As much of the most important news came from Washington and other large Eastern cities, even these rates were a hardship to publishers. "We are in hopes to see a reduction made in the charges," said the Wheeling *Daily Argus*, "before all the printers in the West are broken down by the enormous expense to which they are put by its operations"; for of course telegraphic news had rapidly become a necessity, an obligation; the publisher must have it or go out of business.

But Western papers now began to learn the trick of cooperation, and found that O'Rielly did not object to it. In a city large enough to support two or three papers the burden of each was thus considerably lessened. The Pittsburgh *Commercial Journal* remarked in 1848:

A few days since, we received the Message of Governor Shunk by telegraph in company with two other city papers. The Message contains at least 10,000 words, and the transmission of it cost but $16:—such a Message over the Boston line, a distance not so great as that between Harrisburg and Pittsburgh, would have cost $330, the Eastern newspapers not being allowed to combine for the purpose of receiving intelligence.

He added that 300 messages a day between Pittsburgh and Cincinnati were attesting the popularity of the O'Rielly lines; that while Smith and Kendall were trying to squeeze as much as possible out of their patrons, O'Rielly had been content with a modest profit and good service. The Morse patentees, under Smith's influence, kept up for several years this stupid battle with the press, thereby planting in many an editorial breast seed which bore acrid fruit when the contest between O'Rielly and the patentees came on. In some places they and their concessionaires were actually in competition with the newspapers—posting in telegraph-office windows bulletins of much later news than the editor could command—bulletins which were an excellent advertisement for the wires, but courted the powerful enmity of the Fourth Estate. In some other places, especially where there was telegraph competition, news was presented free of charge to the editor who would give the most fulsome public acknowledgment of the favor, not failing, of course, to mention the name of the polite manager of the telegraph office.

Finally, the Morse lines radiating from the great Eastern ports, New York and Boston, established what they called a regular daily news service, for which provincial newspapers paid weekly rates ranging from five to ten dollars, depending upon distance and other considerations not always quite clear to the editors. But that this service was anything but satisfactory is proven by numerous complaints from the sanctums. The Toronto *Examiner* said in 1847:

We entered into an arrangement on Monday for the Telegraphic reports, and we will now give our readers an idea of the value we have received for our money. On Monday evening there was no report; Tuesday, the report was anticipated by mail; Wednesday there was about six lines of a report; and Thursday the wires were broken!

About the same time the Utica *Daily Gazette* was reporting:

The Telegraph is in complete order to-day, but after dancing attendance for hours, we can only get from New York the gratifying intelligence, "No report this A.M." So it goes. When there is any news, the Telegraph is down; when it is in order, there is no report, or "it can't be sent," or it slips through without being taken. We pay ruinously, are as vigilant as possible, but get little for our pains but vexation of spirit. The Telegraph has great capabilities, but its particular province seems to be to tantalize those who depend upon it.

A few weeks later the *Gazette* was charging that false information had been sent by the telegraph—a complaint which became rather common. After the arrival of a steamer from Europe, the cities in central and western New York were notified that flour was selling at 60 shillings and corn 80 shillings at Liverpool—a rise of 10 shillings for the former and 20 shillings for the latter; when as a matter of fact, there had actually been a decline of 10 shillings on each. In Rochester, contradictory information brought the market to a standstill for hours. It was hinted that speculators might have bribed the operators. Correction of the false report was prevented until well along in the afternoon by a break in the wire between Albany and New York. Editors hinted that this might be a "convenient excuse"—what to-day we would call an alibi.

There were some crooked operators in those days, who gave the editors and press associations trouble. The New Orleans *Picayune* alleged a "regular system of swindling" practised upon that paper by some of the operators:

In the office in this city there used to be a transcribing clerk who made a business of retailing out our dispatches, which were procured at great expense whilst we were running an express, its contents, as telegraphed from Mobile, were regularly rifled by this individual, who sold the news to sundry parties in this city—who will have to pay for it yet, or else the town will be much edified by revelations which will take place in one of our courts of law. Five others in this city daily complain of foul play.

The superintendent of the O'Rielly line between Philadelphia and Pittsburgh publicly admitted the catching of a dishonest operator:

A dispatch proceeding to Mr. Jones, the agent of the associated press of New York, containing news from Mexico, was used in the compilation of a message by an operator employed by us at Pittsburgh, which he addressed to Mr. Johnson, news-agent at Philadelphia. We have the further proof of a disgraceful conversation held upon our line between that operator and Mr. Johnson, in which the latter agreed to pay the former ten dollars per month for collecting items of news, at first intended to be local, but which the former proposed, in the most reprehensible manner, to extend to foreign items, procurable from other press reports going to other parties.

Pennsylvania passed a law in 1851, making telegrams secret, to prevent betrayal of private affairs by operators. When, therefore, an operator was called into court in Philadelphia a little later, and ordered to produce certain telegrams which would prove an act of fraud, he refused to do so, saying that the state law forbade it. The circuit court, shocked at this development, proceeded to override the law, saying:

It must be apparent that, if we adopt this construction of the law, the telegraph may be used with the most absolute security for purposes destructive to the well-being of society—a state of things rendering its absolute usefulness at least questionable. The correspondence of the traitor, the murderer, the robber and the swindler, by means of which their crimes and frauds could be the more readily accomplished and their detection and punishment avoided, would become things so sacred that they never could be accessible to the public justice, however deep might be the public interest involved in their production.

The judge therefore ordered the operator to produce the telegrams.

Another sort of nuisance to the editor was complained of by the Troy *Daily Post* in 1847. Newspapermen in those days sat in the telegraph office with paper and pencil, taking down the news as it was read aloud to them by the operator from the paper tape or the click of the instrument; and the *Post* complained that there were too many greedy listeners:

The Telegraph offices all along the line are constantly crowded with strangers and news carriers. The reports for the press, for which they are charged an enormous price, are almost invariably listened to by men who delight to carry news, and two of whom will circulate it faster than a steam press. At night, we receive a market report, and oftentimes the very men who will not take a paper, are permitted to stand by and swallow down the news we are paying for.

But this reading aloud by the operator to the scribes once proved a boon to one editor. When the President's message was about to come through in 1849, the editor of the Milwaukee *American,* the local Know-Nothing organ, could not afford to pay for it; so for a nominal sum he rented for a few days a vacant room directly over the telegraph office. He had previously ascertained that there was an old stove-pipe hole in the floor, through which the pipe from a stove below had formerly passed, to heat the upper room. As the time for the reception of the message approached, he stole by a back stairway into his secret lair, and lying on the floor with his ear at the hole, wrote down the message as the operator read it aloud to the other newsmen.

There was yet another grievance. The telegraph companies were paid supposedly for reasonably full and coherent news reports; but to save themselves money, they condensed them so that the resulting staccato jumble often left the editor bewildered, and unable to fill out—as he was supposed to do—the true picture of happenings in other cities and lands. For example, in 1849, when Garibaldi was raging through Italy, when that whole peninsula was in turmoil and transition, when the news from there was or should have been as colorful as a Dumas novel, the New Orleans *Commercial Times*—and of course, other papers as well—received one day this crisp résumé of current events in that country:

Rome—people rising—Swiss Guard—palace surrounded—new ministry—triumph—the Pope—French brigade—General Cavaignac —personal safety Pontiff—no alliance—Count Rossi assassinated— Deputies in session.

One would be inclined to suspect that Mr. Alfred Jingle himself was writing the news telegrams in those days were it not for a certain lack of clarity in them which even Mr. Jingle's most disjointed dialogue displayed. The *Commercial Times* man said glumly that it would puzzle a more astute and better informed person than the average American editor to get a true picture of what was happening in Italy then; he just had to guess at it.

The first "waiting for the returns" was done on election night, November 7, 1848. Telegraph offices remained open through the night—an unheard-of thing—and before morning it became apparent to many that the Whig candidate, General Zachary Taylor, had been elected. Ezra Cornell, listening at Ithaca, said he was sure of the result by 11 P.M. Nearly all Whig papers announced it as a settled fact next day, though Democratic papers still denied it. Even eighteen days later, on November 25th, the Davenport, Iowa, *Banner,* a Democratic organ, was still in doubt as to the outcome, refusing to believe the telegraph.

Democratic editors, by the way, for some reason became much disgrunted with the telegraph system in 1848-9, calling it the "Tel-lie-graph" and "a Whig affair"; to which the Whig editors retorted by pointing out that Kendall, Fog Smith and O'Rielly were none of them Whigs, but "all Locofocos."

There were some remarkable displays of newspaper enterprise in those primordial days. In November, 1847, Henry Clay delivered an important political speech at his home town, Lexington, which, it was believed, would sound the Whig keynote for the campaign of 1848. There was then no telegraph line at or near Lexington. James Gordon Bennett the Elder, of the New York *Herald,* wishing to have first publication of the story, had express riders ready with relays of horses all along the eighty-mile road from Lexington to Cincinnati. The speech was delivered on a Saturday afternoon, and like all the great orators of his day, Clay spoke without manuscript. A shorthand reporter sent from New York took it down as delivered and passed the notes to another, who hastily transcribed it back into English. When the transcription was completed, an express rider galloped with it into the dusk towards Cincinnati, where O'Rielly's telegraph operator was waiting to send it on. It was relayed from Pittsburgh, "during a heavy rain, and while a thunder shower was passing over a portion of both the eastern and western lines," and Bennett was receiving it at 4 A.M. on Sunday. "Could a better illustration be wished," he asks, "of the perfection of the telegraphic art?"

Presidential messages to Congress were great events in those times, and all newspapers that could afford such luxuries printed them in full. Polk's message of December, 1848, occupied thirteen columns of small type in those newspapers with the largest pages—and type was smaller and pages larger then than now. Its transmission began on a Tuesday afternoon at from 2 to 6:30 P.M. in various cities, and for some of them it was not completed until the small hours of Thursday morning. As usual, a widespread rainstorm pestered the lines through Pennsylvania and the Middle West. The O'Rielly wire west of Zanesville did not work for several hours just after midnight on Tuesday; some papers published about half of the document on Wednesday, and the rest when it came. James D. Reid, the O'Rielly superintendent at Pittsburgh, was sharply criticized by some editors for holding up the message for five hours on Wednesday to send other telegrams through. It was a rule of the companies that no one was to be permitted to monopolize the wire for more than ten or fifteen minutes at a stretch; but when editors wanted to tie it up for hours to get a Presidential message—why, that was quite a different matter!

Reid, in defense, pointed out the great trouble and cost to the companies of handling the message. Watchmen patroled the line over the Laurel and Alleghany Mountains to see that no breaks occurred. A saddled horse stood at the door of every office, to carry instalments to the next office in case there was a break. All of Tuesday night, rain poured in torrents, while the operators nursed the feeble current and asked again and again that indistinct words be repeated. Next day there were many accumulated messages of such vital import to sender and receiver

that Reid considered that they must be sent—messages telling
of dying kinspeople, messages appealing for help to save business or individuals from ruin, and many others more important
than a Presidential harangue.

Columbus editors were among the most ebullient and violent
of the critics of the telegraph. The Ohio *Statesman* in a furious
editorial of 1849, complains of his failure to receive the foreign
news the day before:

We believe the Telegraph Company could be made to pay heavy
damages for these shameful derelictions of duty, and they will not
be submitted to any longer. The way the thing now works is a
disgrace to the whole system—ruinous to the publishers and discreditable to our city, that the foreign news can be read in St.
Louis and the whole West, and circulated among the people hours
before the Capitol of Ohio knows what is going on!

And what is the excuse set up by the Telegrapher here? Why,
HE WAS AT HIS DINNER WHEN THE NOTICE WAS
GIVEN THAT FOREIGN NEWS WOULD BE SENT
THROUGH ! Do other Telegraphers here never EAT DINNER?
Yes, and supper, too, we presume, but they notified other officials
of the hours when they would be performing that operation.... It
is just as easy for them to have their HOURS as Railroads theirs,
and their stopping places....

In an age when long-time credit was common in all businesses, the Magnetic Telegraph Company was particularly rigid
with newspapers, as witness these orders of 1847:

The accounts of Newspaper Editors using the Telegraph must
be made out and presented every morning, except Sundays, including Saturday in Monday's bills, and if the amounts due be not paid
and no good reason given therefor, no communications will be
delivered thenceforth to such delinquent Editor, unless prepaid at
the station whence forwarded; and notice of the delinquency will
be given to all the Stations, that nothing more may be sent to said
Editors without such prepayment.

In Boston, Topliff & Blake were succeeded in the ownership
of the News Room by D. H. Craig, one of the most noted men
in American newspaper history. Craig began life in 1825, as an
apprentice in a New Hampshire newspaper printing office.

While still a young man, he became interested in homing pigeons, and began importing and training them. He saw in them an important adjunct to the business of gathering news. Establishing himself in New York, he gave service to the numerous lottery men of the period (who were among the first to be willing to pay for the quick transmission of news), to Jacob Little, the Jay Gould of ante-bellum days, to Harnden, the first expressman of importance in the country, and finally, to the newspapers, Moses Y. Beach of the *Sun* being one of his first publisher-customers.

Some time before the building of the New England electric telegraph lines, Craig had a pigeon service between Halifax and Boston, to supply some of the papers in the latter city with news, which other pigeons then carried from there on to certain customers in New York. The Cunard steamers then touched at Halifax, and Craig would be there on steamer day, having traveled by land (and boat across the Bay of Fundy) from Boston with his birds in a basket. English newspapers, regularly engaged, were delivered to him by the steamer, and making hasty digests of the leading items of European news on thin paper, he sent them to Boston by the pigeons, which would beat the steamer by anywhere from one to five hours. Relay pigeons flew the news to New York. When the telegraph line had been completed to Boston, Craig used the wire from there to New York.

But presently the Cunard Company ceased to use Boston as its terminus, and after touching at Halifax, boats sailed directly to New York. The New York Associated Press and some Boston papers now chartered a small steamer to meet the Cunarder at Halifax and carry the news to Boston, whence by telegraph it would outrun the big boat to New York. Craig, whose business was principally with brokers and foreign traders craving news as to European prices, must beat this press service in order to maintain his prestige.

Testifying before the United States Senate Committee on Commerce and Labor in 1883, he told how he thereafter took passage on the steamer at Halifax with his basket of birds and a tiny font of type and printing outfit, and condensed the news greatly as the steamer sped towards New York:

I printed it on tissue paper with small type in my stateroom, fastened it to the legs of the birds and flew them from the decks or portholes.... My birds carried the news to Boston several hours in advance of the steamers, where it was used for speculative purposes,

D. H. CRAIG

and subsequently for publication. When it became known that I was anticipating the news brought to Boston by the steamers, the agent of some of the New York journals made representations to the Cunard Company that I was using the news for speculative purposes, and they undertook to prevent me from taking my birds on board their steamers at Halifax. On one occasion, Captain Ryrie seized and held them until after the steamer arrived in Boston. Apprehending this outrage, I had put one of my birds in my overcoat pocket before going on board, and after putting the news on his legs, I went on deck and flew the bird close to the captain's head.

He darted into his stateroom and caught his rifle, but before he had a chance to shoot, the bird was a mile above him, flying to Boston.

The words "speculation" and "speculator" were red rags before the public bull's-eye in those days. We have already told how a false charge of speculative conspiracy in 1828, ruined Dyar's pioneer telegraph invention, which might have developed into something of importance. New York newspapers in 1846, whispered with shocked countenances of how secret news as to stock and commodity prices were wigwagged across the Hudson and telegraphed to Philadelphia. "This," said the *Herald,* "is certaing using the Telegraph for a purpose never contemplated by the inventor, Professor Morse, nor by the immortal Franklin." To-day, such has been the change in the ethical viewpoint, it is quite respectable to sell stocks short or take advantage of secret information and buy from an unsuspecting owner— just as the traditional New England deacon may work off a balky horse on a neighbor, and then go, conscience-free, to church to pray and sing with unabated unction.

Speculation played an amusing trick on the Associated Press one June day in 1848, while the Whig National Convention was sitting in Philadelphia. The telegraph companies were still having trouble in getting messages across the Hudson, and so the Associated Press arranged to have a man in Jersey City get the news from the telegraph office there and display a white flag on the river bank if Taylor was nominated, a red flag if Clay was the choice. The trouble was that the stockbrokers put on a new wigwag system of their own about that time, and the young reporter watching from the Manhattan shore wasn't aware of it. So when he saw a white flag being waved violently across the water, he ran lickety-split to the various newspaper offices and informed them that Taylor was nominated. Taylor was chosen, as a matter of fact, but not until several hours after some of the New York newspapers had announced it— which evoked many chuckles at Gotham's expense.

Early in 1848, Fog Smith's telegraph line from Boston

187

reached Portland. We say "Smith's" for the reason that of the $175,000 stock in the company, he owned $140,000 worth. The small group of papers now banded together in New York under the name of the New York Associated Press thereupon laid plans to speed its service. As soon as the Cunard steamer had dropped its news at Halifax, a horse express carried it to Digby, on the west side of the peninsula, a distance of 149 miles, and a fast boat dashed thence down the Maine coast to Portland. The express rider aroused terrific excitement along the way, and crowds lined the road in the villages as he galloped by on his foam-flecked steed. Several miles out from Digby a cannon was fired as he passed to notify the boat captain, who thereupon got up a full head of steam, weighed anchor and sent a yawl ashore, manned by his best rowers, to get the bag of European papers.

This process, however, was expensive—about a thousand dollars per steamer—and the Associated Press therefore offered financial aid and a guarantee of business to any company that would build a line through the Canadian provinces to Halifax. The Maine Telegraph Company had just been organized, and was building from Portland to Calais, on the Canadian border. Two other lines were constructed in Canada; one, the New Brunswick, from Calais to Amherst, on the Nova Scotian border—F. O. J. Smith appears as one of the directors—the other a Nova Scotian government project, from Amherst to Halifax.

Even while these were under construction, everybody concerned was thrown into a chill by a rumor that the Cunard steamers would soon cease calling at Halifax and head directly for New York. What! Pass up Halifax, the home of Samuel Cunard himself? It was unthinkable! The *Acadian Recorder* warned that such a course would make news a day or two later in reaching the United States, and mournfully predicted that the change would ruin the telegraph line and the town; perhaps even the projected railroad wouldn't be built now. But several years passed before the disaster actually occurred.

From the collection of George B. Sloane

ENVELOPES FOR TELEGRAM DELIVERY, 1850 TO 1860

THE RISE OF THE ASSOCIATED PRESS

The quarrel between Smith and the press was in full heat in 1848, as indicated by headlines taken at random one day from the New York *Herald:*

THE EUROPEAN NEWS
ONE WEEK LATER
ARRIVAL
of the
Steamship Hibernia at Halifax
Telegraphic to Portland
thence by
Winslow & Co.'s Express to Newburyport, Mass.,
and thence over
Bain's Merchants' Telegraph
to the
NEW YORK HERALD
Advance in Cotton
Improvement in Breadstuffs
The Election of Eugene Sue in Paris,
Etc., etc., etc.

It is evident that as late as 1849, Horace Greeley was not fully coöperating with the Associated Press group; for he reports on February 25th that:

Our special agent at Halifax advises us that the Purser of the *America* declined throwing our package over to our newsboat, but notwithstanding this, our agent succeeded in reaching the Telegraphic office ahead of all others. The news came from Halifax to Portland by Telegram—thence by special express to Boston, and thence over Bain's Telegraph line to this city.

The "telegraphic to Portland" was in part a fiction, for the lines through the Canadian provinces were as yet far from complete, and express riders had to bridge the gaps. That an express company carried the messages from Portland to the end of the Bain line proves the breach with Smith.

When the wires reached up towards Canada, Craig tried flying his pigeons to St. John or Portland and sending thence by wire. For a time he ran a horse express across Nova Scotia to Digby, and a fast little steamer from there across the Bay of

Fundy to St. John, from which place the wire was continuous to New York. But this was expensive, and he went back to pigeons again. Meanwhile, he clashed frequently with one John T. Smith, news agent of some of the New York and Boston papers, their dispatches fighting for precedence on the wire. The New York Associated Press, finding him a hard man to beat, offered him the post of European news agent, and he promptly accepted it.

F. O. J. Smith was already incensed at Craig. One difficulty was that Smith himself wanted to sell news wherever he could. In January, 1849, he refused to carry Craig's dispatches, and the Portland *Umpire* lauded him for "refusing the use of his line for dishonest purposes" by "Craig, the pigeon agent of the New York Associated Press and a gang of heartless speculators." Smith, swelling with righteous indignation, classed "the proprietors or hirers of carrier pigeons in the same gambling spirit with wreckers along the seaboard, or with any other class of speculators who deem all to be fair that can be made profitable in business." Coming from Smith, this was delicious.

"The interest of the man who employs or uses carrier pigeons," he went on, "becomes an interest to break or otherwise interrupt the working of the Telegraph line." Mr. Craig's methods, he said, were "alike fatal to the business and reputation of the Telegraph and dangerous to public confidence." He was horrified because Craig said he would sell news to any one who paid the price, "just as I would a string of onions." Just Heaven! Was "intelligence" to be thus bandied about by unprincipled and irresponsible peddlers?

The Maine Telegraph Company, though a Morse organization, was not controlled by Smith, and it calmly continued carrying Craig's dispatches from Calais to Portland, a special boat taking them from there to the end of the Bain line at Boston. Smith tried to induce the Associated Press to dismiss Craig, but failed. He wrote to the Commissioners of the Nova Scotia telegraph that "the infamous Gisborne" was acting in violation of their charter; he had sent other people's dispatches to Portland with instructions that they were to be held there until Craig's "pigeon messages" could reach Boston by steamer. He declared that the operators of the Main line at Calais and Portland had confessed the receipt of messages with instructions that they were to be held overnight before forwarding.

The Associated Press asserted publicly and somewhat mendaciously that not a carrier pigeon had been used since Craig became their agent. Smith was trying vainly to buy a controlling interest in the Maine Telegraph Company. Kendall wrote to James Gordon Bennett that he did not approve Smith's refusing service to the Associated Press, and did not propose to let him get in control of the Portland-Calais line. "I made up my mind that we ought not increase his power by such means"; and therefore he, Morse and Vail refused to sell their stock to Smith.

To Smith, Kendall had written a biting letter, excoriating him for his course, and saying in part:

A message comes to your line, after having passed over three legitimate Morse lines, and you assume a right to stop it. For what reason?... simply because the agent of the Associated Press at Halifax is, in your opinion, a bad man, not to be trusted by the public.... No overt act has been traced to him; it is not shown that he has employed carrier pigeons, or cut the wires; he is sustained by the public authorities of Nova Scotia and his employers in the United States.

Under these circumstances, it seems to me you assume a high prerogative when you undertake to stop messages, for no other reason than suspicion or dislike of the person who sends them. You virtually condemn the public authorities of Nova Scotia, and attempt to dictate to the customers of the telegraph whom they shall not employ as their agents....

Whether the managers of the Nova Scotia line ought to receive and send messages which may have been brought to Halifax by carrier pigeons, is one question; and whether the manager of a line in the United States ought to stop them on that account, is another. Certainly the manager of a line in Wisconsin would hardly venture to give, as a reason for refusing to forward an item of news, that it had been brought to Halifax by a carrier pigeon, or that he had not a good opinion of the man who sent it.

OLD WIRES AND NEW WAVES

Believing Smith's position to be "essentially wrong and fatally injurious to all interests connected with Morse's patents," Kendall concluded, "I decline selling you our stock in the Maine line, or taking any other step which may strengthen you in so mischievous a controversy."

It will be discovered from the above letter that Craig was now meeting at sea, a hundred miles or more from Halifax, certain ships which did not stop at that port and sending news brought by them from his little dispatch boat to Halifax by pigeon. But Fog Smith was not yet ready to admit defeat. Suddenly Craig's old opponent, John T. Smith, appeared in Halifax, and announced himself as agent for the New York and Boston Associated Press. In reality, said Craig, he had been hired by Fog Smith, with the connivance of a few papers in Boston, Portland and elsewhere. When the next steamer came in, he succeeded in beating Craig to the telegraph office, got possession of the wire and sent a batch of news to New York and Boston.

The New York Associated Press quickly repudiated him, and Craig laid plans to beat him on the next steamer day. He had a dummy package of newspapers made up, with a copy of a well-known Liverpool journal on the outside, its name being visible, but its date carefully concealed. As the liner cast anchor in the harbor, a young fisherman soused this package of papers in the water and then ran with it at top speed to the telegraph office, where he cried breathlessly, "Here's Craig's parcel of European news." A few minutes later Smith was seen dashing through the street in a buggy behind a fast horse. He leaped out in front of the telegraph office, and up the stairs, three steps at a time; but before he could say a word, the operator pointed to the dripping parcel on the counter.

"Craig's beaten you," he said.

With one glance at the package, Smith uttered a furious blasphemy, turned on his heel, hurried back to the steamer and took passage on it for New York. Craig meanwhile prepared his digest of the news in leisurely way.

Fog Smith's rage increased as O'Rielly's Bain line pushed

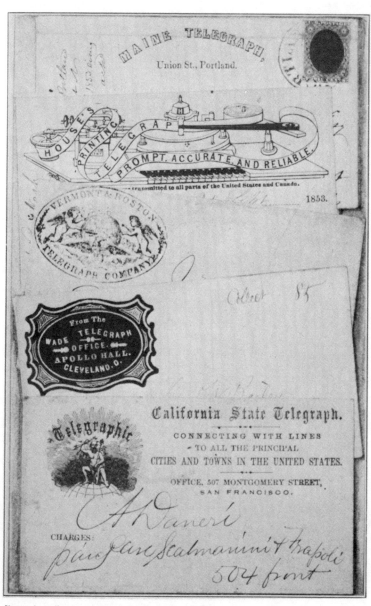

From the collection of Frank E. Lawrance

PRE-CIVIL WAR TELEGRAPH ENVELOPES

its way up to Portland. He tried to get possession of the New Brunswick line; he tried to induce the New Brunswick Legislature to act against the Associated Press; he protested again to Nova Scotia; at one time he refused to receive private messages for Halifax or let anything from there pass over his line. "God forbid that by any act of mine," Kendall wrote to him, "the people of the United States should ever justly come to consider the pirates upon Morse's patents their friends and deliverers" —by which he meant the Bain and House enterprises. "In behalf of my principals, I protest against the further use of their property in this warfare."

The resourceful Craig was now called to New York, where he began developing his scheme to make the Associated Press all-powerful. Foreign and market news service was to be supplied to papers all over the country—perhaps later a general news service. The machinery was soon put in motion, and editors here and there began buying, but it was long before the amateur news vendors learned to send out news entirely uncolored. Until that time, their reports frequently gave dissatisfaction. The Rochester *Democrat* said caustically in 1852, that when this news agency "sends us the speculations of a hired scribbler of the Herald in regard to future political movements, we desire him to give his authority, and not impose such stuff upon the press and public as news." The Buffalo *Commercial Advertiser* thought that, "The gentleman who makes up the reports is evidently unfit for the post, and ignorant of the wants of the papers which have the privilege of paying a considerable amount of money for the trash which he transmits over the wires."

Craig had by that time gotten the lines in the Canadian provinces pretty well under his thumb, and Smith was temporarily baffled. The New York *Herald* on August 21, 1852, had the effrontery to boast of the Associated Press's mastery of the wires in an article sneering at some small rival newspaper groups which promised to receive foreign news as soon as or sooner than the A. P.:

These parties have never received, and they *cannot receive* a single word of news over the Halifax wires, from the time the steamer is signaled until *after the receipt by the associated press of this city of their despatch of three thousand words.* Nor can any other party, under any but the most urgent necessity, and then only with the consent of the Association. Any one, therefore, who professes to have received the foreign news via Halifax, in advance of, or even simultaneously with the Associated Press, may be put down as a cheat.

The *American Telegraph Magazine* saw danger in this power:

The foreign news comes to the agent of six papers in this city and to no other person. For satisfactory reasons, it is sometimes retained in his hands quite a number of hours before publishing. Now, during this interim, *what is to prevent this Agent from corresponding with cotton and provision dealers in distant cities and posting them up on foreign prices,* a little in advance of the newspapers? He or any of his clerks or associates could easily do it in a "cypher" that no one could detect, and might realize something handsome by so doing.

The growing arrogance of the Associated Press even communicated itself to its agent in England, John Hunter, who advertised in British papers that telegraph dispatches to or from England or Europe would be punctually forwarded if confided to his care. He promised that dispatches for America entrusted to him would be sent over the wires in this country ahead of all other private communications on arrival of the steamers at Halifax, Boston or New York. This aroused a storm of indignation here at the impudence of such promises, and the A. P. was called upon to disown them.

Boston, which was trying to get the news from Fog Smith's agency, was not receiving good service. A remonstrance posted by a number of leading merchants in the Exchange Reading Room in 1852, complained that:

We have for a long time borne the mortification of seeing our neighbors furnished with news many hours in advance of ourselves; and it is well known that dispatches of foreign intelligence from

Halifax frequently pass through this city to New Orleans and back before a syllable is allowed to be made public here. This we consider highly improper, and we are astonished that it should have been submitted to so long. . . . A change must be made; we call for it at once, and have it we must.

The only remedy for Boston appeared to be a connection with the Associated Press.

But the A.P. had to fight hard for its privileges. Many editors were opposed to it, and the telegraph heads, Morse, Smith, Kendall and others, were highly antagonistic, fancying that a news monopoly would mean a great decrease in business to the telegraph. But in practice, it worked just the other way. Until Craig extended the service, provincial editors never received by telegraph the details of important news events from a distance. Only a few words, a skeleton outline was sent them, and they "blew it up," drawing upon their imaginations for the details. When the A.P. began supplying the news in full, it was nothing less than revolutionary.

When the Bain and House lines were completed between New York and Buffalo, the Associated Press gave them a share of the business, depriving the older Morse company of some revenue. Thereupon the president of the Morse line, T. S. Faxton, a smaller edition of F. O. J. Smith, decreed that unless all A.P. news was sent over his wire, he would decline handling it at all save when prepaid at private rates. The A.P. firmly insisted on dividing the business; so Faxton refused its telegrams and set up a little news agency of his own, offering lower rates. Fog Smith joined hands with him in forwarding news from New England.

The A.P. also had trouble on the Morse New Orleans line. Boats then brought much California news via Panama to New Orleans, whence it was telegraphed to New York. On one occasion, an important California dispatch for the A.P. left New Orleans half a day ahead of other reports, but never reached New York. When the St. Charles Hotel burned, the A.P. item regarding it was offered first at the telegraph office, but the opposition placed the news even in Boston before the A.P. dispatch reached New York. The Merchants' Exchange in New York thereupon repudiated the Morse line to New Orleans, and requested the A.P. to transmit all its New Orleans news via Louisville and the O'Rielly line; if that wire wasn't working, to send none at all.

"It required several years to force our news reports on to the editors of the country," said Craig, twiddling his short beard complacently as he faced the Senate Committee thirty years later, his cool gray eye no more placid in old age than it was when in the midst of his most desperate battles. "From about 1853 ... every daily journal in the country and in Canada was compelled to submit to our rules in regard to telegraph news reports."

He placed the date just a little too early. Even in the latter '50's he was still having opposition in the northeast. An amalgamation, the American Telegraph Company, then owned the wires from New York to Amherst, on the Nova Scotian border. A rival news agency was still contending with the A.P. and had the backing of Smith, still a large telegraph stockholder. Craig procured the assurance of Peter Cooper, President of the American Company, however, that first come should be first served. The Nova Scotian government quarreled with the A.P., and whenever a steamer arrived at Halifax, the opposition news always seemed to get on the wire first.

Craig thereupon resorted to strategy. As soon as a steamer was sighted off Halifax, his agent or some one employed by him in Halifax sent a cryptic message to another agent at Amherst, who immediately handed a copy of the Bible, open at the first chapter of Genesis, to the American operator, saying, "Associated Press steamer news." With a sigh, the operator began, "Associated Press, New York, N. Y.: In the beginning God created the heaven and the earth. And the earth was without form and void." Meanwhile, the agent at Halifax started the bundle of European papers by horse express towards Amherst. It took five hours for that express to arrive, and during that time, the Amherst operator continued sending Scripture to New York. Sometimes he got plumb through Deuteronomy and into Joshua before the local A.P. man received his papers and began picking out the items to be sent as actual news. A few days of this broke up the opposition and brought about a compromise. Similar tricks have been practised many times since then by correspondents who were trying to beat rivals with news of great importance.

In 1854, Craig tried hard to induce the A.P. to buy one of the ramshackle telegraph lines from New York to New Orleans, and another to Boston as the nucleus of a great news telegraph system. He said that a million dollars would have bought those lines then, as there was so much competition that none of them was making any profit. But the Associated heads, after long pondering, decided that telegraphy was outside the province of a newspaper business, and turned down Craig's suggestion:

Had they assented to my wishes [said he in 1886], the Western Union Telegraph Company (organized 1855) would have been buried in its infancy, or if permitted to live, would have been as the tail to the A.P.'s kite, instead of the other way about, as it is and has been for the past sixteen years. I will admit, however, that as it was my mission to build up a monopoly of news ... and as I was armed with arbitrary power to this end, it is unlikely that the public would have been served with any more tenderness than it has since been served by the Western Union Telegraph Company, who entered the field of telegraph monopoly after I had failed to enlist the Associated Press in my scheme to do what the Western Union has since accomplished.

When the Western Union was organized, covering all the Middle States from the Great Lakes to the Ohio River, and touching the Atlantic Seaboard on the East and the Missouri River on the West, the Associated Press made an alliance with it, by which each agreed to do nothing to prejudice the other's interest. The A.P. promised that members of the association "will not in any way encourage or support any opposition or competing telegraph." "That clause," said a circular of the Press Association, "was to the telegraph company a valuable consideration for the favorable terms upon which they contracted with us."

Ruthless suppression of opposition became the rule. On one occasion Craig learned that a morning newspaper in a certain city was buying news from another source as well as the A.P. dispatches. He warned the proprietor, but the practice was continued, whereupon Craig entered into negotiations with an evening newspaper in the same city for the publication of a morning edition, promising it financial aid and free and exclusive news service for one year. This came to the ears of the offending publisher and quickly brought him to his knees, begging to be forgiven and reinstated on his master's own terms.

The last clash of the A.P. with the eastern telegraph lines occurred in 1859, and so great had its power become that this embroglio proved perilous to the American Telegraph Company. One R. W. Russell, an Englishman, had become secretary and counselor to that company, and fancied that he could make the American, with its vast territory, a powerful opponent to the Associated Press. He therefore incited the organization of a rival news agency, Johnson & Zabriskie, who began to create a considerable stir. At one time they had succeeded in enticing all the newspapers in Philadelphia away from the A.P. At which that old war-horse, Craig, sniffing the battle from afar, pawed the earth and said, Ha, ha!

Russell had maneuvered two prominent expressmen, E. S. Sanford and Cambridge Livingston, on to the Board of Directors of his company, thinking they would be favorable to his schemes. But they were wiser than he; they knew the difference between a hawk and a handsaw, and they also knew that bucking the Associated Press was likely to prove a wearisome and an unprofitable job. The upshot of it all was that Russell lost his job; and presently we find Johnson & Zabriskie writing plaintive letters to Abram S. Hewitt, President of the company, complaining that their steamer dispatches from Halifax were held up until the A.P. news got through. Their service did not last long thereafter.

THE RISE OF THE ASSOCIATED PRESS

Next it is Craig, writing that same summer to Hewitt, complaining that the service through Nova Scotia is "infamously bad." The wire had been extended to Newfoundland two years before, and the Associated Press had a boat cruising off Cape Race in that island to intercept incoming steamers and thus place European news in New York one or two days sooner than when it came through Halifax. Craig writes to Hewitt June 7, 1859:

> Our agent at Cape Race boarded the *City of Washington* last Thursday P.M. We heard nothing of the fact till late Saturday P.M. and then got 300 or 400 words. Then the Nova Scotia line caved in again, and we heard nothing more till Monday P.M. when it again resumed work, but almost immediately went down again, and finally the balance of our report (1,200 words) reached Sackville this afternoon, 18 or 20 hours after the arrival of the steamer—say five days from New Foundland.
> This is not all, but the miserable wretches in N.S. compel us to pay the tolls over their line, even under the circumstances I have narrated.

He suggested as a remedy that Nova Scotia be cut out of the system, and the cable from Newfoundland be brought directly to New Brunswick, via Prince Edward Island. But Nova Scotia presently improved its service.

The entrance of journalism into telegraphy brought about some interesting developments as the years went on. One of these was the syncopated language in which news dispatches came to be sent; not a code, in the sense in which the word is known to commerce and diplomacy to-day, in which a totally non-relevant word stands for a whole phrase or sentence, but a mere self-explanatory telescoping of words, whereby from one to three letters may sometimes stand for a word of three or four syllables, or even a phrase.

Morse and Vail began in a mild way to do this, abbreviating in some of their first sending between Washington and Baltimore. The custom progressed as the newspaper business grew, until finally Walter P. Phillips, for many years head alternately of the Associated and United Presses, went through the whole ordinary English vocabulary, reducing long words to short ones and compiling what is known as the Phillips Code, which has become a newspaper standard.

As a few examples, *pmy* in his language means prominently; *pnr*, prisoner; *pskv*, prospective; *pwf*, powerful; *cgsl*, Congressional; *kfc*, conference; *krpn*, corruption; *fp*, philanthropist; *sx* is the dollar mark; *aljnc*, allegiance, and *uxl* must be much used nowadays, for it means unconstitutional. Words also mean phrases—*potus* is President of the United States; *scotus*, the Supreme Court; *5* means "that the"; *ogt*, "on the ground that"; *cbi*, "covered by insurance"; *yam*, "yesterday morning"; *ssb*, "star-spangled banner"; *rapib*, "filed a petition in bankruptcy"; *gx*, "great excitement."

Fancy this telegram: "Washn 27—t scotus tdy cmfd t stc o fv ys d pen impsd on j smith, a bnkr o squamus ore cnvctd o stealg sx 228tnd o sta fnds." Which is, being interpreted: "The Supreme Court of the United States to-day confirmed the sentence of five years in the penitentiary imposed on J. Smith, a banker of Squamus, Oregon, convicted of stealing $228,000 of state funds." The receiving operator is thus called upon at high speed to make simultaneously two translations—finding letters of the alphabet in the mere clicking of an instrument, and turning syncopated gibberish into readable English.

CHAPTER X

THE TELEGRAPH AND THE RAILROAD

We bring glad news to inland homes
Of ships upon the sea.
We hurry along the murderer's trail,
His Nemesis are we.
We watch all night the roaring trains
When the sleepless needle clicks;
A caution for Number 7 fast
To wait for Number 6.

"ALLID," 1870

WHEN in June, 1845, Editor William Cullen Bryant of the New York *Evening Post* declared that he had seen a machine (whether Vail's or House's—which had not yet been patented—we do not know) which printed "with the usual letters of the alphabet and as legible to a child as the clearest type, executed at one end of a magnetic wire through directions given at the other," the *United States Saturday Post* of Philadelphia reproduced the paragraph, with the comment: "Such a statement as this quite surpasses all belief, except that based upon the evidence of the senses. Without intending any doubt of the veracity of the Editor of the New York *Evening Post,* we confess to our incredulity."

But by 1850, the uses of the electric current were multiplying so rapidly that sophisticated people no longer doubted any new reports about it. Everything done through a wire was called "telegraph." In England, Colonel Pasley had planted gunpowder in the sunken hulk of the *Royal George,* which had long been a menace to navigation at Spithead, and fired the charge with voltaic electricity. In January, 1843, a huge slice of Round Down Cliff at Dover was sheared off by 18,000 pounds of

201

powder, ignited through a wire. Bain invented a method of taking soundings at sea by electricity in the 1840's. All these were considered triumphs of the telegraph. In the late 1830's, Morse, Davy and Wheatstone all designed machines for detecting and reporting the position of a railway train at any point along the line.

In 1844, Morse and Captain Charles Wilkes checked up on the longitude of Baltimore, and found the Battle Monument in that city to be 1 minute, 34.868 seconds east of the Capitol at Washington. The correction of the former figure as recorded in the American Almanac was .732 of a second. Further work in longitude was reported in 1848. O'Rielly had run a wire from downtown Cincinnati up to the observatory on Mount Adam, where the first "electro-chronograph" or "telegraphic clock for longitude," invented by Dr. John Locke of that city was installed. Locke's simple yet ingenious idea was that of causing a clock pendulum to make and break an electric current momentarily at each swing. If the pendulum beats seconds, as astronomical clocks usually do, time and longitude could be checked by it. An astronomer in Washington, for example, observing when a star crossed the hair-line in a transit instrument, tapped a telegraph key at the moment of transit. The comparison of the time of transit in other cities would determine the longitude east or west of Washington.

Lieutenant Maury, quickly impressed by the value of the idea, induced Congress to appropriate $10,000 to buy one of the clocks from Dr. Locke for the Naval Observatory, of which Maury was then director. The United States Coast Survey took it up, and its success was so great that within a few months it was being taken up by several European astronomers, among whom it was known as "the American method." Forty years later it was in every observatory in the world, and was everywhere admitted to afford the most accurate known method of determining longitudes.

When a criminal was pursued by telegraph and captured, the snappy reporter of the day spoke of him as being "struck by lightning." Everybody was looking forward hopefully to the elimination of crime by this method. A fire alarm designed to be set off automatically when the blaze had heated the room to a certain degree was a new marvel in 1850. Moses G. Farmer, then an employee of the New York and Boston Magnetic Telegraph, invented an electric fire alarm in 1848, and in collaboration with Dr. W. F. Channing developed it in 1851 into a city fire-alarm system similar to that of to-day, which was installed in Boston in the following year, with Farmer as its superintendent. There were as yet no official fire bells, and so the bells of nineteen churches in the city rang the alarms. To-day the city of New York alone has enough telegraph wire in its fire-alarm system to girdle the globe one and a quarter times.

Farmer continued to invent devices more or less telegraphic, and some entirely unrelated thereto; an electric clock in 1849, later a burglar alarm, electric locks, an electroplating process, elementary duplex and quadruplex telegraphy, and many improvements in telegraphic apparatus being among them.

Even a sort of telautograph was invented then. Bain's invention for sending script by wire—in which he seems to have been a pioneer—was mentioned in Chapter VIII. An Englishman, Bakewell, produced a closely similar machine in 1851, and exhibited it amid great acclaim at the London Exposition. To pursue this branch further, it may be mentioned that an Italian-born priest, the Abbé Jean Caselli, aided financially in his experiments by the Emperor Napoleon III, developed the idea into an efficient system of telegraphy soon after 1860. It was he who began telegraphing pictures, one of the first ones sent being a portrait of the French Empress. As the system had not been perfected then, the picture was considerably interrupted by messages traveling the same course, and had dots and dashes all over it, but was nevertheless recognizable. The accompanying reproduction from an old telegraph handbook of one of Caselli's telegraph pictures does not do justice to it, the lines (for reproduction purposes) being redrawn much coarser than in the original. For a few years there were offices in France for the sending of messages by "pantelegraphy" in the sender's own writing, a stunt which telegraph companies, late in 1935 were just taking up again, after seventy years. The charge for sending was fifteen centimes per square centimeter.

PICTURE SENT BY TELEGRAPH BY THE ABBÉ CASELLI'S PROCESS, 1865

In 1849 an American, R. E. Monaghan, invented a "legislative telegraph," each member of an assembly having a button or key on his desk and voting by a touch, the result being a perforation either on the yea or nay side of a printed list of the members' names on the clerk's desk. This was installed in the State House at Harrisburg, and votes on a bill were thereby completed in two seconds.

In a circular dated June 1, 1850, J. M. Francis announces his Telegraph Express Agency, headquarters with the O'Rielly lines at 181 Broadway, New York: "Agents wanted everywhere. Information obtained and business transacted by telegraph. Orders promptly dispatched and on reasonable terms." And in 1853, New York City for the first time connected all its police stations by telegraph.

Notwithstanding all these ingenious developments of electricity which blossomed so rapidly, full seven years passed after Morse's patent before any American railroad official awoke to the possibility that the telegraph might be useful in the operation of trains. William Fothergill Cooke published a book on the use of telegraph signals for English railways in 1842, so they were undoubtedly utilizing it long before we were. O'Rielly claimed to have suggested it to America in 1845, but if he did, no one heeded him. To-day we find it hard to conceive how a railroad was operated without it. A Michigan Southern train conductor named Haskins in the winter of 1849-50, once telegraphed to Monroe, on Lake Erie, asking that a boat be held for some passengers on his train, which had been delayed by an accident— perhaps the first instance of the sort in our history; but this incident passed unnoticed. It seems inexplicable that railroads did not grasp the fact that the telegraph was a natural ally, the complement of the railroad, without which in future it could not be operated. But not until 1851 did a glimmer of this begin to percolate through the brain of a railroader.

In 1851 Ezra Cornell was still poor. In 1849 he had organized a company and constructed a line from Troy, New York, to Montreal, where it touched the Canadian telegraph lines, recently completed under the Morse patents from Quebec and Montreal through Toronto and Hamilton to Niagara. But Cornell's chief work during those years was the building, in collaboration with J. J. Speed, Jr., of the New York and Erie

Telegraph, to which he was incited by "Fog" Smith. Kendall objectedly strenuously but vainly when Smith prepared to create this competition to the New York, Albany and Buffalo Company, in which they· were all interested. But Smith had cogent reasons for overriding his wishes. Firstly, he wanted his own line from New York to the lakes, to connect with his lines to Detroit and Chicago. Secondly, he picked up a nice little sum at the very start by one of his favorite tricks. He made a contract with Cornell and Speed, by which they built the single-wire line for $50 a mile. The three of them then sold it to the newly organized company at $250 a mile, in stock, for the first wire, and $100 for each additional wire. Only $27,000 in cash was raised, although Cornell solicited assiduously all along the line, and induced his friends around Ithaca and elsewhere to go in on the scheme. What with the padded construction assessed by Smith, it is easy to see that the cash subscribers held a minority of the stock.

The line ran from New York up the east side of the Hudson River to the summit of a mountain above Cold Spring then called Bull Hill, but now more elegantly, Mount Taurus. From there it crossed the river in a 2,000-foot festoon (which broke whenever ice formed on it), to the summit of a hill on the west shore. All the way to Buffalo it followed country roads, roughly parallel to the New York & Erie Railroad, sometimes close alongside it, sometimes several miles distant.

It was this line which, so Reid says, was ruined by Cornell's iron hat insulator filled with brimstone; which, after it had stood in the weather a while, was no insulator at all, but an actual conductor. Cornell threw out several feeder lines—to Auburn, to Poughkeepsie, to Albany, to Corning, and so on, none of them profitable. The great scheme was a failure almost from the start.

The telegraph line paralleled the railroad from Goshen through Port Jervis to Narrowsburg. At Goshen in 1849, the telegraph instrument was placed in a corner of the book-store and printing shop of Lebeus Vail, and two of Vail's sons became operators—Nathaniel taking charge of the Goshen office and Hector of Port Jervis. Cornell was so hard up that he had to forage in the cash drawers of the various offices at times for personal expense money. Mr. Vail in after years remembered occasions when there was none in the Goshen office drawer, and he himself advanced a shilling to "Old Bones," as Cornell was nicknamed along the line, to buy himself a square meal—though frequently a slice of bread and cheese had to suffice. [1] He had much ado at times to stave off creditors and the sheriff. When he received a letter, he would open the flap carefully and then spend several minutes in turning the envelope inside out, so that he might use it again.

Smith meanwhile was disgruntled because he had not received his share of the construction profits. Cornell ought to have all these outstanding matters squared up, he thought. "His death would involve his family, myself, Kendall, Morse and Vail in a doleful melange. Die he must, like all the rest of us." In later years, when Cornell became wealthy, he paid Smith's share of those construction costs out of his own wallet.

While Cornell was building stretches of his line within sight of the railroad, a far-seeing man, Charles Minot, superintendent of the Erie, was watching him and beginning to suspect that this new gadget might be of value in the operation of a business like his own. Railroad traveling then was a slow and fatiguing experience. Trains needed from two to four days to cover distances which they could negotiate in twenty-four hours after they had the telegraph.

On the Erie in 1850, a "leading train"—what might be a "limited" to-day—had an hour's right of way over trains of the same class going in the opposite direction; that is, the other train had to wait an hour at the specified meeting point before it could proceed. The leading train, having lost its rights, must then wait. The only alternative for either was to wait five or ten

---

[1] Edward Harold Mott, *Between the Ocean and the Lakes; the Story of Erie* (New York, 1899), which is drawn upon in this chapter for much material regarding the Erie Railroad.

minutes and then proceed "under flag"; which means that a brakeman was sent ahead on a dog trot with a red flag, and after waiting fifteen or twenty minutes, the train followed him. Stopping when it caught up with him, the tired fellow was taken aboard to rest and a fresh man sent ahead with the flag. After another interval, the train proceeded again. Mott in his Erie history tells of one train which thus flagged its way for 34 miles. Its conductor remarked that he had more than once flagged the entire length of the Delaware Division.

The road's eastern terminus was then at Piermont, nearly twenty-five miles up the Hudson from New York City. Steamboats carried all passengers, mail and freight between there and the company's dock at the foot of Duane Street. Quantities of live stock and other heavy freight must be transferred at Piermont from freight trains to barges, requiring a large force of men; who, however, were idle between trains. These men must be at the pier at train time, but might have to wait for hours before the train arrived. Or the boat coming from New York might bring the news—which had traveled by commercial telegraph—of an accident and consequent delay of the train.

After studying the construction of the Cornell line, Minot coolly induced his company to build a line of wire with its own construction crews along the railroad right of way. Cornell supplied him with a full equipment of Morse machinery to operate it—which greatly incensed the patentees. Minot then offered—naming his own terms—to purchase Morse patent rights for the railroad's use. Smith refused to sell to him, and made the counter-suggestion that the Erie buy an interest in the telegraph company; which Mr. Minot smilingly declined to consider, remarking that "he understood the Telegraph Company to be in a very doubtful state." He added that it had been his notion that on completion of the railroad's line, it might induce the telegraph company to "work it for us." Anyhow, while Smith, Kendall, Cornell and Minot were bombarding each other with letters, some of them threatening, the railroad calmly put its wire and Morse machines into service. Some think that Minot had a secret understanding with Cornell before he began stringing the wire.

Early in 1851, before the Erie had put its wire into service, the telegraph achieved its first significant feat in the reporting of an accident. Nat Vail, the operator for the commercial line at Goshen had, in the carefree manner of the period, gone on a trip to New York one day, leaving his instrument masterless. There was little to occupy its energy, anyhow. The westbound day express on the Erie chose that particular moment to jump the track two miles east of Goshen and pile itself up in a wreck.

An hour or more after it should have reached Port Jervis, some official there became curious as to its whereabouts and asked Hec Vail, the commercial operator there, to find out something about it, if he could. Hec began calling Goshen—the first place to eastward where railroad and telegraph coincided—to ask whether the train had passed that point. Working in the print-shop was a third and younger brother, Wilmot Vail, who had never done any telegraphing, but who had watched and heard his brother operating, and had picked up a few rudiments. He knew by the click of the instrument that Port Jervis was calling; he was aware of the wreck, and he guessed that Hec might be asking about the train, but he was not a telegrapher, so he went on with his own work.

But after the calling had continued intermittently for two or three hours, Wilmot, thinking the thing over, decided that he would venture to try answering it. In the shop there was a manual containing the Morse alphabet and other information. Wilmot studied it and marked out in dots and dashes a brief message, telling of the accident; then slowly, stumblingly, he did the best job he could at sending it. Hector couldn't quite identify all the lacerated words that came creeping over the wire, but he gathered that the train was wrecked. "What damned fool sent this?" was his retort.

When the railroad's own wire came into use, even Minot did not at first seem able to figure out practical uses for it; and as under-employees were contemptuous and still more ignorant regarding it, its service grew but slowly. For a long time, all telegrams sent over it began with "Dear Sir," and ended, "Yours Respectfully."

One of its first advantages was found in greater expedition at Piermont. It had never been known there, for example, just how much live stock was coming on a given train, and the boat captain never knew how to arrange and calculate upon his deck space until the train arrived. One day young Conklin, the wide-awake operator at Piermont, telegraphed the conductor of a freight train and asked how many cars of cattle he had for the boat. The conductor replied, the boat captain arranged his deck space accordingly, with the result that the boat left for New York only thirty minutes after the train's arrival, instead of being detained for hours as usual.

It was in June of 1851, that the epochal event which revolutionized railroading took place. Train Number 1 was clattering westward one day with Superintendent Minot aboard. By the schedule it was to pass Number 2 at Turner's, a village now called Harriman, a few miles east of Goshen. After waiting patiently for an hour at Turner's, Minot directed the operator to ask Goshen whether Number 2 had passed there. The reply was, "No." Minot then wrote on a scrap of paper—which should be preserved in some museum to-day in a glass case—a message, and handed it to the surprised operator, who read:

To agent at Goshen
DEAR SIR
    Hold all eastbound trains until I arrive.
Chas. Minot, Supt.

Goshen acknowledged receipt, and then Minot, to make sure, asked, "Do you understand?" "I understand that I am to hold all eastbound trains until you arrive," said Goshen, "and will do so." Minot next wrote an official order:

To Conductor and Engineer, Day Express
    Run to Goshen, regardless of opposing train.
Chas. Minot, Supt.

THE TELEGRAPH AND THE RAILROAD

He handed the slip to Conductor Stewart, whose eyes widened with astonishment. Here was something that simply wasn't done! :

I took the order [said Stewart to the Erie historian], showed it to the engineer, Isaac Lewis, and told him to go ahead. The surprised engineer read the order, and handing it back to me, exclaimed: "Do you take me for a damned fool? I won't run by that thing."

I reported to the Superintendent, who went forward and used his verbal authority on the engineer, but without effect. Minot then climbed on the engine and took charge of it himself. Engineer Lewis jumped off and got in the rear seat of the rear car.

He wanted to get as far from the inevitable collision as possible! Again speaking of rugged individualism. . . . Well, anyhow, the Superintendent drove the iron horse to Goshen, where he inquired of Middletown whether Number 2 had passed there. Finding that it had not, he ran on a similar order to Middletown, and from there to Port Jervis, where he entered the yard from the east just as Number 2 came in from the west. An hour or more in time had been saved, and a new use for the telegraph had been found.

It took some time, of course, to establish a system of dispatching. There were no precedents, and no one had the faintest idea how the thing could be done; but gradually it was worked out. Station calls were adopted, such as PO for Port Jervis, XN for Lackawaxen and so on. Syncopated language began to appear, and presently operators were asking another who was slow in answering, "Wr u bn" (Where have you been?) or "Wy dnt u ans" (Why don't you answer?).

A few editors drew attention to the Erie's innovation, remarking that such "might be expected from the sagacity and energy which characterize its operations generally." Said one:

We invoke the attention of all Railroad Companies to the propriety of speedily supplying themselves with lightning ... so as to prevent those awful accidents which too frequently make sad inroads upon the limbs and lives of passengers, as well as upon the credit and cash of too many companies.

But for several years, so slowly did ideas penetrate the brains of railroad executives, little attention was paid to the Erie's new system. Henry O'Rielly wrote an enthusiastic article upon it in 1852, and in the following year the New York Legislature took cognizance of it. Railroad disasters, often with great loss of life, were appallingly prevalent then, and lawmakers were somewhat concerned about it, but the railroads distributed so many favors among the more impressionable and responsive of them that little was done. John T. Clark, the New York State Engineer, covered the subject at length in a report to the Legislature in 1852, describing in detail how, when the time-table became disarranged, "the telegraph is used to disentangle trains and move them forward."

Superintendent McCallum, who succeeded Minot, remarked in his first report to the directors that "I should greatly prefer a single track railroad with a telegraph by its side to direct its trains, than a double track without it." The Delaware, Lackawanna & Western was the second road in the country to show interest in electric train dispatching, and that several years after the Erie had taken it up. D. H. Conklin, the clever young Piermont operator, was called from the Erie to be the Lackawanna's superintendent of telegraphs. He was later Mayor of Decatur, Illinois. It was fully ten years after the Erie's experiment that the Chicago, Burlington & Quincy adopted train dispatching, and it is said to have been the pioneer in the mid-West in that particular.

A veteran railroad man, writing in the *Express Gazette* in 1898, said:

With the old telegraph register then used in receiving, it took 30 minutes or more to make meeting points by wire. The train orders were written on any kind of paper and rewritten several times, being sent to one office at a time. Each would in many cases get a different wording, and frequent were the collisions from a lap order. During the prevalence of the single order, the dispatcher spent about a third of his time checking up his orders to see if he was going to have a collision, and at about what point on the line it would occur. The Standard Code, later adopted by the American Railway Association's Train Rule Committee . . . made the service more efficient, and took away the terrific strain on the mind, of the old system.

Undoubtedly, these errors and failures of train dispatching had much to do with the slowness with which it was adopted by the railroads of the country. Even in the latter '60's General Anson Stager of the Western Union, who had been a noted Civil War telegrapher, had to do much missionary work among railroad men, explaining its uses and advantages. He put on a spectacular demonstration one day on the Pittsburgh, Fort Wayne & Chicago which gave the telegraph much publicity. The engine of the train on which he and General T. T. Eckert, also of the Western Union, broke down. After some delay, Stager asked the conductor if he would call for a locomotive from the nearest division point if the request were sent by wire. The latter agreed. The commercial wire near by was cut, a short piece of it was thrust into the ground, and Stager sent the message by tapping the end of the line wire against this. He received the answer by holding the end of the line wire against his tongue.

It was during that decade that the welding of telegraph and railroad interests began to be extensively carried out. Telegraph lines were now moved to the railroads' rights of way, and the same operator served both railroad and commercial company. The earliest contracts contained these stipulations:

The telegraph company agreed to supply poles and wire for the entire line, both for itself and for the railroad, and Morse instruments for certain specified stations which it was believed would be valuable commercially; and it would maintain the main battery for operation, day and night. If the railroad company desired telegraph connection at any smaller towns, it must furnish its own machinery and local battery.

The railroad company was to convey free all poles, wire and other equipment where needed, for building the line, and pay $30 a mile for the original construction and instruments. It would also haul poles, wire, and so on, thereafter for repairs, and would give free transportation to officers and employees of the telegraph company when on business.

The railroad company watched the line, straightened and reset poles and mended wires. It paid the operators' salaries. It agreed not to send any message free save for its own agents on its own business. All receipts for public messages at any office opened by either party were the property of the telegraph company. The companies were to reciprocate in the use of wires when that of either was out of order, but the railroad wire was never to be interrupted when sending railroad business.

Finally, the railroad company agreed not to permit any other telegraph company to build a line upon its property.

With some small changes as the years went on, these continued to be the general points of agreement.

It was not long after the Erie Railroad began operating its own wire when the name of the telegraph company was changed from New York and Erie to New York and Western Union. In the following January, the line was leased to the New York, Albany and Buffalo, which means that it was passing out of existence as a commercial concern. During 1852-53 its wire was transferred from the wagon roads to the railroad's right of way, and the corporation was absorbed by the railroad company.

There was much ado along the Erie railroad when it was discovered that some reckless operators were reading messages by the mere click of the instrument—as operators in general did for so many years afterward. One day at Addison, New York, says Mott, a train conductor was waiting for an order from the dispatcher. Charles Douglas, the operator, wrote it down from the sound alone. The conductor, who was standing by his table, noticed that Douglas had not even glanced at the tape, and he refused to accept the order until Douglas had recopied it from the tape.

The conductor reported the incident to the Division Superintendent, Tillotson, who was aghast at such trifling with the lives of trainmen and passengers, and called Douglas to his office at Elmira to receive a reprimand. Douglas stoutly insisted that messages could be read by sound as accurately as from the tape. There is no telling how many other operators beside himself were already doing it. Douglas offered to stand any test desired, and he spent the entire afternoon in reading by ear all the different messages which Tillotson and the Elmira operator could devise. Tillotson then ordered him back to Addison, and sent him, as rapidly as it could be tapped out, a long message which he was to take by sound in the presence of witnesses and repeat. As soon as the last word was ended, Douglas began sending it back, and completed it without an error. From that day forward, reception by sound was officially permitted on the Erie.

Again, it seems strange that this flurry should have occurred, for some commercial telegraphers had been receiving by sound for several years, and there had been items in the papers about their achievements. Even into our day, discussion has raged as to who was first to receive by sound alone. The Filson Club, that fine old historical society of Louisville, devoted an article of considerable length to proving that James F. Leonard, a Kentucky boy, was first to receive by ear. An amazing number of mere boys in their teens were telegraph operators in those days. Jimmy in 1847, at the age of fourteen, entered the service as a messenger boy with the Frankfort, Kentucky, office. Within a year he was an operator and was reading by sound. Not only that, but he could send and listen to an incoming message at the same time, writing the latter out between sendings.

It was soon decided that he was too great for Frankfort, and O'Rielly officials took him to the Louisville office in 1848, where crowds went to see him. P. T. Barnum, then attaining renown as a showman, heard of the remarkable cleverness of this fifteen-year-old boy, journeyed to Louisville, saw his work and offered him a contract for exhibition in the museum which the impresario had installed in New York City. But Jimmy refused to commercialize his art. When he died as a Civil War soldier in 1862, he was buried at Frankfort, and the monument over his grave was adorned with sculptured telegraph poles and wires.

But there is plenty of evidence that Jimmy had been superseded by at least a year or more by other operators. In fact, even Morse and Vail in the first few months of their primitive sending, learned to distinguish most of the letters of the alphabet by the clicking of the little bar as it bobbed up and down in its recording. It would seem that any intelligent operator would begin to acquire this facility after very brief experience; yet many of them paid no attention to the sound and did not think of receiving in that way until after news had spread widely that it could be done.

On May 1, 1847—the date is recorded in the files of the Albany *Evening Journal*—while operator Carter in that city was receiving in his office in the Delaware House, the tape became twisted in his machine, and he had difficulty in translating the message. W. C. Buell, an Albany business man who was sitting near by—and had evidently spent many hours in sitting there—said, "I think Utica asks if the nine o'clock train has arrived," scarcely knowing how the knowledge had come to him. Carter was astonished to find, upon a repetition of the message, that Buell was right. Whereupon Editor Ten Eyck of the *Evening Journal,* who also was present, wrote an excited article which reads as if Buell had performed a feat of clairvoyance. That article was copied even in Europe.

But about the same time, the Philadelphia *North American* was saying, "The Pittsburgh *Gazette* gives a statement of an exceedingly delicate operation performed by Mr. Brooks, the telegraph operator in that city. This consisted in writing out a long message from the sound alone." To which a Rochester editor retorted that Mr. Barnes of his town frequently did this. "We have often known him to give a report without looking at the characters on the paper, and answer questions of customers at the same time." Julius Cæsar outdone!

Reid in his reminiscences tells of several early day operators who could send and receive by sound simultaneously. One of his pleasant recollections is that of the operator at Pontotoc, Mississippi, on the O'Rielly line to New Orleans. When Reid rode into that village in a buggy on a hot August day, he found the fat operator smoking and lolling comfortably in a chair in the shade outside his office. While they talked, the instrument just inside the window began to click; Nashville was calling Pontotoc. Without rising from his chair, the operator reached through the window to his key and told N to GA ("Go ahead"). Still without moving, he smoked and listened dreamily while two messages came in, then thrust his arm through the window and acknowledged them. For a few minutes more he sat at ease, then said, "Guess I'll go in and write out those messages. No danger!" with a grandiose wave of the hand to Reid's gentle remonstrance. "I never forget."

When a broker in Louisville sat in the telegraph office in 1847, and received market reports from the East by ear—of course, without paying for them—Manager Shaffner had him arrested as a violator of the Morse patent, for receiving without a license. He was fined and given a heavy jail sentence, but the telegraph company relented and asked for his release, merely stipulating that he be put under bond to do so no more.

Even in 1845-46, the earliest operators could detect by ear some of the signal letters then in use—the office call, SSS, meaning "the end" or "no more"; SFD, "Stop for dinner"; SFP, "Stop for paper"; OK, "correct," and so on. The telegraph companies at first forbade any sound reception, deeming it hazardous, "eliminating the evidence of transmission and preventing the ready detection of the sources of error." But it rapidly proved itself superior to that of the machine. In the first primitive Morse recording system, the operator must gently pull the paper tape through the machine with thumb and finger, and then, when the message or several messages had ended, gather up the yards of tape, study the shallow dot-and-dash undulations, and write out the words, or, if in a large office, read them aloud while a copyist set them down. In a year or so, a weight hanging from a cord was devised to pull the ribbon through the machine, which was considered a great improvement; but still, as a veteran operator of those days said:

The reception by register, the constant winding, the mistakes made by the copyist, caused by imperfect hearing, the whirr of the wheels, the breaking of the weight cord and the howl caused by damaged toes, the rough copy retranslated for delivery, the delay, the labor of all this was palpable and sought deliverance.

How curious that the mere clicking of an instrument, a purely casual sound, at first supposed to be of no more consequence than the rattle of a wagon wheel passing over a stony road, should have come to be for decades the most important function of a telegraph instrument, the only way by which a message was received! But now a cycle has been completed, and the once burning question as to who was first to receive by sound is no longer important; for we have come back to printing telegraphs, and the old Morse brass key, though still clinging valiantly to existence, has been reduced to a very minor position in the business of telegraphy.

CHAPTER XI

THE FIRST ATLANTIC CABLE

Ere they have riven our continent in twain
To wed the widest seas at Panama;
Ere they have cut, at Suez, thro' the band
  That ties the East to Africa,
They weave a thread in History's flowing robe,
Worthy the rapturous strain of Pindar's lyre;
They bury far beneath the changing tides
  Their inter-hemispheric wire.
We joyed when distant nations of the globe
To England's Thames their skill and fabrics sent;
Joy more when Europe bends to whisper words
  Into the ear of great Occident.

FRANCIS LIEBER, 1858

A S far back as 1798, Señor Salva, creator of that mysterious telegraph already mentioned, suggested that a telegraph wire might be laid under water—although a practicable system of telegraphy was yet in the future. Morse and Wheatstone both thought it a possibility, and Morse tried it between New York and Governor's Island, as we have related. That grand old magazine, the *Scientific American,* was in 1846 "not yet satisfied of the impracticability of extending telegraphic communication through broad rivers." Colonel Colt, inventor of the revolving pistol, had succeeded in carrying a wire across the East River in a leaden pipe, though the results were not satisfactory.

The *Scientific American* had its own formula for insulating submarine wire. First wrap tightly with flannel, then with cotton cloth; cover this to a depth of half an inch with a mixture of rosin and beeswax, applied hot with a brush. Swathe again with cotton cloth, and varnish over the cloth with melted rubber. Attach enough lead rings to the wire to sink it in water.

Tal. Shaffner's recipe for under-water insulation has been given. Tar, asphaltum and other substances were tried. In 1847, Alexander Jones conceived the idea of encasing the wire in a glass tube, with ball-and socket joints. But nothing work'd until gutta-percha was discovered, and then, for the first time, the problem appeared soluble. This valuable substance, the exudation from a tropical tree, was first noticed by an English surgeon at Singapore, who found natives using it for tool handles. Letters patent were granted in England in 1844 to 1847 for its use in various ways. It was brought to America in 1847, and Downing tried it in the form of pole insulators for wires, but found that the sun's heat melted it. It was chiefly valuable as under-water insulation.

Its first successful use in this country was in 1849, when a gutta-percha-covered wire was laid by the Bain New York-Boston line across the Connecticut River at Middletown, and worked most satisfactorily. In a prospectus of the Canada Grand Trunk Telegraph Company, published in 1853, is found the stipulation, "Capital Stock limited to £25 per mile, excepting over water courses where Gutta Percha is used, for which part the Capital Stock is limited to £125 per mile."

Professor Wheatstone drew up a plan for a submarine cable between Dover and Calais in 1840. In 1845, John W. Brett and his brother Ronald entered at the British Government Registration Office a project for uniting England and America by cable, using a route similar to that actually adopted a decade later; and in the same year they registered a project for uniting Britain with her colonies. Such schemes, however, were as yet too vast for human comprehension, and nothing was done about them.

In 1847, John Brett procured King Louis Philippe's approval of a cable union between England and France, but for three years could find no backers for so wild a project. Finally, in 1850, the cash was raised and the cable laid, coated only with gutta-percha. The instrument used was a printing telegraph, and Brett sent the first message through it to Louis Napoleon, then President of France. But the coating of the wire was imperfect, and the waves in the restless strait, abrading it against stones and gravel, ruined it. On the following morning, the cable was dead. It was denounced as a gigantic hoax and swindle in the British newspapers. But in September of the following year Brett laid a new cable with gutta-percha and lead covering, and this proved to be permanent. It cost £360 per mile, but was well worth it. It was once broken by an anchor, but quickly repaired.

During the '50's several submarine cables were laid, including three between England and the continent, the other two terminating at Ostend and The Hague. Two were laid between England and Ireland, others between Denmark and Sweden and one across the Bosphorus. During the Crimean War a line about 400 miles in length was laid across the stormy Black Sea from Varna to Balaklava by Newell & Company of London, one of the two great cable manufacturing and construction concerns of the time, for the British-French war service. This was a single wire, insulated only with gutta-percha, and the whole said to be no thicker than a lead pencil! That it endured at all seems well-nigh incredible. Maréchal Vaillant, French Minister of War, exclaimed: "I send by dispatch to General Canrobert, and I have an answer sooner than I would have it by letter from a town half way to Lyons or Bordeaux or Strasbourg. I have not yet recovered from my amazement at this prodigy."

In 1854, Brett was in charge of the laying of cables connecting Italy and France with Sardinia and Corsica, and thence with Algeria, and began to discover some of the hazards and difficulties of such work. The sea's depth had not been charted, and a great deep surrounded by cliffs between Italy and Sardinia made itself evident when the cable began to rush out from the vessel at such terrific speed that for some time it could not be checked, and then only by damaging the insulation for a great distance. Again between Sardinia and Algeria there occurred an alarming flight of the cable, when two miles of it, weighing sixteen tons, rushed into the depths in four or five minutes. It was finally stopped by snubbing it around a timber in the hold. But in trying to raise it, the capstan broke; rough weather had come on, the vessel became unmanageable, and for safety the cable was finally cut and lost. Another attempt was made in 1856, and again the cable, after many narrow escapes, was broken. It was not successfully laid until 1860. Glass, Elliott & Company were the contractors for this and a number of other cables laid around the European coast during the first two decades of such building.

The first sea cable successfully laid on the coast of the United States was that connecting the islands of Nantucket and Martha's Vineyard, completed in 1857. Of its 35-mile length, 11 miles was on poles, 13 submarine and 11 underground. The wire was aërial until it neared the beaches, when it burrowed into the sand and then under water. It crossed three small islands between Nantucket and the Vineyard entirely underground. In 1860, Martha's Vineyard was connected with the mainland by the Cape Cod Telegraph Company.

The germ of the idea which grew into the Atlantic Cable had its inception in the mind of Reverend John T. Mulloch, the Roman Catholic Bishop of St. Johns, Newfoundland. In the St. Johns *Courier* in 1850, he wrote, protesting against that city's being overlooked as a telegraph station between the old world and the new. He called attention to the fact that the Atlantic liners passed near Cape Race, and said that the telegraph system of the United States should be extended to Newfoundland, so that news boats might meet the vessels off the Cape and place the European news in the United States and Canada two days earlier than if it went through Halifax.

F. N. Gisborne, manager of the Nova Scotia line, was intrigued by the suggestion, and resolved to put it through. The British mail authorities and Mr. Cunard agreed to collaborate, with the stipulation that the vessels must not be delayed nor asked to alter their course. Gisborne gave up his post in Nova

Scotia and went to Newfoundland, where, with a grant of £500 from the Legislature, he had a line 400 miles long surveyed through one of the roughest and bleakest of wildernesses from St. Johns to Cape Ray, at the southwestern point of the island. From there he planned a cable to New Brunswick.

But first the money must be procured. Newfoundland had granted a charter to the Newfoundland Electric Telegraph Company, with an exclusive right of way for thirty years. Gisborne hurried to New York and found the necessary capital. With this he laid, in 1852-53, the first American cable, between Cape Ray and Prince Edward Island, and thence across Northumberland Strait to New Brunswick. But he had built only thirty miles of the land line in 1853, when the cable ceased to operate, probably having lost some of its insulation, and the New York stockholders refused to produce any more money. The company thereupon went into bankruptcy, and Gisborne gave up all he possessed to pay some of the debts.

In 1854, he returned to New York to endeavor, if possible, to recreate interest in the project. Among the men he now met were Lieutenant Maury, hydrographer, and Matthew D. Field, an engineer, who was at first not greatly interested, but courteously introduced Gisborne to his brother, Cyrus W. Field. The latter was a retired paper manufacturer, only thirty-five years old, it is true, but already fancying himself through with business. However, having just returned from a trip to South America, he found himself restless and dissatisfied with leisure. His talks with Gisborne gave him a new interest. Standing beside a globe just after one of the interviews, he noticed the comparatively short distance, as it seemed, between Newfoundland and Ireland, and said to himself, "If a cable to Newfoundland, why not a cable all the way?"

The findings of Lieutenant Matthew D. Maury of the United States Navy, had just been published. In 1852-53 this scientist made extensive soundings in the Atlantic, and found that between Newfoundland and Ireland there was a plateau which seemed to be designed especially as the bed for a cable. The water there was neither too deep nor too shallow; deep enough to place the cable beyond the reach of anchors, icebergs and drifts, yet shallow enough to make the laying of it feasible. The depth to this plateau was very regular, gradually increasing from the shores of Newfoundland to nearly 2,000 fathoms as you approached the other side. The microscopic shells brought up from the bottom, unbroken and unabraded by gravel, indicated that there were no currents at those depths to fret the cable.

Field was now fired by a great ambition. He saw in an Atlantic cable the greatest achievement of the age, with himself as its chief creator. He consulted Morse, who, without knowing much of the difficulties involved, declared offhand that the project was entirely feasible. He consulted his neighbor, Peter Cooper. Field lived at the corner of Lexington Avenue and Gramercy Park, and Mr. Cooper's home (still standing in 1936), was the next house north of his. Cooper agreed to come in on the project, and so did Moses Taylor, Marshall O. Roberts and Chandler White, prominent business men of New York.

Little time was lost. Newfoundland promised much greater privileges. Accordingly, after several meetings in Field's dining-room, the New York, Newfoundland and London Electric Telegraph Company was organized on May 6, 1854, with Peter Cooper as President and an authorized capital stock of $1,500,000. Newfoundland granted a fifty-year exclusive right to lay cables, £50,000 to aid the work, fifty square miles of public land, and fifty more when the cable should be successfully laid. Prince Edward Island also granted a liberal charter.

Matthew Field was appointed engineer of the company, and at once went to Newfoundland and pushed the construction of the land line through the rocky wilds of that island. Cyrus Field hurried to England to place an order for cable and to talk with those who had successfully laid such lines in the waters of Europe. Among these was Brett, who took some shares in the Newfoundland company and gave much valuable advice.

It was planned to lay the cable from Newfoundland to the

Photo loaned by Museum of the City of New York; original painting in New York Chamber of Commerce

THE PROJECTORS OF THE ATLANTIC CABLE: PETER COOPER SEATED AT LEFT,
MORSE IN CENTER BACKGROUND, FIELD STANDING IN RIGHT FOREGROUND

nearest land to southward, Cape Breton Island, instead of running it to Prince Edward Island, where the first line had connected. Across the strait to Cape Breton, the distance was only 55½ miles. The cable arrived from England in the summer of 1855. It was made up of three copper wires, each gutta-percha insulated, the interstices filled with rope yarn and a gutta-percha covering over the whole; then twelve iron wires coiled around that, and tar smeared over all.

A party of New Yorkers went up to Cape Ray to witness the start of the project. Among them were Messrs. Cooper and Field, Professor Morse, three or four prominent clergymen, and, to celebrate the occasion in prose and verse, Bayard Taylor and Fitz-James O'Brien. Unfortunately, the sea was so rough that the picnic was somewhat sicklied o'er with a pale cast of *mal de mer*.

The cable laying was a great disappointment, too. The little barque, *Sarah Bryant,* which had brought the cable from England, was to be towed over the course by the steamer *James Adger,* paying out the cable as she went. There was a two days' delay at the start because of heavy fog, and then a strong wind made it difficult to moor steamer to barque. When they started, both were so light that the sea threatened to smash them against each other, and they were cut apart. Then the *Bryant* began to drift toward the rocks and was saved with difficulty, finally having to cut the cable and lose two miles of it.

Next morning the cable end was picked up and spliced to that aboard the ship, and a new start made; but they had not gone far when the cable parted at the splicing point, and the day's work was lost. A fresh start was made next day, but a few miles out, the *Adger* began to veer from the prescribed course—because of the captain's stubbornness, Mr. Cooper says, though the captain's story is that a strong current was setting to northward. After several remonstrances from Mr. Cooper, he drew up a document in legal form, warning the captain that he would be held responsible for any trouble with the cable. At that, the stubborn mariner turned and veered just as much too far the other way—again using the excuse of an irresistible current. He also ran too rapidly, so that the cable kinked dangerously two or three times. Finally, in mid-channel, a gale came up, and as the *Bryant* was about to be thrown on her beam-ends, the cable was cut to save her, and forty miles of it lay useless in the sea. The rest of it was turned over to the underwriters, and the enterprise for the moment was abandoned.

More capital was raised among the original investors, and in July, 1856, with a more capable vessel, the cable across the strait was successfully laid. It had now cost more than a million dollars all of which, says Field, had come from "our own little circle. . . . Those who came first into the work stood by it to the end." But now the group had put up as much money as they could spare. Great Britain itself should be asked to take a hand in the connecting of the two countries, so Field crossed to London as soon as the connection was made with Nova Scotia. There John Brett, Michael Faraday, Brunel (builder of the *Great Eastern),* Stratham of the London Gutta Percha Works, Glass of Glass, Elliott & Company, Charles Tileston Bright, noted cable builder and others were his friends and practical adherents.

Field asked Faraday how long he thought it would take an electric signal to pass between London and New York. "About one second," answered the scientist. (To-day, radio signals shoot across in a fiftieth of a second.) Brunel, pointing to a picture of the *Great Eastern,* said: "Mr. Field, there is the ship to lay your cable"—prophetic words, for the big vessel, nine years later, finally did lay the successful strand.

Morse, who was in London, went with Field to see Lord Clarendon, the Foreign Secretary, who said, "But suppose you do not succeed; that you make the attempt and fail, your cable lost at the bottom of the sea; what will you do then?" "Charge it to profit and loss," replied Field, promptly, "and go to work to lay another." Robert Stephenson, engineer and famous bridge builder, cheerfully predicted that the cable could never be laid in deep water.

Morse had been given a sort of honorary appointment as electrician of the Newfoundland line—though cable telegraphy was not his specialty—but resigned in 1858, when he found himself maneuvered off the Board of Directors, and presently began to have suspicions that the cable wouldn't work. There was not a vestige of the Morse system, by the way, in the cable telegraph. His signals would not have passed through so long a wire with no opportunity for relay stimulation. Instead, the system was founded on that early needle type of telegraph developed by Schilling and Gauss, in which the signals consisted of right and left deflections of a very delicate reflecting galvanometer. Professor William Thomson, who long afterwards became Lord Kelvin, developed the system, producing what he called the marine galvanometer. In his instrument, momentum and inertia were almost wholly eliminated by use of a needle weighing only an ounce and a half, combined with a tiny mirror reflecting a ray of light and indicating deflections with great accuracy. A system of characters somewhat similar to those of Morse was sent by the pressure of a key, the letter being indicated at the other terminus "by the number of oscillations of the needle, as well as by the length of time the needle remained in one place. The operator who watched the reflections of the deflected needle in the mirror, had a key communicating with a local instrument in the office, which he pressed down or raised, as the needle moved." Another operator meanwhile transcribed into longhand the characters thus produced on a strip of paper.

In December, 1856, Field accomplished the organization of the Atlantic Telegraph Company of Great Britain, with a capital of £350,000. Field asked for 100 shares, $500,000 worth, but as the stock was oversubscribed, he was allotted only 88 shares. He had intended selling the majority of it in America, but could place only 21 shares, some at a loss to himself.

The British Government pledged official business amounting to £14,000 per annum to the line until its net profits reached 6 per cent, when the subsidy would be reduced to £10,000 annually. However, if actual government business amounted to more than the promised subsidy, it must pay for the excess at the regular public rates. Britain asked for priority in conveyance of its messages over all other business, subject to exception only of the Government of the United States in the event of their entering into a similar agreement with the company, in which case the messages of the two governments should have priority in the order in which they reached the station.

Our Congress began its contemplation of the subject about the same time, amid a clamor of opposition. A fifty-year monopoly of ocean cable building was asked by the company. This had been bitterly but vainly opposed in Nova Scotia, and many editors, even some telegraph companies in the United States, denounced it, as "odious and abhorrent." "Is it politic if lawful," asked the Boston *Journal,* "is it lawful if desirable, to grant such an exclusion of all competition to a single company? We believe every voice must be raised in the negative on both inquiries."

Nevertheless, after hard fighting, the bill passed the House in February, 1857, and scratched through the Senate by one vote on March 3rd. President Pierce, with Field standing by his side, signed it next morning just before going to the Capitol to see his successor inaugurated. The charge was made that the Act was unconstitutional, but the Attorney-General decided against this, and no test was made in the courts.

The bill had given Field all that he asked. The frigate *Niagara,* largest and finest vessel in our Navy, was detached to do its share of the laying, with the *Susquehanna* as tender. The British ships were the *Agamemnon* and *Leopard.* Field went to England in July, and on August 4th, the vessels reached rugged little Valentia Bay, on the western coast of Ireland, which was to be the eastern terminus of the line. Here next day the end of the cable was taken ashore amid much cheering from the peasantry. There were speeches by Mr. Field, by the Lord Lieutenant of Ireland and other noble personages. The shore end was fixed, and on the morning of the 6th the ships weighed anchor and steamed out to sea, paying out the cable. Communication through the cable was frequently made with Valentia, where Professor Thomson was watching over the instruments.

On the 10th, four days out, word was sent back that all was going as satisfactorily as could be desired. They had now laid about 360 miles, and were in a depth of 1,700 fathoms—about two miles—which made heavy braking necessary to keep the cable from rushing out too rapidly. At 9 o'clock that evening, for some unknown reason, the signals ceased; but at midnight the current returned, and officers and electricians went to their bunks with a feeling of vast relief. There was a strong wind blowing, however, which buffeted the cable ship severely, and eventually brought disaster. At 3:45 in the morning there came a shout from the stern, "Stop her! Back her!"

"What's the matter?" wondered the officers, leaping from their berths as the stoppage of the engines awoke them—and then came the dread response, "The cable has parted!" The vessels signaled to each other, half-masted their flags and returned dolefully to Valentia.

The futile attempt had cost the company a half-million dollars, but the promoters were not deeply cast down. It was decided not to make another essay until the following summer. The directors increased the capital stock, and ordered 700 miles more of cable. Field now proposed that the ships start in mid-ocean, each with about half of the cable, and proceed in opposite directions, both laying simultaneously.

This was agreed to, and on June 25, 1858, the *Niagara* and *Agamemnon,* with their attending vessels, met. On the following day, while they lay connected with a hawser, a hundred fathoms apart, their two ends of the cable were spliced together, and they started. They had gone only three miles when the cable caught in the machinery of the *Niagara* and broke. A new splice was made, and again they started. This time forty miles were laid when the cable suddenly became lifeless and was adjudged to be broken.

On the 28th, the ships met for the third time, connected the cable and parted. A little more than 200 miles of line were laid, and once more there was a break, this time about twenty feet from the stern of the *Agamemnon*. It had been agreed that if this occurred after more than a hundred miles had been paid, the vessels would have to return and make a fresh start because of the low state of the *Agamemnon's* coal supply. Accordingly they turned eastward and once more cast anchor in the little Irish Inlet.

The Directors met in London, this time in an atmosphere of dissension. The ship captains heard that it was proposed to abandon the enterprise. One prominent director did not attend the meeting, but wrote, "We must all deeply regret our misfortune in not being able to lay the cable. I think there is nothing to be done but dispose of what is left on the best terms we can." Another, the Chairman, who had warmly supported Field a few months before, now resigned and left the room rather than listen to a proposition to go on. But the remainder of the Board, moved by Field's impassioned optimism and pleadings for another chance, voted Yes.

Action was had quickly, but this time there was a noticeable lack of enthusiasm on the part of many. The vessels left Valentia on July 17th, with Field aboard the *Niagara*. A huddle of country folk silently watched their departure; there were no notables present, no cheers, not an optimistic word.

Twelve days later, on the 29th, the splice was made and the ships bade each other farewell. At 2:21 P.M. on the 30th, the *Agamemnon* signaled that she had laid 150 miles, and fifteen minutes later the *Niagara* made a similar report. At 5:30 P.M. on the 31st, the forward coil on the *Niagara's* main deck was exhausted, and she halted while the coil in the hold was attached. At 7 A.M. on August 4th, the lookout in the crow's nest shouted, "Land ho!" and at 2:30 P.M. the ships entered Trinity Bay, Newfoundland. The *Agamemnon* at the same time was within sight of the Irish shore.

Cyrus Field left the *Niagara* at 8 o'clock in the evening with another man and walked fifteen miles to reach the nearest station of the New York, Newfoundland & London Telegraph. At 2:30 A.M. they awoke a sleeping operator and sent several messages—to the cable company directors, to Mrs. Field, to the Associated Press, and one to President Buchanan, informing him that Queen Victoria would send him a message as soon as the two ends of the cable were connected with land wires.

The New York *Evening Post* that afternoon, announcing "Success of the Atlantic Telegraphic Cable," said editorially:

We find it difficult to believe the report, for recent events have prepared us for a very different result, and yet the dispatch comes to us through our regular agent, who would not deceive us. He may have been imposed upon, but that is quite unlikely. If the few coming hours shall confirm the inspiring tidings, and the cable is landed and in working condition, all other events that may happen through the world on this day will be trifles.

To-morrow the hearts of the civilized world will beat in a single pulse, and from that time forth forevermore, the continental divisions of the earth will in a measure lose those conditions of time and distance which now mark their relations....But such an event, like a dispensation of Providence, should be first contemplated in silence.

Just before the cable was laid, the company's stock was quoted in London at from £300 to £350 per share. A few days later, it was bringing from £800 to £1,000.

Longfellow wrote in his diary: "August 6th. Go to town with the boys. Flags flying and bells ringing to celebrate the laying of the telegraph." Writing to Sumner, he called it, "the great news of the hour, the year, the century. The papers are calling Field 'Cyrus the Great.' "

The end of the cable was carried ashore at Trinity Bay, the instruments connected and feeble signals began to be exchanged. On August 12th, at 5:35 P.M., *Valentia* received the first intelligible signal from Newfoundland. It read in part, "Coils signals too weak. Work relay. Try drive slow and regular. I have put intermediate pulley. Reply by coils." At a little past midnight that night, after more struggling, Newfoundland asked Valentia to "Send word Atlantic." Valentia responded, "Atlantic." This was the first word received in Newfoundland through the cable. During the following day some other intelligible signals were received. On August 14th, at 1:53 A.M. Valentia hears Newfoundland say "Send faster," and an hour later gets the word through, "Understand, send faster. Now try message. We get your signals on delicate detector by tapping and marking the paper with pencil, for the time the needle is held over on either side."

At 10:20 that night De Sauty, the Trinity Bay operator, got a message of some length through to Valentia, directed to the secretary of the American Telegraph Company, telling of the impatience of American stockholders over the "unexplained delay." He added that he had replied in part, that "instruments require great care and adjustment. Doing fast as possible. You should not look on cable as on ordinary short line, as we encounter many little difficulties, but think all soon overcome."

On the 15th, scarcely anything intelligible was received on either side. But meanwhile, America was in a frenzy of rejoicing over the "success" of the project. Editors jeered at those who had so persistently predicted failure, and had called Field a fool. Bells were rung, guns fired, buildings illuminated all over the country. Henry Ward Beecher delivered one of his loftiest orations on the subject. But when twelve days passed with no news of any real message, the public was becoming impatient. On the 16th, however, Newfoundland received without a break a message of congratulation from the British directors to those in America, which revived enthusiasm. It was reported that the Queen's message would come through immediately. It began at 4:15 that afternoon, but so many repetitions were necessary that by 6:29 only this much had been received:

The Queen desires to congratulate the President upon the successful completion of the great international work, in which the Queen has taken the greatest interest.

At this point Valentia interjected, "Wait repairs to cable," not informing Newfoundland that the greeting was not complete. The fragment was therefore given out in the United States that night as the complete message. Later in the night, Valentia resumed sending, and at 6:48 A.M. the remainder was completed:

The Queen is convinced the President will join with her in fervently hoping that the electric cable... will prove an additional link between the two nations, whose friendship is founded upon their common interest and reciprocal esteem. The Queen has much pleasure in thus directly communicating with the President, and in renewing to him her best wishes for the prosperity of the United States.

It was a bit dampening to find that the thing had dribbled through in sections because the cable was still working so poorly. Nevertheless, the celebration, planned to take place as soon as the Queen was heard from, began in New York that morning. Church bells jangled, factory whistles blew, huge bonfires leaped heavenward, guns and fireworks added to the uproar, which continued until next day, when the City Hall was set afire. Parades carried banners full of delirious enthusiasm and wise-cracking, and business houses displayed transparencies gotten up in the smartest vein of after-dinner toasts of the day. One of hundreds read, "LIGHTNING—Caught and tamed by FRANKLIN—Taught to read and write and go on errands by MORSE—Started in Foreign Trade by FIELD, COOPER & CO.—with JOHNNY BULL and BROTHER JONATHAN as Special Partners." Another was, "The Old Cyrus and the New—One Conquered the World for Himself—the Other the Ocean for the World."

On the 17th, the first news dispatch went over the cable, though not sent by newspaper men. It was a telegram (repro-duced herewith), sent on behalf of the Cunard Company, telling of the bumping together of two vessels near Cape Race, and allaying fear by explaining that it was not a serious disaster.

On the 18th, notwithstanding the strenuous efforts of oper-ators and electricians, not one readable word passed through the cable. Next day, however, Valentia hears De Sauty say, "See to adjustment. Can you receive President's message? Been here since yesterday"; and then "We can't read." "Currents too weak to read"; "Very good currents, but can't read." Finally, Valentia's signals became audible, and the President's message labored through:

The President cordially reciprocates the congratulations of Her Majesty the Queen on the success of this great international enterprise, accomplished by the science, skill and energy of the two countries. It is a triumph more glorious because far more useful to mankind, than ever was won by conqueror on the field of battle. May the Atlantic Telegraph, under the blessings of Heaven, prove to be a bond of perpetual peace and friendship between the kindred nations, and an instrument designed by Divine Providence to diffuse religion, civilization, liberty and law throughout the world. In this view, will not all the nations of Christendom spontaneously unite in the declaration that it shall be forever neutral, and that its communications shall be held sacred in passing to the place of their destination, even in the midst of hostilities?

JAMES BUCHANAN

"President's all right," Valentia acknowledged in receipt, which Newfoundland did not get:

NEWF: "Your current much stronger, but cannot read your signals. Repeat." "Received. Send a few words." "Your current very weak. Repeat."
VALENTIA: "How now? Can you read?"
NEWF: "Understand. Better than ever. Please always commence by attack and give final signals, as we receive on galvanometer. Relay won't work."

Thus they toiled on from day to day, spending most of their time in trying to establish good connection and to locate the reason why they couldn't. Orders and advice went back and forth about "larger galvanometer," "gutta-percha tube and siphon" and other items. On August 20th, Field entertained the officers of the *Niagara* at his home and read from a window to a crowd in the street his telegram of congratulation from the company's secretary in London. Cooper replied that day to the felicitations of the British directors. After much difficulty, a message from the Mayor of New York to the Lord Mayor of London was gotten through on the 22nd. But that morning,

Newfoundland had asked, "Can you receive message?" and then, after an hour's silence, "How do you receive?" But seven

From International Telephone and Telegraph Corporation

FIRST NEWS MESSAGE SENT BY THE CABLE OF 1858

hours more passed before a word was heard from Valentia. Next day the Lord Mayor's reply was transmitted. On the 25th, De Sauty told Valentia of America's rejoicings, and said, "Pray give some news for New York; they are mad for news."

Valentia replied, "Understand. Have sent to London for news." But next day most of the sentences were, "Can't read your signals." "Send slower and repeat all." "Your signals very weak. Have twenty messages for you. Can you take them?" "Try only one galvanometer in circuit," and so on.

On the 27th, Valentia sent to the Associated Press a staccato dispatch of news hints from Europe: "Emperor of France returned to Paris Saturday. King of Prussia too ill to visit Queen Victoria. Her Majesty returns to England 31st August. Settlement of Chinese Question; Chinese Empire open to trade; Christian religion allowed. Mutiny being quelled, all India becoming tranquil." And so on.

Next day Newfoundland replied with a batch of American news, including yellow fever statistics from the South, and announcement that the formal celebration in honor of the cable (the other one, it appeared, had been just an impromptu preliminary) on September 1st and 2nd, would be "the greatest gala ever known in this country." On the 30th, Field cabled London, saying that messages were being offered the company, and asking when the line would be open for business; also requesting some official messages which he might read at dinners and publish during the great celebration.

On the 31st, Valentia called: "I have two Government messages. The first to General Trollope in Halifax from the Military Secretary. 'The Sixty-second Regiment is not to return to England.'" Then the cable turned perverse, and the second message did not get through until late at night: "The Thirty-ninth Regiment is not to return to England." These two messages were highly important afterwards as proof that the cable had actually operated. They are said to have saved the British government £50,000 in the cost of transporting troops.

The signals by this time were growing very weak. The second message could not be distinctly read in Newfoundland, and at midnight De Sauty (when did these fellows ever get any sleep?) was saying to Valentia, "Repeat from 'Canada' to 'return.'" The morning of September 1st, began with:

THE FIRST ATLANTIC CABLE

VALENTIA: "Canada. The Thirty-ninth Regiment is not to return."

NEWF: "Understand. Will you take a service?"

VALENTIA: "I will try. Slow."

A long blank ensued, and then:

NEWF: "We have received nothing since you repeated last."

VALENTIA: "Can you take message?"

NEWF: "Yes."

And then came with tolerable clearness the requested publicity message:

"C. W. Field, New York: The directors are on their way to Valentia to make arrangements for opening the wire to the public. They convey through cable to you and your fellow-citizens their hearty congratulations and good wishes, and cordially sympathize in your joyous celebration of the great international work."

NEWF: "Forty-eight words. Right, right!"

These were the last words received at Valentia.

Meanwhile, the celebration, or what the New York *Herald* called the "Glorious Recognition of the Most Glorious Work of the Age" began in New York that morning with a Te Deum at Trinity Church. The Episcopal Bishop Doane of New Jersey had written a poem for the occasion. The cannon, the parades, the whistle-blowing were just getting well under way when the last words came whispering over the wire from Valentia—so feeble that the little mirror could scarcely be seen to move, and indeed, a part of the message was lost:

"C. W. Field, New York: Please inform.... government we are now in position to do best to forward...."

The rest was silence. The first Atlantic Cable had done its poor best, and now was speechless. For weeks afterward it was like a slowly dying person whose breathing is scarcely perceptible, whose lips at time move faintly, but form no intelligible words which those bending lovingly over the wasted form can detect. But America for some time had no hint of this, and in all its cities the celebration went madly on on those first two days of September. The day's festivities were as usual, succeeded at night by dinners, fireworks, illuminated signs, torchlight parades and hullabaloo. The New York newspapers declared that the scene along Broadway on the first night "altogether transcended

New York, Aug. 21ˢᵗ 1858

This is to certify that I have sold the balance of the Atlantic Telegraph Cable now on board of the U. S. S. F. "Niagara" to Messrs Tiffany & Co. Jewellers No. 550 Broadway of this city, and that the piece which accompanies this, is a genuine section thereof.

Cyrus W. Field

Original from Erskine Hewitt

CERTIFICATE ACCOMPANYING SOUVENIR PIECES OF THE
ATLANTIC CABLE SOLD BY TIFFANY'S

238

description." Some of the banners and transparencies carried delirious predictions that the cable would "elevate labor and refine the heart"; and that it would "make muskets into candlesticks." (Was it not the late eminent philosopher, Will Rogers, who noticed that the more intimately people know each other, the more they fight?) Other *bon mots* were "The Cables of Tyranny are blighted by the Cables of Intelligence," and

> Through the cleft waters of the sea
> Resounds earth's anthem, "Man, be free!"

And now, three-quarters of a century later, let any reader look us over and judge how much of this has come true. In much more recent years we have heard similar idealistic vaporings as to economic Utopias, New Social Orders, the elimination of poverty, making the world safe for democracy, science freeing man of all labor, and so on, and so on, and so on. Only the student of history can appreciate the futility, the fatuity of prophecy.

On September 2nd, a grand banquet was given by the Common Council of New York in honor of Field and the officers of two cable-laying ships, at which 600 guests confronted a menu embracing twenty-five meat and game dishes, twenty pastries, seventeen "confectionaries" and other things too numerous to mention. Field read his telegram from the directors amid great cheering, but his soul must have been gnawed deeply by worry. For a month the effort to establish clear connection had been fruitless. Lately the signals had grown weaker, and he knew that for twenty-four hours since the last poor fragment came fluttering through, not a word had passed. The days which followed deepened his gloom. De Sauty could report nothing but blankness. But America still beamed and waited. On the 11th, *Harper's Weekly* carried a jingle, "How Cyrus Laid the Cable," by John G. Saxe:

> Bold Cyrus Field, he said, says he,
> "I have a pretty notion
> That I can run a telegraph
> Across the Atlantic Ocean."

> Then all the people laughed and said
>   They'd like to see him do it.
> He might get half-seas-over, but
>   He never could go through it.
>
> To carry out his foolish plan
>   He never would be able;
> He might as well go hang himself
>   With his Atlantic Cable.

Describing the first futile attempts, the rime went on:

> "Once more, my gallant boys!" he cried;
>   "Three times!—you know the fable—
> ("I'll make it thirty," muttered he,
>   "But I will lay the cable.")

By that time, this must have begun to have the appearance
of prophecy to Field. But the poem continued:

> Once more they tried—hurrah, hurrah!
>   What means this great commotion?
> The Lord be praised! The cable's laid
>   Across the Atlantic Ocean!

But the days of silence dragged on, with crews on both sides
patiently tapping their keys, adjusting, trying fresh batteries
and new combinations and straining their eyes to make something out of the slight trembling of the tiny mirrors. De Sauty,
concealing the true state of affairs from the public, gave out only
an occasional brief and exceedingly vague bulletin. But to Field
on the 24th, in answer to a question, he said: "We have received
nothing intelligible from Valentia since the first of September,
excepting feeling a few signals yesterday. I cannot send anything
to Valentia." On the following day he again reported "some
weak reversals of the current" from Valentia, but nothing readable. On the 30th, he made his last entry in the service message
book, but continued faithfully trying to get something through
for weeks thereafter.

Field sadly made his dispatches public a few days after they
were received. On October 20th, there was a flurry of hope in
England, after weeks of pessimism. When Valentia announced

that it had that day deciphered four words from Newfoundland
—"Daniels (meaning a Daniell's battery) now in circuit." But
that was the last gasp. Not another word traversed the cable of
1858.

In America the reaction was one of terrific disappointment,
followed by ugly gossip. It began to be rumored—and many
fully believed it—that not one word had ever passed over the
cable. Within a few weeks the story had progressed to the point
of denying that the cable had ever been fully laid. Those who
had jeered at the unbelievers now in their turn had to endure
unmerciful ridicule.

Under the heading, "Was the Atlantic Cable a Humbug?" the
Boston *Courier* in January, 1859, carried a letter signed
"Observer" and occupying three columns of small type, which
voiced the slanders of the opposition, of disgruntled stockholders
and mere mischief-makers. It declared that not one intelligible
word had ever passed through the cable; sneered at the claim
that the collision of the *Arabia* and *Persia,* or other news from
Europe or America had gone by cable—tried to prove that it
was all stale news, anyhow, and could have been received by
mail; asserted that President Buchanan had had a copy of the
Queen's message for weeks before it was allegedly telegraphed;
hinted that De Sauty was "a sort of myth—not sufficiently
identified to be yet known by a positive name, or his reality to
be positively credited"—which inspired Oliver Wendell Holmes
to one of his most delightfully humorous poems; a pity that we
have not space to reproduce it here.[1]

"Observer" finally charged that the pretense at operation of
the cable was done to enable Field to sell the $375,000 worth
of stock which he had on his hands. He quoted from a still more
reckless letter written by Lieutenant Francis Higginson, R.N.,
owner of £1,000 of stock in the Company, to the London *Daily
News,* which asserted that:

The cable was broken in the attempt to submerge it on the 29th
of July, at 7¾ P.M. between the *Agamemnon* and the *Niagara,* when

[1] In *The Professor at the Breakfast Table.*

electrical signals *immediately and finally* ceased; nor were the broken ends of the cable ever afterwards recovered or repaired. It is therefore needless to say that no message of any kind whatever, public or private, could ever have been passed along the telegraph wire rope....

I have nothing to do with *motives,* but am at any time prepared to produce evidence on oath, by eyewitnesses, to substantiate the facts herein defined, and until that can be done, request you will thus disabuse the public of a dangerous delusion into which it has gradually and unavoidably been misled; it being almost impossible to credit the extent to which individual oppression and popular deception have been carried.

In America, the wind was rather taken out of the opposition's sails by an incident which took place one night at a meeting of the New York Chamber of Commerce. A member had arisen and denounced the enterprise in a furious speech, saying, "It was all a humbug! No message ever came over." Whereupon Mr. Samuel Cunard, who was present, arose and said, "The gentleman has no right to say that; he doesn't know what he is talking about. I myself both sent and received messages by the cable."

George B. Prescott,[1] a noted telegraph authority, charged that when the cable was in process of manufacture at the Glass-Elliott plant, coil after coil of it was left exposed for days to the glare of a summer sun, although strict orders had been given that it must be protected from such exposure, and the intense heat had melted the gutta-percha covering until the wire was actually bare in spots. The injury, he said, was partially revealed before the cable left the factory, and thirty-five miles of it was condemned and cut out. But there were flaws in the remainder, on which all parties concerned took a chance, and found that they had gambled unwisely. It was evident that leaking insulation had been the undoing of the great and costly project.

[1] In his book, *History, Theory and Practice of the Electric Telegraph* (1860), published at Boston.

CHAPTER XII

THE TREND TOWARDS MONOPOLY

The public has been slow to learn how disastrous opposition to the Western Union Telegraph Company has been. Competitive lines cannot make a go of it, and they may as well quit trying.

ERASTUS WIMAN, Western Union Director, 1884

IN the first two or three years of its existence as a business, the principal lines of telegraph were highly profitable. The Albany *Knickerbocker* remarked in September, 1846:

> The Magnetic Telegraph between this city and New York, and in fact, between here and Buffalo, is coining money. They have more business than they can well attend to, just now. We told Albanians a year ago that this enterprise would pay well and begged some of them to go into it, but like donkeys as they have proved, they wouldn't take our advice.

There were other companies, too, which throve mightily. In 1847, when the line from Philadelphia through Reading to Pottsville had been in operation only six months, the directors declared a 5 per cent dividend. Wherever there was no competition, rates went up as soon as the people became accustomed to using the wires. On the other hand, the employees were often miserably paid. We have seen that many offices were kept up for from $100 to $200 per year, including the operator's salary, rent and all. Even operators in large cities might draw no more than $25 to $35 per month. The messenger boys for several years were permitted to ask a two-cent fee for delivering a message, and this was their only pay, save that the telegraph company boarded and lodged them. In 1848, the New York, Albany and Buffalo line decided that they were making too much money, and reduced their pay to a flat $4.00 a month and board; the two-cent fee thereafter went to the company.

Operators must carefully preserve every fragment of platinum, zinc, wire, paper, and so on, to be sold for the benefit of the company. Telegraph offices (this from a Magnetic document of 1847) were kept open from sunrise until 10 P.M. every day in the week; save that they were closed during "the ordinary hours for morning and afternoon service on the Sabbath"; and this, of course, represented the working day and week of each operator, messenger and battery man, save for the brief moments he could snatch for his meals.

The *National Telegraph Magazine* in 1853 pictured the operator as a *rara avis:*

> The telegraph operator becomes, after a few months' work, a mere machine; he either does not realize the sense of the letters he writes, or forgets the purport of the message ten minutes after it has passed through his hands. In general, he is a taciturn, suspicious-looking individual, gifted with great clearness of head and a precision in judgment in examining faces, far above the average.

With such high talent and machine-like efficiency, it does seem that he might have been paid a little better salary.

Amos Kendall, in a deposition in the United States Courts in 1848, admitted that the "Magnetic," the Washington and New York line, was yielding 20 per cent profit on the capital actually employed, of which one-half went to the patentees. But when competing lines paralleled it, its income rapidly declined. In 1850-51 its annual dividends were only 2 per cent.

The other Morse lines suffered similarly. Weak, independent companies had thrown out lines in the East among cities and towns of no great size, as O'Rielly did in the mid-West, and these, too, though hurting the larger companies, were themselves in a constant state of crisis. In 1853, the telegraph lines between New Haven, Waterbury and Fair Haven were let to customers by the hour or minute, at the rate of ten cents for five minutes, and one cent for each subsequent minute; and you might have as much talk as you could crowd into your time; while for twenty-five cents you could send as much as you pleased. All of which indicates that those lines must have been pretty hard up.

That same year the New York and New England Union Company took over the Rhode Island lines, connecting Providence with Worcester, Bristol, Taunton, Fall River and New Bedford, for a sacrifice price of $5,000, though the mere cost of constructing them was several times that much. The House line between New York and Boston was offered to the Associated Press about this time for $40,000, and was a part of Craig's ambitious scheme.

The Magnetic directors, seeking a scapegoat, threw out their President, B. B. French, in 1853, and elected in his stead William M. Swain, principal owner of the Philadelphia *Public Ledger*. The Philadelphia *Sunday Dispatch* gave at the time this frank description of Mr. Swain's personal appearance:

> His countenance is not prepossessing to a stranger; it wears a forbidding, morose, distrustful, taciturn and thoughtful expression. Good living and a life of comparative indolence have modified of late to a great extent, this general expression of his face. Some years ago, when he was but little known here, none who merely glanced at his looks, would have given him credit for anything but cunning and an arch spirit of business intrigue. In good sooth, he had an unquestionably dubious face, to which his cold, frowning habit of countenance lent a doubly sinister appearance.

The editor then proceeded to explain that Mr. Swain wasn't really as bad as he looked. But with that sort of mien he was bound, in some degree, to improve the condition of the Magnetic. He could not, however, bring it back to its former prosperity while it was so short a line and with growing competition. But a curious combination of circumstances presently brought about the consolidation of all the companies along the Atlantic seaboard.

In 1855, the industrious D. H. Craig unearthed a new printing telegraph, that invented by David E. Hughes, a professor of music in Kentucky. It was the most highly sensitive instrument yet produced. An experimenter, says James D. Reid, "worked it by aid of a battery composed of a cherry pit and the ordinary metals and fluids." It dispensed with the step-by-step movement on which House's machine was founded. The revolution of the type wheel was continuous; it did not stop to imprint a letter, as House's did. At Craig's suggestion, Peter Cooper and associates bought the North American rights. The instrument was still not quite perfect in its functioning, and George W. Phelps brought it to a fine state of practicability. Hughes later took it to Europe, where it was widely introduced, and in addition to emolument, the once obscure music teacher became a Baron.

Craig and two associates had come into possession of the House New York-Boston line, as well as three minor ones, connecting with it. This was done with the assistance of the Associated Press, to combat Fog Smith's opposition and rival news dispatches. In 1854, Craig induced James Eddy, head of the Maine Telegraph Company and others, to buy the House New England lines, with the idea of extending them to Halifax. Cyrus W. Field had conceived a similar arrangement, as a tail to his Atlantic Cable. This being known, it seemed the part of wisdom for the two parties to combine, which they did late in 1855 as the American Telegraph Company. Field, Peter Cooper, Abram S. Hewitt and Wilson G. Hunt were among the men most prominent in the company's operations in the next few years. The Maine Telegraph line at once became a part of the new system, and the charter of the New York, Newfoundland & London, carrying a fifty-year cable monopoly, was eventually made over to the Atlantic.

After a futile effort to buy or lease the House line from New York to Philadelphia, the American strung its own wire between those cities and began to make things difficult for the two older lines. The House company held out for a little more than two years and then, in February, 1859, was absorbed by the American. On November 1st of the same year the Magnetic, the pioneer company of telegraphy, yielded to the inevitable, and was merged with the new giant. Its leading stockholders, including Morse, Kendall and Swain, accepted $500,000 worth of the American Company's stock in exchange for that of the Magnetic. Along with this consolidation went leases of the Washington-New Orleans line, and the Western Telegraph Company from Baltimore to Marietta, Ohio, with a connecting wire to Cincinnati. At the other extremity, a lease of the New Brunswick Telegraph Company gave the American a continuous line from the Nova Scotian border to the Gulf of Mexico.

Smith's New York and New England Union, as might have been expected, fought stoutly against benevolent assimilation. The negotiations were long and full of Yankee horse-trading tactics. After several months of this, Smith finally accepted $165,000 for his interest (the largest) in the company, and $301,108 for all his proprietary rights in the Morse patent. Several other companies in the United States and Canada contributed to this sum to stop Smith's royalties from their treasuries. And as might have been expected, he had scarcely deposited his checks in the bank when he began "gum-shoeing" about among capitalists of his acquaintance, trying to promote the building of an opposition or "nuisance" line from Boston to Washington, in order to sell it, too, to the American! But sad to relate, the scheme would not jell. The same tactics became highly popular from one to two decades later.

The American Company now had seven wires between Boston and New York, four between New York and Philadelphia, and three between Philadelphia and Washington. In 1860, it gathered in the Nova Scotia wires on a fifty-year lease, and now controlled the entire Atlantic Coast. It strove in vain for a lease of the prosperous New York, Albany and Buffalo, and that line finally fell to the Western Union.

The last great conquest of the American—though not until after the Civil War had temporarily broken each of them in twain—was that of the Southwestern, a prosperous system which had arisen south of the Ohio River. Its nucleus was the two parallel wires between Louisville and New Orleans, O'Rielly's "People's Line," and the New Orleans & Ohio (Morse patent), whose builders raced O'Rielly's crew into Nashville so hotly that Shaffner, its construction boss, wrote exultantly to Morse of the possibility of a clash, saying, "My men are well armed, and I think they can do their duty"; which so horrified the peace-loving inventor that he wrote a hasty reply, begging Shaffner to avoid a collision, saying, "I want no man to fight for me. Let the other fellows put up their poles and wires if they like. I have no patent on poles and wires."

But the injunction and the destruction by court order of O'Rielly's line through Kentucky gave his company a worse backset than Shaffner's bully boys could have done. And later on, its flimsy construction, Ol' Man River (who arose in wrath and obliterated the line now and then), "Bronze John" (yellow fever), rustic malice, competition and debt—which brought sheriffs swooping down upon line and offices again and again—finally completed the ruin of the People's Company, and in 1853 it passed into the control of its competitors, the New Orleans & Ohio, which was in but little better case. Under this management, both wires were still operated, as they took different courses below Nashville.

But disaster and debt still hampered the concern, and in 1856 a group of lessees, among whom we find for the first time the name of Dr. Norvin Green, took over the wires. Under their management, conditions improved. They acquired interests in connecting companies which had built westward from New Orleans into Texas via Alexandria, with branches to Baton Rouge, Vicksburg and Natchez. One line between Shreveport and Natchitoches used cow's horns as insulators on which to string the wires! In Texas, Houston, Austin, Galveston and San Antonio were reached; in Arkansas, Little Rock and Hot Springs. Southeastward, the lessees extended their wires to Chattanooga, Montgomery and Mobile.

In 1860, the lessees were incorporated as the Southwestern Telegraph Company, with Dr. Green—a jolly Kentucky physician and politician, who had poled and steered flatboats down the rivers to New Orleans in his teens—as President. And then came the Civil War!

That there was a community of interest among telegraph companies began to be realized, and in 1853, Amos Kendall

Cape Cod from Frank E. Lawrance; Nevada and California from Albert Dressler; others from Norvin H. Green

TELEGRAMS, 1850 TO 1881

called together the first telegraph convention at Washington, which was attended by the representatives of sixteen companies, nearly all of the most prominent ones in the country. The problems which the meeting took up were such things as rights of priority among messages, some changes in the alphabet, rate-cutting, standardization of signals and abbreviations, and the mutual responsibilities of the lines to each other, though the establishment of a central fund for returning money demanded by irate patrons for non-delivery or too late delivery of messages was not yet accomplished. The project of establishing a telegraph newspaper in opposition to the Associated Press also failed.

One of the (to us) curious items on what our modern chronic conferees are fond of calling "the agenda" was the term O K—which some youngsters of to-day fancy is a bit of modern slang, but is older than most of their grandparents—as an acknowledgment of the correctness of a message. During the half century and more when it was seldom spoken, but was a formal symbol of acceptance or approval of the correctness of an estimate, a proof sheet or other calculation or document, it was always written "O K." President Wilson was apparently the first to lengthen it into a manufactured word, his version being "Okay." At the present writing, some self-breveted pundits are insisting that "Okeh" is the proper form. It began as popular slang, and hence has completed a cycle.

Shaffner, speaking of it as a telegraph term approving the correctness of a message, says it existed before the telegraph era; that it was in widespread use at the time of the Presidential campaign of 1840, and again in 1844. One theory is that it was thus written—either humorously or in ignorance—as an abbreviation for "Oll Korrect," by Andrew Jackson or some other backwoods hero. Another theory is that the Indian chief Keokuk learned to scrawl laboriously the English letters "O.K." on a treaty, meaning "Old Keokuk."

As a response to the reception of a message, Morse used "I I," but the popular O K became the favorite with operators, being more distinct telegraphically than I I, and the stamp of approval was placed upon it by the Telegraph Convention of 1853.

It will also be of interest to notice the elaborate ceremony, explanation and apology with which a new word was sometimes introduced then. The Albany *Evening Journal,* in a long editorial in 1852, of which we can quote only a part, said:

A friend desires us to give notice that he will ask leave at some convenient time to introduce a new word into the vocabulary. The object of this proposed innovation is to avoid the necessity, now existing, of using two words, for which there is very frequent occasion, when one will answer. It is TELEGRAM, instead of Telegraphic Dispatch or Telegraphic Communication. The word is formed according to the strictest laws of the language from which its root comes. Telegraph means to write from a distance—Telegram, the writing itself, executed from a distance. Monogram, Logogram, &c., are words formed upon the same analogy and in good acceptation.

The "friend," who was a certain Professor Smith, furthermore remarked that the House Company ought to call their messages *Teletypes,* since they were printed, not written. And here we discover another word which we had thought was new, suggested nearly a century ago, though the meaning then was entirely different from that of the accepted word of to-day. Telegraphery (an office) and telegraphage (rate for sending) were also invented in 1848-49, but did not last.

Yearly conventions were decided upon by the telegraph companies, and they drifted slowly towards a closer rapprochement, finally resulting in 1858 in the formation of the North American Telegraph Association. But before that date, a new colossus had arisen among their members, one destined eventually to engulf them all.

Rochester, New York, produced the most remarkable group of telegraph promoters and builders in the history of that means of communication. Among these were Judge Samuel L. Selden and Hiram Sibley. Sibley had run a machine-shop near Rochester and been Sheriff of the county before he became interested in telegraphs. When he went down to Washington in 1841 to see William Henry Harrison inaugurated as President, he met Morse and became so much impressed with his instrument that he pleaded with Congressmen in the inventor's behalf. Later, he was one of the earliest investors in the New York, Albany and Buffalo line.

When the House machine was patented, Judge Selden bought rights for the northwestern territory, and suggested to Sibley that they organize a company to operate under it from Buffalo westward. Sibley's reaction to the idea was a suggestion that they buy some of the weak Morse and O'Rielly lines in the territory to westward, and weld them into a system. Isaac Butts, a third Rochester man, joined with them in the project, and in 1851, the New York and Mississippi Valley Printing Telegraph Company was organized, with a board of directors on which Rochester citizens predominated.

But organizing the company proved to be easier than getting stock subscriptions and collecting the money on them. Competition was already hurting the older companies, and their conditions grew worse from year to year. New lines were being airly tossed together in all directions, and on sober second thought, the outlook for another new company seemed dubious. Resort was finally had to watering the stock; giving two shares for one to every subscriber who would pay over his promised cash. This brought in some money, but not enough, and the company was reorganized in 1854.

Sibley had shrewdly analyzed the telegraph business, and saw that its trouble was too much competition, especially in a sparsely settled country where business and individuals had not yet reached the point of dependence upon quick communication. He himself had some money tied up in it, and so he resolved to try eliminating the competition. He saw how the process had already begun in New England and along the coast. In the Middle West were dozens of weak telegraph lines, simply begging for some bigger corporation to take them over and either rejuvenate them or chloroform them. Sibley accordingly

251

planned his reorganization of the New York and Mississippi Valley in 1854 with the intention of accumulating more capital and beginning to absorb the sickly wires which were fighting each other westward from New York State and Pennsylvania.

He talked himself hoarse, trying to make other Rochester capitalists see the beauty of his idea, but found most of them amazingly short-sighted—and yet not amazingly, either, for it is a common condition of the human race. Because most telegraph companies were making little or no profit, they decided that there was no money to be made in telegraphs, nor ever would be. Again and again he called these moneyed neighbors together in his office and argued, pleaded, cajoled, but with no result. They listened with interest to his impassioned speeches, evidently wishing that his bright visions might be made to come true, but they would put up no cash.

"If I do invest in it, Sibley," said one of these friends, walking home with him one night, "promise me it shall be a secret between us forever. I'll loan you $5,000—that means give it to you, for you'll lose it, of course—but you are never to tell that I was such a fool. I believe in you, Sibley, but I don't believe in this telegraphy." [1]

One evening Sibley called a final meeting in his office, offering a last chance for Rochester men to get in on the ground floor. If they did not sign his subscription paper that night, he would leave town next day to find the money elsewhere. After his usual oration, Aristarchus Champion, an extremely conservative millionaire, demanded whether he would not admit that the telegraph business in general and the various companies in particular were so far a financial loss.

"I do," said Sibley, frankly.

"Then how is this consolidation of failures to escape failure? If there is nothing in the result which is not in the cause, where is the element of success to come in? Would collecting all the

---

[1] The dialogue relating to Sibley's promotion is drawn from *How Men of Rochester Saved the Telegraph*, by Jane Marsh Parker, in Rochester Historical Society Publication Fund Series (1926), Vol. 5.

paupers, the social failures of Monroe County, into one organization composed entirely of paupers, insure their success and make them men of fortune?"

It was useless for Sibley to point out the irrelevance and absurdity of Champion's would-be analogy, for the latter would not sign.

"Admitting all that you have said, Mr. Sibley," said Judge Addison Gardiner, "admitting that this organization, by the investment proposed, may reap a certain and increasing success, is it at all probable that you or I or any one here present will live long enough to see your prophecy fulfilled, to reap the benefit of faith in your seership?"

Sibley would make no promise as to this. He only knew that triumph and emolument would come at some time, either to this generation or the next. Judge Gardiner decided to take a chance, and signed for $10,000. His signature was the first.

George H. Mumford, the next to be appealed to, sat for a while, twirling his thumbs.

"It looks to me like a nest of boxes," he said at last. "We must open a great many before coming to the one that holds the treasure, and we may find nothing, after all. We must buy up line after line—the purchase of each the sequence of a preceding purchase." He pondered a while longer in silence, and then signed the paper.

"I agree with Mr. Champion," said the next three in rapid succession, and, says Sibley, "I began to think my cake was dough, after all."

Don Alonzo Watson sparred for time. "I'll tell you in the morning," said he. "Perhaps I'll take all I can pay for." He did take $5,000 worth, but not because he didn't expect to lose it eventually. Sibley says:

The $90,000 subscribed at that meeting was all the money ever paid. The balance was money loaned on bonds of the company, and individual loans. Isaac Butts promised the other $10,000 and paid it in stock of other lines. That $100,000, with what was gained by the consolidation with the House lines outside of the State of New

York, constituted the property of the Western Union Telegraph Company, and soon exceeded in value the whole assessed value of the property, real and personal, in the city of Rochester.

One of the first acts of the reorganized company was the leasing of the wires of the old O'Rielly line, the Lake Erie Telegraph Company, a T-shaped system, with its shank from Pittsburgh to Cleveland and its cross-bar from Buffalo to Detroit. Some of the stock of this company was bought for what is commonly known as a song. Next, Sibley went after bigger game—the Erie & Michigan, which paralleled their just-leased line from Buffalo to Detroit and went on to Chicago and Milwaukee. This company had a number of valuable contracts with connecting lines touching the Ohio and Mississippi Rivers, and owned stock in most of them. Sibley proposed consolidation with this company under a new capital stock of $500,000. Ezra Cornell was now the chief power in Erie & Michigan, and in agreeing to the terms, he stipulated that the reorganized company should be known as the Western Union Telegraph Company. It will be remembered that the languishing line which he created along the Erie Railroad had finally been re-christened New York and Western Union. He liked that name; and in fixing it upon the new company, he perpetuated a name destined to become one of the most noted in all business history.

The three genii of the Erie & Michigan were Cornell, J. J. Speed and Jephtha H. Wade, the latter a pious-looking party with a Methodist preacher's shaven upper lip and beard, who is said to have had "a peculiar faculty for negotiation." In other words, he could horse-trade an opponent plumb out of his eye-teeth. All Morse patent rights held by Cornell, Wade and Speed went into the deal (which eventually meant the elimination of the House machines), also stocks in companies which fed the Erie & Michigan, and whose lines extended to a dozen points on the Ohio and Mississippi Rivers. Here enters another name destined to be heard frequently in our history—that of Thomas T. Eckert, who had been partner with Wade in the construction of several of these lines, and who thus acquired a block of Western Union stock.

The Western Union Telegraph Company was given legal birth by the New York Legislature on April 4, 1856. Nobody, not even Sibley, even began to realize the gilded future which lay before it. Many of those who had been inveigled by Sibley into putting up cash regarded it as just another shifting of some worthless scenery. Most of the men who signed his subscription list on that memorable night in his office, unloaded their stock when and as they could, usually, of course, at a heavy loss. Sibley paid par value for some of it whenever he could raise the cash, confirming many in the belief that he was slightly insane. From time to time he received letters from these and other early stockholders, begging him to take over or dispose of their interests. "If nothing I can say will touch your heart," wrote one of these, later a millionaire, "have pity on my wife and children." To such letters Sibley, when he could not buy, would reply only with an exhortation to hold on—the golden dawn was coming.

The original stockholders, the signers for $5,000 and $10,000, could not have escaped becoming millionaires, says Sibley, if they had had the courage to cling to their stock. Only four of them did so—Sibley, H. S. Potter, Joseph Medbury and D. A. Watson. These four even added to their holdings. Sibley in those days traveled about from town to town on a still hunt for telegraph stocks. He carried a little hand-bag full of cash and rapidly replaced it with stock certificates picked up at nominal figures, some as low as two cents on the dollar. The entire stock issue of a company capitalized at $240,000 was acquired at about that rate.

"As fast as we could make a line pay 7 per cent," says Sibley, "we put it in." In 1857, the company took over 488 shares of stock which Cornell owned in the Michigan Southern Telegraph Company, operating from Toledo to Chicago. "By this and other settlements with Mr. Cornell," says James D. Reid, "What was in 1857 adjudged as worth about $50,000, required in 1865 the issue to him of nearly two millions of Western Union Telegraph Company's stock."

At the early age of one, the new company was a lusty young giant whose power began to be felt. It paid a dividend of 8½ per cent on December 1, 1857. On the first of the following April another 5 per cent was distributed; on July 6th, 8 per cent more, and on July 24th, 20 per cent. The profits now began to roll up, snowball-like, until the secretary said he sometimes doubted his own sanity.

It was deemed essential that the company effect an entrance to New York and Philadelphia, and now there began to appear some of the familiar tactics of monopoly. The Atlantic & Ohio, first built by O'Rielly between Philadelphia and Pittsburgh was a strong, prospering organization, and had no notion of selling out or of submerging its identity in another concern. Its stockholders wouldn't "listen to reason," so Wade began whispering in the ears of Pennsylvania Railroad officials. That road had a wire of its own strung along its right of way for official purposes, and Wade won the right to attach two more wires to the company's poles for commercial use, on condition that nice, new House printing machines be installed in the railroad executive offices—chief and divisional—for its perpetual use. The railroad company was delighted; it hauled the wire and the telegraph company's employees free, and aided the new project in every way. Thereby, the Atlantic & Ohio suddenly found itself confronted by a competitor, the Pennsylvania Telegraph Company, with a capital of $500,000, and none other than an offshoot of the young ogre which was steadily devouring the A. & O.'s connections west of Pittsburgh.

There could be only one outcome. After much fencing and face-saving, the two companies were merged into one, with a capital of $650,000, which was presently exchanged for $833,-400 worth of the stock of the Western Union. The New York, Albany and Buffalo, after some more jockeying, was next to fall, giving the coveted entrance into the metropolis; and the Pittsburgh, Cincinnati and Louisville, an old O'Rielly line, was

next. Notwithstanding the New York terminal, the headquarters
of the Western Union remained at its birthplace, Rochester,
until near the close of the Civil War.

Thus, before the war began, the W.U.T.'s system stretched
from the Atlantic to the Mississippi and from the Great Lakes
to the Ohio. By sheer good luck, it had no wires into southern
territory, to be cut off, and the war merely poured money into
its lap in a golden stream. In the autumn of 1858, its capital
stock was suddenly enlarged from $385,700 to $2,263,300; with
the result that no more than a 2 per cent dividend could be paid
in 1859. The slack was quickly taken up, however, and in 1860
and 1861 the dividend was 5 per cent annually. Then came the
happy days! In 1862, there was a cash dividend of 9 per cent
and a stock dividend which raised the capitalization to nearly
$3,000,000. In March, 1863, a 100 per cent stock melon was
cut, and another of 33 per cent in December. These stock dividends, we are told, "were based on actual mileage of restored
property at a fair valuation."

By May 1, 1864, the capital was $10,066,900, and Western
Union had become the most popular of extravaganzas, a dream-
world come true. The stock rose to 200, despite its frequent
dilution, and then to 225. In Rochester, its home town, Reid
says that homesteads, mortgages, businesses, furniture, pianos,
guitars, anything that could be turned into money at no matter
what sacrifice, was sold, and the cash invested in those beautiful
W.U. stock certificates. While this excitement was at its zenith,
the directors, intoxicated by their own and the public enthusiasm,
flung another 100 per cent stock dividend—"every dollar of
which was clear and unmixed water"—into the giddy mael-
strom. By 1865, the capital of the company was $21,063,400.

Such fantastic success brought its inevitable consequences.
Promoters and capitalists, with chops dribbling for a taste of
such rich gravy, were organizing more telegraph companies,
and because of the shining example of the Western Union,
were readily finding money with which to do it. The United
States Telegraph Company, organized in 1864, was the first of

these. It combined the lines of three smaller companies, and with a well-stocked war chest, threw out new lines, until in the summer of 1865 it had 16,000 miles of wire in service, including a line which had been pushed eastward from San Francisco to Salt Lake, and was intended to bridge the continent.

It called to its presidency that year William Orton, a former collector of internal revenue. Orton found, upon sitting down at the executive desk, that the company, despite its flashy performance, or rather, because of it, was losing money steadily, and that there seemed no chance of correcting the situation. The result was that on April 1, 1866, after a meteoric career of twenty months, the United States sold itself to the Western Union for an issue of $3,885,200 worth of the latter company's stock.

Two months later, on June 12th, $12,000,000 more in Western Union certificates poured from the printing-presses, and was handed over as the purchase price of the last great rival, the American Telegraph Company, which, only a short time before, had swallowed the whole Southwestern system. Thus the Southwestern President, Dr. Green, became a Western-Union director, and took his first step towards the headship of that mighty organization; and thus the Western Union spread its tentacles from Nova Scotia to Texas, and acquired a share in the Atlantic Cable, then about to be successfully laid.

The American's capital being only $4,000,000, its purchaser had given it three dollars for one. Sibley afterwards declared vehemently that, "There was never a drop of water put into Western Union before the consolidation with the American"; in which he is contradicted by other authorities and by the facts themselves. He had been President of the company from its organization until 1866. That year, because of ill health, he resigned, but accepted a place as Vice-President. In his stead as head of the company was chosen the silent, invisible Jephtha Wade, a perfect antithesis to his predecessor. "When Sibley started on a crusade," says Reid, "like the Israelites of old, he blew his horn lustily until the walls fell, and took a complacent toot after they were down. . . . Wade carried no horn. He was a sapper and miner." In other words he was like the mole, whose presence you never suspect until you see his ridge across your garden path, and even then, you can never catch him nor see him. Sibley in later years turned to an entirely different business, and became one of the greatest of American seedsmen. Millions of flower and vegetable gardens have blossomed and borne from seed of his production.

But Wade, too, was in bad health, which continued contemplation of the Western Union books and balance-sheets may have made worse. His incumbency lasted but one year. In 1867, William Orton was called to the Presidency, to be confronted by a capital stock of $41,000,000, and a half-dozen vigorous competitors which had sprung up within the past two years, as if from the dragon's teeth of fable. Nothing else in all business history is comparable to the mushroom expansion of this company's capital. Only $369,700 in 1857, it had, within the following decade, swelled by about 11,000 per cent!

Its original investors and promoters were all millionaires— each many times richer than Inventor Morse. Before the middle '60's they had begun giving their money away. Cornell took half a million dollars and founded Cornell University at his home town of Ithaca. Later, he gave it nearly as much more, besides a considerable acreage of land. Sibley presented it with a college of mechanical engineering, and donated other buildings, both to Cornell and the University of Rochester. Amos Kendall built a $120,000 church for the Baptist congregation in Washington of which he was a member, and when it burned a few years later, he replaced it. And these are but a few of the benefactions which dropped from the magic beanstalk.

CHAPTER XIII

THE TELEGRAPH IN THE CIVIL WAR

—When foe with foe contending,
Man against man and steel 'gainst steel,
Then from loaded mules outsending
An iron wire from off the reel, . . .

Dots, dashes, dots—the word's spoken
From corps to corps, from post to post,
"Hip, hip, hurrah! their line is broken;
We have beaten the rebel host."

Z. P. HOTCHKISS, 1863

NEWS telegrams hurled over the land on April 13, 1861, brought with most poignant force to Washington, and especially to the gaunt man who had sat only a little more than a month in the White House, the bitter tidings of the fall of Fort Sumter before the rebellious guns of Beauregard. As always, there was a generation ignorant of history, unable to comprehend the horrors of war until it had suffered them, ready to leap blithely into the conflict.

Now that war was come, however, both North and South learned for the first time how valuable the telegraph is in such an emergency. In the North, President Lincoln's call on April 15th, for 75,000 troops was broadcast to the four quarters of the land by wire, and at once messages began flashing back from State Governors: "What portion of the 75,000 militia you call for do you give to Ohio? We will furnish the largest number you will receive"; "We will furnish you the regiments in thirty days if you want them, and 50,000 men if you need them," said Zachariah Chandler of Michigan. When Indiana's quota was set at 5,000 men, the Governor retorted that 10,000 were ready.

Instead of 75,000, more than 91,000 were immediately offered. Banks and capitalists telegraphed offers of money and credit; manufacturers offered their product. Units of the regular army were quickly summoned and shifted by means of the magic wire.

Massachusetts was quickest of all. A telegram to Governor Andrew, calling for twenty companies, was flicked across the State, and that night and next day, four regiments assembled on Boston Common. While they were assembling, an appeal came for them to hurry, and save Washington. The Sixth Regiment entrained immediately. Five Pennsylvania companies, 530 men all told, also summoned by wire, preceded them into Washington and were added to the handful of regulars and volunteers which General Scott, the aged Commander-in-chief, was able to scrape together. On the 19th, the Sixth Massachusetts was assaulted by mobs while passing through Baltimore, and although it lost a few men, made its way to Washington. The telegraph and the railroad played a large part in the saving of the Capital from enemy hands.

On the afternoon of April 17th, William B. Wilson of the Pennsylvania Railroad ran a wire into the executive chamber of Governor Curtin of Pennsylvania, setting up the relay on the window-sill—which is claimed to have been the first telegraph for military purposes on the American continent.

Late on the 19th, a company of militia seized the Washington office of the American Telegraph Company, the only one in the city, driving all the operators from their keys. Waiting in an adjoining room, the operators could hear Richmond and other southern offices calling, and commenting sarcastically upon their failure to receive replies. The Government was naturally worried as to the loyalty of some of the men at the keys and wished to check up on them. Colonel Thomas A. Scott, general manager of the Pennsylvania Railroad, had been called into consultation on the subject by Secretary of War Cameron, and he in turn called two or three of his best men to Washington, among them the superintendent of the Pittsburgh Division, a young man named Andy Carnegie.

Eleven years before, in 1850, the manager of a telegraph office in Pittsburgh was looking for a lively boy to sweep out the office and do messenger work, and a certain Mr. Carnegie, hearing of it, took his stocky fifteen-year-old son, Andy, around to ask if he would do. Andy got the job at a salary of $2.50 per week. He soon began practising on a key in the office when it was not in use, "talking with the boys at the other stations who had like purposes to my own." One day when he was alone in the office, he took an important message from Philadelphia. Before he reached his seventeenth birthday, he was a regular operator at $25 a week. He had not been at this dizzy height more than a year when he was taken into the service of the Pennsylvania Railroad at a $10 raise, and at the age of twenty-five was superintendent of the Pittsburgh Division.

Secession mobs were dominant in Baltimore as Carnegie traveled towards Washington. It was deemed best to detour that city, he and his companions going down Chesapeake Bay to Annapolis, thence by rail to the Capital. On the way from Annapolis, while riding on the locomotive, he noticed that some vandal had loosened a telegraph wire from the insulators and pinned its slack to the ground with wooden stakes. He stopped the engine, dismounted and thoughtlessly pulled up one stake, whereupon the liberated wire snapped upward, knocking him backward and cutting a gash across his face. He therefore jestingly claimed to have been the first in the telegraph service to shed his blood for the cause.

On April 22nd, Carnegie wired the superintendent of telegraphs of the Pennsylvania Railroad, asking that four of his best operators be sent to Washington at once for Government service. Four youths named Strouse, Brown, O'Brien and Bates were immediately forwarded. The ages of the quartet ranged from eighteen, that of Bates, up to twenty-three, at which figure Strouse was the dean.

On the night before Carnegie's telegram was sent, a fright

had been given the Government when the telegraph wires towards Philadelphia were cut north of Baltimore. They were the only connection with the North, the other wire, that along the B. & O., having been severed when Harper's Ferry fell into enemy hands two days before. A squad of 160 militia and Baltimore policemen set out to destroy railroad bridges and ferries to northward. Just outside the city they captured the night mail train coming from Philadelphia and turned back with it, picking up on the way two boy telegraphers—James M. Swift, aged fourteen, operator at Magnolia, and William J. Dealey, but slightly older, operator at Black River who, by the way, had been on duty fifty-six hours without sleep. These were among the very first political prisoners of the war. The irregulars proceeded towards Havre de Grace, intending to burn the ferry there, but met a freight train whose conductor frightened them back to Baltimore with news of an advancing Union force. The two boys were released, and Dealey's name appears frequently during the four years that followed as one of the most reliable of Union army telegraphers.

One of the most remarkable phenomena in the early history of the telegraph is that of the boy operators. Carnegie and young Jimmy Leonard, an early sound reader, have been mentioned. J. J. S. Wilson, a noted Civil War telegraph chief, was an operator and office man in Wisconsin at fourteen; and at sixteen was actually appointed manager of the line between Madison and Chicago. His youth betrayed him, however, and he had to give up that job in the following year because of the strain on his nerves. But only a few months later we find him a division superintendent for the Illinois and Mississippi Telegraph Company.

Many boy telegraphers will be noticed in the course of this sketch of the Civil War. It seems inconceivable to-day that the safety and strategy of great armies should have depended upon the courage, accuracy, acumen and cool heads of mere adolescents. The private soldier in his teens is not one-tenth as remarkable as the boy army telegrapher. In many cases, his position was even more exposed than that of the fighting men. His responsibility was enormous. There may have been instances of cowardice and neglect of duty among them, but we have yet to find them. Yet for more than thirty years after the war, their services went unrecognized by the Government, and are unrecognized by historians to this day.

Twenty-three-year-old Strouse was given power to erect and maintain such Federal telegraphs as should be necessary in Washington and vicinity, but with the charming inconsistency of governments, no money or materials accompanied the order, and for seven months he and his successor were dependent upon the bounty of the American Telegraph Company for everything needed. E. S. Sanford, President of that company, honored all requests, hoping that some day his company would be recompensed—as eventually it was. Strouse ran lines from the War Department office to the Navy Yard, the Government arsenal, the B. & O. Railroad station, and to Chain Bridge, a few miles above the city, where Charles W. Jacques, a sixteen-year-old, was the operator; a somewhat precarious post, for the enemy had soldiers at the other end of the none-too-long bridge. There were some cavalrymen with Jacques, but he had no horse. Many times, in an emergency, telegraphers had to take care of themselves, with no help from the army.

This was the first great war in history in which the telegraph was used in the field. At the beginning, the Government, having no experience whatsoever in that line, had only the most elementary notions regarding it, and actually thought that the commercial companies would and should take care of the business—even extending lines to the battle front, if that should be found necessary. To the modern military mind, a stranger fallacy can scarcely be imagined. The commercial companies were willing enough to loan men and build lines for the Government, but they frowned on any suggestion of military organization of the service, and their word was law with Simon Cameron, the politician who was playing at being Secretary of War.

On May 20th the Government seized the telegrams of the

past twelve months in many city telegraph offices, especially those in the border States, in order to discover, if possible, how long disunion had been under way. On the following day, northern and southern officials of the American Telegraph Company held a conference on the Long Bridge across the Potomac, and telegraph communication between Washington and Richmond ceased from that hour, though Richmond continued in touch with Alexandria until that town was taken by Union forces a little while afterwards.

The whole southern half of the American's system was thus cut off and lost for the next four years, being reorganized as the Southern Telegraph Company, under Confederate Government influence. The Confederate Postmaster-General Reagan was, "because of military necessity," in nominal control of all telegraphs in Southern territory, but actually interfered very little with their private operations, save in a military emergency. The southwestern system was likewise cut in two, the part remaining within the Southern lines being at first the larger. Theoretically, it operated as two corporations; President Green directed the northern section from Louisville, and appointed John Van Horne, the General Superintendent, as Acting President of the part within the southern lines.

There was no such thing in the Confederacy as a governmental military telegraph system, like that developed in the North. A few generals carried telegraph outfits with them, but for the most part relied on the commercial lines. Beauregard was the first Southern commander to appreciate the telegraph's importance, and quickly built up a system around Charleston in the spring of 1861; but for the most part, private companies loyally strove to keep the armies supplied with service, and succeeded fairly well at it.

On April 12th, the day when the southern guns opened on Sumter, the canny Governor of Ohio, Dennison, telegraphed Anson Stager, General Superintendent of the Western Union Telegraph Company, with headquarters at Cleveland, asking him to come to Columbus. Stager went, and was asked by the

Governor to assume a military management of the telegraphs in southern Ohio, especially along the Virginia border (West Virginia had not yet been created), where Captain George B. McClellan was to be the commanding officer of a military department. Dennison and McClellan were among the very few who were alive to the possibilities of the telegraph in war. Stager consented, and went to Cincinnati to consult McClellan.

The latter was appointed Major General in May, commanding the Department of the Ohio, which included western Virginia, Ohio, Indiana, Illinois, and later, Missouri. In turn he immediately made Stager "superintendent for military purposes of all telegraphic lines" within that department, adding, "his instructions will be strictly obeyed." This merely meant at the start that military messages superseded all other business on the commercial wires. The telegraph stockholders patriotically agreed to the arrangement; but in a country as yet happily unused to regimentation, still looking upon private enterprise as superior to the military, save by its own voluntary consent, Stager's position was considered extremely delicate, in that he, still superintendent of a private telegraph company, was placed in control of the lines of several other companies.

He had yet another impediment; some of McClellan's staff officers, inspired by conservatism, jealousy and ignorance, insisted that the telegraph could not be of any practical use in war, and opposed the commanding officer's efforts to introduce it—but in vain; and before that summer's west Virginia campaign was over, some of those same officers were praising the telegraph's achievements.

On May 27th, W. G. Fuller, superintendent of the American Telegraph Company's lines between Baltimore and Cincinnati, was called to Cincinnati, where Stager gave him instruction in "the first army cipher ever used telegraphically in war." [1] Stager

[1] So says William R. Plum in his *The Military Telegraph during the Civil War in the United States,* one of the finest works on the Civil War that the writer has ever seen, which has supplied much material for this chapter. Other chief sources are William B. Wilson, *A Glimpse*

himself had worked it out, and as elaborated by D. Homer Bates, Albert B. Chandler and Charles A. Tinker, the three young cipher operators in the War Department at Washington, it became the standard cipher for the army. More than a dozen new ciphers were devised during the war—whenever the one in use was captured by the enemy or it was suspected that they had solved it. The Confederate ciphers were simpler than those of the Federals, and they were therefore far more unfortunate in finding them frequently solved by northern experts and used against them.

The first field action of the war occurred in McClellan's department, at Philippi in the western Virginia hills, on June 3, 1861. When McClellan himself advanced, early in July, from Clarksburg through Buckhannon, "the first field telegraph," says Plum, "that ever advanced with an army in America kept pace with this one;" likewise the first portable printing office—a miniature affair, a fad of one of the telegraph operators, J. L. Cherry. But McClellan found that hobby useful, too, particularly in the printing and dissemination of a Napoleonic, Soldiers-I-am-proud-of-you proclamation which he issued after his victory at Rich Mountain. He was highly pleased with the service of the telegraph, and said that without it, his work would have been much slower. Confederate prisoners brought into the lines were astounded to find wire strung and a telegraph instrument clicking, perhaps in works which they had abandoned but a few hours before.

In Missouri in 1816, there were but few commercial telegraph lines, especially in the southern half of the State. The arsenal in St. Louis was saved to the Union by a telegram from General Wool to Governor Yates of Illinois, asking him to send some troops to capture it. The Confederates destroyed the Stebbins line, which ran from St. Louis through Springfield to Fort

of the United States Military Telegraph Corps (1889) ; David Homer Bates, *Lincoln in the Telegraph Office* (1907) ; also by Bates, *Lincoln Stories* (1926), and Charles A. Dana, *Recollections of the Civil War* (1899), and others.

Scott. The Union General Lyon, when he marched southward in the summer of 1861 to engage the enemy, had no telegraph equipment, and from the time when he left Boonville on July 3rd until he was defeated and slain by a superior force at Wilson's Creek on August 10th, he had no telegraph communication with any higher authority. This knotty, red-bearded little Yankee zealot, who had driven the pro-slavery State government into exile and saved Missouri for the Union, was a martyr to the neglect of his Government and the lack of telegraph facilities. Thereafter, an effort was made to provide wire service when General Curtis's army marched southward during the following winter to clear Missouri of disunionists; but when the two-day Battle of Pea Ridge was fought in March, 1862, in Arkansas, the Union wire-end was still ten miles from the battlefield, and the Confederates had no telegraph at all. Thereafter, young R. C. Clowry, in charge of the Federal Western Department, made a record for building and efficiency which set his feet on the road to the Presidency of the Western Union nearly forty years later.

From April 25 to November 15, 1861, there were built for military purposes in the several departments, 1,137 miles of telegraph line, mostly in the East. Strouse, who had charge of the building in the Department of the Potomac, was physically too frail for the job; his lungs gave way, he was retired on furlough in July and died in November. He was succeeded by James R. Gilmore, a nineteen-year-old youth, but just as efficient as the other boy telegraphers of the period all seemed. Off duty, they were not averse to a bit of skylarking, just like other boys; but on duty they displayed a maturity, a stern devotion, carefulness and patience which to-day we would be apt to regard as far beyond their years.

Gilmore, by way of backing up his authority, at once began growing a beard. The most remarkable achievement of the early months of this incumbency was the rapid building of a line from Washington to General Banks's army in the Shenandoah Valley, mostly through hostile territory, where the farmers had to be

ONE OF THE FIRST ARMY TELEGRAPH STATIONS IN THE FIELD, 1861

SETTING UP A LINE ON THE BATTLE-FIELD, CIVIL WAR

forced to supply poles; but with the aid of his whiskers, Gilmore accomplished even that.

Even in midsummer of 1861 the Government had not yet comprehended either the importance or the method of a military telegraph. The telegraphers were hampered by the inevitable jealousy and clannishness displayed by the military towards civilian employees. Signal-corps officers thought the telegraph should be under their direction, and gave orders which the telegraphers ignored. When Major Myer, a Signal-Corps officer, obsessed by this notion, "inspected" the telegraph office at Hampton, Virginia, in the autumn of 1861, he found the two operators, Bunnell and Smith, both boys in their teens, sitting on the floor in shirt-sleeves and bare feet, playing seven-up with a greasy pack of cards. Worst of all, they did not spring to their feet and assume the posture and dead countenance of clothing dummies upon the Major's entrance, which made it quite clear to him that the wisest of all moves would be the abolition of the army telegraph service.

When General Patterson moved with 16,000 troops across the Potomac above Washington in June, 1861, theoretically to keep the Confederate General Johnston busy, no telegraph was taken with him. There were commercial lines to Hagerstown and Harper's Ferry, and from one or the other of these points, despatches were carried by courier to Patterson's headquarters. General Scott, the aged Commander-in-chief, actually lost track of Patterson for a time. Meanwhile, Beauregard, then digging in along Bull Run, telegraphed Richmond, asking that Johnston join him; and Johnston, notified by wire, did so, unbeknown for two days to Patterson. When Patterson finally notified Washington on the 20th that Johnston had slipped away from him, the information was not even relayed to General Irvin McDowell, who had been given the job of whipping Beauregard.

When General McDowell, with his rabble of raw troops and a few regulars, moved out from the Potomac in the middle of July to attack Beauregard, a telegraph line was strung behind his army as far as Fairfax Station and Fairfax Court House, which latter place was McDowell's headquarters. Still amateurs at the business, it seemed impracticable to them to extend the line ten miles further, to the battlefield. By a bevy of couriers, McDowell received news from the field and gave orders, and was expected to telegraph the War Department every fifteen minutes.

In the War Department telegraph office that Sunday afternoon, a more or less complacent party sat ready to listen in on the concluding scene of the rebellion. There were President Lincoln, Secretaries Cameron, Chase, Welles, Secretary Seward (who had set the duration of the war at thirty days) calmly blowing smoke rings from his cigar, General Mansfield, commander of the defenses of Washington, and several members of General Scott's staff. Patterson's admission by wire the night before of Johnston's departure did not seem to worry anybody; McDowell could take care of both Beauregard and Johnston, if necessary. The only group more fatuous than this was that of the Congressmen and Government officials who had driven out in carriages, some taking ladies along, to see the fun itself.

For the first few hours that afternoon, all news was encouraging. Everything was moving according to plan; the enemy was steadily being pressed back. In a short time all would be over. But as the hot, still summer dusk approached, the clicking of the instruments ceased. A long silence, and then Washington asked Fairfax for news. The reply was that no courier had arrived from the front for some time. Again a long wait, a query, and again the reply, "No news." The only plausible theory propounded in the waiting group was that the Union troops by this time were chasing the Southrons so hard and fast that they had gotten far out of touch with the telegraph, and hadn't time to write messages, anyhow.

Darkness had fallen when at last the instrument clicked the Washington call, and Bates began to write. A shell from one of Beauregard's guns hurled into their midst could not have created more consternation than did that one sentence. The dreadful words were "Our army is in full retreat."

270

Thereafter, the signals became more rapid, more excited, as broken bits of reports from officers told of the slaughter, the rout, the jamming of troops, artillery, baggage wagons and Congressmen's carriages in the narrow roads and bridges, the confusion and panic in the darkness. It was a sickening recital, and the Administration found later that the half of the muddlement had not been told.

Correspondents of some metropolitan newspapers were on the field, and had sent a despatch or two by courier to Alexandria or Washington during the afternoon. These first messages were, of course, eloquent of victory. Far along into the latter part of the night, dispatches began to pile up on the American Telegraph Company's table at Washington, telling the final sad story. General Scott, when in the small hours he could at last be convinced that the army had been defeated, sent an aide in a buggy, galloping down to the telegraph office, to cut out all the bad news. The result was that all over the North that morning, big headlines, jangling bells, cannon and hurrahing announced a glorious victory. But the absurdity of withholding the truth was soon realized, and thus, when it was told, the reaction was made twice as harrowing. Calls for more troops were being wired to every capital in the North early that morning, and the story of the disaster brought 60,000 enlistments in two days.

That battle made it clear that there must be some changes. McClellan replaced Scott as Commander-in-chief of the armies (only to be replaced in turn by Halleck a few months later). Cameron retired in January and was succeeded by Edwin M. Stanton, a Pittsburgh lawyer who, though far more able and vigorous, yet had no more knowledge of warfare than Cameron, and was a tactless man of strong prejudices, often wrong-headed, obstinate, unjust, ruthless, boorish.

Anson Stager was asked to submit a general plan for a military telegraph; and upon his doing so, it was adopted and he was made its chieftain in October, 1861. McClellan accelerated the building of lines when he became commander, and Stager in turn furthered the work.

At first, no military titles were considered for the telegraphers, but some action was immediately made necessary when Quartermaster-General Meigs refused to honor Stager's requisitions for money and supplies, because he had no military rank. Stager was therefore created a colonel and assistant quartermaster. He appointed Thomas T. Eckert as his assistant, and Eckert received the rank of major. Gilmore and nine other department chiefs were made captains. Eckert, already referred to as a telegraph builder and superintendent in the Middle West, had left that service in 1859, and gone to manage a gold-mining project in North Carolina. He was perhaps the ablest of the telegraph chieftains of the war, and during its last three years had a heavy responsibility; for Stager, oddly enough, retained his job with the Western Union, and remained at his office at Cleveland, which made his management rather remote.

The operators and cipher men had to get along with no rank at all, no military standing. They were subject to taxation and draft. General A. W. Greely says of them:

> The telegraph service had neither definite personnel nor corps organization. It was simply a civilian bureau attached to the Quartermaster's Department, in which a few of its favored members received commissions. The men who performed the dangerous work in the field were mere employees—mostly underpaid, and often treated with scant consideration.... During the war there occurred in the line of duty more than three hundred casualties among the operators—by disease, killed in battle, wounded or made prisoners. Scores of these unfortunate victims left families dependent on charity, for the Government of the United States neither extended aid to their destitute families, nor admitted needy survivors to a pensionable status.[2]

The linemen had hazardous jobs, too, particularly in the mountainous region of southern Missouri, where a hostile population constantly menaced the wires, making it necessary

[2] From article on the "Military Telegraph Service," by General Greely, in *The Photographic History of the Civil War* (1911), published by Review of Reviews Co., New York.

for repair men to ride the line daily. How many of these were shot from ambush on their rounds there is no means of knowing, for no record was made of such incidents; they were far less in importance to the governmental mind than the sparrow is said to be to God. Plum remarks that their knowledge of their danger never deterred them from their desperate duty:

If one was killed, another took his place, and being a mere civilian, no notice was taken of his fate by the Government in whose service he died. No provision was ever made for his wife and little ones; no slab ever erected at Government expense; no military salute was fired over his grave. If the corps in his district, from motives of sympathy, made up a purse out of their hard earnings, and mention of his fate was made by the officers in their annual reports, that was the most that could be expected. But what became of those reports? Those for 1864 and 1865 were printed along with the Quartermaster-General's; but none other ever saw the light of day, and astute historians have even overlooked those that were printed. Indeed, some who pretended to write up the history of the Civil War, seem to have been strangely ignorant of the fact that there ever was a Military Telegraph Corps; much less did they ever hear of the repairer, who dared and died for his country.

Those operators who were attached to the staffs of commanding officers incurred the jealousy of all other officers of lesser grades, because they were so close to the big chief, on such unconventional terms with him, and knew secrets which were in some cases kept even from them, officers in the same command. The General's telegrapher and cipher expert was, in effect, a private secretary. Being a civilian, he did not have to notice the General's entrance, nor salute when he met him outside. The General was apt to call him Sam or Joe. Other officers frequently tried to pump him for news, but usually failed. The thought that a mere civilian, sometimes just a broth of a boy, should have this intimacy with the General and this privity to many important secrets which were denied to them was very mortifying, and the smaller among them vented their displeasure upon the telegrapher in petty ways whenever convenient. This feeling, carried into the decades following the war, had much to do with the steady refusal of the Grand Army of the Republic to recognize the army telegraphers as brothers-in-arms.

Among the most noteworthy of these private secretaries was A. Harper Caldwell, chief cipher operator of the Army of the Potomac from the winter of 1861 to 1862 until the end. This efficient youth served at the headquarters of five Generals of that army—McClellan, Burnside, Hooker, Meade and Grant. Another was S. H. Beckwith, Grant's chief operator, who served with him in the Vicksburg and Chattanooga campaigns, and went thence with him to Virginia, where he divided responsibilities with Caldwell.

Telegraphers frequently suffered from the irritation, misunderstanding and cross-purposes of commanding officers, aggravated by the chronic dislike of civilian co-laborers. Linebuilders and operators were threatened with shooting because they did not perform miracles. General Hovey, in command at Memphis, early in 1862, claimed the right to read telegrams passing between General Halleck, then in command in the West, and two generals in Arkansas. The Memphis operator refused to let him see them, whereupon Hovey ordered him under arrest. When Halleck heard of this, he wired Hovey sharply, "Release the operator at once. He did perfectly right in disobeying your orders."

In the course of building thousands of miles of military telegraph line, cables were laid across Chesapeake Bay and all the large midwestern rivers. Some of these river cables, hastily laid, gave trouble. The long circuit from Cairo to Corinth, Mississippi and Decatur, Alabama, worked heavily; that is, much current leaked through "grounds," and at times, the line wouldn't respond at all. Sweating operators, trying to get messages through when transmission was bad, not only burst into vocal profanity, but sent it over the wire in execration to the fellow at the other end. Plum says that operators on some occasions rode thirty or forty miles on horseback or by train to lick others who had cursed them by wire. Pat Mullarkey, an operator at Memphis, once went all the way to Cincinnati to attend to a chore of this sort.

Telegraphers in the field, if not attached to a great army commander's headquarters, led a lively and hazardous existence. Every operator carried a portable instrument and usually a short piece of wire with him. He clung to the instrument to the last moment, but if he saw that capture was inevitable, it was his duty to smash it, so that he might not be forced to use it against his own side. In the Shenandoah Valley, where cavalry was the principal fighting force, and movement was rapid, operators in the heat of action were often left behind, notifying Washington or Richmond or some distant general of the progress of affairs until too late for them to escape. Just a few years ago a Negro farmer, plowing on the old battlefield of Spotsylvania, turned up the rusted remains of one of those portable telegraph instruments; and as it happened, the Union operator who had lost it there in one of the fluctuations of that terrible conflict, was still alive to claim it.

When Forrest was raiding along the Mobile & Ohio Railroad in the winter of 1862, operator after operator was captured, though most of them succeeded in hurling their dispatches and sometimes their instruments into the office stove just as the cavalrymen appeared on the scene, much to the latter's indignation. At Kenton, Tennessee, a boy named Stephen Robinson, only fifteen and small for his age, was the operator. There were three companies of Illinois infantry in the town, and the major promised to take Stephen along if they had to flee. But after dark one night Forrest dashed in from the south, and the infantry fled northward, forgetting the telegrapher, who was at the southern edge of the village. Stephen detached his instrument, rolled it up in his little shoulder-shawl and walked away, right through the enemy troopers. A small boy walking along the street attracted no attention from the raiders, though perhaps some of the family men among them meditated disapprovingly that he ought to be in bed. Alone, Stephen walked out of town, crossed the long trestle over the Obion River in the darkness, and near the next station climbed a pole, cut in on the wire and telegraphed news of the situation to a general's headquarters at Columbus, Kentucky. A locomotive with half a dozen box cars was sent out immediately; stopped by a fire built on the track by refugee Negroes, it picked up Negroes, infantry and telegrapher and took them safely back to Columbus.

Secretary Cameron, as soon as Eckert became telegraph head at Washington, instructed him to deliver army messages to the commanding general, and to no one else. Eckert therefore walked up to General McClellan while he stood talking to President Lincoln and handed him a message, telling of the Battle of Ball's Bluff and death of Colonel E. D. Baker, the President's close friend; and though McClellan read the telegram immediately, he did not tell the President of its contents. Secretary Stanton, when he came into office, was naturally irked to find army news which he never received, going to the Commander-in-chief, and occasionally being given out to the newspapers. Instead of asking frankly for a show-down on the matter, he busied himself to "get something on" Eckert, and sent forth a private snooper, who reported that Eckert was neglecting his duties. Thereupon Stanton was about to dismiss Eckert incontinently, when President Lincoln, backed up by Sanford, the American Telegraph President (whom Stanton had asked to take Eckert's place) and the Governor of Ohio, interceded and assured the Secretary that Eckert was faithful and efficient and was acting strictly under orders. Daunted by such championship, Stanton apologized to Eckert and later became one of his warmest admirers.

The Secretary immediately detached Eckert from McClellan's staff and ordered him to make his headquarters at the War Department, and connect all wires save one with that building to the General's office. This of course angered McClellan, and the incident probably marked the beginning of the ill feeling between the two men. Stanton likewise appointed Sanford censor of telegrams—the first functionary of that sort that America had known.

276

FEDERAL TELEGRAPH BATTERY WAGON IN THE FIELD NEAR PETERSBURG, 1864

THE TELEGRAPH IN THE CIVIL WAR

When McClellan moved the Army of the Potomac to Fortress Monroe for its attempt on Richmond, it was not feasible to connect it directly with Washington through Tidewater, Virginia, because of enemy menace, so a cable was laid across Chesapeake Bay from Fortress Monroe to the eastern shore, and a land line led thence via Wilmington, Delaware, to Washington. Richard O'Brien was the operator at Monroe, his assistant being his young brother John, only fourteen years old in 1862, and the youngest operator in the Government service. He had had three years' experience when he went to Monroe, where General Wool was amazed to see him receiving by ear. John was on duty when the dreaded Confederate iron-clad, *Merrimac,* appeared among the Union war vessels like a lion among sheep. He saw its smoke and signaled its coming to Newport News. The operator there, George Cowlam, watched the first day's slaughter of the wooden ships and reported it, point by point, to John, who relayed it to Washington. Cowlam's broken messages sound like a hideous parody on a modern radio announcer's description of a football game: "She is steering straight for the *Cumberland.* . . . The *Cumberland* gives her a broadside. . . . She keels over. . . . Seems to be sinking. . . . No, she comes on again. . . . She has struck the *Cumberland* and poured a broadside into her. . . . God! the *Cumberland* is sinking. . . ." Before the fight was over, shells were shattering Cowlam's own office.

One may wonder at a telegrapher's becoming exclamatory by wire, but it became almost as natural as vocal invective. When Grant and Sherman began their movement on Vicksburg in December, 1862, there was a private telegraph line built by a wealthy planter from De Soto, opposite Vicksburg, to the owner's largest plantation, near Lake Providence, some seventy-five miles up the river, which was a valuable Confederate aid. On Christmas Eve the operator at the plantation was playing Old Sledge in his quarters with a friend when they became aware of the beat of paddle-wheels and the coughing of many steamboats. Stepping out on the "gallery," where they had a view of a long stretch of the river, they saw it absolutely crowded for miles upstream, with boats hastening southward.

The two counted boats for a few minutes and then the operator rushed to his instrument and called Philip Fall, the operator at De Soto. "Good God, Phil, sixty-five transports loaded with troops have already passed," he said. "There must be as many more, for hundreds of lights can be seen up the river." Fall left his key and hastily rowed across to the city with the news, carrying a green light in his boat by pre-arrangement to protect himself against the gunners in the fortifications. And then ensued a repetition of the scene in Brussels on the eve of Waterloo. "There was a sound of revelry by night," and General M. L. Smith, the Confederate commander, and his officers were tripping light-heartedly through the polka, the lancers and the schottische when the news burst upon them. Within ten minutes the ball had evaporated. That message sent by the plantation telegraph line was its last, for Federal soldiers cut the line next day. But it had done its work well; Sherman's repulse at Chickasaw Bluff four days later was largely due to its vigilance.

McClellan thrice had reason to thank the telegraph for saving him from the claws of his enemy, Stanton. Once in April, 1862, while he was on the Virginia Peninsula, a prominent New York Democratic National Committeeman sent him two or three long telegrams, urging him in general to disregard the fools at Washington and do as he pleased, and he would be sustained by the people of the North. Eckert happened to be at Fortress Monroe when these telegrams arrived, one after another, and they were of such vicious character that he would not let them go to McClellan through the army wire, but held them until he could deliver them in person; whereupon McClellan fervently thanked God that a man of Eckert's intelligence and courage had been there to suppress those missives which might have been his ruin.

Among the other unwise friends from whom McClellan suffered was his father-in-law, Colonel Marcy, who was his

278

chief of staff. The Seven Days' Battles had just begun when a flamboyant pæan of triumph came to the War Department, purporting to have been signed by McClellan, followed very shortly by another which told of the troops being driven back. The two reports were so absurdly incongruous that Stanton, of course, was all for throwing McClellan out at once. But Eckert pointed out that the first message was not at all in McClellan's style, and suggested that it might be a forgery. President Lincoln was of this opinion, too, and Eckert was sent in person to McClellan's camp on the Pamunkey to demand an explanation. The General, routed out of bed at 2 o'clock in the morning, said he had never seen the first message and could not account for it. Caldwell, his operator, was then aroused, and remembered at once that the first message had been sent by Colonel Marcy, and as he was chief of staff, the operator had every reason to believe that it was genuine. It developed that Marcy had sent the telegram just to give Son-in-law a boost.

McClellan, angered because the Administration had refused to reinforce him with the forty thousand men under McDowell before the Seven Days, wrote a long telegram of complaint and defense to Stanton as he was being driven steadily backward during those engagements; a message which was fairly temperate until its close. Then all his pent-up rage and gall burst forth in its last two sentences: "If I save the army now, I tell you plainly that I owe no thanks to you or to any other person in Washington. You have done your best to sacrifice this army." That telegram fortunately fell into the hands of Sanford, the censor, and he unhesitatingly decided, not only for McClellan's good but for the general good, to cut out those final sentences. Stanton did not know of them until long afterward. President Lincoln may never have known of them.

When the Confederate General Hood invaded Tennessee late in 1864, General George H. Thomas was sent to oppose him with an army hastily thrown together from every direction— some of it raw troops, some poorly equipped, and especially short of horses. While he was toiling night and day at Nashville to get this nondescript force into fighting trim, the pundits in the East, especially Grant near Richmond, were bombarding him with telegrams, wanting to know why he didn't go out and annihilate Hood, who lay within easy reach. Grant, who was inimical to Thomas because the latter had been placed over him for a time after the Battle of Shiloh, tried three times to unhorse Thomas. His first telegram, on December 9th, was squelched by Lincoln. On the 13th, Grant sent General Logan via Washington and Cincinnati to replace Thomas, and late on the following day, he started for Nashville himself.

That same day the wires north of Nashville were cut, and for twenty-four hours nothing was heard from Thomas. Grant reached Washington on the 15th, and wrote a telegram removing Thomas. Lincoln and Stanton strongly opposed such action, but finally yielded to Grant's insistence, and the message was handed to Eckert. The latter returned to the telegraph office, where, between 9 and 10 P.M., he learned that one wire to Nashville had been repaired, but nothing had yet been heard from Thomas's headquarters. With the telegram in his hand, Eckert hesitated. Knowing how strongly Lincoln and Stanton believed in "Old Pap" Thomas (and with reason), he wanted to hear from Nashville before sending that cruel and unjust order. Where else than in semi-pioneer America would a military subordinate have dared thus to think for himself and to take a situation into his own hands? For more than an hour he waited nervously. At last, at 11 o'clock, two telegrams came clicking through; the first from Thomas, dated the night before, saying that he would attack on the following morning; the second, dated 10:30 P.M. on the 15th, describing the first day's battle, with the smashing of Hood's left wing and the capture of one thousand prisoners and sixteen cannon.

Eckert ran downstairs with the dispatch and drove to Stanton's home, who was overjoyed at the news, and went immediately with Eckert to the White House to tell the President. On the way, Eckert showed the Secretary Grant's dispatch, said that it had not been sent and told him why. "I fear that I have made myself liable to court-martial," he said. Stanton put an arm around his shoulders. "Major," said he, "if they court-martial you, they will have to court-martial me, too. The result shows that you did right."

Many and varied were the experiences of telegraphers. General Sumner's operator on the Peninsula was seventeen-year-old Jimmy Nichols. One night Sumner, on the march, wanted to talk to McClellan. A line ran near by. Nichols had only three feet of wire with him, and did not want to ground the line and interfere with other officers' service, so a pyramid of cracker boxes was piled up for him nearly to the top of one of the ten- or twelve-foot poles, and sitting atop of it, he hooked on his wire. To read Sumner's messages and write McClellan's replies, he had to have a lantern. This made a delightful target for the enemy's gunners, and shells by the dozen sang around him, occasionally splintering or knocking some of the boxes out from under him, but otherwise doing him no damage.

As the Union troops fell back from Mechanicsville, Jesse Bunnell, the stripling operator for General Fitz-John Porter, having no horse, was left behind and separated from his head-quarters staff. Crossing the brook just east of Gaines's Mill, he saw that the two armies were forming lines of battle in front of and behind him. Knowing that Porter had no operator with him, Bunnell cut the wire which ran through the woods to his former headquarters, and squatting behind a tree, he called "Mc," the call for McClellan. Caldwell, several miles away, promptly answered, and Bunnell told him of the situation. McClellan was delighted at having connection with the battlefield; he told Bunnell to stop the first officer or soldier passing by, and in the General's name, order him to take a message to Porter, who was to detail fifteen mounted orderlies for Bunnell's use, and communicate at once with McClellan by wire. This was done, and for several hours the boy sat behind that none-too-large tree, with a hail of lead and iron around him, reporting the battle, sending Porter's call for reinforcements, transmitting McClellan's orders and news of other troops on the way. Some of Bunnell's orderlies were killed or wounded, some of the messages he handled were spotted with blood.

Brilliant service was often rendered by operators who tapped wires and learned of enemy plans or who impersonated operators in the enemy service. This last was usually a difficult feat, for an operator's personal touch in sending by the Morse key was just as distinctive, as characteristic as his voice; and the telegraphers along a railroad line, for example, knew instantly the touch of every other operator on that line. General John H. Morgan, the noted Confederate cavalry raider in Tennessee and Kentucky, and even north of the Ohio River, had always with him an operator named Ellsworth who was a demon at getting information, either imitating other operators' styles, or dashing into their offices and forcing them at his pistol's muzzle to send what he directed. Even so, he was detected and out-witted many times.

Late in 1863, two Union operators, Pat Mullarkey and Frank Van Valkenburg, sent out by General Rosecrans, spent thirty-three days inside the Confederate lines in eastern Tennessee, tapping wires and listening in on the enemy's military secrets, which were seldom sent in cipher. For this reason, Federal wire-tapping was usually more successful than Confederate, for 90 per cent of the Union dispatches were enciphered. Mullarkey and Van Valkenburg were protected to some extent by Union sympathizers among the country folk, and the Confederate authorities, who were aware that there was a bad "ground" somewhere, and were searching for them, were never able to catch them. When the two heroes, after adventures and narrow escapes unsurpassed by the best pulp-paper fictioneers, finally fell in with Union pickets, both were in rags, with naked, bleeding feet and half starved.

It was Rosecrans, by the way, who made an unusual use of the telegraph on the eve of Chickamauga. According to Charles A. Dana, who was at his headquarters, he notified clergymen all over the North that a great battle was impending, and requested their prayers in his behalf.

A Confederate telegrapher tapped the wires between the War Department and Burnside's army, only a few miles below Washington in the winter of 1862, and listened in until Union operators, suspecting his presence, advised him to "clear out." Operators on the two sides frequently exchanged amenities. W. K. Smith, General Crook's telegrapher, once cut in on a wire in the Shenandoah Valley. When the alert operator at Dublin heard his "ground," he called, "Sign," but Smith, not knowing the Dublin call, disconnected. An hour later he tried softly to cut in again, whereupon the Dublin man promptly challenged, "Oh, we know you're there, Smith, you damn Yankee." Smith laughed and admitted his interference, and the two joked each other for several minutes. When Crook captured Dublin a few days later, the operator had fled, but had left a request with the railroad agent to treat his friend Smith courteously.

One of the most remarkable jobs of wire-tapping was that of C. A. Gaston, General Lee's operator, who entered the Union lines at City Point, Virginia, while Grant was besieging Richmond and Petersburg, and for six weeks listened to the messages passing over Grant's wire. Most of them he could not read, but one not in cipher which told of the coming of a beef herd for the Union army, when sent by one of Gaston's couriers disguised as a countryman to Lee's headquarters resulted in the capture of the herd by Wade Hampton's gray-coated cavalry. An eighteen-year-old Confederate operator in Arkansas was executed as a spy by his enemies because he happened to have in Morse characters in a notebook in his pocket some notes on the Union forces and fortifications around Little Rock.

The Union army had the only woman operator in military service, who, incidentally, was the first woman telegrapher west of the Mississippi. Louisa Volker, at Mineral Point, Missouri, did valiant service in checking guerrilla movements by keeping

Union headquarters informed and detecting the places where lines had been cut.

President Lincoln spent much of his time, especially afternoons and evenings, in the War Department telegraph office. Soon after his noon dinner, his tall, top-hatted figure would be seen striding across the lawn between the White House and the old War Department building, if in cold weather, with his gray plaid shawl around his shoulders. Arriving at the office, he turned over and studied the stack of telegrams that had come since his last visit, and his understanding of the military situation was about as keen as anybody's in Washington. In times of crisis, he sometimes stayed in the office all night. There was a little side room where he rested on a lounge at times. The place was a refuge for him from office-seekers and bores. He wrote the Emancipation Proclamation there, sitting at Eckert's desk.

Charles A. Tinker, one of the cipher men, while a boy operator at a hotel in Pekin, Illinois, in 1857, had explained to the lank country lawyer, Abe Lincoln, who was there in attendance at court, the workings of the first telegraph instrument that Lincoln had ever seen. Now the President was delighted to find "Charlie" in the War Department. To him Eckert was not Major but "Tom"; the other operators were "Homer," "Bert" and so on, save that some of the very younger ones were often called "Sonny"—ones such as little Willie Kettles, for example, the fifteen-year-old who received the message from General Weitzel on April 3, 1865, announcing the fall of Richmond. Secretary Stanton lifted Willie bodily and exhibited him to crowds in the street below, who were cheering over the news. In the excitement of the moment, the Secretary exclaimed, "Boys, I consider the telegraph my right arm, and if ever I can do anything for you, don't hesitate to ask it." But neither he nor his successors ever did anything for them. Thirty years after the close of the war, Andrew Carnegie was caring for more than a hundred Civil War telegraphers or their widows who were in need.

CIVIL WAR TELEGRAPHERS (IN LATER LIFE)

DAVID HOMER BATES   ALBERT B. CHANDLER

ANSON STAGER

ANDREW CARNEGIE   R. C. CLOWRY

THE TELEGRAPH IN THE CIVIL WAR

This war was likewise noteworthy as being the first in which telegraphing was done from a military balloon. Professor T. S. C. Lowe and his captive balloons were an important adjunct of McClellan's army on the Peninsula, and during the Battles of Fair Oaks and the Seven Days he made a number of ascensions, connected by wire with the earth, and sent down news of his observations of the opposing forces. When McClellan was demoted, the balloon service disappeared from the army.

The Federal Government built 15,000 miles of telegraph lines during the war, and 6,500,000 messages passed over them. Some achievements in building were remarkable. During the month's campaign from the Wilderness to Cold Harbor, Dennis Doren, the construction boss, averaged building twenty-four miles of line a day, some of it under fire, some of it at night. When Hancock's Second Corps groped its way in pitch darkness for three miles to a new position near Spotsylvania on the night of May 11th-12th, operator L. A. Rose accompanied it and at 2:00 A.M. opened an office on a cracker box just back of the line. Plans for assault were discussed with Meade over the wire, and two hours later the terrible but successful struggle for the Bloody Angle began.

Grant in Virginia kept in constant touch with all the other Union forces in the field. "Hardly a day intervened," says Sherman, "when General Grant did not know the exact state of facts with me, more than fifteen hundred miles off, as the wires ran." Burnside said of the Telegraph Corps, "I never knew a body of men who possessed more integrity, industry and efficiency." McClellan spoke of the "loyal and invaluable devotion displayed by the men of whom Caldwell was so excellent an example." Several other generals spoke quite as feelingly, as did the Comte de Paris, the French military observer, in his history of the war. But though, at the peace, Stager and Eckert were brevetted Brigadier-generals, and the department superintendents and chief operators Lieutenant-colonels, nothing was done for the rank and file.

With the surrender of the southern armies, the Federal Government took charge of all telegraph lines throughout the southern states, Colonels Gilmore, Clowry, Caldwell and others assuming the superintendency of various areas, in which for seven months they exercised a semi-military control of the wires, in order to combat guerrilla warfare and other lawless and disturbing activities. The commercial lines were restored to their former owners on December 1, 1865.

CHAPTER XIV

THE OCEAN IS CONQUERED

O lonely Bay of Trinity,
O dreary shores, give ear!
Lean down unto the white-lipped sea,
The voice of God to hear.
From world to world His couriers fly
Thought-winged and shod with fire;
The angel of His stormy sky
Rides down the sunken wire....
For lo! the fall of ocean's wall
Space mocked and time outrun,
And 'round the world the thought of all
Is as the thought of one!

JOHN G. WHITTIER, 1866

CYRUS W. FIELD was not invariably the unquenchable optimist, the indomitable will. There was in his life at least one moment—of the sort which must now and then come to all great doers—when his iron control gave way. Descendants of some of the original promoters of the project have heard from their grandfathers of a meeting of the American directors immediately after it was known that the cable of 1858 had failed, at which Field, his soul sapped by the long strain, broke down and wept as weakly as any child. It was Peter Cooper who rose to the occasion and put iron back into the spirits of those present by saying, "We will go on." Then Field, recovering from his momentary weakness, took up again the chief burden of promotion.

Wilson G. Hunt was one of the stockholders who favored trying to recover their losses by going forward; but Mr. Cooper says, "it was like pulling teeth out of Roberts and Taylor to get more money from them." However, money was soon raised to pay Field's expenses on another trip to England—he never asked any salary for these labors—and he crossed in May, 1859. Many people in Britain ridiculed the idea of another gamble with the Atlantic. The company was held in such low esteem by many that a man was once able to buy a £1,000 certificate of its stock for 30 guineas. Worse still, a New York man showed Field a certificate for $10,000 worth of stock in the New York, Newfoundland and London, which he had bought for $10.

But on June 8th, the directors held a meeting in London, and voted to raise £600,000, with which to lay another cable, and if possible, repair the old one. It was easy enough to vote money, but collecting it was another matter. By January, 1860, only £72,000 had been raised, and the directors were discouraged by the lack of interest. The British Government had guaranteed the Red Sea cable, which had proved a failure, and the disgruntled ministers therefore refused to back so great a hazard as a challenge to the Atlantic.

A panicky feeling spread through American business in 1860, because of the threatened separation of the Union, and Field's paper house, in which he was no longer active but in which most of his small fortune was invested, was so near bankruptcy that it had to suspend payment. The breaking out of the war made it impossible to go ahead with the cable project, but stimulated capitalists with the determination to push it as soon as the war was over. Its importance now began to be more manifest. Field wrote from London to Secretary of State Seward in June, 1861, "I never had more confidence in the ultimate success of the Atlantic Telegraph Company than I have to-day."

When in November of that year, a zealous Federal warship captain took from a British steamer Messrs. Mason and Slidell, two men commissioned by the Confederate Government to go to England and persuade that nation to recognize their government, war was threatened for several weeks, and was averted only when the Federal Government disavowed the act. Field again wrote to Seward, pointing out how easily and quickly the matter might have been settled by telegraph, had a cable existed, instead of dragging on by mail for weeks and months, while partisans on both sides fomented the war spirit. The London *Times* remarked, "We nearly went to war with America because we had not a telegraph across the Atlantic." Seward, in a letter to Ambassador Adams, suggested that when Adams found opportunity, he might tell Earl Russell, then Prime Minister, that President Lincoln highly approved the project.

Field went to England again in 1862, and was received by Russell, but the Cabinet would promise nothing towards helping the project. Good politicians as they were, they wanted to sit tight and see what happened first; in fact, a majority of official England were convinced that the Confederacy were going to win and set up a permanent government. Gladstone and Bright, who foresaw the North's ultimate victory, were partisans of Field. George Saward, secretary of the company, wrote a magazine article on the subject, in which he remarked that Mr. Field had crossed the ocean twenty-five times, and had never asked for a shilling of remuneration for his time. Professor William Thomson wrote to him, "If any degree of perseverance can be sufficient to deserve success, and any amount of value in any object can make it worth striving for, success ought to attend the efforts you and the directors are making for a result of world-wide beneficence."

Julius Reuter, whose news agency was rapidly rising to greatness in those days, told Field that he did not believe that one wire between Newfoundland and Ireland would be enough for the business, and that his own agency, he thought, would send through the cable in its first year as much as £5,000 worth of messages. All this was a strong tonic to Field, and his enthusiasm was such that he became a nuisance even to some of his friends. He used to tell in after years of seeing men hastily cross the street or dodge into doorways when they would see him coming.

In December, 1863, he sold his interest in the paper business, in order that he might give his whole time and thought to the cable. On the following February 6th, the London *Telegraphic Journal* reported that "The Atlantic Telegraph project is again attracting public attention. Mr. Cyrus W. Field, one of the leading spirits of the undertaking, is again among us, full of hope and ready to embark once more in the gigantic enterprise."

Field remained in London through that spring, scheming, boosting, slowly building up the stock subscriptions. At a dinner in April, he announced that the owners of the *Great Eastern* had agreed to lease the vessel to the cable company until the end of the year 1865 for a compensation of £50,000 in shares of the company, if the cable was successfully laid; if not, there would be no charge. It was a generous offer, but would not have been made had not the ship been a sort of white elephant on the hands of her owners. This noble vessel was a symptom of a sort of giantism which is again afflicting shipbuilders in the fourth decade of the twentieth century. Like some human beings, she was born half a century ahead of her time. She was 680 feet long over all, 83 feet wide and had a displacement of 27,000 tons. Her interior was arranged to accommodate, if necessary, 4,000 passengers and 400 officers and crew. All other vessels of her period were mere toys beside her. She was intended for the England-Australia trade, around the Cape of Good Hope, but never ran in it. Among her troubles were the facts that there were then no piers large enough to accommodate her comfortably, and not enough business for so large a vessel. She had made some passenger trips across the Atlantic, but had proven most valuable as a troop-ship for the British Government, in which service she carried as many as 5,000 soldiers at a load. With the laying of the Atlantic Cable she at last found her true vocation, and continued in it for many years.

In the latter part of 1864, she berthed at the Medway, and three great tanks for the cable were built into her below decks. No other ship afloat could have carried 2,300 miles of cable. The tanks alone weighed 2,000 tons, the cable 7,000, and she stowed 8,500 tons of coal in her bunkers. These preparations were carried forward because of Field's implicit confidence that Grant would soon take Richmond, and the Civil War be at an end.

It so fell out, and in July, 1865, the Irish end of the cable was landed in Foilhummerum Bay, one of the inlets of Valentia Harbor, and spliced to one of the big coils aboard the *Great Eastern*. Again there were ceremonies; the Knight of Kerry, Glass, the cable-maker, Field and others delivered orations. At 7:15 P.M. the huge vessel's paddle-wheels and screws began to revolve—for she used both kinds of propulsion—and she moved majestically away into the sunset, with three small satellite vessels, the *Hawk*, the *Terrible* (whose name must have seemed comic when one compared her with the monster leader) and the *Sphinx* accompanying her. Captain James Anderson was on the bridge, and among the authorities aboard were Cyrus W. Field, Professor Thomson and C. V. De Sauty, chief electrician of the expedition and representative of the Telegraph Construction and Maintenance Company, which was owned jointly by Glass, Elliott & Company and the London Gutta Percha Works. No longer was De Sauty a "myth," a mere mysterious voice whose very name was a puzzle to compositors. A newspaper humorist of 1858, had thus apostrophized him:

> Thou operator, silent, glum,
>   Why wilt thou act so naughty?
> Do tell us what your name is—come!
>   De Santy or De Sauty?
>
> Don't think to humbug any more,
>   Shut up there in your shanty,
> But solve the problem once for all—
>   De Sauty or De Santy?

As usual, communication was kept up with the shore through the cable. No less than four times within the first ten days out did the signals cease. Each time the cable must be cut, the great bulk turned ponderously around, the cable shifted to the bow and slowly reeled in as the vessel back-tracked until the fault was found. Three times short pieces of wire were found thrust through the insulation so as to destroy its effectiveness. At the first discovery this was thought to have been an accident. When a second precisely similar damage was found, all decided that some workman had committed sabotage; but at the third discovery, the majority of the experts veered once more to the belief that these bits of wire had gotten thrust into the cable while it was being reeled. After another break, on August 2nd, a great disaster occurred—the end of the cable slipped from the vessel while it was turning, and was lost in the sea. The *Great Eastern* was then only 660 miles from Newfoundland.

For nearly ten days the big ship slowly cruised back and forth, dragging the bottom with a grapnel, in search of the cable. At length, on the 11th, it was hooked, and slowly the winch began to raise it. It had been hoisted 765 fathoms through the green water when a hawser broke, and down it went into the depths again. With it sank the hope of all on board of completing the task that year; for the grappling apparatus was now recognized as far from being as efficient as it should be.

Field's disappointment must have been racking, though externally he had all through the crisis been seemingly the calmest man on the ship. "I shall never forget the day," said Thomson, then Sir William, in an address at Dundee, Scotland, two years later, "when we last gave up hope of finishing the work in 1865. On that day Cyrus Field renewed a proposal for the adoption of the plan which has been adopted, and which has led to the successful completion of the enterprise. Field's last prospectus was completed in the grand saloon of the *Great Eastern* on the day when we gave up all hope for 1865."

On the morning of the 12th, the *Terrible* was directed to proceed to America with letters telling of the failure, while the *Great Eastern* and the other vessels turned back towards England. There was one bright ray of hope through the murk; the smooth functioning of the big steamer had convinced all of the party that she could lay the cable if it could be done at all. Field returned with her, for he must again convince British capital that the project was practicable. He returned to America the following month, but commuted again to London in December. "Mr. Field," said Thomas Brassey, one of the large English stockholders, to him, "don't be discouraged. Go down to the company and tell them to go ahead, and whatever the cost, I will bear one-tenth of the whole."

It was decided that the best course was the organization of a new company. Despite the numerous failures, promotion was easier now; there was a growing conviction that the task was feasible, and success just around the corner. Ten men sat down around a table in London, and after a brief talk, agreed to put up £10,000 apiece. Those who rail at Capital as timid and pusillanimous must revise their adjectives a bit when they study history. One cannot be too categorical on such subjects. Capital is often rabbit-like in its fear at times of crisis, but at other times it has dared greatly and performed services of inestimable value to civilization.

The Telegraph Construction and Maintenance Company took £100,000 worth of stock in the new corporation. Then the books were opened to the public through the banking house of J. S. Morgan & Company, and within two weeks the whole £600,000 was subscribed. The new company's organization was completed on the first day of March, and within five months from that day, the cable had been laid and was carrying messages.

The new corporation, known as the Anglo-American Company, contracted with the preceding one, the Atlantic Telegraph Company, to manufacture and lay a cable in 1866, for doing which it was entitled to what was virtually a preference dividend of 25 per cent. As surety for this, a first claim was secured by the Atlantic Telegraph Company to the new concern upon the revenue of the cable (or cables) to the extent of £125,000 yearly. The New York, Newfoundland and London also agreed to contribute from their revenue a further annual sum of £25,-000, on condition that a workable cable be laid in 1866. An agreement to all these points was signed by Field, subject to ratification by the companies in America, which was quickly obtained.

The cable was manufactured at the rate of twenty miles per day, and at noon on June 30th, the *Great Eastern* sailed from Sheerness with 2,375 miles of it on board. On July 12th, the shore end in Valentia inlet was spliced to that aboard the vessel, and once more she sailed for America, with the ever-buoyant Field aboard. Day after day, night after night, her great pistons glided in their channels, and the cable poured over her stern without a hitch. At last they had learned how it was done! All through the journey, she avoided by several miles the course of the previous summer. Ten days out, she passed near the place where the cable of '65 had been lost.

On the morning of the 23rd Field telegraphed Glass, "Please obtain the latest news from Egypt, China, India and distant places for us to forward to the United States on our arrival at Heart's Content." The Seven Weeks' War between Prussia and Austria was raging when the vessel started, and the news now came that Austria was to be driven out of the German confederation. "Please send us on Thursday afternoon," asked Field, "the price that day for cotton in Liverpool, and the London quotation for consols, United States five-twenty bonds, Illinois Central and Erie Railway shares, and also bank rate of interest. The above we shall send to New York on our arrival, and I will obtain the latest news from the States, and send you in return." Next day, Tuesday the 24th, he notified Glass that, "We are within 400 miles of Heart's Content, and expect to be there on Friday. When shall the Atlantic Cable be open for public business?" To which Glass replied, an hour and a quarter later, "If you land the cable on Friday, I see no reason why it should not be open on Saturday."

At 7 o'clock on Friday morning, the 27th, the tiny hamlet of Heart's Content in Trinity Bay, the cable terminal, was in sight. At 8:15 Field, undoubtedly the happiest man living at that moment, went ashore. All the way across, he had been the most confident man on board. The day was spent in splicing the shore section of cable on one of the smaller vessels, and at 5 P.M. it was successfully landed and connected. Immediately it began working perfectly.

Justin McCarthy, in his *History of Our Own Times,* says, "The history of human invention has not a more inspiriting example of patience living down discouragements and perseverance triumphing over defeat." And Field now proceeded happily to another confutation of his critics. On August 9th, the *Great Eastern* (still with the promoter aboard) and one escort, the *Medway,* set out to find, if possible, the end of the lost cable of '65. They had better grappling and hoisting equipment this time. The other two small ships had already preceded them to the spot. For three weeks they fished and searched the ocean's bottom. Three times they hooked the cable and drew it up some distance, then lost it. Finally, they brought up several miles of it which had become detached from the rest. Then they moved farther eastward and tried again. At last, on September 1st, they got a firm grip on it about 720 miles east of Newfoundland, and at 2:15 the following morning, they had the end aboard.

No one on the ship was asleep when the end was taken into the electricians' room, and the test made to see whether the wire was alive or dead. The London *Times* of September 5th, pictured dramatically the scene at Valentia:

The recovery of the cable of 1865 from the very lowest depth of the Atlantic seems to have taken the world by surprise. It is not, however, too much to say that no class of the community has felt more astonished than those who are best acquainted with the difficulties of the task—the electricians....

Night and day for a whole year an electrician has been on duty, watching the tiny ray of light through which signals are given, and twice every day the whole length of wire—1,240 miles—has been tested for conductivity and insulation.... Suddenly last Sunday morning at a quarter to six, while the light was being watched by Mr. May, he observed a peculiar indication about it which showed at once to his experienced eye that a message was near at hand. In a few minutes afterwards, the unsteady flickering was changed to coherency, if we may use such a term, and at once the cable began to speak:

"Canning to Glass—I have much pleasure in speaking to you through the 1865 cable. Just going to make splice."

"Never shall I forget that eventful moment," said Field, "when in answer to our question to Valentia whether the cable of 1866, which we had a few weeks previously laid, was in good working order, and the cable across the Gulf of St. Lawrence had been repaired, in an instant came back those six memorable letters, 'Both OK.' I left the room, I went to my cabin, I locked the door; I could no longer restrain my tears."

One of the first things which he did was to send word to his wife of their success via Valentia and the new cable. The recovered strand was spliced to the surplus in the hold of the *Great Eastern,* and once more it turned back to Newfoundland. On September 8th, the second wire was landed at Heart's Content, and began working flawlessly. The *Times* was right; the recapture and putting to work of that cable lost a year ago appealed to the public imagination more powerfully than the laying of the new line. Field was no longer a fanatic, but a world hero. There was one noted French scientist, however, Bobinet, who had never believed that the Atlantic could be spanned by telegraph, and refused to concede that it had been done, even after the cable was in service.

The directors of the company granted each man on the ships a month's pay on their return to England. Professor Thomson, Glass, Captain Anderson of the *Great Eastern,* and the chief electrician. Thomson, by the way, contributed another important item to the cable system—the siphon recorder—wherein a slender curved metal tube but slightly larger than an old-fashioned knitting needle, siphons ink from a reservoir and automatically records a Morse message on a tape in a zigzag line resembling the serrations of Morse's early sawtooth type. This gradually supplanted the mirror galvanometer everywhere. Go into a cable office to-day, and you will still see that thin, intelligent little steel finger tracing its crooked ink mark on an endless ribbon of tape.

Lord Derby, then Prime Minister, in announcing the honors in behalf of the Queen, said that only the fact that Americans were forbidden to receive such honors prevented Mr. Field's being one of the knights; and the Government very sincerely regretted its inability to show its appreciation for his achievement in this permanent and traditional way. However, during the great celebrations on both sides of the water, he was banquetted, praised, given honorary degrees and be-medalled again and again.

The Anglo-American Company started out with highly exaggerated ideas as to prices of service, the charge for messages at first being £20—nearly $100!—for a minimum of ten words. This continued from July 28th, until October 31st, during which time, even at that outrageous rate, the company handled 2,772 messages, and had an average daily intake of $2,500. Then the rate was halved to £10 or about $48.60 for ten words. In 1867, Peter Cooper wrote to the New York *Tribune* that the two cables were working at only five per cent of their capacity; to which Greeley retorted bitingly that if the exorbitant rates were cut, the company would do an enormously greater business. Even at the rate then obtaining, the income had risen to more than $2,800 daily.

Taking the editor at his word, on December 1, 1867, the rate was almost halved again, this time dropping to a five-guinea minimum; and again the income rose. From the time the first cable opened in July, 1866, until August 31, 1868, 63,985 messages were sent, and the average daily income for the whole period was close to $3,000. More than $2,400,000 profit over cost of operation was shown, and cable shares were soaring. On September 1, 1868, the total business still occupied only one cable no more than six hours daily. That day, the minimum for ten words was reduced to £3 7s. 6d.—a little over $16—which gave another boost to receipts.

It was no wonder that Field, in 1867, was able to pay off in full all creditors with whom he had compromised in 1860, and add 7 per cent interest, distributing in this way a total of $171,000. There was a memorable dinner given him at Willis's in London in 1868, with the Duke of Argyll in the chair and John Bright, Ferdinand de Lesseps and other notables present, on which occasion it was remarked that Field had then crossed the ocean forty times in behalf of the cable. He himself, speaking of the fluctuations in cable stock, pointed out that the man already mentioned who had paid only thirty guineas for £1,000 worth of stock was now receiving £160 interest per annum on it.

In 1870, he was again agitating in behalf of an ocean cable, this time a projected bridging of the Pacific. The idea had been taken up by the New York Chamber of Commerce that year, and Field sponsored a memorial to Congress, asking aid for such a line. The route selected was that over which a cable was eventually laid: via Hawaii and Midway Island to China and Japan. But the Pacific was too vast, our connections with the Far East as yet seemed too unimportant to gain any considerable support for so costly and hazardous a project. In 1871, Field changed his plan of attack, and attempted to interest the Czar of Russia in a cable whose western end should be on the island of Sakhalin or the adjacent Siberian coast. He even made two trips to Russia in the hope of furthering the scheme, but without result. Thirty years passed before that Pacific cable was laid.

In 1868, the Anglo-American Company was much perturbed to learn of the organization of a company, part French and part British, to lay a cable from France to the United States. The company was promoted by Julius Reuter, the news-agency man, and Baron Emile d'Erlanger of Paris. The capital was fixed at $6,000,000, and so high in favor were cables just then that in less than eight days the stock was all subscribed for by leading banking houses of Europe, and the shares were at 2 and 3 per cent premium. The plan was to lay the cable from Brest, on the Breton coast, to the Island of St. Pierre, just off the shores of Newfoundland, and thence to Duxbury, Massachusetts; a total distance of 3,333 miles, or more than twice as long as the line from Newfoundland to Ireland.

When the company asked for a landing privilege from the United States, the Anglo-American and New York, Newfoundland & London Companies fought against it, and in turn tried to wring from Congress an exclusive right to land their own wires on the shores of Massachusetts. A bill was introduced in Congress by Senator Sumner, giving the old company a twenty-year monopoly. Peter Cooper asked the Attorney-General whether the N. Y., N. & F. would have a right to lay a cable from Newfoundland to the shores of the United States if it just did so without asking permission. The Attorney-General said No. Newspaper opinion was divided on the subject. The New York *Herald* took up the cause of the French company, called the others "the telegraph monopoly ring," and characterized the bill introduced by "that eminent inside jobber, Hon. Charles Sumner," as "about the meanest swindle ever before Congress."

In the end, Congress granted the concession, and in the summer of 1869, the *Great Eastern* laid the cable without a hitch. Her tanks had been so increased in size that she could carry 2,752 miles of cable. This covered the 2,584 miles from Brest to St. Pierre, and a smaller vessel had preceded her to St. Pierre with sufficient cable to finish the job to Duxbury, which place was reached July 23rd.

Just four years after it was laid, the French cable was gathered in by the Anglo-American Company. Long afterwards another French company laid another cable to the United States, which still endures and is independent. The story of the '70's is one of rapid increase of cables across the Atlantic. The Anglo-American owned most of them, though the Western Union laid a couple—for it now began to be apparent that the wisest course was to lay them in pairs, so that when one was out of service—as it frequently was—the other could bear the burden. Finally, the Western Union absorbed the Anglo-American, and thereby gained a predominance in Atlantic Cable business. Of

John W. Mackay and his Commercial Company's Atlantic and Pacific cables, we shall speak at a later moment.

The South Atlantic was bridged in 1873, by a cable laid from Portugal to Pernambuco, Brazil. But several years before that, the United States had begun reaching out towards her southern neighbors. Late one summer afternoon in 1865, just before dusk, Captain James A. Scrymser of New York, and his friend, Alfred Pell, Jr., were rambling along the then fair rural banks of the Harlem River or sitting under an apple tree near by. Scrymser saw a great future in ocean cables, and called attention to the fact that a vast untilled field lay to southward. Pell agreed to give him some backing, and with that encouragement, Scrymser became the chief promoter of the International Ocean Telegraph Company.

Congress in 1866, granted to the company a fourteen-year monopoly for a cable to Cuba, while the State of Florida did better still by giving the company a twenty-year concession, as well as the right to construct land lines throughout the State. General William F. ("Baldy") Smith of Civil War fame, was the first President of the company. On August 29th, of the same year the Spanish Government blessed the project with a concession in the name of Queen Isabella II ("Whom God guard") to General Smith ("God guard you many years") as representative of the company. The cable was made in England and laid in July, 1867. There were two stretches of it—one of 133 miles from Punta Rassa, Florida, to Key West, the other of 101 miles from Key West to Havana.

In 1870, the company decided to connect Cuba with Jamaica and Panama; then Puerto Rico and Trinidad were brought into the chain. The governments of these various islands and states promised handsome subsidies, which were not always regularly paid. But the Western Union was looking with a jealous eye on the rapid growth of this prosperous concern, and by 1873, it had succeeded in getting a clutch on a controlling interest in it. A "reorganization" thereupon took place, William Orton being made President and Norvin Green Vice-President.

COILING THE CABLE IN THE HOLD OF THE GREAT EASTERN

THE GREAT EASTERN LAYING THE CABLE

Scrymser, dissatisfied with subordination to a great monopoly, sold out of the company in 1878, and went about the organization of cable communication with Mexico and South America. At that time, all messages from the United States to South America must be sent via Europe, which was so expensive as to be usually impracticable. But by this time, cables had become so numerous that their prosperity had declined somewhat, and Scrymser had much trouble in putting over his new idea because of the skittishness of capital. But at last he succeeded in filling up the subscription books of the Mexican Cable Company with a capital of $500,000, and in 1879, organized the Central and South American Cable Company, capital, $3,000,000. Later, the word "telegraph" was substituted for "cable" in the names of both companies.

The Mexican Government gave the Mexican Company a half-century monopoly. Its original cable, 738 miles long, ran from Galveston via Tampico to Vera Cruz, from which port a land line led to Mexico City. Service was inaugurated on March 11, 1881, and President Garfield, then just one week in office (and so soon to leave it!), sent the first message to President Gonzalez of Mexico. For the Central and South American Company, a land line from Vera Cruz crossed the Isthmus of Tehuantepec, on the Pacific coast, where cable took up the work and proceeded down the coast, touching at ports in Salvador, Nicaragua, Panama, Colombia and Ecuador, and ending at Callao, Peru, whence a land wire led to Lima. And thus was begun the powerful company later known as All-America Cables.

In 1890, the South American cable was extended to Valparaiso, Chile; and in the following year the Transandine Telegraph Company, with 1,200 miles of line connecting Chile with Argentina was purchased. By 1905, three cables instead of one connected Galveston with Vera Cruz, and still could not handle the business. It was therefore deemed essential to lay a cable directly from New York City via Cuba to Colon in Panama, cross the isthmus and there connect with the South American wire. This was achieved by August, 1907, and in later years the cable was duplicated and triplicated. In 1917, after many years of contention, a decision of the Brazilian Supreme Court gave Scrymser's company the right to enter that country; and as the shortest means of reaching it, cables were thrown northward from Buenos Aires to Santos and Rio de Janeiro.

Scrymser died in January, 1918, and was succeeded by John L. Merrill, who had entered the company's service thirty-four years before as an office boy. In December of that year the two companies were united under the name of All-America Cables. The subsequent history of that company is told in another chapter.

The gradual improvement in the quality of cables, beginning with those earlier ones, is shown in the testimony of Manager Carson of the Anglo-American Company in London in 1896, before a committee considering the feasibility of an all-British cable across the Pacific. He said that the cable laid in 1865 and completed in the following year suffered no interruptions for more than three years. In the fourth year, 1870, there were 31 days when it was out of commission; in the following year there were 171 days blank; in 1872, it functioned without a break, but in 1873, it died forever. By that time the gutta-percha insulation had gotten in such bad condition that it would not stand lifting to the surface of the water for repairs. This cable lasted only seven years.

The cable of 1866 started off badly by being off duty for 99 days in 1867; in 1868, 69 days; in 1869, 93 days; in 1870, 153 days; in 1871, 154 days. Then it worked happily along for two years without a murmur; but in 1874 it lost 92 days. Again it braced up and worked without a break, though more and more feebly, until 1877, when it, too, breathed its last. Its life had been ten years. Carson said that the breaks always occurred where the cable passed over rock; that there were two stony ridges in the Atlantic which gave them all their trouble.

Each cable seemed a little better than the last. The one laid by the French company in 1869, ran for three years with no trouble, and then the hiati began. But this line lived for twenty-four years, passing out in 1893. During that time it had had twenty interruptions, one of which continued for ten months. The next cable laid by the Anglo-American—in 1873—and the next one—1874—had neither of them any interruptions until 1880. But breaks began in all of them, however, sooner or later.

From Harper's Weekly

NEPTUNE—"AHOY, THERE! GET OFF OF THAT THERE CABLE, CAN'T YER? THAT'S THE WAY T'OTHER ONE WAS BROKEN."

In 1900, there were thirteen cables crossing the North Atlantic, and seldom were all of them in working order at once.

In 1896, Mr. Carson was gloomily certain that gutta-percha was being adulterated and was no longer what it used to be. But cable builders by that time had learned that it must be carefully protected from contact with the sea's rough floor and from marine borers, such as the teredo. It is still the standard insulation for deep-sea cables, though some shorter ones use rubber.

The modern cable is a built-up affair of many layers. Around the copper conductor through which the message passes, there is often wrapped nowadays a thin ribbon of nickel-iron alloy, which greatly increases the speed at which the cable may be worked. Next comes the gutta-percha insulation; and to protect it against borers a brass tape is wound around it, save in water too deep for the borers to exist. Next comes a winding of jute yarn which serves as a cushion for the armor or sheathing wires. These wires, of high tension galvanized steel in deep water, and galvanized wrought-iron of larger size in shallower soundings, are wound in a long spiral. The armor increases until near the shore it is doubly heavy—this to protect the cable against ships' anchors, trawling gear, and in northern latitudes, against ice. An outer double wrapping of jute yarn or tape dipped in a compound of tar and pitch preserves the armor wires from corrosion. In deep water the cable, wrapping and all, is only an inch in diameter, and weighs two tons to the nautical mile, but near the shore, it may be three and one-half inches in diameter and weigh as much as thirty tons to the mile. Cable made in this fashion has been lifted after forty years' submersion and found to be in excellent condition, even to the tarred outer wrapping.

A British cable laid between Halifax and Bermuda in the early '90's was the first to plumb a depth of 17,000 feet of water. The Atlantic is now webbed with cables, several of them crossing each other at various points. In the Eastern Hemisphere, not only European waters, but those around Asia and Africa and through the East Indian Archipelago, are a maze of cables, most of the mileage being dominated by British capital or influence. All told, there are nearly 300,000 miles of cable in the great network encompassing the globe.

The submarine cable has other enemies than those already mentioned. In that popular outdoor sport called war, which the world is still too uncivilized to give up, cables are ruthlessly hooked up and destroyed, if there is any chance of the so-called enemy's deriving any aid or comfort through them. In the World War, for example, the Allies quickly cut the German cables leading towards America, thereby causing the Reich much inconvenience.

Earthquakes are another occasional menace. In November, 1929, a violent tremor agitated a long, narrow area extending northward and southward just south of Newfoundland. A tidal wave rushed up on the shores of that island, killing many people. Twelve out of the twenty-one cables crossing the North Atlantic were broken. Nowadays every cable company maintains a fleet of big cable-laying and repair ships, and from every direction, numbers of these rushed to the scene at once. Their experiences during the next few weeks would be worth a chapter in themselves if one had room for it. The winter was particularly unpropitious, and they worked in bitter gales and mountainous seas, menaced at times by icebergs. Many weeks passed before all the cables were in repair again.

Modern cables may cost $2,000 per mile to build, and from half a million to a million dollars a year are required to maintain one across the Atlantic. Furthermore, competition has reduced the rate from the $9.75 a word or thereabouts of 1866 to 25 cents a word to-day. Hence a high capacity for wordage is necessary. Duplex cabling, that is, sending a message in each direction simultaneously on the same wire, was introduced in 1871, and has been a great boon to cable owners. From a maximum of 15 words per minute in 1858, the capacity of a cable has been increased in one way and another to more than 2,500 words per minute at the time this book is written.

CHAPTER XV

WESTWARD TOWARDS THE PACIFIC AND ASIA

> Sink the poles, boys, firm and strong,
>   Deep and close together.
> Solder the joints of the mystic thong
>   And let it stand forever.
> Shouting still, by rock and rill,
>   In morning's crimson glow,
> "Four thousand miles already up,
>   And thousands more to go!"
>
> JAMES D. REID

THE first telegraph wire—O'Rielly's—had not yet reached St. Louis in 1848 when the *New Era* of that city opined that "A streak of lightning ought to be established to form an instantaneous and constant communication between St. Louis and the coast of the Pacific." The treaty of Guadalupe Hidalgo had just confirmed us in the possession of the far Western lands seized by us early in the Mexican War—California, and indeed, all the territory west of the Rockies not included in the Louisiana Purchase. But gold had not yet been discovered in Sutter's mill-stream, and the demand of the St. Louis editor therefore had a touch of the prophetic about it.

The westward surge of '49, the magical development of a new world west of the Sierras of course increased the desire for quick communication. In 1852, Senator Stephen A. Douglas of Illinois presented in the Senate a petition from that inveterate promoter, Henry O'Rielly, described as "a man of great experience in the business of telegraphs throughout the United States," who desired to establish a line from the Missouri River to the Pacific sands. He asked no subsidy, either in money or land; only desired that he might be protected from the irascible

306

Indians. He received no encouragement, but from that time forward, the notion of a transcontinental telegraph was never permitted entirely to lapse. California senators and representatives introduced bills for the aid of such enterprises from time to time, but for years, nothing was done with them, save to lay them on that mythical Table which is the grave of so many projects.

In 1853, James Eddy, a New England telegraph man, spurred by that other busy brain, D. H. Craig, suggested to Congress the laying of a wire underground to California. It was to be encased in gutta-percha and then in a metal tube, and sunk three feet below the surface. This was the only feasible way, said the promoters, to maintain an unbroken line of communication, secure from storms, Indians and other hazards—as if Indians couldn't have dug up the wire in five minutes! But the project did not develop further, perhaps because it was learned that Europe was having trouble with its subterranean telegraph wires. Mr. Eddy and his co-promoter, H. O. Alden, as recompense for their building of the line, asked the Government for only 1,500,000 acres of land!

California that year began building her own system of telegraphs. How that vivacious, up-and-coming community, with its unlimited means, had endured the lack of instantaneous communication during the four years past is beyond our conception. Hubert Howe Bancroft says that the first telegraph on the Pacific Coast was erected by two members of the Merchants' Exchange of San Francisco, and completed in September, 1853. It was six miles in length and ran from the Exchange on Sacramento Street to Point Lobos, where (as well as on Telegraph Hill) there had been a semaphore to announce the coming of ships. The new electric telegraph had the same object. There was a considerable celebration at its opening, with all the San Francisco editors, foreign consuls and other notabilities present.

An attempt had been made in 1852, to organize a company to connect San Francisco by wire with Sacramento, Stockton, Marysville and other places, but the scheme did not burgeon satisfactorily. In 1853, Nevada City, Grass Valley and Auburn raised enough money to string one wire on trees connecting those three towns, and this was the first real interurban telegraph in the Far West. In that autumn of '53, the dormant company of the previous year was reorganized as the California State Telegraph Company, and built a line around the bay, via San José, through Sacramento to Marysville. Rates were high— $2.00 for ten words to Sacramento or Marysville, a dollar for ten words from San Francisco to San José, only a few miles distant.

Another company, the Alta Telegraph, was organized shortly after this, and ran a wire from Sacramento to Nevada City and adjacent mining towns. In 1856, the Northern Telegraph Company built from Marysville to Yreka, far in the north; another concern threw a line down the coast to Los Angeles; and there were yet other, smaller projects. An important undertaking of 1858, was the organization of the Placerville, Humboldt and Salt Lake Telegraph Company, headed by Frederick A. Bee, which hoped to construct a line across the Sierras and through the Humboldt Valley to the Great Salt Lake. In the spring of '59, their wire reached Carson City, Nevada, and in the following year Virginia City and Fort Churchill, 150 miles to eastward, which was as far as it could afford to go. One of the company's directors had been sent to Washington to solicit Government aid in building to Salt Lake City, but his mission was unsuccessful. This line was facetiously called "Bee's grapevine" ("grapevine telegraph" was a popular slang term for rumor), because it was pegged to trees instead of poles wherever possible. Storms and falling boughs wrecked it every few days, and the tangled wire was pulled from the thickets by wagoners and used in mending their harness and vehicles, they pretending to think that that was why the wire was strung along the road. This line was a highly useful agency, however, during the early days of Washoe silver mining, and eventually became the pioneer unit of the transcontinental telegraph.

During the "Utah War," the trouble with the Mormons in

LANDING THE CABLE AT HEART'S CONTENT, 1866

1857-58, Henry O'Rielly, John J. Speed and Tal P. Shaffner offered to build a line to Utah for the service of the United States troops sent there, if they were given protection against the Indians by a line of military posts. O'Rielly also stipulated for protection against the Mormons, "who are resolved on maintaining their rocky fastnesses." They promised to have the instruments clicking within a hundred days from the time of breaking ground—which offer was a detriment to their cause, for it sounded too much like moonshine; most people declared it absurd.

But Secretary of War Floyd believed in them, and tried to induce Congress to provide the desired protection, but in vain. However, the three promoters quickly changed their strategy, and offered for a subsidy to build a line through to California. This time they had Senator Broderick on their side, and so much noise was made over the subject that Acting Governor Thomas B. Cuming of Nebraska told the Legislature in his annual message on December 9, 1857, that the arrangements had been perfected, and that they might congratulate each other on the actual commencement of the work. But Broderick's bill, introduced in the following May, failed because, as Bancroft says, Gwin, the other California Senator, "was opposed to whatever Broderick favored." And thus O'Rielly's last effort at telegraph promotion failed.

Meanwhile, the thought had been taken up by another Rochester man, a sounder planner than O'Rielly, with no lesser vision, but more careful in his steps, and with better backing. Hiram Sibley was one of the few men living with sufficient will power and vigor of intellect to grapple fearlessly with the problem of bridging the continent by wire. He proposed it again and again in the middle '50's to his Western Union Board of Directors, but they were too timid to attack it; it seemed too hazardous, too great an opportunity to risk a fortune and probably gain nothing. They thought it ought to be done by an outside organization; the sinews and prestige of the Western Union should not be hazarded. Finally Sibley, after wasting many heated words, including even profanity, on them, said, "Gentlemen, if you won't join hands with me in this thing, I'll go it alone."

In 1857, he brought his project before the North American Telegraph Association, hoping to find enough men of vision there to put the thing through; but though committees were appointed to ponder the matter, nothing was actually done. The American company and Senator Gwin favored the southern route through Arizona just about to be adopted by Butterfield's Overland Mail coaches; while Sibley, Cyrus Field and others argued for a central route, via the Great Salt Lake.

For three or four sessions, Sibley camped on Congress's door-step as a seeker of aid for a western wire line. By this time California was becoming loudly vocal in its demand for some better means of communication than the plodding three-weeks-and-more of the Overland Mail between St. Louis and San Francisco. Russell, Majors & Waddell started the Pony Express that year, which was some improvement, but still did not quite fill the bill. Had the express promoters had the faintest idea as to how quickly a telegraph line could and would be strung along their route, they would never have sunk that million dollars in their gallant, dauntless but inevitably doomed enterprise. But few people believed that a telegraph line would become a reality under five or ten years' time.

When Sibley went down to Washington in 1860, he took with him as aides two noted journalists, Samuel Bowles of the Springfield *Republican* and Isaac Butts, editor of the most influential Democratic newspaper in western New York. The time was now riper and telegraph progress elsewhere had made the project seem more feasible. Even some Western Union directors were warming to it. After some vigorous lobbying, and with the support of Secretary of the Treasury Howell Cobb, an act was passed on June 16, 1860, "to facilitate communication between the Atlantic and the Pacific States by electric telegraph."

The bill as first drawn was an outright concession to Sibley;

but in its final form, it directed the Secretary of the Treasury to advertise for sealed bids for the construction of a line to be completed within two years after July 31, 1860, from a point on the Missouri River to San Francisco. The Government was to have preferential use of the line for ten years, and pay the owners not more than $40,000 yearly, which was to be "taken out in trade." If more Government messages than that passed over the line, the excess was to be reported to Congress for allowance. The rate from the Missouri River to San Francisco was not to be more than $3 a word. The subsidy did not begin until the line was in actual operation. Messages for the Coast Survey, the Smithsonian Institution and National Observatory were to be carried free. The contractor had the right to the same terms whenever he should extend the line to Oregon.

Although by the terms of the act, the concession was to be given to the lowest bidder, by some singular chance it went to the highest—Sibley, at $40,000. Ben F. Ficklin of the Pony Express offered to do it for $35,000 a year, and two others for $29,000 and $25,000 respectively. But oddly enough, before the time came for giving bond for the fulfilment of the contract, all of the other three had withdrawn from the competition. Associated with Sibley as bondsmen and later as stockholders when he turned his concession over to a corporation, one finds such names as Jephtha D. Wade, Norvin Green, Fred A. Bee, Charles M. Stebbins and several of the old Rochester neighbors —nearly all connected with the larger telegraph companies of the land, but with Western Union influence largely predominant. In fact, the new company was but the Western Union under another name.

The new organization was incorporated by the Territory of Nebraska on June 11, 1861, as the Pacific Telegraph Company. Edward Creighton, a very successful line builder had, as early as 1859, examined the southern or Overland Mail line via Fort Smith; then, early in 1860, he rode a mule over the central route, from Omaha via Fort Kearney, Laramie, South Pass,

Salt Lake and Fort Churchill to Sacramento, and reported his willingness to undertake the building by that route.

Meanwhile, another clever idea was put in motion. The California telegraph companies were notified that if they would all consolidate, with a capital of, say, $1,250,000, they might build the western end of the line to Salt Lake City and share in the profits. The silent Mr. Wade and A. W. Bee went all the way to California to bring the thing about, and did so. It was finally agreed that the eastern company should take 60 per cent of the proceeds, the western 40 per cent, until the total yearly revenue passed $70,000, when the California company's share should be reduced to 30 per cent. The California consolidation was made under the name of the Overland Telegraph Company. Western Union directors promptly began acquiring stock in it, and the outcome was easily foreseen.

Late in May, 1861, this company began rebuilding the line from Placerville to Fort Churchill; but it was not until July 4th, that the Pacific Telegraph Company formally "broke ground." Sibley had already gambled on his luck by building a line from Omaha to Fort Kearney during the previous autumn. Among his company's aides were nearly a thousand oxen and a hundred teams of mules. Each company employed two crews and began simultaneously at both ends of its route. A bonus had been agreed upon for the company which first completed its line to Salt Lake. Brigham Young, by the way, was a prominent sub-contractor, supplying poles, subsistence and transportation.

Even in the early winter of 1860, the eastern news brought by the Pony Express had begun to be telegraphed to San Francisco from Placerville. The Government concession for the Express had limited its life as "until the completion of an Overland Telegraph"; and its owners now saw with dismay that this would not be long. As the Pony riders galloped over their course, they saw at every trip the telegraph builders at a startlingly greater distance on their course. One day in August the western crew were 100 miles east of Fort Churchill; a week

From Harper's Weekly, New York Public Library

ONE OF THE LAST RIDES OF THE PONY EXPRESS, JUST BEFORE THE TELEGRAPH LINE
ELIMINATED IT

later, 50 miles farther; in another month, 75 miles more. Meanwhile, the Pacific's eastern crew, having a more level country to work in, were progressing at still greater speed. By August 9th, they were 50 miles west of Fort Kearney; by September 14th, with more experience, they were getting well into their stride, and 115 miles more had been added; and by October 8th, 368 miles more. As the lines advanced, the Pony's ride became shorter and shorter.

The problem of poles on the prairie had been foreseen as a serious one. In fact, some poles were hauled 240 miles over almost non-existent roads. But near Cottonwood Springs, about a hundred miles west of Fort Kearney, or half-way between there and Julesburg, the builders found in little cañons leading into the Platte, quantities of cedar trees, which supplied poles for hundreds of miles of line. A number of telegraph offices, stage stations and stables were built of cedar logs. Old Julesburg burned cedar, brought over a hundred miles, for firewood.[1] But the first telegraph station at Fort Kearney (there was no room for it in the military headquarters) was set up in a sod house built for the purpose by the postmaster and news-dealer at the fort.

The Pacific, the eastern company, won the race to Salt Lake, opening its line to that place on October 24th, while the western crews, because of more serious difficulties, did not complete their job until two days later. From the moment of the beginning on the Placerville line in May, it had been just four months and eleven days under way. All America was stricken breathless with amazement and admiration by the feat. Newspaper headlines blazed with wonder and congratulation. Felicitations were shot back and forth over the new wire by President Lincoln, the Governor of California, the Acting Governor of Utah, Brigham Young, the telegraph presidents and other dignitaries. Brigham Young told the President of the Pacific Telegraph Company that "Utah has not seceded, but is firm for the Con-

[1] F. A. Root and William E. Connelley, *The Overland Stage to California* (Topeka, 1901).

stitution and laws of our once happy country." There were great rejoicings, bell-ringing and gun-firing, not only in California, but in the East. And with the joining of the wires, that debonair adventure, the Pony Express, faded out forever.

In the first enthusiasm over quick communication between the two oceans, the line was swamped with telegrams, for which the company unblushingly charged a dollar a word between San Francisco and the Missouri River, notwithstanding the law specifying a maximum of $3 for ten words. The first rapture soon slackened, and within a week there was a "readjustment" of rates. From San Francisco to St. Louis the first ten words now cost $5, and each additional word 45 cents; to Chicago, the rate was $5.60 for ten words, and 50 cents thereafter; to New York and Washington, $6 and 75 cents; to Boston $7 and 60 cents. And in the first ten words were to be included the month and day of sending and the name of place from which sent, leaving only seven words for the message. The sending of the President's annual message in 1862 cost $600. This outrageous violation of law was ventured upon because the magnates believed that the Government was too busy with the Civil War to notice their chicanery. Only bankers, brokers, large merchants and freighters and the well-to-do could afford to use the telegraph under such conditions.

The growls of protest over this piracy swelled to a storm by 1863, and an effort was made in Congress to revoke the subsidy. The Overland Company of California thereupon came whimpering to the Capitol with a plea of poverty and high costs, saying that it was compelled to depend upon local business for its dividends. This is contradicted by (among several others) James D. Reid, a corporation advocate if ever there was one, who says that, "No line ever constructed on the continent became so immediately and largely profitable. . . . It was the basis of several fortunes." The Western Union was too influential in Congress to permit its favorite child to be curbed in its fun, so nothing was done about the rates. An attempt about the same time by a

California senator to break the grip of the Associated Press on California journalism was likewise a failure.

The two companies had their troubles, it is true, and these were all cited in their pleas to Congress. The great flood of the winter of 1861 to 1862 in the Sacramento Valley put the telegraph out of business over a wide area. Two repair men, striving to learn the extent of the damage, left Stockton one day in a skiff rigged with a sail, headed for Sacramento, and found the water for miles almost up to the telegraph wires, while in one place they actually sailed over the wires!

Save for the Gos-Utes of Nevada, who were rather pestiferous, the Indians did not give the line-builders much trouble, but they made up for this afterwards. The plains Indians remained very friendly for a time. Some of the chiefs were given electric shocks and other experiences by the builders to make them fear the wire. Another device was that of calling a number of chiefs, big and little, of a tribe together, telling them to agree among themselves upon a story and sequel, not telling the white men a word of it. Then they were to separate, go to two stations many miles apart, and one group was to tell its story to the operator. When it was repeated to the group at the other station and the sequel was brought back, the Indians were convinced that the telegraph was indeed big medicine.

But presently a brave came along who had been among the white people east of the Missouri. He assured them that their dread of the telegraph was nonsense, and that the wire might be made very useful in tethering ponies and tying tepees together. Under his direction, the wire was cut, and a number of mounted braves, taking hold of it, started their ponies and tore a long stretch of it loose and dragged it away. But, as the story goes, when once a group of them were doing this during a thunderstorm, lightning struck the wire, and the surviving bucks decided that there must be something diabolical about the device, after all, with the result that it was immune from harm for some time thereafter.[2]

[2] *Kansas State Historical Society Collections*, Vol. XIII, p. 28.

But eventually, they lost their respect for it, and furthermore, there were other tribes who hadn't heard of the lightning disaster; so in the outbreak of 1862, the line was damaged on several occasions. The Indians soon learned that it was a pale-face means of communication; therefore, if it were severed, troops could not be called against them so quickly, hence the one frail wire was cut again and again. In the war of 1864, they simply devastated the line, burning stage and telegraph stations and killing their staffs.

Early in February, 1865, they felled and burned more than fifteen miles of poles between Julesburg and Fort Laramie, and ten miles of them on the branch line to Denver. Denver had at first refused to pay the high bonus demanded by the company for a branch telegraph line, and got along for two years with an express rider service to Julesburg; but in 1863, under more favorable terms, the line was built. Army officers reported that poles for replacements in these gaps made by the Indians would have to be hauled in some cases 130 to 145 miles.

This whole period presents a chronicle of thrills. One day, 150 Indians attacked St. Mary's, a lonely station in Wyoming, where there were only five men to oppose them. They succeeded in setting fire to the station buildings, and the little garrison retreated to an old, dry well a few yards away, where they fought off attacks for some thirty hours, finally slipping away from their enemies at night by a miracle of cleverness and luck, and escaping to South Pass. They saved only their guns, and the operator his sounder, relay and a coil of fine wire, with which he cut in on the telegraph line at a few miles' distance, and notified Fort Bridger of their plight. With the close of the Civil War, the Government was able to send more troops to protect the stage and telegraph lines, and the Indians could not inflict so much damage, though they did their best.

Notwithstanding their harassments, everybody, especially among the higher-ups, in the Western telegraph was happy. The promoters in particular, for they were their own contractors, and made huge profits. Stebbins admitted that line represented to the public and charged up to the enemy as having cost $250 a mile was, through Nebraska, built for $67 a mile. Creighton, the builder of the Pacific line, became a banker in Omaha and died a Crœsus. In 1864, the Pacific Telegraph was benevolently absorbed by the Western Union; and in 1866, the Overland went down the same gullet. This answered the sarcastic suggestion of a California editor that the same paradox seen on California rivers, i.e., the more boats there were, the higher the rates, appeared to obtain in the telegraph business.

In 1867, the Western Union took over the California State Telegraph Company, and thereafter pursued a pleasant and profitable existence along the coast, picking up nice sums here and there for giving service to towns and counties. For example, San Bernardino had to scrape together $250,000 to get an extension of the line from the next county in 1873. One reason for assuming positive rather than indirect control of the Western companies was that competition, stimulated of course by Western Union oppression, was growing and threatening. The United States Telegraph Company, organized late in 1864, had by the spring of 1866 built a line from San Francisco to Salt Lake, and then was taken over by the Western Union, which could always afford to issue a few more millions of stock for such purposes. But by this time the Atlantic & Pacific Telegraph Company had been organized, controlling a right of way along the infant Union Pacific Railroad westward from Omaha, and was likewise chartered in California and began to build eastward from San Francisco. It gave trouble for years to come, especially after Jay Gould became a power in its management.

The telegraph, among other things, was accused of being a tool of speculators. A San Francisco correspondent of *The Telegrapher,* writing in 1865, said:

The Overland line is "out of order" about three-fourths of the time, being either "interrupted by lightning between here and Salt Lake," or else "down somewhere east of Salt Lake," if we may believe the official bulletins of the Agent. Malicious and evil-minded persons trace some remarkable coincidences between the ups and downs of this wire and similar fluctuations on the part of gold. Of course, being a member of the profession, I ascribe it to the "pesky Injins." Possibly, if a competing line were established and a lively opposition inaugurated, such as you have at the East, the "Overland" would work with greater regularity, the friendly attention of the red-skins and the "Atmospheric" being divided between two lines instead of being concentrated upon one, as at present.

In the meantime, another great project was under way. Perry McDonough Collins, a Californian, had for some time during the '50's been United States consul at Nikolaievsk, at the mouth of the Amur River in Siberia and after that, our commercial agent in Russia. He conceived the idea of connecting America with Europe by means of a telegraph line through Alaska—then a Russian possession—and Siberia; Bering Strait, of course, to be crossed by a cable. He first brought the matter to the attention of Congress early in 1861, but the Government was then too busy with the rising tide of war to think of an Asiatic telegraph. Collins got in touch with President Sibley of the Western Union, and of course received a quick and enthusiastic reaction from that dynamic dreamer. It was soon agreed between them that a company should be organized as soon as feasible, to build the line. For his services in promoting the affair and obtaining the coöperation of the Russian Government, Collins was to receive $200,000—half of it in stock of the new corporation.

The Russian Government in the '60's was building a 7,000-mile line from Moscow across Siberia to the Pacific Coast. The promoters foresaw lines to China—where Count de Lanture was even then struggling with the problem of reducing the 44,000 characters of the Chinese language to a possible telegraphic form (he finally gave it up)—to India and elsewhere. Sibley visited Russia in 1864 to discuss the telegraph and was cordially received by the Czar. In conversation with a high Russian official, he is said to have received the first intimation that Russia would be willing to sell Alaska to the United States.

He reported this to Secretary Seward, and that gentleman consummated the deal three years later.

In 1864, the California State Telegraph, under the direction of its master, the Western Union, prepared for the Asiatic venture by building a line from California to Victoria, British Columbia. This proved to be the most arduous and the costliest job of the sort yet undertaken in America; yet parts of it were done at amazing speed. Over much of the course the builders had to construct their own roads, and for a considerable distance had to carve their way through the densest forests on the continent. Nevertheless, when the party entered Olympia, Oregon (now Washington), it had built 120 miles of telegraph line and 40 miles of road in two months. North of Seattle, conditions were still worse—an untouched wilderness of mountains, forests, thickets, cliffs and deep rivers, which made wagons useless; so a small steamer on Puget Sound was utilized as the base of supplies. A long delay occurred because the steamer bringing the cable which was to cross the Gulf of Georgia to the city of Victoria had been lost off Cape Horn, and another cable had to be sent by the same circuitous course.

That same year, 1865, the great inter-continental project was begun. The company organized by the dashing Sibley consisted almost entirely of Western Union directors. Colonel Charles S. Bulkeley, the man who twenty years before had been just a clerk in the Magnetic office in New York, was in charge of the construction, and pushed it with amazing speed and efficiency. The Fraser River gold rush in 1855 had brought about the making of roads along the lower reaches of that stream, and the telegraph line followed it northward for 450 miles. Thence the surveyors struck off through the mountains to the Skeena and Stikine Rivers, reaching the latter at the mouth of a little stream which, together with a village at the spot, bears the name of Telegraph Creek to this day.

The Indians in that region proved friendly and peaceable, and though the severe winter caused a long stoppage (save for exploration of the route with reindeer and dog teams) working conditions were no worse than they had been just south of the United States line. A right of way 50 feet wide was cut out and a good trail made over the whole route.

By the end of July, 1866, 850 miles of line had been strung by Bulkeley's crew. The builders were of course in constant touch with the East through the new line. One evening there came ticking through it to Bulkeley a paralyzing message: "Stop all work at once. Atlantic Cable successfully laid."

The project had been pushed thus far only on the assumption that an Atlantic Cable was not possible. In this light, the adventure to-day seems foolhardy in the extreme. A directors' meeting was held, and it was decided that 16,000 miles of land telegraph could not compete with 1,600 miles of cable, and the job was therefore set down as a magnificent failure. Crews were also working in Russian territory, and two or three weeks passed before the stop order reached them. By that time, 300 miles of wire had been strung in Alaska and 350 miles in Siberia. The cable for Bering Strait was at the spot, ready to be laid. The futile gesture had cost, all told, about $3,000,000, but its millionaire promoters pocketed the loss without a murmur. The Western Union continued to operate 450 miles of the line, to Quesnel on the Fraser River until 1870, when they sold it to the British Columbian government, which in turn ceded it to the Dominion Government in the following year.

Beyond Quesnel the wire was left standing until the poles fell into decay. But meanwhile the Indians, finding that it was no longer wanted, began cutting out lengths of the wire to use in tying their shacks together, to make into nails, fish-spear points, traps and swings. They even built some crude but ingenious semi-suspension bridges, which were partly swung, partly tied together with the wire. When the Klondike gold excitement arose in the latter '90's, the Canadian Government strung a line to the gold-fields, mostly over the old right of way as far as it went. In 1905, a surveying party of the British

From Harper's Weekly, New York Public Library

VIGILANCE COMMITTEES IN THE WEST FOUND TELEGRAPH
POLES USEFUL FOR OTHER PURPOSES THAN TELEGRAPHY

From Report British Columbia Minister of Mines, 1915

BRIDGE BUILT BY INDIANS OF BRITISH COLUMBIA, PARTLY OF
WIRE FROM THE ALASKA-ASIA TELEGRAPH LINE

Columbia Bureau of Mines were much interested to find two or three of the original poles still standing, and some miles of the wire, uncorroded, lying across rocks or trodden into the earth by the hooves of pack animals working their way towards the far northern Eldorado.

CHAPTER XVI

THE FIGHT FOR A GOVERNMENT TELEGRAPH

With the channels of thought and of commerce thus owned and controlled by one man or by a few men, what is to restrain corporate power or fix a limit to its exactions upon the people? What is there to hinder these men from depressing or inflating the value of all kinds of property to suit their caprice or avarice, and thereby gathering into their own coffers the wealth of the nation?

SENATOR WILLIAM WINDOM, 1881

THE Western Union was kept fairly busy after the Civil War fighting off competition. New telegraph companies sprang up as did armed giants from the dragon's teeth of Cadmus. Some have been discussed in the preceding chapter. The Franklin Telegraph Company, organized in 1865, a well-managed concern which overspread New England and pushed into the other Atlantic States, was another. Some of these companies were palpably intended to be sold to the Western Union. The region around Chicago swarmed with such, according to a pamphlet entitled *The Age of Humbug*, published there in 1869.

There was the Great Western, for example, of which an enthusiastic correspondent of the New York *Herald* said, "They will complete 4,000 miles of line this very year." The Number 1 schemer of this company was a white-haired gentleman from Brooklyn named Josiah L. Snow, whose name was anathema in Canada because of a promotion which he had engineered there seventeen years before—the Grand Trunk Telegraph Company, though it had no connection whatsoever with the railroad of that name. Snow and his son had assured investors that their stock would quickly double in value, that it would be a family heirloom, and so on. The firm of Snow & Dwight were contractors for the line, and the son, W. D. Snow, as engineer for the company,

322

pronounced the job perfect. "The wily Josiah," said the Barrie *Northern Gazette*, "based the price at $250 per mile, whereas a good line can be built for $100." Having collected their money, the Snows left the Dominion, never to return. The line limped along for a few months, but according to the *Trade Review* of Montreal, "the poles were like whipstocks," the wires and instruments cheap stuff discarded by other companies. Most of the wire was eventually sold to farmers along the line to be used for fences and clothes lines. Investors lost about $250,000.

Despite this record, the Messrs. Snow had the consummate nerve to apply, *in absentia*, for a charter for another company in Canada in 1868. It was refused, and then the charter was asked for by H. B. and Sela Reeve. It was granted, and some thousands of dollars had been collected on stock subscriptions when some snooper discovered that the Reeves were cousins of Mrs. Josiah Snow. Canada didn't succeed in catching them, either. Unable to proceed further in the Dominion, the Snows went over to Chicago and started the Great Western.

Of another concern, the Rock Island *Daily Argus* of February 20, 1869, under the heading, "A Swindling Telegraph Company, and an Incompetent or Drunken Superintendent," wrote with the frankness characteristic of the times:

A year or two ago a few sharks in St. Louis organized what they pompously called the "Mississippi Valley National Telegraph Company"—probably for the purpose of covering certain territory and then inducing the Western Union to buy them out. They put up a few poles, and opened here and there an office in some garret with a $2.50 table and one chair for furniture, and employed such boys as they could get for about half wages.

Although these companies exposed themselves to the monster freely, some of them expired without being devoured by it. The National Telegraph Company was another hopeful concern of 1869 which stoutly averred that it would have no dealing with the Western Union. One of its promoters was none other than that Yankee genius, D. H. Craig, who had now parted company with the Associated Press. An Illinois editor breath-

lessly announced that the National's stock—ten million dollars!
—was all subscribed for, that already 6,000 miles of line had
been built and that it would cut rates to one-tenth of the present
scale. *The Telegrapher* jeeringly begged to be informed as to
the location of the 6,000 miles of line.

The National expected to use the automatic telegraph system
invented by George Little of Rutherford, New Jersey. It declared that one wire operated by this system would do as much
business as ten Morse wires. There had been one automatic
device after another introduced since the time of Bain, House
and Bakewell. Hummaston and Allen brought forth machines
in the latter '50's, and in 1872 Wheatstone's automatic, which
was in later years much used in the United States, appeared. Its
telegrams were represented by three rows of round holes
punched in a strip of paper by a machine operated by keys
somewhat like those of a typewriter. This perforated fillet, passing through the sender, closed and broke the circuit, whereupon
at the other end of the wire, two pens worked by electro-magnets
recorded the message in small dots, which were rather difficult
to read.

Bonelli, Simpson and Siemens were others who produced
automatics before 1870—none of them greatly successful. Craig,
answering the question why the Western Union did not adopt
the Little system said, that "the owners and promoters of the
system believe that the public demand a new deal in the telegraph business, and the inventor and his friends determined,
even long before the invention was perfected, that they would
have nothing to do with that unwieldy and essentially bloated
concern"; therefore, "no official of the Western Union had ever
been permitted to see the new machine"—which represents a
plane of integrity so high that our earth-bound lungs can scarcely
breathe its rarefied atmosphere.

The Atlantic & Pacific Company, already mentioned, may
have been one of those originally intended to flirt with the
Western Union. Organized in 1865, it had by the early '70's a
line across the continent from New York, via Buffalo, Chicago,

the Rock Island Railroad's right of way, and thence beside the Pacific Railroads' tracks to San Francisco.

It now actually offered to sell to the Western Union, but the panic of '73 had come on, and the W.U.T. had by that time swallowed so many companies that it was suffering from indigestion, and had been put on a low diet for a time by President Orton. Hence it refused the proffer of the A. & P., which proved a costly refusal in the end; for a new force was now coming into control of the latter company, along with the Union Pacific Railroad—a force which the Western Union had not yet learned to fear, but to which it was destined eventually to bow; and that force was none other than a little black-whiskered, inscrutable demon of intrigue named Jay Gould.

Gould struck up a friendship with General T. T. Eckert, Superintendent of the Eastern Division of the Western Union, and playing upon the latter's dissatisfaction with what he regarded as certain mistaken policies of his company, induced him to leave it. In January, 1875, Eckert was elected President of the Atlantic & Pacific, and at once chose as his three chief aides none other than the three former cipher men in the War Department during the recent war—Albert B. Chandler, D. Homer Bates and Charles A. Tinker. Under Eckert's direction, the lines of the Franklin Company were leased and the company's territory increased until by January 1, 1877, it had 17,759 miles of line, carrying more than twice that much wire.

Meanwhile, cities had grown so large that local telegraphs had sprung up in them, some of these attaining major importance. Henry Bently, a bookkeeper and newspaper scribbler, started the first one in New York in 1854. After one failure, he tried again, organizing the New York City and Suburban Printing Telegraph Company in 1855, and this time was successful. He even laid a cable across the East River near Blackwell's Island and brought Brooklyn and its suburbs into his system. He is said to have been the first to use stamps in payment of telegraph charges. He had a number of message depositories in stores, where telegrams might be left, to be collected frequently and carried to the nearest office by messengers. For prepayment on the messages he printed and sold stamps in one-, two- and three-cent values. Presently he added to his service a "dispatch," by which letters were carried about the city. After a few years, he sold out for a good price and, removing to Philadelphia, started a similar local telegraph system there.

While on the subject of telegraph stamps, it may be mentioned that in the early 1860's they began to be used for the prepayment of telegrams in England, where the telegraph has, of course, always been a part of the postal system. In 1867 France, where the telegraph is likewise a Government monopoly, took them up. In that country, you might affix a stamp to a telegram, put it into an envelop and drop it into a box at a telegraph station or put it into the post-office, marked, "Telegraph Dispatch." But these, of course, were Government stamps. In the United States in the '70's and '80's many companies had their own private stamps for the payment of telegraph fees. The philatelic catalogues show a fascinating array of them. The larger companies also began using stamps for complimentary franking. Most companies, on the first of each year, sent to the politicians and railroad officials whom they delighted to honor, or rather, whom they feared not to honor, a prettily designed card with his name written in, and he had only to show this at a telegraph office to have his message sent free. But the Western Union in 1871 and the Postal, Baltimore & Ohio, Mutual Union and two or three others after 1880, began issuing books of stamps to their honorees; the Western Union continues the practice to this day.

The American District Telegraph Company was a novelty of this period. Organized in 1872, within two years it had 2,000 subscribers in New York City. It offered messenger, policing and other services. Each subscriber had a wire run into his home or office, ending in an instrument resembling the present telegraph messenger call, but on which you might give a few different signals. For this you were charged $2.50 per month. A pamphlet issued by the company in 1875, declared that it had

Originals from Scott Stamp and Coin Co.

PREPAYMENT STAMPS AND FRANKS OF VARIOUS COMPANIES
FOR USE ON TELEGRAMS

then over five hundred uniformed messengers, reporting to twenty-one district offices, some of them apparently with police power:

> The variety of purposes for which our policemen are called, would astonish anyone unfamiliar with our business. They have been summoned to search houses, disperse crowds, arrest drunken people and suspicious characters, to remove drunken servants, to take sick people home, to open doors (servants or others being absent with keys), to watch single houses during absence of all or part of the family, to collect bills, to disperse disorderly crowds of boys, to prevent abuse by impudent or dishonest tradesmen and peddlers, to kill or remove mad or vicious animals, to search rooms and trunks of suspicious persons, to prevent fights ... and perform many other services required.

A turn of the crank, and one or more of their men came running with a Babcock Fire Extinguisher. They watched homes, either inside or outside; they installed burglar alarms and thermostat fire alarms. Dr. Henry Ward Beecher, an enthusiastic patron, testified that "I have had the American District Telegraph Company's instrument in my house for about a year, and nobody can take it out unless he is a great deal stronger than I am." Another clergyman exclaimed, "How did we ever live without it?"

By 1882, a news item stated that they had 5,000 call boxes and nearly a thousand uniformed men and boys, none of them under fourteen. Their service had now broadened; the men attended children to and from school, they were sent home with drunks, or searched saloons and other hangouts for missing husbands. They were employed as spotters of suspected clerks in stores; they took things to the pawnbrokers if you were too modest to go yourself. Dressed in the pink of fashion, they paid New Year calls by proxy, were ushers at fashionable weddings, and managed the carriage arrangements on such occasions.

And here we must notice the phenomenal rise of a company whose existence was built around the stock ticker, a dubious convenience whose inventors and improvers might appropriately be crowned with tasteful chaplets of ragweed. The most remarkable thing one notices in the story is that the seed of the plant was supplied by a Presbyterian preacher. Dr. S. S. Laws, who had resigned the presidency of a synodical college and become a Vice-President of the Gold Exchange in New York, designed an instrument which, by telegraphic impulse, would automatically display the price of gold in a broker's office or elsewhere. The mechanism consisted simply of three overlapping dials, which displayed three figures at once—the last one usually a fraction. Laws patented this in 1866, and soon had contracts with more than fifty brokers.

In 1867, Edward A. Calahan went Laws one better by devising a telegraph machine which printed not only gold but other commodity and stock prices on a fillet of paper. The Gold and Stock Telegraph Company was organized that year with a capital of $200,000 to give service through Calahan's machine. It presently took over Laws's device also, and in 1868 increased its capital to $500,000.

Those eight years following the fall of the Confederacy constituted a post-war gilded period closely comparable to the vertiginous nineteen-twenties. There were the same imbecilic stock-gambling, the same fatuous belief that good times would never end, the same pie-crust palaces of dreams reared upon quicksands through which crawled sullen currents of debility and decay. Stock-market joy was reflected in the meteoric growth of the Gold and Stock Telegraph Company—its rapid expansion rivaling that of the Western Union. Marshall Lefferts became its President in 1870, when the capital leaped to a million—then to a million and a quarter in 1871.

The Western Union was naturally not insensible to the rapid growth of the young giant. In collaboration with the Associated Press, it had been operating a commercial news department, but the Gold and Stock, with its automatic machines, was cutting into that business. So Western Union directors bought some more G. and S. stock, and then proceeded with what modern gangdom might call putting on the heat. The G. and S. was "offered" the W.U.'s commercial news department on condition that it double its capital stock and hand the new issue over to the W.U. in payment therefor. This was done; the Gold and Stock now had a $2,500,000 capital and was a tentacle of the octopus. One after another, it took over new printing machines, or improvements upon them, designed by George Phelps, Thomas A. Edison, Frank L. Pope, Elisha Gray and others; and from these, "preserving the best features of each," as newspapers say when they combine, has been developed the modern ticker.

The Gilded Age also saw the rapid spread of private wires. The first one known was installed in 1849 by R. M. Hoe, the printing press manufacturer, between his downtown office in New York and his East Side factory, a mile or so distant. In 1853, a telegraph machinery manufacturer named Norton had a private wire between his office and his factory, and did his own operating. In 1869, two companies were organized in New York to string private wires to the offices of bankers, brokers and merchants. One, the American Printing Telegraph Company, used the Pope and Edison Printer. It sold out to the Gold and Stock Company two years later, while the other company, the Manhattan, after a few years more, leased its system to the G. and S. Thus the private wire and the ticker were joined in a matrimony which still endures.

The high rates, the huge profits and the swollen capital of the Western Union, its rapid swallowing or crushing of competing companies, had brought about an ugly public reaction which might have been expected, and which, even if some of the magnates did foresee it, they had become too arrogant to fear. During those eight years following Appomattox, the great public communication services—railroads, express companies and telegraph companies—became colossi; they combined or collaborated, fixed high rates, watered stock, manipulated the market, made millionaires of their officials. But among all these, the nearest to a complete monopoly was the Western Union Telegraph. It was therefore regarded by liberal and reform opinion and by a considerable segment of the public, with fear, suspicion, even abhorrence. Its enormous capitalization, its merciless elimination of competition towards the close of the Civil War, brought growls of protest, which swelled into a roar of demand that the Government take over the telegraph service and operate it for the benefit of the people, as was being done, so we were told, in Europe. The Washburn Committee of the House of Representatives in 1870, declared that telegraph rates in Europe averaged less than one-half those in America; in England they were less than one-third, in France less than one-fourth of our rates, mile for mile.

Lincoln's Postmaster-General, Montgomery Blair, favored Government ownership or, as an alternative, the Government's giving aid to a smaller company to combat the Western Union. Following this secondary suggestion, a bill was introduced into Congress in 1866 to incorporate and confer special privileges on an ideal concern, as yet unorganized, to be known as the National Telegraph Company. Postmaster-General Dennison, then incumbent, was against the proposal, and the bill did not pass. But a counter-measure was adopted, giving all telegraph companies the right to build lines along post and military roads, on the following conditions:

First, that the Postmaster-General should fix annually the rates on Government messages, which should have priority over all others.

Second, that the United States, at any time after the expiration of five years from the passage of the act, might buy all lines, property and effects of any or all companies at an appraised value to be decided upon by a board of five disinterested persons.

All the principal companies in the country filed their acceptance of these terms, and the Western Union began to consider seriously the possibility of its dissolution, though it was firmly resolved not to die if money, favors and propaganda could prevent it.

In that same year, however, the Government gave critics a

331

still weightier grievance by handing over to the telegraph companies 14,211 miles of telegraph line and 178 miles of submarine cable, which it had built for military purposes during the Civil War—in compensation, it was explained, for the losses which the companies had sustained by reason of the Government's seizing their lines and sometimes destroying them during hostilities. This was done, it was charged, at the behest of General T. T. Eckert, who immediately thereafter became a Western Union official; and the lines were all given either to the Western Union or to companies which were just about ready to fall into its lap.

Coupled with the Western Union as a subject of attack was another monopoly, the Associated Press. They were firm allies; it was charged before Congress that the Western Union "is a co-conspirator in building a press monopoly." Its President, Orton, admitted to a congressional committee that the A. P. was under agreement to use the Western Union wires exclusively, and that newspapers were forbidden to deal with any other telegraph company. There were many complaints of refusal to give news service by the combined monopolists.

The Western Union naturally held the whip hand, and in the '70's, the Associated Press dared not send anything inimical to its overlord. The Associated Press not only selected and colored the news, but forbade its editor-customers to criticise it. "The Associated Press," said a Congressional committee, "has notified newspapers that they would withhold the news from all papers that criticised such dispatches. This power was exercised in the case of the Petersburg (Va.) *Index*" [1] and other papers, too. The second Ramsay Committee report told of newspapers which had expressed approval of the idea of a Government telegraph, and which had thereupon either lost their news or telegraph service or had their rates raised to such a mark that they could not afford to pay them.[2] "The understanding between the telegraph company and the press association," said

[1] Senate Report, 242; 43-1, p. 3. Senate Report, 624; 43-2, p. 2, etc.
[2] Senate Report, 242; 43-1, p. 22.

From the collection of Frank E. Lawrance

ANNUAL COMPLIMENTARY FRANKING CARDS OF VARIOUS
TELEGRAPH COMPANIES, 1880 TO 1900

another report, "secures to the latter low rates and the power of excluding new papers from the field, and to the former a strong influence upon press dispatches, the support of the papers in such association, and the right to transmit and sell market quotations." As late as 1894 the International Typographical Union complained at the Henderson Committee hearings that there was, "a tremendous bar in the way of starting newspapers, it being practically impossible to launch a daily without the consent of the Western Union Telegraph Company and the Associated Press"; and that "any paper attempting to assert its own individual opinion as against the Western Union would suffer for it."

During the latter '60's, several bills proposing Government construction of wire lines—from Washington to New York and from Washington to Boston, for example—another for the simple purchase of all lines in the country, were introduced in Congress. In the Fortieth Congress first appears Gardiner G. Hubbard, Boston attorney and promoter, with his noble idea for the slaying of the Western Union dragon—nothing less than the organization of a company of his own, which should be called the Postal Telegraph Company, and which should operate all the wires in the Nation under Government auspices. He did not get it through Congress at that time, but he did not lose hope.

Grant's first Postmaster-General, Creswell, was strongly in favor of Government ownership. He said that to destroy rivalry, the Western Union "did not scruple to use any device which the strong can employ against the weak." He quoted Orton as saying to his directors, "The time is not far distant when the Western Union Telegraph Company will be without a substantial competitor in the conduct of a business which, notwithstanding the enormous growth of the last seven years, is still in its infancy."

Congressman Charles A. Sumner of California, a persistent worker for the postal or Government telegraph, delivered a scathing address against the monopoly in Dashaway Hall, San Francisco, on October 12, 1875. He declared that: "The Western

Union has a twin connection with another incorporated thief and highway robber known as the Associated Press. They are banded together in the strong bond of mutual plunder and rapacity against the people." He described telegraph promotions of earlier days—O'Rielly, Fog Smith and others—and declared that there had been more fleecing of innocent investors by these concerns than by wildcat mine promoters in California and Nevada. "I know of prominent men in this city," he shouted, "against whom to-day there are pending in Massachusetts indictments for getting money under false pretenses through the very machinery I have described."

He told of sudden changes in market prices being withheld from San Francisco until insiders could make a killing. He charged that the dispatches of the Western Union and the A.P. "are in the interest of the party which the Western Union and the railroad monopolies own—the Republican Party." He charged that railroad and telegraph influence prevented the publication of a Democratic morning paper in San Francisco, and added that the San Francisco *Herald* had been destroyed by the deliberate breaking of a contract by the Western Union. He defied "that crawling, sneaking, lying pismire of San Francisco monopoly newspapers, the *Morning Call*," and said that it and the *Bulletin,* together with the New York *World,* "Jay Gould's so-called 'Democratic organ,'" were moving heaven and earth to keep the Democrats from nominating Samuel J. Tilden for the Presidency in the following year.

Postmaster-General Creswell pointed out in 1873 some of the absurdities and injustices of Western Union rates. A ten-word telegram went from Washington to Boston for 55 cents, but to Waltham, ten miles from Boston, it would cost $1.75. From Washington to Chicago the rate was $1.75, but to Geneva, forty miles from Chicago, it was $3.00. Victor Rosewater told the Bingham Committee in 1890, that when he was managing the Western Union office at Omaha, the rate from there to Chicago was $3.55, while from Council Bluffs, across the river, to Chicago, it was $2 less. Omaha citizens sometimes went by bus over to Council Bluffs and back, paying $1.50 for the round trip, just to send a telegram to Chicago, and saved 50 cents thereby.

Hubbard's Postal Telegraph bill was introduced again in the Senate in December, 1873. By its terms, the Postal Telegraph Company was to be incorporated by Hubbard and two associates, one of whom, by the way, was a rising young man named Andrew Carnegie of Pennsylvania. Existing telegraph companies would be permitted to sell their plants to the new corporation at a price to be determined by arbitration. The Postmaster-General was to establish telegraph offices in all post-offices on the existing telegraph circuits, and others in any post-office of sufficient importance within ten miles of any circuit. The Post-Office Department was to supply all telegraph blanks, stamps and stationery. Any customer might have his telegram sent ahead of all others by paying double rates. The original capital of the new company was set at $1,000,000; but if it purchased other lines or increased its mileage, increases in capitalization were to be allowed. Trust Mr. Hubbard to see to that!

The alert Mr. Orton promptly pointed out that the Post-master-General was required to "establish" offices; that nothing in the bill required the company to fit these with furniture, instruments, batteries, and so forth, hence it must be inferred that the Government would do it; that as Uncle Sam was paying all expenses, the $1,000,000 capital stock seemed to be "in the nature of an appropriation for the benefit of the promoters of the scheme"; that if the property or business of the corporation was taxed by any state or city, the bill permitted it to add the tax to the telegraph rates; that the company was merely the "agent" of the Postmaster-General, and therefore not liable to prosecution for damages for delay or non-delivery of messages; that there was no guarantee that anything performed by or expected of the company would be performed within a reasonable time, or ever performed at all.

One need not cavil at Congress for not passing such a measure. The selfishness of the Hubbard proposal was evident

OLD WIRES AND NEW WAVES

at a glance. Other things against him were dug up. *The Telegrapher* charged that he was the paid lobbyist of the banknote companies in their opposition to the printing of paper money and stamps by the Government; which puts both Hubbard and the editor in an amusing light, this being a complete reversal of the stand of each with regard to the telegraph.

Neither did Congress seem disposed to take over the wires in any other manner. Perhaps the complimentary franks which the Western Union gave with a lavish hand to the legislators had something to do with forming their opinion. The number of the books of these franks which the company gave away each year ran well up into the thousands; and as President Orton naïvely told his directors in the annual report of 1873:

The franks issued to Government officials constitute nearly a third of the total complimentary business. The wires of the company extend into thirty-seven States and nine Territories within the limits of the United States, and into four of the British Provinces. In all of them our property is more or less subject to the action of the National, State and municipal authorities; and the judicious use of complimentary franks among them has been the means of saving to the company many times the money value of the free service performed.

Nor should all the odium for this state of things rest upon the company. Little men in legislative assemblies can and often do, in the pretended interest of the "pee-pul," harass and damage great properties enormously, unless their consciences are lulled by soothing favors. But on the other hand, as a prominent jurist remarked: "Members of Congress and Senators, having free telegraphy themselves, are not as likely to be impressed with the iniquity of high rates as we who pay them, and the monopoly is alive to the fact that the continuance of their monopoly depends more upon the good-will of Congress than upon any argument they can make."

Naturally, most of the backing of the Western Union Telegraph Company was expected from the Republican Party; but the Democrats got their franks, too. Even in primaries and pre-election fights, books of franks were handed out to bosses and candidates, sometimes both ends being played against the middle. The writer has read the following letter, written by a Western Union official to a prominent New York politician:

10th June, 1880

DEAR MR. ———

I enclose another book of franks, of which I have extended the limits to cover all Western Union lines.

I hope they may help you to make a good nomination. Please use them freely on political messages, and telegraph me when you want a fresh supply. Between ourselves, we have been obliged to help the other side to this extent, and I would like to see fair play.

How deeply the Western Union went into intrigue to make its position safe is shown by the happenings after Horace Greeley's death in November, 1872. A fight for control of the New York *Tribune* soon followed. Sinclair, the publisher of the paper, sold his twenty shares to William Orton, who was believed to be acting in behalf of Roscoe Conkling and others of the Republican Old Guard of New York, the evil genii of Grant. It was proposed to make Schuyler Colfax editor of the paper. But just then the Credit Mobilier scandal exploded, Colfax was disgraced and Orton was baffled in his effort to put the deal through. Fighting against him were John Hay and Whitelaw Reid who, oddly enough, received financial aid from Jay Gould which enabled Reid to obtain control.

The Western Union was accused of crookedly aiding the Republicans against Tilden in 1876 and against Cleveland in 1884. The election of '76, one of the most disgraceful episodes in our history, appears to have been a contest in thievery between the two major parties, with the Republicans proving rather more adept at it than the Democrats. At the instance of Democratic Congressmen, thousands of political telegrams were seized from Western Union offices after the election; but though the buying of an Oregon elector and some minor skullduggery were unearthed therefrom, most of the dirt must have been

337

either well enciphered or kept off the wires. But to the consternation of the Democrats a few months later, some appalling derelictions on their own side were revealed in the telegrams; such things, for example, as a message from a Democratic negotiator to Headquarters in New York, saying that the Florida canvassing board and the Governor's signature could be bought for $200,000—and a reply from Headquarters, saying that the price was too high; also a telegram from another scout in South Carolina: "Majority of the Board have been secured. Cost is $80,000—" and then prescribing the number of parcels to be made of the money, and the proportions in $1,000 and $500 bills. The efforts of the senders of these telegrams to explain them innocuously afforded comic relief to a sordid drama. Democratic editors and publicists thereupon wrote some furious editorials and pamphlets, claiming that William Orton, "an unscrupulous Republican partisan," had hidden from Congress some of the most incriminating Republican telegrams. John Bigelow charges this in his life of Tilden. And it may be true; in the words of our old southern kinsmen, "We wouldn't put it past him."

The battle over Government ownership raged in the magazines through the 1880's and '90's, with a ratio of about ten shots for it to one against. Dr. Norvin Green, then President of the Western Union, contributed one of the few articles in favor of the corporation to the *North American Review* in 1883. John Wanamaker, in President Harrison's administration (1889-93), was the last Postmaster-General who made a real effort to bring about a Government telegraph, and Victor Rosewater told Congress that Jay Gould spent $250,000 to defeat him. Frank Parsons, in his book on *The Telegraph Monopoly* (1899), says that a million dollars was ready to drop into Wanamaker's pocket if he would withdraw the bill. But seemingly, enough effective work was done among Congressmen to make this unnecessary.

Congressional committees appointed for that particular purpose investigated the situation and reported on a postal telegraph

THE FIGHT FOR A GOVERNMENT TELEGRAPH

in 1845, '69, '70, '72, '74, '75, '81, '83, '84, '90 and '96. Nineteen times before 1900, committees of one sort and another in Senate and House expressed their opinion on Government ownership. Seventeen were for it, and two against it. After 1900 the reformers apparently gave up the fight as hopeless. By that time a healthy opposition to the Western Union was being supplied by Mackay's Postal Telegraph, and the greater concern by no means had everything its own way. The Associated Press was also being compelled to divide business with a growing competitor, the United Press. When Congressman Treadway, of Massachusetts, made an almost tearful complaint in the House of Representatives in 1927, "Mr. Speaker, I have been so outrageously, brutally and unhumanly treated by the Western Union Telegraph Company in relation to the reception of cables that I wish to call attention to some extension of remarks I shall incorporate in the *Record* on the subject, in the hope that other people may not receive like treatment from that corporation," Representative Blanton of Texas heartlessly inquired, "Why not use the Postal?"

In conclusion, let no reader leave this chapter with the notion that the author actually favors Government control of the telegraph. It may work well in England, but may that not be because they handle their politics better and more honestly than we do in the United States? Having long weighed all the arguments on both sides, we refuse to believe that any human being is wise enough to say with authority which is better, or rather, which is worse—corporate or government ownership. Having seen as much as we have of the workings of our Government in recent years, of the lost motion and the palsying hand of politics at Washington, it is a nice question with us whether Government inefficiency and partisan putrescence do not outweigh the undoubted evils of a monopoly—a thing, however, which does not at the present moment exist in the telegraph business.

CHAPTER XVII

THE MYSTERY OF THE TELEPHONE

Commerce has made successful strides
From inland towns to ocean tides,
Our railroads have been taxed to bring
Our harvest's bounteous offering.
New lines of telegraphic wire
Flash messages on wings of fire.
And an invention all our own
Is the successful "TELEPHONE."
NEW YORK NEWSBOYS' NEW YEAR GREETING, 1878

THE efforts to increase the range of the human voice have, throughout the history of the race, been a manifestation of that craving for quick communication which has already been mentioned. Just how long ago the speaking trumpet or primitive megaphone was devised, no one can say. The ancient Chinese had something of the sort. A reference to such a trumpet is found in Europe as far back as 1589, and it was then no novelty. Ship captains and mates used them centuries ago. Cooper in that eighteenth-century story, *The Pilot,* pictures Barnstable as pacing his quarter-deck, "dangling a speaking trumpet by its lanyard from his forefinger," while in battle he shouted orders through it "in a voice that might be heard above the bellowing of the cannon." How many pictures have we seen of the old volunteer fire chiefs with their trumpets! In later years Edison made an improved megaphone, whereby voices might be heard at a distance of two miles.

Nor can we say when it was first discovered that a rod, string or wire would, by vibration, carry sound much farther than does the air. Dr. Robert Hooke, that seventeenth-century putterer with all sorts of ideas, speaks of this, though one finds no mention of an actual use of the mechanical or "lovers'" telephone

From Leslie's Weekly, New York Public Library

TEXAS COWBOYS IN EARLY DAYS USED THE INSULATORS
FOR THEIR TARGET PRACTICE

(such as we made when we were children with two old tomato cans and a string) for more than a century after Hooke's time. The word "telephone," concocted from two Greek words meaning "distant" and "sound," is first found in use about 1796 by Huth; but he, queerly enough, was speaking of transmitting sound by means of megaphones and ear trumpets.

Thirty-five or forty years later, Wheatstone was bandying the word about; and that was some forty years before Alexander Graham Bell and his helper first heard words over a wire. Newspapers and magazines of the day speak frequently of Wheatstone's telephone or *speaking machine*. He had what he called an "enchanted lyre"—a lyre-shaped sounding-box connected by a rod or wire with a piano in another room, whereby the piano music appeared to originate in the lyre itself. He also had a glass clock-face hung on the wall, with hands on it but no machinery back of it; yet the hands moved and the clock ticked and struck the hours, both the impulse and the sounds coming through several miles of wire from a clock movement on another floor. But Tegg, the English writer on posts and telegraphs, says that "Wheatstone's experiments had nothing to do with electricity," but merely conveyed sound by mechanical vibration, "as in the familiar toy telephone."

It may surprise some persons who have never tried it to hear of the possibilities of this telephone. Professor Dolbear, an early telephone inventor, wrote of two in New England, one of 500 and one of 1,000 feet in length, over which one could talk and hear distinctly. In the longer one, the transmitting and receiving tubes or boxes were of tin with pieces of sheepskin stretched tightly over one end, and the line was of No. 8 cotton thread, supported at intervals by loops of cord not less than three feet long. The thread pierced the membrane and was held against it by a small button. The greater the tension, the better the transmission, hence wind and rain affected this line to its disadvantage. The other, the 500-foot line, running between a railroad's passenger and freight stations, used copper wire, which could be tightly stretched, and hence was not affected by the weather. To talk over these phones, you stood about three feet from the drum and spoke in an ordinary tone. We even hear of communication between two dwellings half a mile apart, the sounders being holes a foot across in a plank, with drumhead skins stretched across them.

In 1854, English and French newspapers were discussing a report that the cables across the English Channel would be used as "a medium of conversational intercourse." The method was remarkable: "A plate of silver and one of zinc are taken into the mouth, the one above, the other below the tongue. They are then placed in contact with the wire, and words issuing from the mouth so prepared are conveyed by the wire—in a whisper, we suppose, though the account does not say. It has been tried, it is said, with successful results." The journalists had imaginations even then, it seems.

That same year a Frenchman named Charles Bourseul evolved an idea which drew nearer to reality. In an article in *L'Illustration* on the wonders of telegraphy, he said, "I have asked myself if the spoken word itself could not be transmitted by electricity," and then goes on:

Imagine that one speaks near a mobile plate flexible enough not to lose any of the vibrations produced by the voice; that the plate establishes and interrupts successively the communication with a battery. You would be able to have at a distance another plate which would execute at the same time the same vibrations. It is true that the intensity of the sounds produced would be variable at the point of departure, where the plate is vibrated by the voice, and constant at the point of arrival where it is vibrated by electricity. But it is demonstrable that this would not alter the sounds.... In any case, it is impossible to demonstrate that the electric transmission of sounds is impossible.... An electric battery, two vibrating plates and a metallic wire will suffice.

In other words, Bourseul's idea was that of the make-and-break, which later experimenters declared was not the proper system for perfect telephony. Bourseul apparently never attempted to put his system into practice; but a baker's son, an orphan boy in Germany, read his suggestion in the paper and

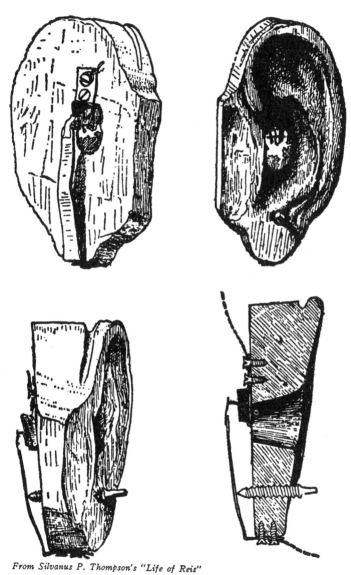

REIS'S FIRST TELEPHONE, IMITATING THE HUMAN EAR

was much impressed by it. This young man, Philipp Reis, began teaching in 1858 at Garnier's Institute at Friedrichsdorf, near Homburg, where he himself had been a pupil. From boyhood he had been deeply interested in physics. In 1860 he devised his first telephone. He knew of no better way than to imitate the human ear, so he cut a crude ear out of oak and tried to reproduce the whole human organ of hearing. A thin membrane, a piece of pig's bladder, took the place of the tympanum, and a little curved piece of platinum wire represented the malleus, or hammer bone. This was attached to the membrane by a tiny dot of wax, so that it quivered with every motion of the tympanum. This piece of metal, at its other end, rested in loose contact with a small vertical spring. The membrane, vibrating when sounds were made before it, moved the platinum lever and caused more or less contact of it with the spring. From the bottom of the spring led an electrified wire towards the receiving instrument, which was a knitting needle, surrounded by a coil of wire and resting on a violin, the latter acting as a sounding board. He improved a bit upon this later, but the receiver was always his weakness.

Dr. Messel, a former pupil of Reis and a witness of his earlier experiments, said [1] that one of the very first of Reis's models consisted of a beer barrel bung with its center gouged out so that it became a hollow cone and with its small end covered with a sausage skin. The platinum lever affixed with wax and the other paraphernalia were the same in this as in the ear telephone. He strung wire from one floor to another or across the playground of the school, and gradually developed his telephone until it attained the form of a box, with the membrane in a sunken circular orifice in the top, and a mouthpiece in the side. Thompson traces similarities in Bell's and Edison's work to Reis's. Bell mentions Reis's telephone in an early account of his own, when he quotes a report on it written by Inspector Wilhelm von Legat of the Royal Prussian Telegraphs. This

---

[1] In a letter to Silvanus P. Thompson, author of *Philipp Reis, the Inventor of the Telephone* (London and New York, 1883).

report was put into the hands of Thomas A. Edison by the Western Union, when they set him to work to produce a telephone. Edison himself said that in Reis's instruments, "single words uttered as in reading, speaking and the like were perceptible indistinctly, nevertheless here also the inflexions of the voice, the modulations of interrogation, exclamation, wonder, command, etc., attained distinct expression." [2]

Reis made in all, ten or twelve models of his telephone. Professors lectured and read papers upon it before the scientific societies of Germany, and accounts of it were published in scientific journals. The later models were to be seen in the physical laboratories of several German universities. A firm in Frankfort was given the contract to manufacture the instruments for sale, and a few were sent even to Great Britain and other foreign countries. But success was small. The instruments were imperfect, and conveyed little save musical sounds. The manufacturing firm told Professor Thompson twenty years later that it was impossible to find membranes all of equal goodness, and that those buyers who happened to get a poor one "could hear but little, while those who happened to have a good instrument were astonished at its performance." As a matter of fact, no telephone with a skin or membrane tympanum could ever succeed. Reis hoped eventually to use a metal tympanum, but though he tried it, he could never make it work.

As against the charge of later inventors that Reis's telephone never reproduced anything save musical notes, Professor Thompson (himself an eminent British scientist and for many years professor of physics in University College, Bristol) procured some interesting testimony from those who had heard it tested. Professor Quincke of the University of Heidelberg "heard distinctly both singing and talking. I clearly remember having heard the words of the German poem, 'Ach! du lieber Augustin, Alles ist hin!'" Professor Bohn of Aschaffenburg said it was known to him that Reis intended to transmit words (later denied in America). Legat's report said the same. Bohn

[2] Proceedings in Dowd suit, Edison's second answer.

said that "words sung, especially well accentuated and peculiarly intoned, were somewhat better (or rather less incompletely) understood than those spoken in the ordinary manner." He mentioned a boy "with a rather harsh North German dialect" who was particularly well understood on the telephone. Leon Garnier, son of Burgomaster Garnier, founder of the Institute, remembered hearing such phrases spoken as "Good morning, Herr Fischer!" "What time is it?" "What is your name?" and "Pay attention!" through the wire. But another professor, believing that these commonplaces would be too easily recognized, decided to try nonsense, so said to Reis, listening at the receiver, "Der Sonne ist von Kupfer" (The sun is made of copper), which Reis understood as "Der Sonne ist von Zucker" (sugar); not so bad.

The imperfections of the instrument and the total inability of the public of that day, especially in Germany, to see any possible utility in the telephone, deprived Reis of the credit that was his due. He seemed to have reached the limit of his progress by 1865, and the scientific world rapidly forgot him. He died a disappointed man in 1874, not yet forty years of age. In 1877, when Bell's invention began to be seen in Europe, the Germans belatedly awoke to the fact that they had had an unrecognized genius among them, and within a year they had collected the funds to erect at Friedrichsdorf a monument to Reis, upon which he is honored as "the inventor of the telephone."

However, the fact remains that Reis did not succeed in producing a practicable telephone. Two of his greatest fundamental crudities were his receiver and his skin tympanum. On the other hand, it is unbecoming in the Bell people to deny—in the face of such evidence as we have adduced—that any articulate speech ever passed through a Reis telephone. It does not sound well to the historian when they say that the first words ever transmitted by wire were Bell's "Mr. Watson, come here. I want you." It does not detract from the merit of Bell that he was not actually the first to send speech over a wire. His arduous toil, his devotion, his conception of an idea and battling through to its realization, deserve credit. As we have already suggested, no so-called invention is ever entirely original. To a mere layman, it appears that if Bell's patent should have been invalidated because spoken words had been dimly and imperfectly heard over Reis's crude concoction, then Morse's should also have been thrown out because European scientists had previously transmitted messages by wire, and Marconi's because other men before him had sent signals through the air. The man revered by future generations as the "inventor" of a device is usually the man who finally got it into practicable or semipracticable form, and thus was enabled to place it before the public. This historian, it may be remarked, is a bitter opponent of Big Name worship—of singling out one man and bestowing upon him all the laudation for an achievement, disregarding the many who aided him or paved the way for him. A sentence of good old Sir Thomas Browne's recurs to us almost daily: "Who knows whether the best of men be known, or whether there may not be more important persons forgotten than any that stand remembered in the known account of time?"

In 1869 a European scientist, Van der Weyde, exhibited in New York a telephone, probably Reis's or an imitation of it, which *The Telegrapher* called "one of the most remarkable recent inventions connected with telegraphy." It said that the singing or playing of a musical air could be "heard and distinguished plainly" through it; but it added some important qualifications: "No harmony, nor different degrees of strength or other qualities of tone can be transmitted . . . much less can articulate words be sent—notwithstanding the enthusiastic predictions of some that now we would talk directly through the wire. . . . The receiving instrument sings the melodies transmitted, as it were, with its own voice, resembling the humming of an insect." If this was a Reis instrument, it must have been inferior to some shown in Europe, for two men in Dublin who tested the latter in 1865 told Professor Thompson that they could instantly recognize the voices of acquaintances through it.

OLD WIRES AND NEW WAVES

In 1885, Professor Edwin J. Houston wrote a series of articles for the *Journal of the Franklin Institute,* attacking Bell's claim, and quoting letters to him from a number of American scientists who had tested the Reis instrument. There were then several of them in this country—one in the Smithsonian Institution, and others in physical laboratories here and there. The majority of the experimenters, nearly all professors of physics, such as Ogden N. Rood of Columbia, H. S. Carhart of Northwestern, William A. Anthony of Cornell, Charles S. Hastings of the Sheffield Scientific School, John B. De Motte of De Pauw and several others, declared that the Reis transmitter actually would transmit articulate speech. Most of them, however, admitted the weakness of the receiver.

De Motte said that with a Reis transmitter and a Bell receiver, he and others carried on a conversation so well that some of the group would not believe that they were not using a full Bell outfit. Anthony asserted that his Reis outfit reproduced speech so well that "if we had not had something better, it would be considered a thoroughly successful instrument." Here we have scientists upholding Reis's instrument and praising it more categorically than his contemporaries! What is the explanation? In the first place, probably better batteries or magnets, better wire and so forth than Reis had. In the second place, some of these professors had made their own reproductions of the Reis equipment. Did they—unintentionally, of course—make them just a little better than the original? The clamor of asseveration and denial is all very confusing, fifty to seventy-five years later, and the historian can only quote some of the testimony on either side and let the reader take his choice.

While Reis lay dying over in Germany in those first few days of 1874, two men in America were laboring to produce a harmonic telegraph, each of them for a time unknown to himself, drifting towards the creation of a telephone. Elisha Gray is the first one publicly heard of; an Ohio farm boy, an orphan and a mechanic in his teens, who paid his way through Oberlin College by carpentry. His particular interest was electricity.

THE MYSTERY OF THE TELEPHONE

Between 1867 and 1873 he invented an automatic self-adjusting telegraph relay, a telegraph switch and annunciator for hotels, a private telegraph line printer and a telegraph repeater. He settled in Chicago in 1872, where he later organized the manu·facturing firm of Gray & Barton, out of which grew the Western Electric Company. For a time he labored hard at his dream of a "harmonic" telegraph, in which, by means of different musical tones, several messages might be sent over a wire at the same time.

Early in July, 1874, the Western Union, then engaged in combating and ridiculing the automatic telegraph invention of George Little, displayed, with much gong-beating, Gray's instrument in New York (calling it a telephone), and announced that by its medium, every wire belonging to the company would be increased fourfold in capacity, and little new wire need be strung for years. But at the test, nothing beyond the musical achievement of Reis was in evidence; music played on a melodeon or piano went through (so we are told) 2,400 miles of wire, to be reproduced on a violin as a sounder. A. B. Chandler, then a Western Union official, claimed to regard it as "the first step towards doing away with manipulating instruments altogether, and . . . he believes that in time the operators will . . . talk with one another instead of telegraphing." This has come to pass in train dispatching and several other fields.

The editor of *The Telegrapher* ridiculed these visions, but oddly enough, he had a semi-sarcastic vision of modern broadcasting, though it was to be done by the telephone: "Our symphonies will be on tap like Croton, and we will turn on Theodore Thomas and the Philharmonic, and pay our bills quarterly. . . . Inevitably, we shall have telephonic reports of every new opera crashing in the walls."

Gray had discovered that a sound produced in the presence of a magnet would cause another magnet of similar adjustment to respond to the tone. He then found that by the same wire, another note might be transmitted by another magnet, and be reproduced by a receiving magnet adjusted in harmony with it.

349

This could be done many times on the same wire; he even sent sixteen tones over it at once. He presently began to develop the hope that he might cause it to transmit the voice. But as a telegraph, it was not greatly successful. The argument against it, as against previously invented duplexes, was that every time you doubled the number of messages passing over a wire, you slowed up the speed; so that by the time you had a quadruplex, your gain in capacity was almost *nil*. The first really successful quadruplex was that of Edison, made practical shortly after this, and the Western Union, having acquired that, quickly lost interest in Gray's harmonic idea. But he continued to work at it, and in July, 1875, obtained two patents on it. He was now forty years of age, and he had now fully made up his mind that a logical development of his system was a speaking telephone. He therefore swerved towards that goal.

The other man who was toiling over almost precisely the same course was a younger and luckier man than Gray; luckier because he started with little knowledge of electricity, yet brought forth a telephone; luckier because his attorney is said to have reached the Patent Office two hours ahead of Gray on that momentous St. Valentine's Day in 1876. Moses Farmer, that veteran inventor who for a quarter century past had been improving the telegraph, said—just a bit grumpily—that if Bell had known anything about electricity, he never would have invented the telephone. The trouble with himself and Gray was that they knew too much about it.

Alexander Graham Bell was born a Scotsman. His grandfather, also Alexander, was a teacher of diction and had a private school in Dundee. Old Alexander's son grew up in the same profession, and devised a system of alphabetics known as "visible speech." Alexander Graham represented the third generation expert in speech and sound, and his prime interest for many years was that of aiding the deaf and those with lingual impediments. When he was a very young man, he visited London and there met two men, Ellis and Wheatstone, who unconsciously had much to do with shaping his career. Ellis told him of the experiments of Helmholtz with vibrating tuning forks actuated by electro-magnets, and thus planted a seed which germinated several years later.

Young Bell's lungs were delicate; in fact, a physician predicted an early death from tuberculosis, and in search of a more salubrious climate for him, his parents and he removed from Scotland to Brantford, Canada, in 1870. He was then twenty-three. By the following year he was so much improved that he went down to Boston and began teaching the family's system of visible speech in the city's school for deaf-mutes. His success was so great that he won a professorship in Boston University, but did not remain there long, for in 1872 he established a school of his own for the correction of stammering and other defects.

About this time he made two contacts of great importance to his life and work. Little Georgie, the son of Thomas Sanders, a prosperous leather merchant, had been born deaf, and consequently, without speech. Bell took him on as a private pupil, and was invited to live in the Sanders home at Salem—as part payment for his services, it is said. There, while commuting daily to Boston, he was permitted to have a workshop in the basement, which he turned into a jumble of wires, batteries, magnets and what-not. He was an indefatigable experimenter, and when not working on ideas for the improvement of speech and aids to the deaf, he was tinkering with another notion which had found lodgment in his brain, one similar to Gray's; namely, that with eight magnets, each fitted with a reed tuned to one of the notes of the musical scale, he might send eight messages simultaneously to eight similarly equipped magnets at the other end of the wire.

The other contact which he made just a little later was with Mabel Hubbard, a fifteen-year-old girl who had lost her hearing, and with it her power of speech, from an attack of scarlet fever when she was an infant. When she met Bell, however, she had learned lip-reading and could speak in the labored, imperfect way which such unfortunate people acquire. Her father, Gardiner G. Hubbard, became interested in Bell's work, and Bell in turn became interested in Mabel. She was a pretty girl and winsome despite her misfortune, which did not repel the young Scotsman as it might have some other people. In fact, for him it may have given her an added interest.

Her father was that same long-bearded Boston attorney and promoter, long interested in telegraphs, who was at that very moment trying to persuade Congress to aid him in creating a pseudo-Government telegraph monopoly. Both he and Sanders became rather excited over Bell's harmonic telegraph experiments, and encouraged them. As Bell more and more neglected his teaching and gave the time to his telegraph vision, they agreed to supply expense money for him. Sanders, with the inventor in his home, had rather the worst of the bargain, for Bell, "his black eyes blazing with excitement," would rout the tired business man out of bed in the middle of the night to make a test. Yawning but patient, Sanders would stumble down to the workshop in the basement, while Bell would rush out, perhaps through a winter storm, to the other end of his wire in the barn, to send signals. If Sanders noticed any improvement since the last test, Bell "would do a war dance." If not, he would go back to work.

It was in 1875 that Thomas A. Watson, who became his co-laborer in the development of the telegraph, first met Bell. Watson, the son of a stable foreman, had gone to work at the age of eighteen in Charles Williams's machine-shop in Boston, where work on electric parts and appliances was a specialty. A youth with little opportunity for education, Watson became interested in electricity, bought a book on it and studied it with zest. One day in 1874 (he was then twenty) he was working on a device for Moses G. Farmer, a regular patron of the shop, for exploding submarine mines by electricity, when "there came rushing out of the office door and through the shop to my work-bench a tall, slender, quick-motioned young man with a pale face, black side-whiskers and drooping mustache, big nose and high, sloping forehead, crowned with bushy, jet-black hair."

Edison from New York Edison Co.; Gray from American Telephone and Telegraph Co.; Dolbear from Tufts College

TELEPHONE INVENTORS

THOMAS A. EDISON   ELISHA GRAY
PHILIPP REIS   AMOS E. DOLBEAR

Bell was bringing two parts, the receiver and transmitter of his harmonic telegraph, on which Watson had been working, and which had not been made precisely according to his idea; and in his impetuous way, he violated the rules of the establishment by going directly to the workman, instead of stopping in the office. Thereafter, Watson gradually gave more and more of his time to Bell's instruments, and finally, all of it—Sanders and Hubbard paying him a salary of $9.00 a week. A large attic space over the Williams shop was rented, and there they conducted their experiments. They worked through the winter and spring of 1875-76, finding the receivers perversely determined to pick out the wrong messages much of the time, and before spring, Watson's faith in the gadget had waned considerably.

But meanwhile, to Bell as to Gray, a new and dazzling idea had grown out of the experiments. "If I can make a deaf-mute talk, I can make metal talk," he said to Sanders; not a very logical ratiocination. He showed Hubbard one day how, when he sang the note A near the strings of a piano, the A string responded with faint vibration. "This is an indication," said he, "that some day we shall have a vocal telegraph. If I can project my voice over musical strings, why can't I project my voice over a wire?" But this was beyond the compass of Hubbard's unscientific mind, and as he and Sanders saw Bell becoming more and more infatuated with the idea, they feared that, genius-like, he was flying off on a tangent, leaving behind his most valuable idea. They threatened to cut off the financial assistance they had been giving him if he dropped his harmonic telegraph and went in pursuit of this phantom. Thereafter, he conscientiously gave a part of his time to the telegraph, but his heart was no longer in it.

On February 27, 1875, the three had put their previously informal agreement into writing. The covenant was that Sanders and Hubbard should supply one-half the money needed by Bell to carry on his experiments and to procure patents, and that the three should own the patents in equal shares. It was never the idea of Sanders and Hubbard to include the telephone in this agreement. They regarded that as just a foolish little flyer of the inventor, a wild oat which he was bound to sow, but which had no financial value, and which it was hoped he would soon forget. The stated basis of the written agreement was that "said Bell has invented certain new and useful methods and apparatus for telegraphy." Had Bell chosen to hold them to it, the courts would doubtless have sustained him in the claim that the telephone was not here contemplated. In fact, in 1876, when the telephone patent had been obtained and the instrument seemed headed towards success, Hubbard admitted this, and offered to relinquish all claim on it to Bell. Cynical persons might cast doubt upon his scrupulosity by pointing out that by this time Mabel Hubbard was betrothed to Bell, and the money would be in the family, anyhow. But Bell, with undoubtedly true magnanimity, retorted that he had never for a moment considered that the telephone was not included in the agreement, although he was well aware that his two partners did not so regard it. Out of their shares, however, came a one-tenth interest which had been promised to Watson. All agreements were kept by the group, and so far as we know, there was no friction among them afterwards.

Bell had now discarded all his pupils save two, and these barely provided him with the necessities of life. He was worn thin by nervous strain and lack of sleep. Copying a human ear as did Reis, he made words spoken near the tympanum trace a record with a bristle on smoked glass. But he could not reproduce speech. Early in 1875, he went down to Washington and saw the aging but still mentally virile Joseph Henry. He told Henry of his experimental groping towards the telephone, and how, when he passed an intermitted current through a helix of insulated copper wire, a sound could be heard in the coil. Henry was much stirred. He asked to see and hear the experiment and sat for a long time with the coil at his ear, listening. He asked to be permitted to publish a report in the Smithsonian papers. "You have the germ of a great idea," said he to Bell. "Work at it!"

Bell replied that he appreciated the mechanical difficulties in the way, and feared that he had not the electrical knowledge wherewith to overcome them.

"Get it!" replied Henry, laconically. The words were a tonic to Bell. He returned to Boston, fired with new zeal. Ever afterwards throughout life, he never refused to see or listen to an inventor who asked his advice, no matter how silly his ideas seemed. "I don't want to discourage him," he would say. "There may be something in it. But for Joseph Henry, I should never have gone on with the telephone."

But months more passed with little or no encouragement. On June 2, 1875, he felt that he had gained a step. He and Watson were working on the harmonic telegraph, trying to get the steel reeds in the receiving instruments to vibrate in consonance with the sending ones. Bell, in one room, was receiving, and Watson, about sixty feet away, in another, was plucking the reeds. One of them stuck, and he kept plucking at it, trying to start it vibrating. All at once he heard a shout from Bell and the inventor rushed in with, "What did you do then? Don't change anything! Let me see."

Instead of getting a reaction from his reed, he had heard the sound—the first sound through his telephone. By accident, the current had been flowing continuously through the electromagnets and the line. Watson's plucking had varied the intensity of this flow and caused the thin strip of steel at the other terminus to vibrate and produce a tone. It would seem that success was now within the eager inventor's grasp. He immediately gave Watson instructions for the building of a telephone; a small drumhead of goldbeater's skin mounted over the receiver, the center of the drumhead joined to the free end of the receiver spring, and a mouthpiece just a short distance outside the drumhead to direct the voice against it. But try as he might, four-fifths of a year passed and a change was made in the instrument before he could induce it to talk.

Bell had a sinking spell of discouragement that year, but rallied. By this time Hubbard and Sanders had become convinced that he "had something" in that telephone dingus, and Hubbard advised simultaneous patenting in America and England. Bell knew a prominent man in Toronto, George Brown, who agreed to take over the job of getting an English patent and to pay Bell a nominal sum for half of the foreign rights. Brown was to sail about the first of January, but his departure was delayed, and Hubbard became impatient, fearing that Gray or some one else would anticipate Bell.

Here the stories of the telephone begin to diverge, and thenceforward, one may, on many points, find diametrically contradictory statements, often solemnly sworn to on the witness stand by reputable persons. Bell's biography written by Catherine Mackenzie says that Brown did not sail from New York until January 25th, and that Bell saw him off. Another version has it that it was on the 25th that Bell, Hubbard and Pollok, the Washington patent attorney, met Brown as he was returning from England, having failed to get a patent over there. Miss Mackenzie, on the other hand, says that by the time Brown reached England, his courage had evaporated, and he did not dare ask for a patent, lest he be ridiculed, so he let Bell's papers lie untouched in the bottom of his trunk during his stay. This account says that he was to have cabled Hubbard as soon as he had made application for the patent, but that he failed to send any word at all, and finally, by February 12th, Hubbard feared to wait any longer and notified Pollok to go ahead. Bell's description of his devices had been drawn up some weeks before and sworn to on January 20th. He insisted afterwards under oath that he did not change it afterwards, and that the variable resistance clause which caused all the trouble was in it all the time. Opposing forces just as stubbornly maintained that it was not.

On one momentous Monday, February 14, 1876, Bell's attorney entered the Patent Office in Washington, and filed his application in the Department of Electricity. The entry and the receipt of the fee were duly entered on the blotter. The hour of entry was not noted; for who could have guessed that two inventors would try to patent that rather absurd device, the telephone, on the same day? Yet it was on that same day—a stormy one, it is said to have been, and truly it was for the other fellow—another man, Elisha Gray in person, entered and filed, not an application for patent, but a caveat on a telephone—a mere warning that he has gotten the invention well under way; a warning which gives him the right to be notified if any one else asks for a patent on the same article.

Had the clerk entered on his blotter the hour when each of these applications was filed, much litigation and bitter feeling might have been averted in the years that followed. As it was, it was believed by some for years afterwards that Gray was first with his application. It was charged under oath that being filed first, it lay near the bottom of the day's papers, and therefore, at the close of the day's business, was entered among the last on the records—Bell's entry being the fifth and Gray's the thirty-ninth. This theory was repudiated by the Patent Office officials, and the averment was gradually built up that Gray had arrived at the office two hours later than Bell's attorney. Thirty-four applications for patents and caveats must have made that an unusually busy two hours for the office. All charges, counter-charges and denials were made long after the event. Gray at first and for months afterward meekly accepted the theory that he had been beaten.

What a crude system is ours for handling such matters! What a discredit to the boasted human ingenuity and justice! Why must invention be always a race in which the prize and the only prize is awarded to the swift, or a battle in which all the honors and emoluments are handed over to the strongest and most ruthless mauler? Haroun-al-Raschid would have thought of a better plan.

Let it be noted that the sketches and description included in Gray's caveat showed a variable resistance feature which was produced by a cup of acidulated water, into which dipped the end of a short wire, attached to the diaphragm. Wire and diaphragm were in the circuit; the current entered at the side of the transmitting box and ran down into the liquid. The depth of the wire's immersion in the water-and-acid, and the consequent resistance of the circuit were varied as the voice caused vibration of the diaphragm, this in turn making the galvanic current undulate, and produce speech at the other terminal. No evidence exists that Bell had experimented with such an instrument previous to this time, though he claims that it was comprehended in his patent application.

Another odd thing is seen in the fact that Bell's application did not promise speech by his instrument; only the transmission of "noises or sounds." Truth to tell, his device had not yet reproduced speech. Gray, on the other hand, though more cautious in asking only for a caveat, was more confident in that he claimed to have invented an "art of transmitting vocal sounds telegraphically," and added: "It is the object of my invention to transmit the tones of the human voice through a telegraphic circuit, and reproduce them at the receiving end of the line, so that actual conversation can be carried on by persons at long distances apart." From this it was reasoned by many in the decade that followed—and not without logic—that Gray had been the first to transmit speech.

Now come the five days claimed to have been sullied with dark intrigue. The charge as made by Lysander Hill, eminent counsel speaking in behalf of the People's and Overland Telephone Companies in after years, is that Bell's attorneys were permitted to see Gray's caveat, which was a gross violation of law, if true, and that between the 14th and the 19th, as a result of this "unlawful and guilty knowledge," Bell's application was withdrawn and a new one substituted, in which the acid cup and the variable resistance feature were embodied. Gray was notified on the 19th that there was an "interference" with his caveat, the points given by Patent Examiner Wilbur being: (1) The receiver set into vibration by undulating currents; (2) the method of producing the undulation by varying the resistance of the circuit; (3) the method of transmitting vocal sounds telegraphically by causing these undulatory currents," and so forth.

358

Bell's attorneys were also notified of an interference. In the Dowd case in 1879 Bell swore that when he heard of the interference:

I went to Washington to examine into the matter, for I understood that an applicant in interference had a right to see that portion of the interfering application which conflicted with his invention. I therefore went to the Patent Office and requested the Examiner to explain to me the exact points of interference between my application and the other. I found that there had been two interferences declared with my application. The first was with a caveat filed the same day as my application, and had already been dissolved. The Examiner declined to show me the caveat, as it was a confidential document, but he indicated to me the particular clause in my application with which it had conflicted. I therefore knew it had something to do with the vibration of a wire in liquid. I do not now remember what it was that led me to suppose that that liquid was water.

"Amazing intuition!" sneered the anti-Bell factions. "The truth of the matter is that he was told the exact nature of the interfering caveat, perhaps permitted to read it; and then he approved and signed the altered application which his attorneys had drawn for him." By a strict interpretation of the law, Wilbur did wrong even in indicating to Bell the point of conflict in the two applications. Perhaps it was just a magnification of this statement when witnesses swore in later years that Wilbur had actually admitted in their presence that he revealed the contents of Gray's caveat to Bell. How is one to decide fifty and sixty years later which of the millions of words of testimony in the telephone cases is truth and which is perjury; which is cold, sober fact, and which are statements warped by prejudice, influence, selfishness, envy, malice, toadyism, bad memory, lack of concentration, necessity for holding a job and the thousand other enemies to truth?

In his long deposition in 1892 in the Government's suit against his patent, Bell was not asked by his attorneys about the Gray interference. Led by their questioning, he said that his attorneys wrote him that the Examiner had the impression that in a certain clause in his application, he was infringing upon his own patent application of February 25, 1875, on a harmonic telegraph appliance; in other words, that he was asking the Government to patent the same thing over again; and suggested that he come to Washington and explain the difference to the Examiner. He said that he reached the Capital on the 26th. On the previous day the Examiner had written to his attorneys, formally eliminating Gray's caveat, and stating that it had been declared an interference "under a misunderstanding of applicant's (Bell's) rights." Bell testifies that he explained to the satisfaction of Wilbur that his new idea did not overlap his former one, and Wilbur suggested that he put the explanation into writing and attach it as an amendment to his application. This was completed by the 29th, and miraculously enough—that is, it seems a miracle to any one who knows official Washington—the patent was allowed three days later. Bell then returned to Boston, and the document, Number 174,465, perhaps the most valuable patent in our history, was handed to his attorneys on March 7th. This almost unheard-of celerity supplied another ground for suspicion. Where else does one find such alacrity? demanded the critics. Berliner's telephone transmitter waited fourteen years for a decision, and Edison had two applications for telephone patents which were held up for fifteen years!

One of the most interesting features of the story is that no word of speech was transmitted by a telephone devised by Bell until twenty-five days after his patent application was filed, and three days after the patent had been granted. On the evening of March 10th, Bell and Watson were tinkering away in the attic room of Bell's new lodgings at 5 Exeter Place, Boston, to which they had removed some of their apparatus. Watson, at Bell's direction, had made a new transmitter in which a cup of acidulated water was included in the circuit, precisely as Gray had stipulated in his caveat. Watson asserts that "Neither of us had the least idea that we were about to try the best transmitter that had yet been devised." But he also claims that "Bell knew from the first that he could produce stronger undulations" (that is,

Top—BELL'S FIRST INSTRUMENT, 1875
Left—HIS LIQUID TRANSMITTER
Right—HIS CENTENNIAL RECEIVER
Bottom—HIS CENTENNIAL TRANSMITTER

in the instruments he was then trying, in which the undulations were magneto-electric, the voice being the source of power) "and as perfect in form, by a more complicated telephone so designed that the voice varied the resistance of the circuit through a galvanic battery, and some of his earliest experiments included work on such a battery transmitter." In short, he tells us that the use of the acid cup at this moment was just a coincidence; but if so, it was a coincidence which a malicious Fate devises to mock at men and set them by the ears.

It was so necessary that Bell produce speech through the instrument upon which he had already received a patent that he and Watson had agreed to work all of that night of March 10th, if necessary, to show an inch of progress. They filled the cup with a mixture of sulphuric acid and water and hooked it up to a battery and to a wire connecting the two attic rooms. Then Watson went into Bell's meagerly furnished bedroom, shut the door and stood with the receiver pressed to his ear. Almost immediately he heard Bell's voice, faint but distinct through the receiver, "Mr. Watson, come here! I want you." Bell had upset some battery acid on his trousers, and in his excitement, forgot that Watson had shut himself up in the next room. But he also forgot the disaster to his scanty wardrobe when Watson burst into the room with popping eyes and cried, "Professor Bell, I heard every word you said!" Watson, it will be noted, had no transmitter, only a receiver, and therefore, could not reply to Bell by wire. Bell, jubilant even with ruined breeches, ran into the other room and listened while Watson talked. Within a few days an iron wire was run from Bell's rooms to Williams's shop, half a mile distant, and much experimenting went on over it.

Some time after the granting of the patent, Bell said to Gray, "I do not know about the nature of the caveat to which you referred as having been filed two hours after my application for a patent, excepting that it had something to do with the vibration of a wire in water, and therefore conflicted with my patent. My specification had been prepared *months* before it was filed, and a copy had been taken to England by a friend." This paper entrusted to Brown, allegedly the original, was displayed and sworn to in the telephone trials in after years. In it is a rude sketch of the telephone as it existed in December or January; this is captioned, "First attempt to transmit the human voice. The varying pitch of the voice could be discriminated, but not the quality. A sort of muttering effect was perceived at the receiving end when a person talked very loudly at the other end." No wonder Brown hesitated to ask for a patent on it in England!

As for the variable resistance feature, there was on one page of this description given to Brown, a very crude drawing by Bell (who was obviously no draughtsman) of the instrument and circuit, though no cup of water is shown. The accompanying text mentions condensers as a means of lessening or destroying the spark when the circuit is broken, and says that: "The same effect may be produced by introducing between the points where the circuit is broken an *imperfect conductor* which will offer great resistance to the voltaic current, but afford a free passage for the induced current which occasions the spark. Such a substance is water, especially when slightly acidulated." Retort carbon, plumbago, animal or vegetable tissue and other substances would do, he added, but he preferred water, which could be decomposed by the passage of the current.

From this it would appear that Bell had then thought of impeding the current with acidulated water, though oddly enough, he had not yet tried it, or perhaps had not found out how to try it. That this paper did not show a sketch of the instrument which first transmitted speech with its watercup and lacked other features of the patent application was charitably attributed by the Supreme Court eleven years later to the assumption that it was just a rough draft, hastily prepared.

During the patent trials a file jacket and copy of Bell's specification enclosed in it bobbed up, with a number of pencil notations on the margins, embodying the variable resistance idea. The anti-Bell attorneys pounced upon it and theorized that this was the original Bell application and its envelope, and that the corrections were written thereon by Bell when he went to Washington to approve and complete the trick which his attorneys had put over—a fresh copy with the corrections incorporated therein being substituted for this one. The Bell attorneys retorted that this was merely a certified copy of the application obtained for their use in the trials, and the pencil writing was their own memoranda of the differences between this copy and the specifications sent to England by Brown. So it would appear from their explanation that after all, the Brown description did lack some items which were in the patent application. In short, that Bell's machine just before and at the time of patenting was in a state of nervous, hurried alteration and experiment, and that he had not actually produced a workable instrument when he received his patent.

CHAPTER XVIII

STRUGGLE AND TRIUMPH OF THE BELL PATENT

Great contest follows, and much learned dust
Involves the combatants; each claiming truth
And truth disclaiming both.

COWPER, *The Task*

IT WAS Hubbard who persuaded Bell, early in the summer of 1876, to exhibit at the Centennial Exposition at Philadelphia. A much better looking set of instruments was prepared, but he was so late in entering that he was crowded out of the electrical department and into the adjacent educational section. Bell himself, who was now doing more teaching, was busy with his speech classes, and Hubbard superintended the exhibit and explained the instruments to those who could be induced to stop and listen. Along towards the 20th of June, Hubbard wrote Bell that the judges would reach his exhibit on Sunday, the 25th, and he must be present.

Bell, who, now that he had won his patent, had begun to give evidence of that curious waning of interest in the telephone which finally approached totality, protested that his class examinations were set for Monday, and he could not spare the time to go to Philadelphia. It was only through the urging of his fiancée that he was persuaded to go. Meanwhile Hubbard, tired and wilted by the heat, had come home, leaving his young nephew, William Hubbard, in charge of the exhibit.

Bell, too, hated hot weather, and he was very uncomfortable in his best black suit as he nervously awaited the coming of the judges that forenoon. They were long in coming, and when they appeared, they too, swathed in heavy woolen suits, as men thought they must be in those days, were perspiring and anxious

364

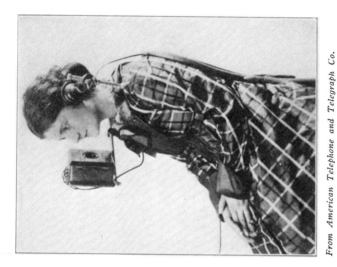

From American Telephone and Telegraph Co.

AN EARLY TELEPHONE OPERATOR'S HEAD-SET; WEIGHT MORE THAN SIX POUNDS

THE BRAZILIAN EMPEROR AND BELL AT THE CENTENNIAL EXPOSITION, FROM A MOTION PICTURE VERSION OF THE SCENE

to have done with the morning's task. They were a distinguished group; led by Professor George F. Barker of the University of Pennsylvania, it included Sir William Thomson, the great cable authority, Professor James C. Watson of the University of Michigan, Professor T. Sterry Hunt, Dr. Koenig, a noted inventor, and others, including none other than Elisha Gray, whose harmonic telegraph they had already seen.

As they neared his stand, Bell, to his consternation, heard them agree that the next exhibit would be the last they would honor that day. The next exhibit was the one just before his own. He feared that that destroyed all hope of an award for him, for without his presence, the instruments would not be adequately explained to them. But lo! there was another man with the judges—Dom Pedro de Alcantara, second Emperor of Brazil, who was making a long visit to the United States and was at that moment the star guest of the Exposition. This scholarly, high-minded gentleman, whom Brazil dishonored herself by banishing thirteen years later, had visited Bell's classes in Boston a few weeks before and been much interested. Now he recognized the black-whiskered young man standing wistfully by an exhibit several yards away. The judges were just turning to depart, but the genial Emperor strode towards the young man with outstretched hand. "How do you do, Mr. Bell," he exclaimed. "And how are the deaf mutes of Boston?"

The judges, much impressed, but anxious to get away, waited while Dom Pedro talked with Bell. The latter told his friend of his great disappointment at the judges' failing to reach his exhibit, for he must return to Boston that night. "Ah, then we must have a look at it now," exclaimed the Emperor, and taking Bell's arm, he led the way to the booth, while the bored judges trailed along after him.

Transmitter and receiver were 500 feet apart. Bell went to the transmitter, while Willie Hubbard superintended the listening of the judges. Sir William listened for a few moments as Bell recited *Hamlet's* "Soliloquy," then he, too, hastened to the transmitter; he wanted to talk himself. As he took the instrument from Bell and continued the soliloquy, Professor Barker, who was listening at the moment, said to the others, "Sir William is now talking." That struck them as a most wonderful thing—that an individual voice could be distinguished. The Emperor took his turn at listening. A legend has it that when he heard the first words, he explained, "My God, it talks!" but this may be apocryphal.

The judges were deeply impressed by the test, and asked to have the telephone removed to Judges' Hall next day for further trials. Willie Hubbard did this, and reported that Sir William and Lady Thomson ran back and forth between the instruments "like a pair of delighted children"; while the assembled scientists made so much hubbub over the apparatus that the police thought a disaster must have occurred. But newspaper reporters of those days were not alert for such occasions as these, and the telephone received but little notice from the press.

Sir William Thomson went to Boston and made some more tests of the instruments. Bell presented him with a set, but he packed it badly in his trunk, and when he reached home and tried to give a demonstration before his brother scientists, a small part was displaced, and the thing would not work. Great physicist though he was, Thomson could not discover what was wrong, and the British decided that he had simply been humbugged by those slick Yankees. But he wrote a report on the subject, in which he said: "I need hardly say I was astonished and delighted, as were the others who witnessed the experiment and verified with their own ears the electric transmission of speech. This, perhaps the greatest marvel hitherto achieved by the electric telegraph, has been obtained by appliances of quite a homespun and rudimentary character"—which hurt Watson's feelings considerably.

Bell went to visit his parents at Brantford, Ontario, that summer, and a test was made over telegraph wires between that place and another eight miles distant, with fair success. Nobody had yet learned that telegraph wires and equipment were too coarse and their power too strong for so delicate a mechanism as the telephone. The power required to operate a telephone is almost infinitesimal, yet without it there is no transmission. Herbert N. Casson remarks in his story of the telephone, "Catch the falling tear-drop of a child, and there will be sufficient water-power to carry a spoken message from one city to another." In October of that year, Bell for the first time substituted a thin plate of iron or steel for the skin tympanum, and a little later he ceased using a battery, and substituted a permanent magnet for the electro-magnet, obtaining a patent on this in January, 1877.

The somber face of Elisha Gray at that Centennial exhibit is to this writer a pathetic part of the picture. He has been accused of insincerity because he changed his mind so often, but we do not concede that. At first he did not believe that Bell's instrument was a real electric telephone. He argued with Professor Watson of Ann Arbor, one of the judges, that it was just another acoustic instrument. Watson apparently convinced him to the contrary. Newspaper accounts of a lecture which Gray delivered in Illinois during the following winter, however, led Bell to believe that Gray was questioning his title. He wrote to Gray, and the latter, on March 5, 1877, replied frankly (referring to his lecture) : "I gave you full credit for the talking feature of the telephone. . . . I described your apparatus at length by diagram. . . . I do not, however, claim even the credit of inventing it, as I do not believe a mere description of an idea that has never been *reduced* to *practice*—in the *strict sense* of that phrase—should be dignified with the name, invention."

But rougher times were coming. With about a dozen inventors producing telephones, not to mention a few would-be's and pretenders, a storm of litigation presently arose, and advisers convinced the simple, serious Gray that he was a greatly wronged man. Now he heard for the first time of the alleged skullduggery in the Patent Office—some that we have mentioned and some not yet told—with the result that he went to his grave convinced that he had been robbed of his deserts.

Dolbear says of the instrument exhibited at the Centennial

that, "The one who was to talk had to shout himself hoarse in order to be heard at all." But after Bell had begun using the metal tympanum and made some other improvements, he conducted some tests over a two-mile stretch between Boston and Cambridgeport which attracted much attention. Watson says humorously that by this time the telephone, "was talking so well that one didn't have to ask the other man to say it over again more than three or four times before one could understand quite well, if the sentences were simple." It was evident to those best informed that it needed a better transmitter; but when such transmitters were designed, Bell did not design them. He did make changes in them. By 1878, transmitter and receiver were precisely the same—an instrument closely resembling the latter-day receiver now gradually being displaced by the so-called French telephones. You placed it alternately at your lips and your ear, and amateur users often became confused by the quick changes necessary. After a time, persons who could afford it had two of these bells, one to talk through, one to listen through. If hearing was a bit difficult, you helped it while listening by placing one of the pieces at each ear.

Now that Bell had speech going through the instrument, Hubbard, the tireless promoter, took charge. For two or three years, he carried a coil of wire and a set of instruments with him wherever he went, and would demonstrate to any one he could induce to listen to him. He began arranging for lectures to be given by Bell in various New England cities, always with the assistance of Watson, who was to be at the Boston terminus of the wire. There were no telephone wires, of course, so permission was procured from the telegraph companies to use one of their wires, seldom with entirely satisfactory results.

The first lecture, before the Essex Institute of Salem, was considered a success. For these lectures, Bell would have an instrument on the platform beside him, pointed towards the audience, and usually three more in various parts of the hall. They were thus giving the telephone a rather severe test—they were talking over a considerable distance and expecting the reproduction to be loud enough to be heard several yards from the receiver. At Bell's request, Watson in Boston would, after some conversation, introduce in turn a cornetist and an organ player, who would oblige with music; and then Watson, who made no pretensions as a singer, would nevertheless do his best with "Auld Lang Syne," "Hail, Columbia!" or "Do Not Trust Him, Gentle Lady." The audience at Salem was much impressed by the demonstration, and newspaper references to it brought many more requests for lectures.

Other engagements were not always greatly successful. Reporters in Lowell found Bell's lecture "slow and rather uninteresting"; said that the music was heard well enough, but that the conversation "between Professor Bell and somebody in Boston, was not audible to any save those near the instruments." The Providence *Journal,* after his engagement there, said that "his instruments proved their ability to transmit instrumental music perfectly, but were not equally successful in demonstrating their capability to transmit speech with sufficient force to be practicable." Bell was using a diaphragm four inches in diameter then, and it caught too many undesired sounds—not to mention other defects. At Lawrence they were given a telegraph wire which wasn't working well, and the audience heard practically nothing over it. The Lawrence *Daily American* on May 29, 1877, satirized the affair in a clever poem of a dozen or more stanzas, which began:

> To the great hall we strayed,
> Fairly our fee we paid,
> Seven hundred there delayed,
>   But where was Watson?
>
> Was he out on his beer?
> Walked he off on his ear?
> Something was wrong, 'tis clear.
>   What was it, Watson?
>
> Seven hundred souls were there
> Waiting with stony stare
> In that expectant air—
>   Waiting for Watson.

OLD WIRES AND NEW WAVES

As the poet suggested——

> Doubtless 'tis very fine
> When all along the line
> Things work most superfine;
> Doubtless 'tis, Watson—

but when they didn't, when they were bad, like the notorious little girl in the nursery rhyme, they were horrid.

The interest in the lectures was mostly that of idle curiosity. Scarcely any one as yet saw any utility in the telephone, or any future possibilities. Nevertheless, the small admission fees charged for the affairs put a few hundred dollars in Bell's pocket, and gave him courage to marry Mabel Hubbard. They planned to spend their honeymoon in England, where Bell would endeavor to introduce his idea to the hard-headed Britons.

Meanwhile Hubbard, in May, 1877, published the first telephone advertisement. It was he who conceived the idea—taking it from a shoe-machinery concern for which he was attorney—of leasing instead of selling the instruments; and he maintained it stoutly, often against the vigorous opposition of his associates, all through those early days when the infant organization needed money badly, and could have raised it by selling apparatus. His wisdom soon justified itself. His advertisement offered the use of two telephones for social purposes, as between a dwelling and any other building, for $20 a year. For business use, the rental of the two sets would be $40. Instruments were to be kept in working order by the lessors. Several telephones might be strung on the same line at an additional rental of $10 for each instrument; "but the use of more than two on the same line, where privacy is required, is not advised." This announcement, it will be seen, did not contemplate the use of a switchboard or central exchange; but that convenience was soon to come.

The advertisement quickly brought some small result; within a short time after it appeared, a man presented himself at Hubbard's office in Boston and handed over $20 for a year's lease on two telephones—the first money received in history for that purpose. On May 17th, the first switchboard was installed, though it was a private one. E. T. Holmes, another pioneer whose business still lives, had electric burglar alarms in six banks in Boston, and these he connected with his office. The wires were used through his exchange for telephone purposes by day, and became burglar alarms at nightfall.

The shares of the original owners of the telephone patent and of the three patents which Bell had previously been awarded on his harmonic telegraph had been assigned to Hubbard as trustee; and he now created the Bell Telephone Company, he still continuing as trustee. This took place on July 9, 1877, two days before Bell's marriage. The telephone rights were parceled out by Hubbard into 5,000 shares of stock. To make the division "come out even," Bell received 10 shares more than either of his two partners; and he promptly transferred all but those 10 shares to his bride. The ownership now stood thus:

	Shares		Shares
Alexander Graham Bell .	10	Charles Eustis Hubbard .	10
Mabel H. Bell	1,497	Thomas Sanders	1,497
Gardiner G. Hubbard	1,387	Thomas A. Watson	499
Gertrude McC. Hubbard .	100	Total	5,000

The telephone idea seemed to be taking hold that year, especially in New England. The Lowell, Gas Company and several of the textile factories of that city were among the very early clients. By August, 1877, 778 instruments were in service, and the manufacturers could not keep up with the demand for equipment. Williams, in whose loft Bell and Watson had worked, was at first the sole manufacturer, but after a time orders began going to Gray's Western Electric Company, where a more finished product could be obtained. Notwithstanding the increase in business, the company was hard up. Hubbard, Sanders and Watson went to President Orton of the Western Union and offered the whole concern, patent included, to him for $100,000, but he simply smiled. How bitterly the telegraph magnates rued that short-sightedness less than two years later!

Bell cut quite a figure in England that summer. Chaperoned by Sir William Thomson, he exhibited his instruments before some notable gatherings of scientists. He and Mrs. Bell were presented to Queen Victoria at Windsor, and the inventor demonstrated the telephone to her. Connection had been made between the castle and Osborne Cottage, the home of Sir Thomas Biddulph, and first Bell and then the Queen talked with Sir Thomas and Lady Biddulph. Miss Kate Field, journalist and daughter of a famous American family, had been stationed at Osborne Cottage, and sang "Kathleen Mavourneen" over the wire, "for which Her Majesty returned gracious thanks telephonically through the Duke of Connaught." Connection was made in turn with Cowes, London and Southampton, and organ music, bugle calls and other sounds were transmitted. "Her Majesty and the entire Royal Household evinced the greatest interest."

By this time, telephone inventing had become a fad, just as building home radio sets became in recent years. Telephone inventors swarmed upon the Eastern landscape and especially around the Patent Office as the grasshoppers were doing in Kansas; and many of them, as it appeared from their statements, had been working at their idea long before Bell ever thought of a telephone. This might have been true in the case of some of them—James W. McDonough, for example, who applied for a patent on April 10, 1876, only a month after the granting of Bell's patent. He called his instrument a "telelogue or means of transmitting articulate sounds by electricity." The transmitter was about a foot in diameter and looked like a tambourine; its greatest fault was its natural tendency to transmit every sound made within a block or two of it. McDonough swore that he had begun experimenting with it about 1867, and had transmitted speech over it early in 1875. Because of this priority, the under-examiners at the Patent Office were disposed to concede him a superior position in the telephone race, but

Old print from American Telephone and Telegraph Co.

BELL AT SALEM AND WATSON AT BOSTON GIVING A
DEMONSTRATION OF THE TELEPHONE

the chief examiner overruled them on the ground that McDonough used the make-and-break idea, which was not only an imitation of Reis, but which had been declared impracticable when the undulating current system of Bell was accepted by the Office as the only workable method of telephony. But McDonough was not yet out of the running.

A little "Brain Trust" in Providence, Rhode Island, had given Bell quite a scare. In the winter of 1876-77, two professors of Brown University named Eli Whitney Blake and John Peirce, were playing with the telephone idea, and allegedly improving upon what Bell had done. Blake was convinced that Bell was using too large a diaphragm (often four inches across), one which gathered in all the noises in the neighborhood. So he tried a metal diaphragm at first only an inch in diameter; later enlarging it slightly to just about the size used to-day. Blake also conceived the idea of concentrating the sound on the center of the diaphragm by means of a bell-shaped, sunken mouthpiece. He used a ferrotype plate—one of the sort that Grandfather's and Grandmother's pictures were made on—for his diaphragm. In fact, many of the telephone tympani of those days were cut from old ferrotype and daguerreotype plates. Donald Cowell [1] tells of a man in recent years examining an old telephone preserved in Vermont, and finding on the diaphragm a portrait of one of his ancestors.

The Providence group—for half a dozen or more volunteers were helping Blake and Peirce in making practical experiments —believe that they strung the first telephone line used for other than experimental purposes. In fact, they strung two or three of them, one reaching the home of a physician; and when he was called by telephone to attend a factory workman who had been hurt, he was stricken breathless as the possibilities of the telephone burst upon his mind for the first time.

Blake conceived and used the idea of a tuning fork as a call signal. In Bell's telephones up to that time, the only mode of

[1] "Rhode Island's Part in the Development of the Telephone," *Providence Magazine*, May, 1922.

attracting the attention of the other party was that of rapping upon the transmitter with your finger-nail, a pencil or any other convenient object, which produced a series of clicks at the other terminus. Temporarily, the tuning fork was used on the Bell instruments, but Watson soon bettered that.

Bell was much annoyed when he heard of the activities of the Providence group. He wrote a sharp letter to Blake, but the latter heaped coals of fire on his head by promptly shipping him a pair of the Blake telephones, and giving him permission to use any feature of them, adding that he, Blake, had no thought of pecuniary gain. Bell was mollified, but claimed that he had completed experiments resulting in practically the same instrument two or three days before receiving the Blake device. Nevertheless, Providence still believes that it played a larger part in the evolution of the Bell telephone than the Bell clan will admit.

While Bell was lecturing in New England in the spring of 1877 another inventor bobbed up in his path. He received a letter dated May 6th from Professor Amos E. Dolbear of Tufts College, who remarked that he had attended a recent lecture by Bell, and heard the latter make the claim that he was without a competitor. Dolbear desired that in future, Bell recognize his, Dolbear's claim. He said that as long ago as 1864, when he was a college student, he conceived what was substantially his present telephone. He showed it to his physics professor and others, but they were skeptical as to its value, and he had no money with which to promote it. In the autumn of 1876, he read Sir William Thomson's remarks on the Bell telephone, and thereupon dug out his old instrument and added some improvements. He had had no idea that Bell was working along the same line. He could adduce plenty of reputable evidence, he said, to prove his statements. He had thought of writing to Bell and telling him that the telephone could be worked without a battery, but his friends urged him instead to procure a patent on his own ideas. He had at one time thought of contesting Bell's patent, but he realized that this would cost too much money for his slender purse, so he had decided to do nothing. Bell, therefore, need not be uneasy; he would not interfere. All he asked was recognition. He later visited Hubbard and gave an account of his researches in the presence of Bell. They refused to recognize his claim; but he was not done with them yet.

Dolbear did conceive a novel idea, that of the "electro-static receiver." In it, two thin metal diaphragms were separated only by a thin air-space. As the electric current varied by the electro-magnetic transmitter flowed into and out of this condenser, the two disks attracted each other more or less strongly, and thus vibrations were produced which corresponded to the vibrations of the original sound. Bell used dynamic electricity whose motion produced an electric current; Dolbear used static electricity which produced electrical attraction while at rest.

Evidently it was during that summer of 1877 that the Western Union, hitherto distracted by its fight with Gould's rival telegraph company, began to see in the telephone a possibly annoying rival. It could not have had—nobody had—the faintest conception as to the extent of that rivalry in after years. But as the telephone idea began to spread in New England it seemed just as well to get into the game and checkmate a possibly dangerous interference in one way or another. Whether this leaven had begun working on Orton's mind when he was offered the Bell patent for $100,000, we do not know; if it was, he probably thought he knew of a trick worth two of that.

Anyhow, his organization had somehow got wind of Dolbear, and in September of that year, the Gold and Stock Telegraph Company, the Western Union subsidiary, made a contract with the Professor, whereby he undertook to apply for a patent on his telephone and assign it to the company when it was issued—for a nice consideration, of course. Two months later, the American Speaking Telephone Company was organized by Western Union officials, with a capital of $300,000. The new company immediately acquired the rights to all of Gray's patents and applications relating to speaking telephones. The Gold and Stock Company was to act as the agent of the Telephone

Company and to have full charge of its business. In short, the Telephone Company was just a stuffed lay figure.

The Gold and Stock Company installed a big switchboard in its New York headquarters, and began serving hundreds of its clients by telephone as well as through the ticker. The service was not so good, but it was considered marvelous at the time. The company's overlords had made one great and fundamental mistake at the start. They had supposed that their heavy telegraph wire and power could be used for telephony. They strung wires on their poles and in 1878 began opening new exchanges in many cities. But the first public exchange in history had been opened on January 28, 1878, by the Bell Company in New Haven. In June, 1935, Dr. Ernest L. Thomson, the oldest survivor of that first printed directory, died at the age of eighty-four. He was the youngest of the only three physicians in that city who would at the time permit a telephone to be placed in their offices or homes, the others believing that the telephone would make night calls too easy and thus ruin their health. Boston, Bridgeport, New York, Philadelphia and other cities followed with Bell exchange service.

The Bell people were in a serious predicament. Sanders was still financing their operations; he had $110,000 tied up in the business before he began to get any of it back. Nobody as yet suspected that the iron wire they were using greatly impeded the weak current used by the telephone. Hard-drawn copper wire was not discovered for another five or six years. With Bell in Europe, Watson did what he could in a mechanical way. He improved the calling apparatus by devising, first a buzzer, and then the pealing bell which still summons us; and because his landlady objected to his yelling into his experimental telephone, he hung blankets around him to muffle the sound, and so conceived the idea of the telephone booth. That yelling was a sign that the enterprise was still in desperate need of a good transmitter; and better transmitters had by now begun to be invented.

Early in February, 1878, the first Bell subsidiary, the New

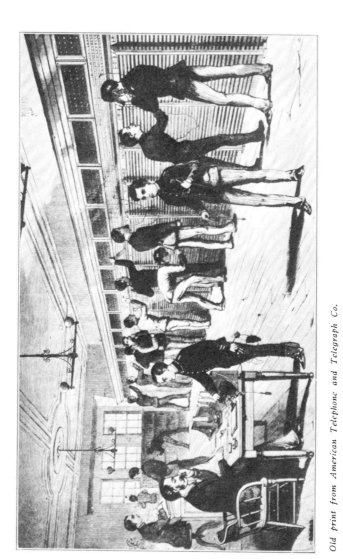

Old print from American Telephone and Telegraph Co.

GOLD AND STOCK TELEGRAPH COMPANY'S TELEPHONE SWITCHBOARD, NEW YORK, 1879. NOTE THE HANDSETS, ORIGINALS OF THE SO-CALLED "FRENCH" TELEPHONE

England Telephone Company, was organized, with the original promoters holding large blocks of its stock. It was followed soon after by a New York company. It was about this time that a letter written in a precise script, indicating that the writer was of Germanic nativity, came from Washington to the Bell attorneys informing them that the undersigned, Emil Berliner, had applied for a patent on a telephone transmitter, which he would sell to the Bell concern for $12,000. They could not afford to overlook any tip of this sort, but in their reply, the attorneys pleasantly "doubted that Mr. Berliner had intended to be serious," inasmuch as the company's resources were but little larger than the price he asked. Nevertheless, Berliner went to New York at the company's expense for a conference, and it was promised that some one would come down and look over his device.

Berliner, a young Jewish clerk in a little dry goods store on Seventh Street in Washington, had come to America as an immigrant from Hanover in 1870. His only instruction in physics he derived from two books, one given him by a friend, another picked up in an old book-shop. His first telephone transmitter was patched together from a child's drum, a needle, a steel dress button and a guitar string. He is called the inventor of the microphone because of the "loose contact" principle for the transmission of sound which he discovered, and which is a fundamental principle of the microphone to-day. This was with his second apparatus (you may see it in the National Museum), a small soap-box with a piece of sheet iron fastened over one end as a diaphragm, and a polished steel button in light contact with the center of it on the under side. Gentle pressure on the diaphragm deflected a galvanometer. The movement of the diaphragm, actuated by the voice, varied the pressure against the button and caused undulations in the current, which were reproduced in sound at the other terminus of a wire. Hitherto, the invariable rule with electro-magnets had been firm contacts.

Berliner converted an electric current of any strength into waves corresponding to sound waves with all their characteristics, great and small. During the telephone trials of the '80's, James J. Storrow, the noted Bell attorney, said, "A thousand inventors have worked on telephones and five hundred of them on microphones. They have improved the details, but have not been able to supersede the Berliner type, so brilliant and daring was Berliner's conception." Professor Barker, the Government's expert in the litigation twenty years later to annul the Berliner patent, confessed that the loose contact theory "passed the limits of scientific credibility" before it was proven true.

Berliner wrote his own caveat, later eulogized by Storrow as a "now classical document, unrivaled for its concise accuracy and completeness," and filed it on April 14, 1877. Two weeks later, Edison filed application for a patent on a transmitter, in which a metal diaphragm vibrated against a large, flat disk covered with graphite. The actuating principle lay in bringing a larger or smaller area of the carbon disk in contact with the diaphragm, as the voice affected the latter.

Berliner was experimenting with a hard carbon button of smaller size at the same time, and considering his instrument to be now practicable, he applied for a patent on June 4, 1877. He had to take some of the patent examiners to his lodging over the store (where his employer's family had long been aiding him in his experiments) and show them his plant before they would believe that it would work. One of the last public acts of Joseph Henry's life was a demonstration of Berliner's apparatus at the Smithsonian Institution. This included the continuous current transformer, on which the inventor asked for a patent in October, and received it in the following January, 1878. But the granting of the patent on his transmitter did not take place until fourteen years later.

In 1877, Edison also applied for a patent on a transmitter employing a series of plumbago cylinders. This and his previous application waited fifteen years for recognition. Early in 1878 he brought forth his best idea yet—namely, a button of compressed lamp-black to rest lightly against the diaphragm. The Western Union puppet had made a deal with Edison for his telephone inventions, and with this transmitter, they now had a tremendous advantage, for the Bell forces had nothing to compare with it. The Western Union also, just to be on the safe side, picked up some other patents, such as the George Phelps receiver, the Short transmitter and the Page induction coil.

But in that spring of 1878, a serious interference (to use official jargon) developed on all telephone applications in the Patent Office—which, in plain language, means that the examiners had gotten into such an addled mental condition over the situation that they didn't know what to do. Hubbard went down to Washington to look after his company's interests; and on one of these trips, he executed one of the master strokes of business history when he persuaded Theodore N. Vail, thirty-three-year-old Superintendent of the United States Railway Mail Service, to give up his job and become General Manager of the telephone corporation. The influence of Vail is seen to this day in the structure and functioning of the American Telephone and Telegraph Company. A cousin once removed of Alfred Vail, Morse's co-worker, Theodore Vail had been a telegrapher and railway mail clerk in his youth, and had made a fine record at the head of the Railway Mail service. Hubbard, who had known him for years, had already made a telephone enthusiast of him, and for some time he had been putting all the cash he could rake and scrape into Bell stock, which could then be had for $25 and $30 a share. His friends and his superiors in the Post-Office Department were appalled at his fatuity in leaving a good, sure job to take up with a "damned Yankee notion, a piece of wire with two Texas steer horns attached to the ends, with an arrangement to make the concern blate like a calf"—thus commented the First Assistant Postmaster-General, who added a prediction that within a year Vail would be wishing himself back in the Government service.

One of Vail's first important acts as manager was the reorganization of the parent company into a corporation, again known as the Bell Telephone Company but minus Hubbard's trusteeship, with a capital of $450,000. He came into the business with full knowledge of the fact that the Bell telephone must have a transmitter as good as Edison's or perish. He came in at the darkest period that it had yet known. The popularity of the telephone was steadily increasing, but the rival concern, with its powerful backing and its arrogant claim to the "only original telephone," was capturing the territory more rapidly than the Bell organizations. The latter were on the verge of bankruptcy. A Chicago company had been organized, but it was so intimidated by the enemy company already intrenched and by the belief of most Chicagoans that Gray and Edison were the real inventors of the telephone that it folded up and quit. Bell himself was already wailing that he was out fully $12,000 in time and money on the thing, and hadn't gotten a cent of it back.

On one of his Washington visits, Hubbard asked Pollok and Bailey, the patent attorneys, to look over the situation and see if there were any telephone patents which the company should buy. They found Berliner's name on the records, saw his apparatus at work, and reported it as worthy the consideration of their clients. Berliner, of course, had nothing to offer them but a caveat and an application for patent not yet acted upon, though he did have a patent on a good transformer or induction coil. However, he entered the Bell organization on a salary and royalty on exported transmitters. Several years later, by the way, the company paid him a lump sum and increased his salary.

He had been with them but a little while when Francis Blake of Weston, Massachusetts, a young man connected with the United States Geodetic Survey, offered to the corporation a transmitter which, without being an imitation, was in effect an ingenious and valuable modification of Berliner's. Blake was placed on the payroll to improve his device; but he soon suffered a nervous breakdown, and Berliner thereupon brought the Blake transmitter to a high degree of efficiency.

Thus fortified, the spirits of the Bell officials rose to hitherto unknown heights. They were now ready for battle—they had a transmitter as good as or better than Edison's; therefore, in September, 1878, they threw down the gage by bringing suit in the Federal Court in Boston for infringement against one Peter A. Dowd, a manager for the American Speaking Telephone Company in Massachusetts. Suits were also brought in other places, and in Boston and Cincinnati, injunctions were obtained against manufacturers, to stop their making unauthor-

A TELEPHONE OF 1878

ized instruments. The Dowd case was the only one tried at length. It did not come to trial for some time, and when it did, it dragged on through the spring and summer of 1879.

Meanwhile, another structural change had taken place in the Bell organization. In December, 1878, a new director appeared on the parent company's roster—William H. Forbes of Boston, son-in-law of Ralph Waldo Emerson. Mr. Forbes soon took steps to reorganize all the Bell interests in one great company. This was accomplished in March, 1879, the new corporation being known as the National Bell Telephone Company. Its capital was set at $850,000.

As the Dowd suit wore on through the summer, the public began to sense the fact that the Bell Company was presenting the stronger case. Its stock in the spring, shortly after the reorganization, was quoted around $50 a share. As summer and autumn passed, it mounted steadily to 100, then to 200. And then came the climax. A thousand witnesses had testified, the evidence was all in, but before the referee could make his decision, George Gifford, the leading Western Union counsel, told his clients that they might as well yield the fight and cease spending money on a hopeless cause; the two Bell patents on telephones were unassailable and undoubtedly had precedence. With that, the suit was halted, and Bell stock rose to 350.

But the Western Union was still unwilling to yield without trying to save something from the wreck. It proposed a compromise; let the Bell Company handle all local business, while the Western Union took over the interurban or long distance traffic, which, as it foresaw, was soon to become important, and would cut into its own trade. But this Vail would not hear to. He himself had his eye on distance telephony. Committees from the two companies met and powwowed in vain; the fight went on, and Bell stock began to decline again. The Western Union was steadily thrusting out more lines, and in some newly entered towns, was giving service free, hoping by its great spread to force better terms.

But finally Vail, by bulldog pertinacity, forced his opponents to yield. In one final conference, high officials from both companies sat down around a table in New York, and after a meeting lasting all day and nearly all night, a treaty of peace was signed on November 10, 1879, which was in effect a complete surrender on the part of the Western Union. By its terms, the Goliath of the two combatants acknowledged Bell to be the original inventor of the telephone, and his patents as valid; and it agreed to retire from the telephone business forever. The Bell Company, on the other hand, covenanted never to touch the telegraph business; it agreed to buy the American Speaking Telephone system at an appraised cost of construction, and to pay the Western Union a royalty of 20 per cent on all telephone rentals. These payments continued for seventeen years, and brought a nice bit of cash into the Western Union strong-box. The Bell Company took over 56,000 working telephones; the A. S. T. had been diligent.

Next day, when announcement was made of the consolidation, Bell stock shot up momentarily to 995! Those who had formerly scorned the telephone, who had had opportunities to buy when the stock was begging to be noticed, were now holding their heads and moaning with remorse. Fancy the feelings of the electrician who had once refused to go from New York to Boston to take a job with the company because he understood that he would have to take part of his pay in stock! The Bell and Hubbard families never had occasion for worry thereafter. Watson soon left the telephone business and founded a shipbuilding plant. Sanders sold his telephone stock for about a million dollars, and lost most of the money in Colorado gold mines. But fortunately, he had given some of it to his mother, and Mrs. Bell, after his disaster, insisted on sharing some of her stock with the family. Charles Williams, the Boston manufacturer, had been taking some of his pay for telephone apparatus in stock. At times he managed to work off small quantities of it for $25 a share. Now he found himself comfortably rich overnight.

In connection with the settlement, Elisha Gray once more renounced his claim to priority, and through his counsel, made formal admission that Bell was the inventor of the telephone. Gossip had it that he received $100,000 for so doing. Nevertheless, like Galileo when he was forced to recant, Gray was unconvinced, and seven years later he opened the subject again.

CHAPTER XIX

STRUGGLE AND TRIUMPH OF THE BELL PATENT
(CONTINUED)

WITH the Bell patent triumphant, a reorganization was inevitable, and it took place only a little more than four months after the settlement, when the American Bell Telephone Company was created, with a capital of $7,350,000. Stockholders of the old National Bell were given six shares of the new stock for one of the old, and could buy more, if they chose, at par. Within a short time, shares in the new company were quoted at 170. Thereafter, telephone stock was watered again and again, but seemingly, could always stand it. The telephone had crowded the Comstock Lode off the map as a Big Bonanza.

One reason for its growing popularity was that improvements now began to appear rapidly. The telephone by 1880 had become a big walnut structure screwed to the wall, with a battery jar in its lower compartment, whose acid slopped over sometimes and made long, hideous streaks down the wall-paper. The earth was still being used for the return circuit, which caused much waste of current and unearthly noises, filched from adjacent telegraph wires and other disturbers. Wires strung between Boston and Providence were so noisy that they could not be used at all. In 1879, an inspector in the Boston office reported thus the process of handling a call:

When a call comes in, it is promptly answered by the man at the switch, who calls out the name of the parties to the clerk. The clerk writes the names on a slip of paper and hands it to a boy, who makes the connection on the switch, then passes the slip to the operator at the table.... The switch boys frequently make mistakes in connections, and ... sometimes seven minutes elapse before the parties get to conversing with each other.

STRUGGLE AND TRIUMPH OF THE BELL PATENT

As will be seen by the accompanying instructions of the Chicago Telephone Exchange, calling a person in a large city around 1880 was a complicated process of pressing black and white buttons or of giving your party's name and street address. Then L. B. Firman invented the multiple switchboard, and Charles E. Scribner, of the Western Electric, began improving it. By 1883, hard-drawn copper wire began ·to be made, and greatly improved conductivity. John J. Carty, a young diploma-less Bell engineer, only recently a switchboard boy for Holmes, the burglar-alarm man, conceived the idea of using a wire instead of the earth for the return circuit, and that promptly eliminated most of the disturbing noises. This was the first major achievement of Carty's career as one of the greatest of telephone engineers. And in 1881, a long step was made towards the per-fect transmitter when the company purchased the American patent of Henry Hunnings, a Yorkshire clergyman, on a trans-mitter which was a narrow chamber with one electrode-wall fixed, the other wall the vibrating diaphragm, and the space between partly filled with crushed engine coke, which supplied a great number of points of microphonic contact. Bell engineers improved this and in 1886, Edison gave it a boost by suggesting, instead of the gas coke, granules of carbonized anthracite—the stuff still being used in transmitters. Anthony D. White gave the final touch in 1890 by designing a transmitter with two carbon disks for electrode walls with the granules between, one disk fixed, the other moving piston-like, forward and backward when actuated by the diaphragm to which it was attached.

After the Western Union surrender, the Bell Company found itself with half a dozen kinds of transmitter patents in its pos-session, most of them in use at one place and another, and for a while it had to let the situation remain so. In the Bell Labora-tory Museum to-day you may see a large, elaborate walnut wall-telephone apparatus, with two transmitter orifices a few inches apart. The story of it is that there was a sharp division in the directorate of the Pennsylvania Railroad as to which was the better transmitter, Edison's or Berliner's. As they could not

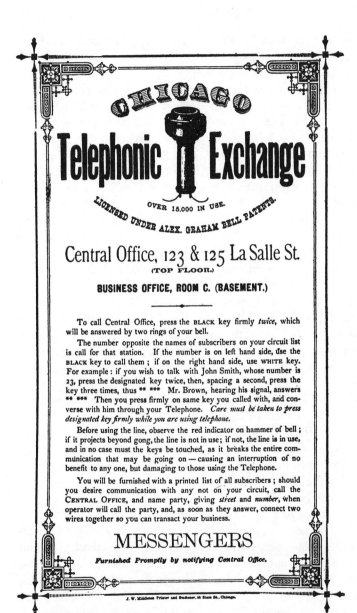

CHICAGO
Telephonic Exchange

OVER 15,000 IN USE.

LICENSED UNDER ALEX. GRAHAM BELL PATENTS.

Central Office, 123 & 125 La Salle St.
(TOP FLOOR.)

BUSINESS OFFICE, ROOM C. (BASEMENT.)

To call Central Office, press the BLACK key firmly *twice*, which will be answered by two rings of your bell.

The number opposite the names of subscribers on your circuit list is call for that station. If the number is on left hand side, use the BLACK key to call them; if on the right hand side, use WHITE key. For example: if you wish to talk with John Smith, whose number is 23, press the designated key twice, then, spacing a second, press the key three times, thus ** *** Mr. Brown, hearing his signal, answers ** *** Then you press firmly on same key you called with, and converse with him through your Telephone. *Care must be taken to press designated key firmly while you are using telephone.*

Before using the line, observe the red indicator on hammer of bell; if it projects beyond gong, the line is not in use; if not, the line is in use, and in no case must the keys be touched, as it breaks the entire communication that may be going on — causing an interruption of no benefit to any one, but damaging to those using the Telephone.

You will be furnished with a printed list of all subscribers; should you desire communication with any not on your circuit, call the CENTRAL OFFICE, and name party, giving *street* and *number*, when operator will call the party, and, as soon as they answer, connect two wires together so you can transact your business.

MESSENGERS

Furnished Promptly by notifying Central Office.

J. W. Middleton Printer and Stationer, 46 State St., Chicago.

From American Telephone and Telegraph Co.

INSTRUCTIONS FOR USING THE TELEPHONE, CHICAGO, 1880

agree, they specified that their system must be equipped with both types on each instrument. If you believed in Edison's transmitter, you yelled through that one, and if you thought Berliner's the best, you used that. As the two were close together, the probabilities are that they slyly helped each other.

With the clinching of the Bell monopoly and the sky-high flight of its stock, every amateur inventor who had ever tinkered with a telephone idea at once became of major importance. Promoters sought him out and pondered ways of proving his prior claim or at least of turning him into a nuisance which the great corporation would pay money to get rid of. McDonough was now taken up by one group of promoters, Dolbear (with a new invention) by another, and there were dozens more. Within a quarter century, some six hundred suits were fought out in assailing or protecting the priceless patents of Bell.

A slippery gentleman, one Dr. Seth R. Beckwith, took up several inventors in turn. He first organized the Overland Telephone Company early in 1883 to promote the patents of Myron L. Baxter of Illinois. The American Bell brought suit and Beckwith, seeing that the situation looked dark, quietly severed all connection with his company, leaving it and Baxter in the lurch, and bobbed up in another company, the Globe, which he had meanwhile organized to handle the patents of George E. Shaw. He had now decided, however, that to succeed, one should have an inventor who could show priority, and presently he discovered one such jewel—an old Italian candle-maker down on Staten Island, a veteran of Garibaldi's wars named Antonio Meucci, who claimed to have invented a telephone—oh, as far back as 1857, and was experimenting with it eight years before that. He had filed a caveat in 1871 and renewed it twice, but never got a patent. The truth is that he appears to have had nothing but an acoustic telephone, though he thought he was using electricity (a medium of which he had little knowledge) and insulated both sender and receiver from the earth by having them sit or stand on glass.

While the case against the Globe Company was in progress,

Dr. Beckwith again saw storm signals and once more slipped out, to go over in New Jersey and organize the Meucci Telephone Company. But all his plans came to naught.

The strangest and most interesting case of all had its beginning on November 14, 1879, just four days after the Western Union settlement, when Abner G. Tisdel filed an application in the Patent Office, claiming "a new and useful improvement in speaking telephones." Four days later, Frank A. Klemm of New York also prayed protection on a telephone device. These inventions, in the excited atmosphere of the moment, promptly found backers—Ernest Marx of New York, Monty Loth of Cincinnati and Simon Wolf of Washington, to whom both patents were assigned. Shortly thereafter, two Pennsylvanians told Lysander Hill, a prominent Washington attorney, that they had discovered in the hills west of Harrisburg a genius who had anticipated everybody—one Daniel Drawbaugh, an obscure village mechanic, who had made and used a telephone years before the subject had ever occurred to Bell. Hill and the other two quickly tied Drawbaugh up in an agreement whereby he was to obtain a patent and give the other three each a quarter share of its ownership.

A few days later—this was in May, 1880—Messrs. Marx and Wolf heard of Drawbaugh, and decided that he was the best bet yet. On the argument of their superior promotional ability, they induced the other quartet to throw in with them in the ownership of all three patents, and a new assignment was recorded in the Patent Office on July 22, 1880, though Drawbaugh's patent had not been applied for. Klemm and Tisdel were now sidetracked. Drawbaugh had become the star.

The publicity department was already at work. On the same day, July 22nd, a flamboyant dispatch from Washington to the Cincinnati *Commercial* declared that a company with $5,000,000 cash (?) capital had been organized (it was not really organized until a month later) and had

bought up all the telephone patents antedating those now in use. . . . In about sixty days they will open up a telephone which will cer-

388

tainly result in the driving out of all telephones in the market save the ones they hold, or else compelling the Gray, Bell and Edison lines to pay the new company a munificent royalty. . . . It will not be long until they have in their charge the telephones not only in this country, but in the world.

The People's Telephone Company, organized in August, began producing telephones even before the patent was granted. The Bell Company brought suit and sent investigators—the other side called them spies—into the hills across the Susquehanna to learn something about Drawbaugh. They found that he had for years run a little machine and repair shop at Eberly's Mills, a hamlet a few miles west of Harrisburg. He had invented and patented several articles between 1860 and 1875—a molasses faucet, a rotary pump and some improvements in stave machinery and nail-plate feeders. He had apparently pretended the invention of an electric clock, and without trying for a patent on it, had palmed it off on somebody for $500. The Bell attorneys pointed to this as proving that he was a faker—that he read descriptions of one thing and another in scientific magazines, made imitations of them and claimed them as his own. He asserted that he had begun experiments with the telephone about 1862; that in '66 he had a workable instrument, made with a teacup as the shell of its transmitter. In the next three years he produced others, with a glass tumbler, a tin cup and a mustard can respectively, for transmitter. By 1870-71 he had a greatly improved magneto instrument; by January, 1875, a perfectly adjusted and finished telephone; and more designs followed during that year. Nearly all these instruments, indexed from "A" to "O" inclusive, were on exhibition at the trial. But the astonishing thing is Drawbaugh's explanation that dire poverty had prevented his ever getting a patent on his telephone. Another theory was that he wanted to develop the receiver to the point where the voice from it could be clearly heard across a room.

The trial of this case was the hardest fought of any in telephone history. Storrow and Dickinson for the plaintiffs and Hill for the defense were masterly in their strategy and argument.

There were 7,000 pages of evidence taken. And this man, perhaps an arrant impostor, came nearest of all claimants to overthrowing the Bell Patent—much nearer than Gray, who may have had a better claim. In August, 1883, newspapers called attention to the

Dan'l Drawbaugh,

Inventor Of

THE FOLLOWING PATENTS.

Stave, Heading & Shingle Cutter.
Barrel Machinery.
STAVE JOINTING MACHINE, Many in use.
Tram & Red-staff for leveling face of Millstone.
Rine and Driver for running Millstone.
Nail Machinery for Feeding Nail Plates.
PUMPS, ROTARAY & OTHERS.
Hydraulic Ram.
THE DRAWBAUGH Rotary Measureing Faucet, very extensivly used.
CARPET RAG LOOPER-- A little device by which rags are looped quick and firm. without Needle or Thread.
ELLECTRIC CLOCK.

MAGNETO ELECTRIC MACHINE,

For short line Telegraphing, Fire Alarm. and Propelling Electric Clocks. It can be applied to any form of Electric movement.
Gives entire satisfaction USEING NO
GALVANIC BATTERY.——
☞For SIMPLICITY it has NO RIVAL,
From U. S. Supreme Court Reports

DANIEL DRAWBAUGH'S BUSINESS
CARD

fact that Bell stock had dropped 50 points within the past month, largely because of fear as to the outcome of the Drawbaugh case.

The defense brought a swarm of witnesses to prove its thesis —friends and neighbors of Drawbaugh, chance visitors, men who had fished in the streams near by and happened to visit his shop. Rounding up all these was really a remarkable feat. The recollections of some of them as to Drawbaugh's telephone went back as far as 1867. No less than forty-nine of them had talked and heard speech through his telephones before Bell's patent date; seventy had either used the telephones or seen and heard others using them; one hundred and forty-nine (including those already mentioned) saw the instruments at one time and another in Drawbaugh's shop, and most of them identified one or another of them in court; two hundred and twenty had either used or seen or heard of their use prior to Bell's application.

By far the greater part of these remembered that Drawbaugh had told them the telephone was actuated by electricity. Many remembered the magnets and the wires running up the wall; some not so well versed in physics recalled "something like a horseshoe" attached to the thing. One Philadelphia man had seen both a horseshoe magnet and a double-spool electro-magnet. Drawbaugh had asked dozens of these to put up some money and aid him in getting the invention on the market. A merchant from Dover, Delaware, who was thus solicited in 1874, said that when he first saw a Bell telephone in Philadelphia three years later, he supposed it was one of Drawbaugh's; that Drawbaugh "had got a man named Bell to go with him," and the moneyed man's name was used.

Nearly all these witnesses appear to have been highly reputable and disinterested persons. It is impossible to believe that they were all committing perjury. But the Bell attorneys delivered some telling counter-strokes. They showed that it was rather absurd to claim that all through those years, Drawbaugh could never raise the sum of $50 with which to procure a patent. They proved that he had had a modest income from his shop and his other inventions; that a company, the Drawbaugh Manufacturing Company, had even been organized and had a shop at Shiremanstown, where it made his molasses faucet and other devices. They brought in three friends of Drawbaugh in Harrisburg, two railway telegraph superintendents (one a member of an electrical supply concern) and a patent solicitor, and these men said that Drawbaugh had never mentioned his telephone to them. Was it because he feared that these experts would see through his sham? To a prominent journalist of Baltimore who had talked to him in 1878, Drawbaugh mentioned his experiments, but said that he had never got speech and did not expect to do so; he was merely trying for a harmonic telegraph. The lawyers brought forth a history of Cumberland County, one of those racket-born volumes in which any citizen's life story, tailored to his taste, may appear for a fee. In this one (fee $10) Drawbaugh's sketch, written by himself with the assistance of the village schoolmaster, spoke of him as "one of the greatest inventive geniuses of this age (so prolific of great men) ... [who] has spent the greater portion of an active life, conceiving and producing, as a result of the conceptions of an unusually fertile brain, a score of useful inventions, machines and devices." He listed them minutely, but—although this volume was published as late as 1878—he did not mention his chef d'œuvre, the telephone!

The only possible explanation seems to be that Drawbaugh merely had an acoustic telephone, that he may have read something about Reis's experiments and tried to vitalize his instruments with electricity or magnetism, but did not know how, though pretending that he did. The deuce of it is that those tumbler and tin-cup transmitters were declared in court to be actually workable electric telephonic devices, and many witnesses identified them as the original articles they had seen and in some cases used in Drawbaugh's shop. Could they have been cunningly improved before they were brought into court?

The Drawbaugh case excited enormous interest. In that antimonopolistic age, the picture of this poor little, hard-working village mechanic in battered spectacles fighting for his rights against a gigantic octopus, was an arresting one, and the "sob" phase of it was played up for all it was worth. Other suits were on the dockets concurrently, and the whole situation was complicated rather than resolved when the Patent Office announced a decision on the telephone "interferences" in 1883. Bell was

Old Print from American Telephone and Telegraph Co.

SOME OF THE FIRST SWITCHBOARD OPERATORS WERE BOYS

awarded priority for the magneto-induction, transmitting and receiving telephone; he was declared to have been first to invent the art of transmitting sonorous vibrations of all kinds and quality by varying the strength of an electric current. In a second category, relating to the transmission of speech by varying resistance in the transmitter, Gray was declared to have been the first to conceive and disclose the invention in his caveat of February 14, 1876, but failed to take action and complete it until others had done so, hence the priority was awarded to Bell. Edison was first in another category and McDonough in another, relating to the receiver. The Bell people claimed to have made a deal for the McDonough patent, but the McDonough backers retorted that the corporation had broken the agreement, and hence the suit over that device was creeping sluggishly through the courts.

The numerous improvements which had followed each other rapidly were greatly increasing the use of the telephone in the cities, though the small towns and villages saw almost nothing of it for ten years afterwards. By the middle '80's, a city physician who did not have a telephone lost much business and was apt to be regarded as a back number. There was even a telephone in the White House during Cleveland's first term, (1885 to 1889), and if you rang up that number, like as not the President himself would answer. Mr. Cleveland hated the telephone, however, and always avoided it as much as possible.

No matter how a suit was decided in the lower courts, it was always carried to the highest tribunal. The Drawbaugh, the McDonough and other cases were pondered by the Supreme Court in the autumn term of 1887, and the digest of them fills a whole volume of its records (Volume 126). Even Elisha Gray had, like Thomas Cranmer, repented of his recantation and in 1886 had asked the law to reopen the case, spreading upon the records the ugly gossip about Bell's alleged guilty knowledge of his caveat, as well as of his applications on the harmonic telegraph during the previous year. Even attorneys who were fighting the battles of other inventors dwelt on the outrage to Gray, to prove their contention as to Bell's fraud. But a majority of the Supreme Court refused to consider such charges seriously. Chief Justice Waite voiced their sentiments in saying that the notion that eminent attorneys and the officials of the Patent Office would conspire to commit such knavery was unthinkable. The chief menace to Bell, in their opinion, was Drawbaugh.

There were only seven justices sitting at that time. One vacancy by death had not yet been filled, and another Justice, Gray, was ill and did not hear the argument. And of the seven who passed on the case, four—only four, mind you!—voted to uphold the Bell patent. The other three, Bradley, Field and Harlan, were convinced that Drawbaugh had anticipated Bell. They were not at all interested in Gray's troubles; he, too, was an interloper. In their dissenting opinion, they said, in part:

We think that the evidence on this point is so overwhelming, with regard both to the number and the character of the witnesses, that it cannot be overcome.... We are satisfied, from a very great preponderance of evidence, that Drawbaugh produced and exhibited in his shop, as early as 1869, an electrical instrument by which he transmitted speech ... by means of a wire and the employment of variable resistance to the electrical current.... We are also satisfied that as early as 1871 he reproduced articulate speech at a distance by means of a current of electricity, subjected by electrical induction to undulations corresponding to the voice in speaking—a process substantially the same as that claimed in Mr. Bell's patent.

Perhaps without the aid of Mr. Bell, the speaking telephone would not have been brought into public use to this day; but that Drawbaugh produced it, there can hardly be a reasonable doubt....

It is perfectly natural for the world to take the part of the man who has already achieved eminence.... It is regarded as incredible that so great a discovery should have been made by the plain mechanic, and not by the eminent scientist and inventor.

But in the opinion of the other four judges, to hold that Drawbaugh discovered the secret of telephony before Bell

395

"would be to construe testimony without regard to the ordinary laws that govern human conduct."

That was the narrowest squeak that the Bell patent ever had. Recently there was produced in New York a play entitled, "If Booth Had Missed," a speculation upon the course of history had Lincoln lived out his life. It is interesting to try fancying what would have ensued had just one of those majority judges been swayed to the other side. Daniel Drawbaugh would now be revered by the world as the inventor of the telephone, and Alexander Graham Bell would be just another contender who failed. Financially, the decision would have been a major calamity; a company with millions of capital and investments would have been ruined, and would have had to make such terms as it could with its conquerors. And in other hands, how different the course of telephone history might have been!

While these matters were being decided, the Bell patents were undergoing another test. In 1883, a corporation called the Pan-Electric Telephone Company was organized with a large capitalization to promote the inventions of a man named Rogers which were the most flagrant infringements yet on that of Bell. General Joseph E. Johnston, an unsuspecting old Confederate hero, was made President of the company, and there were two United States Senators on the Board—Garland of Arkansas and Harris of Tennessee. Garland was the company's attorney. In 1884, a bill was introduced in Congress intended to vacate the Bell patents. It passed the House, but failed to get by the Senate Patent Committee.

Shortly after this, Cleveland became President; Garland was appointed Attorney-General, and other Pan-Electric stockholders occupied important Government positions. The new Attorney-General was asked to begin suit to annul the Bell patents. He declined, but presently left Washington for a vacation at his home in Arkansas. A day or two after his departure, the Solicitor-General of the United States was requested by a Pan-Electric subsidiary, the National Improved Telephone Company of New Orleans, to begin the suit, and after one day's study of

From Illustrated London News, New York Public Library

A NEW YEAR'S PARTY IN LONDON, 1880, WHERE GUESTS RECEIVED AND SENT
GREETINGS BY TELEPHONE

the situation, he did so, starting the action in the Memphis district. He placed in charge of the case as Government prosecutors an official of the Pan-Electric Company, another who was a stockholder, of the same, and two associates.

The Memphis district was declared to be the wrong jurisdiction, and the suit was dropped, but not soon enough to save Attorney-General Garland's reputation. He protested that he had nothing to do with launching the suit, and knew nothing about it. But there was a bad odor about the affair, and his ambition to reach the Supreme Court was forever blighted.

The Department of Justice ceased its prosecution but Secretary Lamar, of the Interior Department, was implacable, and in January, 1887, he brought suit to annul the Bell patents. Before the case was completed, those patents had expired—in March, 1890 and January, 1891—but the suit went on. Bell himself spent nine weeks in the spring and summer of 1892 in giving testimony; and finally, in 1897 the Government dropped the suit.

But three years prior to that, it had attacked the corporation from another angle. By a curious coincidence, only a few months after the Bell patents expired, the Patent Office finally made up its mind and granted the microphone patent of Emil Berliner, which had been hanging fire for fourteen years. No sooner was this publicly known than a roar of indignation went up from editors and anti-monopolists. The Rochester *Herald* voiced their sentiments in its charge that the Bell Company sought to extend its monopoly "by the dishonorable trick of keeping up a sham contest in the Patent Office through the past fourteen years." That such conduct was possible in a bureau of the National Government, said the editor, was a disgrace to the officials and an outrage on the American people. "The time has come for a complete revolution in that office."

On February 1, 1893, the United States brought suit in one of its circuit courts against the American Bell Telephone Company and Emil Berliner to vacate the latter's patent. It had a weak case; it dared not throw mud on its own Patent Office, so it sought to place the blame on the Telephone Company by alleging (despite proof to the contrary) that the Company had made no effort to push the matter along (a rather absurd contention and discreditable to the Patent Office's efficiency), and that the patent was now exhausted, according to a doctrine cited from another case. It claimed that Berliner was not the inventor of the transmitter and that the latter wouldn't work—a charge which was disproved on the spot by the sending of conversation through it between New York and Philadelphia. The Circuit Court decided against Berliner, but the Supreme Court in 1897, in a sweeping decision, completely demolished the Government's case, saying, "There is seldom presented a case in which there is such an absolute and total failure of proof of wrong."

Despite this decision, an attack from another angle was later made upon the Berliner patent, and in 1903 a Court of Appeals narrowed its scope somewhat.

In 1885, the American Telephone and Telegraph Company was formed, to build and operate the long distance lines of the Bell system—which, at that time, meant lines between Boston and New York, New York and Washington and the like; they as yet could achieve no greater distances. Vail, who was becoming dissatisfied because the American Bell directors were more interested in splitting up the income as dividends than in extending the system, resigned as manager of that corporation to become manager of the A. T. & T. At the close of the year 1889, he gave up that job, too, and devoted his time to other investments. Seventeen years later, when the great telephone corporation was in trouble, he was called back to the helm again and gave another twelve of his latter years—years of priceless service—to it, leaving it sound and supreme among the world's communications corporations.

One of Vail's great services during his seven years as manager was the beginning of the placing of telephone wires underground. The first work of the sort was done in New York City, where it was most needed. In the early '80's, the streets of the large cities of America had become, overhead, an appalling maze of telephone and telegraph—yes, and electric light—wires.

Huge, unsightly poles, just rugged tree trunks with the bark peeled off, took up portions of the sidewalk and clustered in ungainly huddles at the street corners. When the first telegraph line entered a prim young State Capital, Indianapolis, in 1848, the authorities specified that the poles must be sawn octagonal and neatly painted; but esthetics soon vanished and poles were erected "as is." In the '80's and '90's it was impossible to get any adequate photograph of a public building because of the mess of wires and crooked poles in front of it. Ice formed on the wires in winter and then fell off, injuring people in the streets and endangering their lives. Firemen had the Fiend's own time with the wires. One recalls seeing a long extension ladder shot up in a narrow street in front of a burning building and leaned against the wires—a fireman with rubber gloves and clippers running up it and calmly snipping every wire until the ladder leaned against the building; a bit rough on telegraph, telephone and light service, but it had to be done. By the end of 1889, the Bell Company had 11,000 miles of wires underground in New York City, though overhead wires continued to curse most cities for two decades and more thereafter.

Just as the Bell patents were expiring, Judge Walter Clark of North Carolina wrote an article for the *Arena* (published March, 1892), urging that the Government take over the telephone system, supposing that the American Bell Company would now relinquish its rich holdings and pass out of the picture. "If the telephone is not now adopted by Government, some gigantic corporation, some vast syndicate, will be sure to utilize it; and when hereafter, Government should be forced to take it up for the public service, Congress will be waived off, as trespassing upon private and vested rights, as is already the case with the telegraph."

But to the surprise of Judge Clark and others, the Bell Company did not choose to die with its original patents. Relying upon the newly born Berliner patent and others recently acquired, upon the further skill of its engineers and upon its great and now well entrenched organization, it continued to

399

function and grow. Independent companies, however, sprang up in all directions during the '90's, after the lapse of the Bell patents. They invaded not only the cities but the villages and rural areas where telephones had never before been seen. The nuisance of two telephone systems in a city was and is at times almost beyond endurance, as anybody who has experienced it can testify, and tends to prove the Bell contention that the telephone is a natural monopoly. If you wanted to reach some one by phone, the odds always seemed to favor his being on the other line. Business houses of any consequence could not get along without having both systems installed. The Independents nearly always leased instruments at a flat rate and a low one; sometimes absurdly low. There were small rural telephone systems which leased telephones at 50 cents per month and made no charge for installation. There is no doubt that the Independents increased enormously the knowledge and popularity of the telephone business. Much of their good-will later became the property of the Bell people; though it was recently stated that there are still 7,000 telephone companies, most of them small ones, controlling nearly one-fourth of the telephones in the country, which are not parts of the Bell system.

On October 18, 1892, with great ceremony, the American Telephone and Telegraph Company inaugurated long distance service between New York and Chicago, Dr. Bell himself speaking the first words. In 1900, that company became the dominant force in the Bell system, the American Bell sinking to the position of subsidiary. In 1915, Dr. Bell again sat at a richly decorated table and for the first time spoke clear, commercially profitable speech from New York to San Francisco, being answered from the Golden Gate by his old co-worker, Watson. This achievement was due in no small measure to the development by Dr. Michael Pupin of the loading coil, which encourages the waves, boosts them along the wire; Pupin, who landed at Castle Garden in 1874, a penniless Serbian immigrant boy with not a word of English to his tongue, and fourteen years

THEODORE N. VAIL   JOHN J. CARTY

NEW YORK TELEPHONE COMPANY'S BUILDING

HEADQUARTERS, AMERICAN TELPHONE AND TELEGRAPH COMPANY, NEW YORK   AMERICAN TELEPHONE AND TELEGRAPH COMPANY LONG LINES BUILDING, NEW YORK

later became a professor in Columbia University, thereafter developing into one of America's great men of science.

John J. Carty, the great self-taught engineer of American Telephone and Telegraph, likewise had much to do with the telephone's longer reach. He was inventor as well as engineer— he had twenty-four patents to his credit; few in number as compared with those of some other inventors, yet all highly important. He had also an incomparable genius for developing and adapting the inventions of others—as when he put De Forest's audion tube at work in radio telephony.

Early in the present century, the independent companies gave the telephone colossus more trouble than it liked to admit; and a management arrogant as to competition, and still thinking more of dividends than of building for the future brought it to a position which gave its stockholders concern. In this emergency, the directors called back to the helm on May 1, 1907, the genius of its earlier years, Theodore N. Vail. They had asked him to come several years before, but he had declined. He was sixty-two years old when he assumed the Presidency, but still the ablest telephone man in America, and with none of his powers weakened.

Vail worked an entire change in the company's attitude towards the public. He banished the "take-it-or-leave-it" arrogance of former administrations, and enforced a rule of courtesy which, under his successors, has become fixedly habitual and perhaps unsurpassed in quality in any other business. His first thought when he assumed office was that of rebuilding and extension; and his first act therefore was boldly to issue $22,-000,000 in common stock, and sell nearly all of it at par or better. His return had given investors confidence. Four months later, when a small-sized panic swept over the land, A. T. & T. stock dropped as low as 88, but it was one of the strongest and earliest to recover.

Vail's next big idea was that of taking over the Western Union Telegraph Company. The original A. T. & T., as its name implied, had been organized in 1885 with the notion that in addition to doing long distance telephony, it would probably also take over a telegraph company. Its parent, the American Bell Telephone, had bound itself to stay out of the telegraph business, and the only way to evade that promise was to organize another company. But thereafter, there were only two companies of any consequence, and of these, the Western Union was rather too big to buy, and the Postal was owned by Mackay, who wouldn't sell.

But by 1909, the Western Union was in a somewhat run-down condition, and the A. T. & T. easily acquired 296,572 shares of its stock, out of a total of 998,171 outstanding. It had long been Vail's dream that a man should be able to sit in his office and without the trouble of calling a messenger, dictate a telegram over the telephone, and have it delivered by telephone at the other terminus; and he believed that this could be done only if the two media of communication were one. In 1909, the deal was completed, and Western Union became a vassal of the telephone. The corporations remained separate, but Vail was elected President of Western Union, and Newcomb Carlton, a telephone man by trade but then President of British Westinghouse, was made Vice-President.

The new arrangement was satisfactory to the parties immediately concerned, resulting in increased earnings and greater power, but it did not suit that section of the public who dreaded monopoly, and another great outcry was raised. After a time, the United States Government began, under the Sherman Anti-Trust Law, to move slowly and ponderously against the combination, with the result that in 1913, the A. T. & T. backed down and agreed to sever the connection. Vail, protesting that there had never been any actual merger—that the two companies were, as it were, complementary—resigned as Western Union President, and his company disposed of its Western Union stock. It also agreed to make arrangements whereby all other telephone companies could get for their subscribers connecting toll service over the Bell lines. President Wilson was much gratified over the separation, but Editor Hearst thought a great opportunity had been lost by the Government to take over the whole outfit, and that Vail was glad that the severance had been enforced, and thwarted this possibility.

Vail retired in 1919 and died in the following year. Under his successors, Harry B. Thayer and Walter S. Gifford, the company has continued to grow until it is now probably the world's most powerful corporation, with its fingers in many other pies than the telephone—even in motion pictures. It has a total of more than eighty million miles of wire (single lines and cable) in operation, and more than thirteen million telephones.

The United States has almost precisely half of the world's telephones—16,710,858 on January 1, 1934, as against 32,445,-855 for the globe. It makes over thirty million telephone calls a year, whereas the rest of the world totals about twenty-four million. Stack the telephone books of London and all the British Isles together, and they will just about equal those for New York City and immediate suburbs. New York City proper has 1,495,922 telephones—more than all Asia, 300,000 more than Canada, nearly twice as many as Chicago (which has 799,122), more than three times as many as Berlin (456,304) or Paris (411,249). London has only 831,800. That the United States, with 6 per cent of the earth's population, operates 50 per cent of its telephones is due in part to the national character and the vast resources which have helped to give it buoyancy, but also in a considerable degree to the scientific and business genius which has guided the great Telephone Trust.

Dr. Bell's experiments in sound transmission did not continue for many years after the success of the telephone was assured. He did nothing else whatsoever for that instrument. He experimented with three other inventions during the early '80's—the photophone, whereby electric impulses were conveyed by light rays, the induction balance and the graphophone, which resembled Edison's phonograph, and which he patented in 1883. Thereafter, he turned his attention to other branches of science. His wife, to whom his devotion was beautiful and undying, believed that the fact that she could not hear had much to do with his loss of interest in devices having to do with sound. Before he died, in 1922, he had seen air telephony become possible, and many other things come into being which were even more amazing to his scientific mind than to many a layman.

From American Telephone and Telegraph Co.

TELEPHONE SWITCHBOARD, RICHMOND, VIRGINIA, 1881

CHAPTER XX

WAR AND PEACE ON THE TELEGRAPH WIRES

For Vanderbilt and Company 'tis indeed a gilded age,
But poverty increases, and 'tis thus that tramps are made.
Shall it, will it be continued when the people's votes are weighed?
      As we go marching on.

No! We'll hang Jay Gould on a sour apple tree,
And bring to grief the plotters of a base monopoly;
From the heartless ghouls of booty we're determined to go free,
      As we go marching on.
                    ANTI-MONOPOLY SONG, 1880

A S the 1870's drew near their close, the most powerful opposition and competition yet offered menaced the Western Union Telegraph Company. Jay Gould was an antagonist whom any one might fear, and under his ruthless marshalship, the Atlantic & Pacific assumed the aspect of a major menace. By January 1, 1877, it had 17,759 miles of poles, carrying 36,044 miles of wire. In addition to Morse apparatus, it used Edison's automatic system very largely. Sir William Thomson reported that in Philadelphia he saw 1,500 words received by it from New York in fifty-seven seconds. The speed attained was calculated at 200 miles' distance as being 1,000 words per minute; at 300 miles, 500 words per minute, and slowly decreasing therefrom until at 1,000 miles only 100 words per minute could be sent. By this system the President's message on December 5, 1876, was begun in the Washington office at 1.05 P.M., and completed in New York at 2:07 P.M. The first 9,000 words were sent in forty-five minutes. The perforations were made in thirty minutes by ten persons, and copied by seven copyists.

The story of the fight between the A. & P. and the Western

405

Union over Edison's quadruplex sheds an interesting light on Mr. Edison's harum-scarum notions of contractual obligation in those days. Edison had asked permission of Orton early in 1873 to make experiments on the Western Union wires, with the idea of improving the duplex telegraph system of Joseph B. Stearns, whose patents the W.U.T. was then using. Edison showed Orton his sketches, and an arrangement was made, whereby his patents, when obtained, should be assigned to the company; compensation to be such as agreed on by the two parties—or if they couldn't agree, arbitrators were to be called in.

Orton directed T. T. Eckert, then general superintendent of the company, to give Edison all needed facilities. Within the next few months, Edison applied for ten patents, all of which were to be assigned to the company. By October, he could send two messages simultaneously in the same direction; he then set to work to double the number.

There was a halt in the work that winter, and when Orton asked why, he was told that the inventor hadn't the proper facilities. Orton then called in George B. Prescott, the company's electrician, and ordered him to give Edison all possible aid. But in March, '74, Orton went to Europe and Prescott to Key West, whereupon Edison ceased work again and took his apparatus out of the building. Questioned again, he said he could do nothing without the presence and aid of Orton and Prescott. All this is Orton's side of the story. He says he then agreed that Prescott should give Edison his personal help. Edison later admitted in testimony that this was material and considerable. He even agreed with Prescott that they should own the patents jointly, though (says Orton) he evidently did not intend splitting the royalty, half and half. Edison's version is that he found he could get nowhere until he agreed to let Prescott have half the glory of the invention.

In the autumn of 1874 the quadruplex was tested, and installed on the lines between New York and Boston and between

New York and Chicago. Edison now wanted some money on account. Orton paid him $5,000, and after some chaffering, agreed to buy his patents for $25,000 in cash and a royalty of $233 per year on every circuit set up. This, Orton says, was somewhere around December 30th. A few days after that, Edison ceased his visits to the company's offices, and when they tried to get in touch with him, they couldn't find him. It was not long before they discovered that he had sold out to the Atlantic & Pacific!

Edison says that all this time he was dreadfully hard up; that the $5,000 he received all vanished immediately in the payment of debts, and within a few weeks he was bribing the sheriff to keep him from attaching the Edison laboratory in Newark. Why he did not tell all this frankly to Orton, he does not explain. At the time, Gould was negotiating with Eckert to leave the Western Union and take charge of the A. & P. Says Mr. Edison:

One day Eckert called me into his office and made inquiries about money matters. I told him Mr. Orton had gone off and left me without means, and I was in straits. He told me I would never get another cent, but that he knew a man who would buy it. I told him of my arrangement with the electrician, and said I could not sell it as a whole to anybody; but if I could get enough for it, I would sell all my interest in any share I might have. He seemed to think his party would agree to this.

Eckert did not tell him who the "party" was, but next morning brought him over to Edison's Newark shop—none other than Jay Gould. Edison admitted in his testimony that this was on December 28th. Gould examined the apparatus and departed. On January 4th Eckert took Edison up to Gould's home on Fifth Avenue. "It was in the evening," said Edison, "and we went in by the servants' entrance, as Eckert probably feared that he was watched." Gould and Edison sparred a bit, and the magnate finally made an offer of $30,000. "I will sell any interest I may have for that money," replied Edison, promptly; it was more than he had expected to get. An interesting feature of the episode is that Eckert then and for a week afterwards was still on the Western Union payroll.

As he would not come near the office, Orton sent Edison a letter by the hand of Marshall Lefferts, intended to close the deal for the quadruplex patents. This was about January 20th. On February 9th, a letter from Edison to Orton (dated Washington, January 26th) was dropped into the New York post-office. In it Edison said that he had made the arrangement with Orton under an error; he found that the quadruplex patents really belonged to one George Harrington, with whom he had agreed away back in 1871 to share certain automatic patents. An assignment to Harrington was recorded at the time in the Patent Office. Gould had now bought Harrington's interest, and Western Union attorneys found that somebody had forged the word "or" on the Patent Office records to indicate that Edison's agreement with Harrington covered his other telegraph patents. A lawsuit was soon under way between the two companies, and the A. & P., barred for the moment from using Edison's quadruplex, used one allegedly invented by their electrician, d'Infreville, which was doubtless a flagrant infringement on Edison's. Before the suit was settled, in 1877-78, the two companies had drawn so near together that further litigation was unnecessary.

The Atlantic & Pacific swallowed up the Franklin Telegraph Company, and increased its power, though not its profits. It was slightly "in the red" in 1875, and in '76 showed only $39,228 profit on a capitalization of $15,000,000. Early in 1877 the Western Union began an offensive, designed to squeeze its chief rival out of business. Rates were cut, small lines were grabbed, and the A. & P. had to fight back in kind. Even Gould confessed that he was breathing hard from the strain of conflict. A treaty of peace was signed before the year was out, by which the Western Union was "permitted" to acquire 72,502 shares of A. & P. stock—mostly from Gould—at $25 a share, for which was paid $912,550 in cash and 12,500 shares of Western Union stock. A pool was formed, whereby the Western

Union received 87½ per cent of all income, the A. & P. 12½ per cent. Gould thus pocketed the better part of $1,812,550, and acquired a nice block of Western Union stock, though this did not necessarily connote loyalty to that organization. In fact, he was not yet done with making trouble for it.

In that same year, opposition arose in other quarters. The Western Telegraph Company, organized in 1847 and holding a right of way along the Baltimore & Ohio Railroad tracks from Baltimore to various places in the Ohio Valley, had been leased by the American Telegraph Company in 1859, and the lease had passed, with the other American assets, to the Western Union. In February, 1877, the Western Telegraph's charter expired, and the B. & O. Railroad ordered it and its lessor to vacate. After a court battle, the railroad was successful, and took over its own telegraph system, which it presently leased to the Atlantic & Pacific.

In 1878, William Orton died and Dr. Green, no less capable, but perhaps a little milder and more genial, assumed the Presidency of the Western Union. On May 15, 1879, Gould touched off another bomb by organizing the American Union Telegraph Company in New York with a capital of $10,000,000; and lo, here were Bates and Tinker, come over with him from the A. & P. to act as co-incorporators. Bates was elected President; a promoter named Owen, who had just succeeded in building a telegraph line from Oswego almost to New York City was made Vice-President because his line would come in handy. Of course he could be discarded at any time. As Treasurer, a name common in Gould's promotions during this period appears—Giovanni P. Morosini, private secretary and confidential clerk to Gould for twelve years and more during the magnate's later life. That his association with Gould was of value to him, a fine old estate in the aristocratic Riverdale section of New York City still bears witness.

A touching revelation was made later by Mr. Gould before the Senate Committee on Labor and Education, which was prying into his entrance into Western Union affairs—the true inside story of the organization of the American Union, which reveals the great, golden heart of the man. Speaking of the alliance of the Atlantic & Pacific with the Western Union, he said, "At that time a very dear friend of mine was the manager [of the A. & P.], and I supposed that he would be made the manager of the Western Union; but after the consolidation was perfected, it was not done, and I made up my mind that he should be at the head of as good a company as I had taken him from. The friend was General Eckert, and for him I started another company, the American Union." A friendship so noble as this, a Jonathan willing to risk such colossal and hazardous strokes as this in order that young David might be given the power and glory that he merited, brings a lump to one's throat, and sheds a new light on the great mogul's character. Eckert, preparing to assume the presidency of the new company, resigned as President of the A. & P. in March, 1879; but the directors of that company, by bluff, bullying and persuasion, induced him to reconsider, and he remained for nine months longer, finally becoming head of the American Union on January 1, 1880.

Mr. Gould, at the organization, took all the stock in the new corporation, giving a $10,000,000 check for it. On the stand four years later, he could not remember whether the check read five or ten million; but no matter, he got it all back, anyhow. That was probably history's most noteworthy instance of a check's flying around in a circle. Bates testified (all this was in a suit brought in 1883 by William S. Williams, a cantankerous Western Union stockholder, who believed that his company had paid too much for the American Union and the A. & P.) that the original subscribers to the stock were Gould, Tinker and himself. "We three subscribed $10,000,000; I subscribed one-quarter, $2,500,000, and paid for my subscription in the shape of Jay Gould's check." In other words, the chief magician said merrily, "Now we'll play like a quarter of this stage money which I am passing from my right hand to my left is yours, Homer, and a quarter of it is yours, Charlie." It was great fun.

WAR AND PEACE ON THE TELEGRAPH WIRES

Mr. Gould now being the sole owner of all the stock, turned over a few thousands of it to Owen for his little York State line, and sold a quantity of it to outsiders; he needed some outside money to pay for the building of new lines. This was done by the newly organized Central Construction Company, of which Washington E. Connor, Gould's favorite broker, was President. The company was made up of Connor, two Owens brothers, Morosini and one Calef, treasurer of another of Gould's companies. Naturally, these men were all dummies, Gould owning nearly all the stock; and of course the telegraph company paid through the nose for line construction.

The American Union, under Gould's magic touch, quickly reached a dominant position. The Dominion Telegraph Company of Canada was leased, and its officials permitted to buy into the new corporation. President Garrett of the B. & O. Railroad did the same and became a Director; whereupon Gould's small, white hand began feeling for the keys of the B. & O. telegraph system. An alliance for foreign business was made with the French Cable Company. Rates were cut, small lines were bought, and more than 5,000 men under Dennis Doren, noted Civil War construction chief, were at work in all directions, paralleling the lines of the Western Union.

Eckert came to the Presidency on January 1st, and under his generalship the company, in true modern style, did not declare war, but precipitated a state of war. Working in secret, it made private arrangements with several railroad companies, and without warning, fired the first gun when it moved into the B. & O. telegraph system, from which the railroad had expelled the lessee, the Atlantic & Pacific. Next the company seized the wires on the Union Pacific and Kansas Pacific, being aided thereto by Gould's domination of those roads. Whenever and wherever there was resistance to the seizures, force was used. The Western Union was knocked breathless for a moment, but recovered its wind and fought back. Temporary injunctions saved its wires for a time along two Gould roads, the Missouri Pacific and the Central Branch Union Pacific. But the American

Union grabbed the Wabash. It was a battle of giants. Bills, injunctions, subpoenas, search warrants, contempt citations and other legal instruments flew about like hail; and there were more illegal than legal actions. Many a warrior was knocked cold and carried away on a shutter. President Garrett of the B. & O. was among the numerous citizens arrested for contempt. Lawyers rubbed their hands and waxed fat.

By the end of Eckert's first year as President, the American Union had 2,000 offices, more than 10,000 miles of poles and nearly 50,000 miles of wire. It had important contracts with many of the great railroad systems from whose tracks it had elbowed the other companies. These included the Gould lines, the Pennsylvania, Pittsburgh, Cincinnati & St. Louis, Cincinnati Southern, Western & Atlantic and many others. On its Board of Directors were seen such names as Jay Gould, Russell Sage, Robert Garrett and Sidney Dillon.

"Impossible!" exclaimed Dr. Green, when it was suggested that the young upstart might yet lick his company. "It would bankrupt Gould and all his connections to parallel our lines, and to talk of harmony between him and us is the wildest kind of speculation." But by that time, the Doctor himself was whistling to keep up his courage. The Western Union was undeniably in trouble. Before the end of 1880 its receipts had been cut by an average of $5,000 a day. Its stock fell to the lowest figures known since the '50's. The Christmas holidays could not have been a very cheerful season for its officials and directors.

At last it was decided to send out a flag of truce and ask for terms. On Sunday, January 9, 1881, Mr. Gould received a brief note from the largest Western Union stockholder.

DEAR SIR; I would like to see you a few moments, at 9 o'clock, if convenient to you, at my house.
Yours very truly
W. H. VANDERBILT

Mr. Vanderbilt had heard a pretty well authenticated rumor that Gould would "listen to reason" if it was put into words;

and so it proved. Negotiations proceeded rapidly. The "grapevine telegraph" spread the news and there was much conjecture, most of it uncomplimentary save among stockholders. Two days after Mr. Vanderbilt's note was written, Western Union stock, already recovering slightly, jumped from 78 to 103, and next day to 114½. An employee's journal, *The Operator,* said that if the two companies combined, "Mr. Gould will make $5,000,000 by the transaction, some hundreds of clerks will be thrown out of employment, and hundreds more retained at a point just above starvation wages. But that is the usual 'divvy' in such cases." An attempt was made to rush a bill through the New York Legislature to prevent the union, but it failed of passage.

Mr. Gould later explained to a Senate committee that when Western Union stock fell to such low figures during the "war," he bought large quantities of it just as you would buy any commodity because it was cheap; and then, with all that cheap stock on his hands, "I found that the only way out was to put the two companies together."

On February 15, 1881, the terms of settlement were ratified by the Western Union directors. To make it a nice melon for everybody, it had been decided to take in the Western Union's subsidiary, the Atlantic & Pacific. The capital of the Western Union—for the old name was to be retained—was to be raised to $80,000,000, accounted for as follows:

To purchase the Atlantic and Pacific Telegraph Company, 140,000 shares at $60 .... $ 8,400,000
To be issued to the American Union Telegraph Company, on its bonds pledged to the Central Construction Company 5,000,000
To the American Union on its capital stock 10,000,000
Western Union Company's capital stock 41,073,410
Stock dividend to represent increase of property by purchase and construction since 1866 15,526,590

$80,000,000

Gould, Dillon, Sage and Eckert were elected directors of the Western Union, four less potent personalities on the Board courteously resigning to give them place.

When the terms of the deal reached the public prints, one of those summer heat-lightning storms of indignation common to the American people burst over the land. The Evil One at last had possession of the monopoly. "The cormorant of the past has been swallowed up," said *The Operator,* "and the Western Union of to-day is only the Western Union in name, and the American Union in fact"; by which it meant that Jay Gould was now telegraph dictator of the continent, and such was the fact. Dr. Green thenceforth had to play second fiddle.

It was pointed out that the shares were merged at a price of about 129 for Western Union, 113½ for American Union and 66⅔ for Atlantic & Pacific—and all watered valuations, of course. Economic and commercial authorities later estimated that the stock issued in payment for the American Union and A. & P. Companies was in face value probably at least five or six times the worth of their plants and good-will.

An excited meeting of the Anti-Monopoly League was held at Cooper Union in New York two weeks after the consolidation, and much oratory was expended. A glee club sang the Anti-Monopoly song, of which two stanzas grace the opening of this chapter. Mention of Jay Gould's name brought hisses and cries of "Hang him!" "Cut his throat!" The Republican Party, supposed to be an ally of the monopolists, came in for a wigging and President-elect Garfield's name was hissed. But seemingly nothing could be immediately and legally done about the matter, and so the public presently forgot it, and nobody save the reformers and a few publicists and politicians (mostly Democrats) kept it alive. There was a revival of the bitter feeling three years later, on election night, 1884, when the result was much in doubt, and flying rumors had it that the Western Union was again aiding the Republicans in stealing the election, as it had done in 1876. A mob surrounded the Western Union

Eckert from William S. Eckert

JAY GOULD   WILLIAM ORTON

WESTERN UNION TELEGRAPH COMPANY HEADQUARTERS,
NEW YORK

NORVIN GREEN   THOMAS T. ECKERT

building in New York and yelled for Jay Gould's blood. But after all, he died peacefully in his bed eight years later.

Stockholders brought suits to prevent the consolidation— among them Williams, already mentioned. In the Williams trial, it appeared that Mr. Morosini, treasurer of the American Union, had been almost a total stranger to the whole episode. He testified that he had been treasurer of the company from the beginning, but had never seen a book nor a treasury, had never drawn a check, never had a bank account nor an office where company books might be kept. Bates went farther and declared that the company didn't keep books. Sounds as if Gould not only did its thinking, but its clerical work. As might be expected, the stockholder-complainant got nothing out of the case but an attorney's bill.

Shortly after this, Gould took Russell Sage, Cyrus Field and Frank Work into a vault one day and opened his strong box. There the goggling eyes of the other magnates rested upon $23,000,000 worth of Western Union stock (then said to be earning $10 a share), $12,000,000 in Missouri Pacific and $19,000,000 in other stocks, mostly those of transportation. Perhaps Mr. Gould murmured as he displayed them, "My jewels!" Despite reports of its earning power, the Western Union continued to make a poor mouth. Erastus Wiman, one of its directors, told a Chicago *Inter-Ocean* reporter in 1884 that there were still too many companies to permit anybody to make any money. He said that in New York City alone there were 232 telegraph offices, of which the Western Union had only 150. As late as 1886, there were still 214 telegraph companies operating in the United States, though about 210 of them were very small fry. The W.U.T. then and for years afterwards was one of the most lucrative businesses in existence.

The wars were by no means over with the great consolidation of 1881. Other dragons' teeth had already been sown. Our old friend, D. H. Craig, had for years been trying to promote a system of automatic telegraphy. He told the Senate Committee in 1883 that he and Marshall Lefferts had promoted such a company in 1870, strung a wire between New York and Washington and sent 1,000 words a minute over it. But one George Harrington got control of the company, and made a deal with Jay Gould, whereby an ostensible $4,000,000 in stock of the Atlantic & Pacific Company was to be paid for the Harrington company and the automatic patent, only Gould was to put a million of it into his own pocket. According to Craig's story, Gould pocketed most of the four millions, Harrington, with his own pockets well lined, fled to Europe, and Gould still owed somebody for the stock.

In 1879, Craig again appeared before the public with an automatic telegraph, a modification of the Bain and Wheatstone systems, and organized the American Rapid Telegraph Company, which announced that, "We confidently expect, within three years, to Telegraph ordinary Business Letters, to all parts of the country, for TEN CENTS." The promised superiorities of this system were amazing. It was "clearly demonstrable" that the company could "build lines which will very rarely, if ever, be out of order." Also "The Company will be so constructed and organized, under the advice and direction of eminent counsel, that it will be impossible for it to be, in any degree, controlled by any set of Monopolists." Even the poles were to be larger and more durable than those in common use. And finally, with sixty-six low-salaried girls to perforate and copy the messages, and with two operators to send them, one wire could carry 60,000 words an hour or 480,000 in an eight-hour day.

A $3,000,000 corporation was formed and the eastern seaboard cities were connected by wire, but the lightning speed promised in the prospectus was never realized. Between New York and Philadelphia, less than a hundred miles, it managed to average 500 words a minute at best, and for two years performed excellent service. But at greater distances the difficulties increased, and the company could show no earning power.

Here we pick up another thread. Two New York capitalists named Case and Crossman, while on a shooting expedition in North Carolina, heard of the big telegraph merger, and decided

416

From American Telephone and Telegraph Co.

TWENTY-FIVE CROSS-ARMS, 250 WIRES ON ONE POLE, WEST STREET, NEW YORK, 1887. A TYPICAL SIGHT IN A LARGE CITY IN THE 'EIGHTIES

to take advantage of the wave of opposition that would be aroused and organize a company of their own. The Bankers and Merchants Telegraph Company was the result. It was incorporated for $1,000,000, a line built over the favorite course —from New York to Washington—and some mileage in other directions; but it lost money, and as the American Rapid was doing the same, they decided to join hands in 1883; whereupon the promoters proceeded to make medicine in the true Wall Street fashion.

First the A.R.T. was to issue $3,000,000 in bonds (about twice the value of its whole plant), ostensibly to pay the B. & M. for the building of some 1,500 miles of new line (which it never intended doing) in the Western states. As soon as the B. & M. received the bonds, it was to trade them back to the A.R.T. stockholders for all the stock in that company; so that the B. & M. would now control the A.R.T. and the latter would have nothing but its own dubious bonds to bless itself with. (Properly handled, this could be made into a good Broadway farce.)

A. W. Dimock, a smooth promoter, was now President of both companies. His next move was to mortgage to the Farmers Loan and Trust Company all property owned or to be acquired by the B. & M. for a $10,000,000 bond issue, of which he at once sold $5,200,000 worth at a discount. That company took over some smaller concerns, including the United States Telephone Company, which controlled the McDonough patent and others. There were scores of other facets to the situation— subterfuges, stipulations, agreements which were denied later by one party or another. Among other things, the A.R.T. consented that the B. & M. string wires on its poles at a yearly rental figure. Under this contract, the B. & M. strung 7,000 miles of wire on A.R.T. poles; the latter even had to set some new poles.

In 1884, the business world was shaken by the failure of the Marine Bank and several big business houses; the banks began calling loans, and presently Dimock and the B. & M. were in bankruptcy, quickly followed by the A.R.T. John G. Farnsworth was appointed receiver for the B. & M. and a man in Hartford named Harland for the American Rapid.

The problem of unscrambling the two companies appeared hopeless. A Boston bank which held the mortgage for the A.R.T. bonds claimed all wire on the poles, under the old doctrine that any improvement on a piece of property immediately becomes a part of the realty. A Federal court in Connecticut directed Harland to take possession of all A.R.T. property, "unless the same or a part of it is in possession of some other person or corporation claiming right of possession." Harland passed the buck by leasing the A.R.T. system to the Western Union. Jay Gould considered himself an Alexander capable of cutting the Gordian knot. On July 10, 1885, a squad of men entered the building in New York where the B. & M.'s offices were located, and while most of them remained out of sight, the two spokesmen entered Farnsworth's office and demanded the delivery of the A.R.T. property to the Western Union.

"I must consult my attorney," said Farnsworth. Telephones were still absent from many offices, and he had to go down street in person to the lawyer's sanctum. No sooner had he left the building than the two leaders called in their huskies, who were armed with axes, chisels, clippers and crowbars; and herding clerks into a corner, they proceeded to demolish all wires and cables, then broke through to the roof and cut all wires loose, so that they fell to the surrounding streets and buildings. This was done in other cities at the same time; the 400 offices of the B. & M. were crippled, hundreds of employees thrown out of work and the company very nearly eliminated from business. Farnsworth procured a court order to the Western Union to hand back the seized property, but what was the good? On July 31st the company's possessions were sold, but it had been so ruined by the destruction that the whole plant brought only $500,000.

With the exception of the Postal Telegraph, which will be treated in the following chapter, the Baltimore and Ohio Telegraph, which was so nurtured by the railroad of that name that it was able to spend sums far beyond the size of its capital stock issue, was the only independent concern to survive this period and continue for long thereafter.

All the telegraph companies had a troubled month in the summer of 1883, when the second telegraph employees' strike in history took place. The first one was called in January, 1870. A Telegraphers' Brotherhood, with secret oaths, had been organized in 1866, but was a feeble union. When the strike was called, only sixty-four operators, including, we are told, seven "ladies," forsook their keys in New York City, leaving many still on duty. The same was true in other cities, and within a few days the strike was an acknowledged failure.

In 1883, the union had greater power and held a charter from the Knights of Labor, which was then the national workingmen's organization. President Green had gone to Europe for a summer vacation when the employees presented their demands to General Manager Eckert. They included—for operators, an eight-hour day and seven-hour night shift, extra pay for Sunday work, a 15 per cent increase in pay and equal pay for men and women. Linemen and others made similar demands. Eckert refused to consider them, and on July 19th the strike began. In the whole country, it is said that 7,000 men and 1,000 women left their posts. For a week or two the service was badly crippled. But again the walkout was not effective, because so many employees did not belong to the union, and even some union members dared not obey its orders. Within thirty days, the union leaders admitted failure, though it had been apparent long before that.

Even in the 1890's, telegraphers in the smaller cities and towns were receiving only from $25 to $50 a month as salary, though the lowest priced ones, as a rule, drew additional pay from railroads or other sources. In New York City, the best male operators were drawing $71 a month, women only $36. But it was not long before the unions began to change those figures.

It may be interesting to mention more fully women's service in communications. Women operators were frequently taken on by telegraph companies as early as the 1850's; and whenever one appeared on a certain line, we find her refining influence on the whole line spoken of; no more cuss words, no rowdy remarks by operators to each other. Andrew Carnegie's sister was an operator in those days, and her office became a sort of school for women telegraphers. Flirtations were inevitable, often between operators who had never seen each other, and some of them developed into romances and happy marriages. President Orton testifying before a Senate committee in 1874, spoke very highly of the women, though we do not find his high opinion reflected in their salary list. Among other things, he said:

The conditions under which it is proper to employ women in the business are so limited as compared with men that we are unable to employ as many as we would like. We use them in the large cities where we have enough business to justify the creation of a separate department. But we cannot, for example, put them in many hotels. There was a time when it was not deemed proper to put them in railway stations; but I believe that between Buffalo and Albany, the telegraph at nearly every station is worked by women. The same is true on other roads.[1]

MR. HUBBARD—Every station in Boston is, I think, worked by women.

MR. ORTON—The number of female operators is increasing. We employ about sixty in the New York office, who do about as satisfactory work as any we have.

MR. HARRINGTON—Are they not put on your city wires?

MR. ORTON—They work the city wires almost exclusively.

In interesting contrast is an early reaction as to the employment of women as telephone exchange operators. Inspector Lockwood reported to Manager Vail in 1879 regarding the Boston telephone office:

The operators are all females, which of course has its advantages and disadvantages.... Notwithstanding the pronounced opin-

[1] These were overstatements.

ACCORDING TO THIS ARTIST OF THE 'SEVENTIES, ROMANCE
BUDDED WHEREVER THERE WERE LADY TELEGRAPH
OPERATORS

ion of resident authorities that female operators are much superior to males, the fact remains, viz., that the office manager, unless an unusually well-balanced man, is liable to form preferences and favor some to the exclusion of others. The young ladies also appear fond of airing their voices, and sometimes prolong telephonic conversation to talk with subscribers, again losing time. On the other hand, they exceed males in civility and general attention to their own tables.

And the fact that they exceed males in civility and tactfulness, and that rules of procedure have ironed out the early frivolities, accounts for the fact that women are universally the telephone operators of to-day.

Jay Gould died in December, 1892, and Dr. Green soon followed him, passing away at his old home in Louisville, in February, 1893. General Eckert, then nearly sixty-eight, was elected President. When he resigned office in 1900, the company had a capital of $99,800,000, and admitted that during its existence its total receipts had been $515,000,000, of which $180,-000,000 was profit. Opposition economists believed that the real profit would be nearer $250,000,000. John Wanamaker, when Postmaster-General under Harrison, remarked that an investment of $1,000 in Western Union in 1858 brought in, in the following thirty years, stock dividends of more than $50,000 and cash dividends of about $100,000, or 300 per cent of dividends per year. But the company's palmiest days were over.

Eckert was succeeded in 1900 by R. C. Clowry, the last of the Civil War telegraphers to reach the top. They had become a tradition; their right to rule was undisputed. It is interesting, by the way, to discover how many leaders in business and industry began as Morse "key-pounders." In addition to the heads of the great telegraph companies, there were, for example, Andrew Carnegie, Thomas A. Edison and Ralph Blumenfeld, the great English editor (American born). In 1910 a reporter found many railroad executives: Marvin Hughitt, President, and W. A. Gardner, Vice-President of the Chicago and Northwestern; A. J. Earling, President, and E. W. McKenna, Vice-President, Chicago, Milwaukee & St. Paul; Henry R. Williams,

President, Chicago, Milwaukee & Puget Sound; F. D. Underwood, President, Erie; Henry U. Mudge, President, Chicago, Rock Island & Pacific; also L. C. Weir, President, Adams Express Company (he once sat by an instrument for six hours and took 3,000 words without a break) ; B. E. Sunny, President, Chicago Telephone Company, and many others.

But with Eckert and Clowry, the Civil War heroes were growing old; under the latter's reign, the company fell into doldrums. A hint as to the reason may possibly be seen in the company's quarrel with the Pennsylvania Railroad in 1901 to 1902. At the expiration of a twenty-year contract with the railroad, the Western Union haughtily refused to consider any modifications in a new contract. When the railroad finally made a deal with the Postal Telegraph for service, the Western Union publicly announced that it would not be inconvenienced by the change, and refused to take its poles and wires off the railroad right of way; whereupon the railroad set locomotives to work at pulling the poles out by the roots. After they had been overthrown, the Western Union refused to remove them. At the expiration of the Postal contract, the Western Union was under a different management, peace was made, and it returned to the Pennsylvania lines again.

Clowry was again in hot water a few years later, when reformers, led by the City Club of New York, made an attack on pool-room race-track gambling, and on the Western Union for its alliance with that racket. The Club placed the Western Union income from race-track gambling at $5,000,000 yearly, and other companies and the telephone took almost or quite as much. Such a stench was raised that the Western Union was forced to withdraw service temporarily, and on May 21, 1904, there was not a pool-room in operation in New York City—a condition which had not been known in thirty years.

But the telegraph barons had no notion of giving up such a rich source of income, so they endeavored to operate in secret. In the summer of 1906, Dr. Thomas R. Slicer took up the fight against them again for the City Club, and matters grew so serious that once more the Western Union made a fake renunciation. This time its racing bureau manager resigned, and together with Johnny Payne, an old pool-room racketeer, organized two corporations, the National News Company and Interstate News Company, which tried in various ways to mask their real object and their sources of information. One of their subterfuges at Chicago is interesting in that it shows the entrance of a new demon into the game—wireless telegraphy. A pool-room ship, the *City of Traverse,* was anchored in Lake Michigan, at some distance from the shore, with which it was connected by the DeForest Wireless Telegraph Company, and many tugloads of the sort of folk who suffer from the gambling mania went out to it daily. Josiah Flynt said in the *Cosmopolitan* in 1907 that the *City of Traverse* paid DeForest Wireless $100 a day for service. He asserted that Payne's income was $50,000 a day, or $15,000,000 yearly, most of which went to the big telegraph and telephone companies.

Times and standards have changed since then, and gambling is in 1936 looked upon with far more indulgence than formerly. A telegraph company may now deal with gamblers and still claim to be perfectly respectable.

In 1914, after the re-separation of Western Union and the A. T. & T., as described in the previous chapter, Newcomb Carlton, then Vice-President, became President, and has so remained to the time of this writing. The company long ago assumed control of the old Field cables corporation, and has laid several strands of its own across the Atlantic, but it has never gone in for air telegraphy, and in these latter days it suffers somewhat from competition—other cables and land telegraphs, the telephone, radio telegraphy and telephony, the teletype, which the A. T. & T. is using largely, and which the Western Union complains is an invasion of its field and a violation of the treaty of 1879. But it still does a great majority of the land telegraph business of the continent. It owns over 216,-000 miles of poles and 1,900,000 miles of wire, besides 30,784 nautical miles of ocean cable.

CHAPTER XXI

THE SILVER KING AND HIS SUCCESSORS

Their line is gone out through all the earth, and their words to
the end of the world.   PSALMS XIX, 4

ELISHA GRAY'S harmonic telegraph was a follow-up of
Helmholtz's discovery that the qualities of sounds were
due to "the intensities of the harmonies which accompany their
primary tones." Gray found that with a free magnet and an
armature, he could develop higher or lower tones, according
to the frequency of the impulses of the electric current actuating the magnet. He found that several tones could be sent
simultaneously over a single wire, and he reasoned that these
tones could be translated into telegrams. He succeeded in sending sixteen signals, though that number was never found practical under his system.

Gray's patent was offered to the Western Union, but rejected.
A Connecticut manufacturer named Chester Snow produced
about this time a new telegraph wire, a thin strand of steel
overlaid with copper, which formed about 3/5 of the total bulk.
This made a wire of great tensile strength, yet having the fine
electrical conductivity of copper. These two patents, the Gray
harmonic telegraph and the Snow wire, were made the basis for
the organization of a new company in New York on June 21,
1881—one destined to play a considerable part in the communications drama of after years. It was christened Postal Telegraph Company, the charge being made by competitors that it
thereby hoped to deceive the public into believing that it was
connected with the Government; and as a matter of fact, many
persons did believe just that. George D. Roberts, a Californian,
with large ideas, was one of the chief promoters. Elisha Gray

and Governor Charles Foster of Ohio are found among the incorporators. It was probably due to Roberts that the capital stock was fixed at $21,000,000, and $10,000,000 in bonds authorized. Erastus Wiman, in his Chicago *Inter-Ocean* interview in 1884, charged that not a dollar was paid in for stock; that Roberts had been given $12,000,000 worth of it, and "what Mr. Roberts has ever done to become possessed of 12,000,000 worth of telegraph stock has never appeared."

Roberts explained the large capitalization by saying that the automatic-harmonic system with the small number of wires necessary, plus the low rates which the company proposed to adopt, yet still making a good profit, would enable the company to capture the whole telegraph business of the country, and thus necessitate the taking over of old plants and the building of new ones.

A line of unusually careful construction was built from New York to Chicago and thence to St. Louis. A flat rate of 25 cents for twenty words anywhere was established, and at this figure the company's limited territory did not permit it to show any profit. Roberts, hoping to enlist Government coöperation to the extent, perhaps, of inducing Government sponsorship or even selling out to Uncle Sam, offered to transmit Government messages for one cent a word for distances up to a thousand miles, and 2½ cents beyond that. By night, the rates were to be even lower. The B. & O. Telegraph offered almost the same rates. The Postmaster-General refused both offers, but used them as a lever to force down rates to the Government from other companies.

"When the line to Chicago was completed," said Wiman to the reporter, "they had floated about $3,000,000 of their bonds, so that the company's issues at that time were $24,000,000, represented by an expenditure of less than $1,000,000." In the summer of 1883, John W. Mackay, silver millionaire, greatest of the bonanza kings of Virginia City, returned from a visit to Paris, and was at once buttonholed by Roberts, an old acquaintance, and induced to invest some money in Postal Telegraph.

Mr. Mackay was the more easily persuaded because he didn't like the rule-or-ruin policy of Jay Gould. Born in Ireland, he had been brought to New York when a child, sold newspapers on the Bowery and went to school briefly on Park Row, within a few hundred feet of the site, years later, of his thirteen-story Postal Telegraph Building. Going to California in 1851, it was a decade before Fortune began to flirt with him as he got a foothold in the silver diggings of the Washoe country. There on the great Comstock Lode, he found many millions of wealth.

Mackay was fifty-two years old, physically and mentally still at the top of his power, and longing for activity. He knew nothing about the telegraph business, but he could learn, and he counted upon the indomitable will and perseverance which had won success for him in the West. He paid cash for a million dollars' worth of Postal stock, and was elected President of the company. He said, however, that he thought it ought to be reorganized and some of the water wrung out of it. This was done at once, and the capital reduced to $10,500,000.

Meanwhile, the new president had conceived the idea of going in for foreign communication. One story is that James Gordon Bennett the Younger, publisher of the New York *Herald,* who spent nearly all his time in France and ran his paper by letter and cable (and who, incidentally, hated Jay Gould) talked him into it. Another contribution is that Mr. Mackay was so impressed by the size of his wife's cable tolls that he thought there must be large profits in the business. Mrs. Mackay, a brilliant and beautiful woman, sojourned in Paris for several years, showing Europe what an American millionaire's wife could do in the way of lavish entertainment, with a dab at culture.

Anyhow, in September, 1883, Mackay and Bennett formed a partnership which two months later became a corporation, the Commercial Cable Company. Mackay put in 70 per cent of the money, Bennett about 25 per cent, and a few acquaintances were permitted to come in for much smaller amounts. Tremendous activity on the part of Mackay followed. Two cables were to be laid. Their manufacture had to be arranged for, cable-laying ships procured and fitted up, four governments—the United States, Canada, England and France—had to be seen, charts of the ocean bed studied, offices opened on both sides of the water, and capable staffs assembled, which last was a difficult job, for the Gould interests had nearly all the capable men cornered, and only the high salaries offered, plus the magic of Mackay's name, could lure them away.

Mackay became an Atlantic commuter, and spent most of his time for months in shuttling back and forth between the two continents. But the effect of his energy was quickly visible. The first stretch of cable—that between Waterville, Ireland, and Canso, Nova Scotia—was landed at the latter place July 19, 1884. It was quickly extended on this side to Rockport, Massachusetts, and Manhattan Beach on Coney Island, near New York City. On the other side, it reached the western coast of England and continued thence by land to London and other cities. A second cable over the same route was completed in October. From Waterville, a branch cable extended to Havre and thus to Paris.

Cable tolls across the ocean by other lines were 75 cents per word. Mackay announced that he believed 40 cents to be a fair figure; but as the Western Union quickly met that rate, he cut his own to 25 cents, in order to introduce his service. This was nothing less than a gage of battle, and the Western Union presently slashed the rate to 12 cents. The Commercial office considered a possible cut to 6 cents, but Mackay turned his thumb down on that and kept the 25-cent figure in force. With his huge fortune as a weapon, he felt strong enough to keep up the fight, even if his opponent was undercutting him.

Gould was furious at this impudent opposition, and in his usual delicate manner, one of the shots he fired was a vicious personal attack on Bennett, copies of which were sent to all the papers in New York save the *Herald*. However, Julius Chambers, managing editor of the *Herald,* heard of the story from a friend on another paper before it was printed; and shrewdly seeing that a clever way to meet it was to print it in his own paper, procured a copy from the friend and ran it in the *Herald* on the same day of its appearance elsewhere. Bennett was not consulted, but was highly pleased by the coup; and incidentally, Gould's assault fell flat. "Indeed," says Don C. Seitz in his book on the Bennetts, "to assail the character of the *Herald's* proprietor was a waste of time. It had long since ceased to be an asset."

Meanwhile, the Postal Telegraph had found itself in serious difficulties, notwithstanding its reorganization. It was unable, even with the aid of the automatic and harmonic system to carry enough business to earn any profits at its low rates. The harmonic system proved a disappointment. It was a good quadruplex, and even six messages at once could be sent over it at short distances, but no more. In the summer of '84 the Postal joined the B. & O. and the Bankers and Merchants in a pool to eliminate competition among themselves and for defense against the Western Union. But scarcely had they done this when the panic came on, the B. & M. became a bankrupt, and the Postal, too, was so badly shaken that it was placed in receivership.

Albert B. Chandler, prominent telegraph executive and former Civil War cipher man, was appointed receiver. Under his management (Mackay being too busy with his cables to pay much attention to the land lines just then), the Postal began to recuperate as the effects of the brief panic wore away. In January, 1886, the company was again reorganized, and Chandler was elected President, though the old Silver King remained the major power in the company. Having picked the other cable companies and dictated peace with the rate restored to 40 cents, he now turned his attention to the extension of the Postal's land lines.

Several small independent Eastern companies were first gathered in. The service as then constituted had its western limit at St. Louis. But the Postal now made a contract with the Canadian Pacific Telegraph Company, operating along the railway system of that name, to carry its messages to the Pacific

From International Telephone and Telegraph Corporation

JAMES GORDON BENNETT, JR.   JOHN W. MACKAY

BRINGING AN AMERICAN-OWNED CABLE ASHORE AT ALGECIRAS, SPAIN

coast. Meanwhile, the Pacific Postal Telegraph Company had been organized, and had built a line from the Canadian Pacific at New Westminster, British Columbia, down to San Francisco, eventually overspreading the whole Pacific slope. By the summer of 1886, Mackay lines had service from London and Paris across the Atlantic and the American continent to the shores of the Pacific. This amazing speed of development was due in no small measure to one-man control, and to the fact that Mackay did not have to ask help to finance his operations, but for the most part used his own money.

Having spanned the continent, he next turned his eyes towards Asia. For years, telegraph magnates and promoters had talked of and sketched plans for a cable across the Pacific Ocean, but the magnitude and the great depth of that water were too much for the nerves of investors. Promoters did not think a cable could be laid to Asia unless Congress would subsidize the owners. In the latter '90's, efforts were made to push a bill through Congress, authorizing the Government itself to cable the vasty deep. The Army and the Navy favored this idea, and there was much wrangling over the route. The nearest possible way was by Hawaii and Midway Island; but opposing factions pointed out that Midway was a barren, desolate atoll, impossible as a relay station because no one could live there in its natural state. This group favored a course hugging the Pacific coast up to Alaska, thence along the Aleutian Islands, perhaps touching the tip of Kamchatka, and so down the Kurile Islands to Japan.

A corporation, the Pacific Cable Company, had been organized, with the Western Union in the background, and proposed to lay a cable to the Orient, provided Congress would grant it an annual subsidy for ten years of—well, at one time it asked $400,000, at another $300,000, and eventually came down to $100,000. While it was lobbying in Washington through two or three Congresses, Mackay quietly made preparations to go ahead on his own. In 1901, he spiked all opposition guns by announcing that if granted a charter, he would lay a cable without asking a cent of subsidy from Government, and would cut the rates from San Francisco to China and the Philippines to $1 a word. The rate from San Francisco to China was then $1.72, and to Manila it had been as high as $2.35. Western Union opponents, thus left without a leg to stand on, threw their influence towards Government ownership of the Pacific strand, but vainly. Mackay's proposition was so fair and attractive that there seemed nothing to do but grant his charter and privileges. He did not live, however, to see his dream realized. He died on July 15, 1902, leaving to his son, Clarence W. Mackay, the carrying out of his plans.

On December 15, 1902, the shore end of the cable was attached at San Francisco, and the construction ship headed for Honolulu, where it landed a few days later. Service to that point was at once opened at a rate of 50 cents a word from San Francisco. On June 19, 1903, the cable reached Midway Island, and on July 4th, Manila, which was already connected with the Asiatic coast by another company's cable. So on that day, for the first time, the globe was completely encircled by telegraph.

Hawaii, Midway and Guam divide the Pacific cable into four great stretches of deep-sea line, respectively 2,276, 1,254, 2,593, and 1,490 miles in length. Midway Island was a tiny dot in the ocean, a mile and a quarter long by half a mile wide. To make it habitable, shiploads of soil were hauled and deposited upon it. Trees and grasses were planted, then flowers. Homes were built, also plants to provide electric light, heat and water supply. Milch cows and poultry were brought; a golf course was laid out and other recreations provided for. A ship regularly and frequently supplies the island with food, clothing, reading matter and whatever else is needed. The radio now adds its amelioration, with the result that an assignment to Midway for two or three years is not considered at all bad by employes of the cable company.

Just as John Mackay was getting his Pacific charter in 1891, a twenty-year-old banker in New York was growing a handsome blond beard, in order that he might look more like the responsible head of a foreign exchange department in a big New York banking house than he did without it. (He has shaved it off since.) The young financier was Sosthenes Behn, a native of St. Thomas in the Virgin Islands, then Danish territory. He and his brother Hernand, two years older than he, had decided when they were small boys to be business men and partners. Their family was well to do. As nearly as blood lineage can be classified, they are half French and half Danish. They were educated in Europe, learned to speak many languages, and became two of the world's most thorough cosmopolites. In 1906 (they had long since become American citizens) they took over their stepfather's sugar business, and Sosthenes went to join his brother in San Juan, Puerto Rico, where they set up their headquarters, and where they also became bankers. Presently, they took over the telephone system of the island from a friend who had had to take it as security on a loan. They did not know it at the moment, but that marked the turning point of their careers. Henceforth they were to be masters of communication.

The World War came, and Sosthenes served ably with the United States Signal Corps in France (thereby learning much more about telegraphs and telephones) and emerged a Colonel, while Hernand kept the business going. During the war and afterwards, their West Indian companies were increasing their plants at the rate of 4,000 telephones a year, which argues good service. In 1920, the brothers made a deal with the American Telephone and Telegraph Company for the joint laying of a new cable from Cuba to the United States. In the following year they organized the International Telephone and Telegraph Corporation. Their aims were world-wide.

Spain was struggling with an antiquated Government telephone system when the brothers boldly sought in 1924 to obtain it as a concession. The reply was that they might have it if they would manufacture all their equipment in Spain. They had no factory anywhere, let alone in Spain, and they wanted American-engineered equipment, but Sosthenes, who was conducting the negotiations, took a chance and signed the contract, hoping to work out the minor matter of manufacture later.

The A. T. & T. had a large subsidiary in Europe, manufacturing telephone equipment—International Western Electric. The Behns asked them whether they would build a factory in Spain and manufacture equipment for I. T. & T. The answer was, No. Siemens & Halske of Germany and the Ericsson Company of Sweden, both of whom had tried to get the Spanish concession, would give no assistance, both hoping, of course, that the Behns would fail to make good. The latter then turned to American Telephone and Telegraph again and said, "Will you sell International Western Electric to us, and if so, for how much?"

The answer was, "Yes, for thirty millions!" It was rather breath-taking, but these daring brothers, whose nerve has seldom been exceeded in business history, bore up under the shock. They persuaded J. P. Morgan & Company to take over a $30,000,000 bond issue (how some of the rest of us wish we had such persuasive powers) and the thing was done. They then proceeded to put the most up-to-date telephone system in the world into Spain. It was even more modern at the time than that of the United States, and its high standard has been maintained. The great majority of it was automatic or dial-controlled, and the reaction to their service was a multiplication of the number of telephones in Spain by two and a half times in five years.

The next step towards their dream of a world communication system was the acquirement of a great cable network. All-America Cables, the North-and-South American system whose building we have sketched in a previous chapter, had in 1922 entered into a compact fraught with curious significance for the future of both parties; it made a traffic agreement with the Postal Telegraph and Commercial Cable Companies which drew them all much closer together. In 1926, All-America, which was evidently finding the going a bit rough, sold its Mexican Telegraph system to the Western Union. In the following year it

CLARENCE W. MACKAY   SOSTHENES BEHN

INTERNATIONAL TELEPHONE AND TELEGRAPH CORPORATION
BUILDING, NEW YORK

HERNAND BEHN   JAMES A. SCRYMSER

agreed to let the I. T. & T. purchase not less than two-thirds of its capital stock, each three shares of A.A.C. to be paid for with four of I. T. & T. And hard upon the heels of that came the next great coup.

The Postal Telegraph had greatly extended its system under Clarence Mackay's direction, and now reached all parts of the country. It had originated various ingenious devices to gain more publicity and traffic—the flowers-by-telegraph idea, for example, and great extensions of the Christmas and other sorts of greetings, so that now, if you wish to send holiday or birthday good wishes to a friend, you don't have to do any thinking about the matter; you just pick out Number 26 or Number 87 from a telegraph company's list, and the company does the rest. But Mr. Mackay, though one of the best beloved executives in America and inspirer of the most intense loyalty on the part of his employes, had never been able to gain much ground against the Western Union. In 1928, the Postal was handling only 17 per cent of the telegraph business of the United States when the I. T. & T. offered it hospitality and took it over.

These rapid strokes, one after another, and the phenomenal growth in assets and profits gave I. T. & T. enormous prestige, and just before the crash of 1929, its stock sold as high as $149 a share. Within six years' time, it had boosted its total assets from $38,300,000 to $535,000,000; its net income from $1,930,000 to $17,730,000. Then came the cataclysm, and the years since have been lean and tough going for so young a company. But it has shown great versatility. Its next move was into the air; and it is now the only company in existence using all five methods of communication—land telegraph and telephone, submarine cable, and air telegraph and telephone. In June, 1930, it sent a telegraph message around the globe in five and a half minutes, beating the record by two and a half minutes.

From North and South America, its wireless stations hurl air messages in both directions around the globe to the Eastern Hemisphere. On its waves, King Alfonso XIII inaugurated radio telephone service across the Atlantic from Spain to America in 1928. It installed in the Vatican the first telephone ever used by a Pope; and reports say that Pius XI took to it readily, and uses it frequently. Under this Pontiff, by the way, the Vatican has gone modern more rapidly than ever before in its history. The Marchese Marconi himself superintended the installation of a fine broadcasting station for its use in communicating with its adherents the world over; and in 1931, the Belinograph, one of the several machines for sending pictures or reproductions by telegraph, was installed there, a 350,000-franc gift from the inventor, Edward Belin. George Seldes, in *The Vatican Yesterday, Today and Tomorrow,* remarks that it "is able not only to transmit photographs by radio, but the texts of diplomatic correspondence, scrambled electrically, which the recipients can easily decipher with the key." A costly and cumbersome diplomatic code system may thus be dispensed with.

The I. T. & T. controls the telephone systems of Spain, Rumania, Cuba, Puerto Rico, Peru, northern Argentina, three-quarters of Chile and Uruguay and parts of Mexico and southern Brazil; of such widely scattered cities as Shanghai, Istambul (Constantinople), Buenos Aires and others. It has telephone equipment factories in America, England, Germany, Austria, Hungary, France, Belgium, Italy, Spain, Argentina, Australia, Japan and China. It connected South American capitals for the first time when it strung wires across the Andes between Chile and Argentina. It is the only company spanning both the great oceans, Atlantic and Pacific, by cable. Six cables cross the Atlantic alone, four via Nova Scotia and two by way of the Azores.

Hernand Behn, then President of the corporation, died in 1933, aged fifty-three, and his brother Sosthenes succeeded him.

CHAPTER XXII

MARCONI, THE WIZARD OF THE AIR

"I'll tell the world."
SHAKESPEARE, *Measure for Measure*

APPARENTLY the first suggestion that telegraphy might be possible without wires came from the German physicist, C. A. Steinheil, just ninety-eight years before the publication of this book. In 1838, Steinheil discovered that a return wire was not necessary to complete a circuit, but that the earth would act as the return carrier. Just what steps his mind took to reach the prophecy we do not know, but he suggested that some day it might be possible to dispense with even the single wire.

Joseph Henry was among the earliest to experiment with electrical action at a distance, without connecting wires. He succeeded, in 1843, in magnetizing needles at a distance of 220 feet. Faraday also found that electrical apparatus may be made to influence a dead coil or wire at a distance. Morse sent a signal through water without wires. Bell, with his "photophone," conveyed a Morse message across a large room by means of a beam of light, thus using the same electrical waves—only that they were infinitely shorter ones—as those later used in wireless telegraphy.

It was Ampère who, far back at the beginning of the nineteenth century, suggested the existence of the ether. In 1865, and after, James Clerk-Maxwell, great English physicist, wrote his famous papers on electro-magnetic phenomena, in which he shows that electrical action passes through space in the form of waves, which travel with the velocity of light. He decided that light waves are electro-magnetic, but that there are also waves that do not make themselves visible, and these were what Henry

435

and Faraday had stumbled upon. As a matter of fact, they are the same sort of waves; it is only the shorter ones that we see. There must be four hundred trillions—or, to be strictly accurate, four hundred million millions (400,000,000,000,000) —of vibrations per second before we can see light. In other words, light waves are so short that there are from 30,000 to 60,000 of them in an inch. The invisible waves whose existence Clerk-Maxwell guessed are those produced when the ether—if that is what it is—is vibrated only a few thousand or a few million times per second. These waves may be anywhere from a few inches to miles in length. Their frequency is so low that they make no impression on the eye, and therefore we have no consciousness of their existence; yet they are the waves which have now been harnessed and which talk to us through the radio, and which soon will make us *see* things as they happen in other parts of the world.

Several Americans in the early '80's groped towards wireless telegraphy, but did not quite reach it. Professor Trowbridge of Harvard was obsessed with the idea that telegraphy through earth and water without wire were possible. He succeeded in sending messages through both media, and strove to find some way by which ships could communicate with each other at sea by trailing ends of wire in the water. But to reach a distance of half a mile by his system, a coil of 800 feet radius would be necessary, and of course that was out of the question. Trowbridge believed that it was possible to use the air as a medium, and prophesied that this would be done, but did not see how it could work well at a distance because of the curvature of the earth.

Bell followed Trowbridge's suggestion as to water, and established communication between vessels in the Potomac River. Professor Dolbear, another telephone inventor, grounded two wires at some distance apart and sent high currents into the earth, but he took a step forward by adding a large induction coil to his transmitting set. He believed that speech would eventually be sent through the air as well as the click of the

Top—WESTERN UNION OPERATING ROOM, NEW YORK, 1890
Below—THE TELETYPE TO-DAY SUPPLANTS AS MANY OP-
ERATORS AS ARE SEEN BEYOND, IN THE CINCINNATI OFFICE
OF 1860

telegraph, and thus was the pioneer in suggesting radio telephony. Had he used a heavy instead of a fine wire in his own apparatus, he would have come nearer to realization.

Several scientists. noting how telegraph and telephone wires by induction picked up sounds from each other although they were feet or yards apart, began wondering whether telegraphy from moving trains might not be possible. Edison succeeded in it in a crude way. He set a plate covered with tinfoil on top of the engine or car on a level with the telegraph wires or nearly so, and found that the current could be lured across the space between them, no matter how fast the train ran. Thus a message could be flashed from train to wire, and along the wire to a station. Edison's interest in this soon slackened as he became absorbed in other subjects, else he might have worked out wireless telegraphy years before Marconi.

Americans now let the wireless idea lapse, and Europe took it up. An Englishman, Sir W. H. Preece, set up in 1885 two great squares of insulated wire, a quarter-mile across and a quarter of a mile distant from each other, and caused telephone messages to leap from one to the other by induction, but this was no great advance over the old accidental induction which had so troubled early telegraphers. Two years later, another Briton, A. W. Heaviside, laid circuits on the surface and others in a coal mine 350 feet below the surface and established communication between the two through the earth. Preece and Heaviside combined their experiments, increased their distance, and decided that the best means of wireless communication was attained by a combination of conduction and induction.

But even this alliance could not convey signals to the distance necessary for worthwhile communication. It was Heinrich Hertz, a modest young German scientist, who finally began to clarify the situation by proving the existence of electric waves around an oscillating circuit. He had two coils or hoops of wire at some distance apart, one of them with a small break in it. He found that when a charge of electricity was thrown into this coil, the spark which leaped across the gap excited currents in the other coil. He placed them farther and farther apart and tried them. He found that the electric waves which leaped from one coil to the other traveled at the speed of light. He found that they could be reflected by large, polished metal mirrors, that they could be focused by large, lens-shaped masses of pitch and that they could be prolonged; in other words, that they were just like light waves, save that they made no impression on the eye. Now, if you have a wave, there must be something to wave. Palpably, these were not waves in the atmosphere; hence the assumption of the ether, a strange, inexplicable something supposed to permeate all space and all matter.

When it was found that you could create these waves, could set them in motion just by jumping a spark across a gap, wireless telegraphy was right around the corner. Hertz's discoveries created a great sensation in the scientific world, and much to his embarrassment, the waves were given his name. He deprecated his achievement, and said that if he had not made his discovery just when he did, Sir Oliver Lodge would soon have done it. Lodge in England, Popoff in Russia and Branly in France carried the experiments further. Branly and Lodge improved Hertz's broken ring. But all these were working in the interest of pure science, and not one of them, almost unbelievable as it seems, ever thought of the Hertzian Waves as a means of communication. Lodge admitted years afterwards that he "did not realize that there would be a practicable advantage in . . . telegraphy across space." Sir William Crookes was the first to see the point, and make the suggestion, this in an article in the *Fortnightly Review* in 1892. He even predicted the tuning to special wave lengths; but the thought of wireless telephony evidently had not occurred to him.

At last came the practical man; not the pure scientist, but the inventor who thought of turning pure, abstract science to practical use. Guglielmo Marconi, son of an Italian father and an Irish mother, was born near Bologna in 1874. From his mother he learned to speak English as fluently as Italian, and his schooling was received variously at Bologna, Florence and

Rugby—all of which was of great value to him in later years. This shy, quiet boy, yet careful and diligent student, had a teacher, Professor Richi, who had studied the Hertzian Waves, and was himself a notable experimenter. From Richi's inspiration and from the scientific books and magazines which he eagerly devoured, Guglielmo was fired with the idea of wireless communication. He wished that he might be the one to achieve it, but realizing his youth and inexperience, he was certain that some older man would beat him to the goal. Had not Sir William Crookes plainly pointed the way in that magazine article? But as months passed with no news of accomplishment, he began experimenting himself, though still half expecting to be beaten. He scarcely dared open a scientific magazine, lest the bad news leap out into his face.

He did his experimenting on his father's farm; the latter, evidently a man of vision, encouraging him and supplying needed materials. The youth set up plates of tin for aërials on top of two posts on opposite sides of the family vegetable garden, and put together such crude sending and receiving apparatus as was then available. Now for the first time, a Morse telegraph key was connected with Hertz's broken coil. A quick touch on the key caused a momentary spark to flash across the gap; a more lingering pressure caused a longer spark; thus dots and dashes were formed.

He soon saw that his receiving device was the part that needed most attention. The telephone had long been using in its transmitter the mass of carbon granules which we have already described; whose particles, when an electric current flashed among them, joined hands as it were, making a linked-chain web or bridge, through which the current passed. Professor Branly, of the Catholic University of Paris, by way of experiment, tried metal filings, instead of carbon, putting them into a small glass tube about six inches long, and arranging a tiny hammer to tap the glass and shake the filings apart after the spark had brought them together. Marconi worked this Branly "Coherer" into his receiving apparatus, experimenting with various metals for the filings until he decided that nickel with a small percentage of silver was best. He plugged the ends of the tube with silver stoppers and attached platinum wires. He had the automatic tapper ready to strike the tube lightly after each dot or dash, and so shake the particles apart, ready to rearrange themselves again. The young inventor was just twenty-one years old when he took another long step forward, arranging Hertz's dipole oscillator by connecting one-half of it with the earth and elevating and prolonging the other half into the air until it began to resemble the modern aërial. To many persons it looked like a huge caricature of an insect's feeler or antenna; and as there was a certain logic in the comparison from a scientific standpoint, the name antenna became attached to it, and has so remained to this day. By this stroke, Marconi was able greatly to increase his distance. That year, 1895, he sent a message a mile and a quarter, and with that event, a new means of communication may be said to have been born.

In 1896, he went to England and there, at the age of twenty-two, was granted the first of all patents on wireless telegraphy. Sir William Preece, who had himself done notable work in that line, was engineer-in-chief for the British Post-Office, which was a fortunate circumstance for Marconi. His work thereby became at once an object of interest for Government, and under the supervision of the Post-Office, the War Office and the Admiralty, he carried on a number of experiments, which were as educational to himself as to others. Some of the work was done on Salisbury Plain, but some of the messages were sent over water along the coast, and he soon found that the latter offered less obstruction than the land. The sea was therefore indicated as the best field for the development of wireless.

In 1897, in experiments on Italian warships near Spezia, Marconi obtained a range of twelve miles. The Lloyd's Corporation of London, always astute, soon saw the advantages of wireless to its own business and to shipping in general, and asked Marconi to make some tests over a seven and one-half-mile stretch between two of their lighthouses in the north of Ireland, where rough terrain and particularly a high cliff intervened. But the instruments worked well. The lighthouse keepers, though they were not electricians and had scarcely heard of wireless, quickly acquired proficiency in the air telegraph, and it was in operation there for a considerable time. In July, 1898, the Kingstown Regatta, held off the Irish coast near Dublin, was reported by wireless from a steamer to the shore. In August, Marconi was asked to establish communication between Osborne House, Isle of Wight, Queen Victoria's summer residence, and the Prince of Wales on the Royal yacht in Cowes Bay. This connection was kept up for sixteen days, to the great entertainment of the Royal family, though it may be guessed that the aged Queen did not spend much time in the room where the sending apparatus was crackling off the nerve-racking explosions peculiar to the wireless spark of those days. The experience was valuable to Marconi in that it enabled him to study the effect of intervening hills on the air waves.

In all this rapid development of the art, Marconi had as yet actually *invented* nothing. He simply used ideas supplied by the men who had pioneered before him; men who discovered principles, perhaps, but did not know what to do with them or were not interested in making them of practical use. Marconi is revered to-day as a great inventor and scientist, mostly because he brought something concrete out of a mass of abstractions; because he took embryonic ideas and developed them or recast them according to his will, because he set himself to work to create a new art of communication, and never slackened in his purpose until he had done so. Later, he did invent other things, as we shall see.

Sir Oliver Lodge helped him in 1897-98 by working on the principle of tuning, making the sending station a huge tuning fork; sending out waves of one electric pitch—that is, wave length—only, and tuning and adjusting the receiving instrument so that it would respond to that note and no other. This was an important step forward. Marconi was granted permission by Lodge to use the idea in his system. He had been having trouble in increasing his distance. It could be done by building antenna masts taller, but obviously there was a limit to that. In some of his experiments, he used kites with a very thin wire trailing from them, but it was plain that for permanent use, something better than that would have to be devised. However, by developing Lodge's tuned circuits and making his receiver more sensitive and selective, he obtained greater range.

Wishing to prove to skeptical and slow-moving shipmasters the value of wireless in their business, Marconi procured permission from the British Government to instal wireless connection between the South Foreland Lighthouse near Dover and the lightship twelve miles distant on the dangerous shoals known as the Goodwin Sands. By this communication with the shore, the lightship was able to save a number of ships and lives. It was proven in Admiralty Court that £52,588 worth of property was salvaged as the result of one message telling of a steamer aground on the Sands. It was from this lightship that the first wireless distress call in history was sent on March 3, 1899, when the little vessel itself was rammed by a freighter during a fog and was in danger of sinking. In fact, the East Goodwin beacon ship had to call for help twice within a year.

Winston Churchill tells of an experience in that year, 1899, which should have impressed indelibly upon the public mind the need for the new communication then being developed. War with the Boer Government was then threatened and just about to flare up in South Africa. General Sir Redvers Buller, the British Army Commander-in-Chief, together with Churchill and some others, left England one day at the end of summer in the steamer *Dunnottar Castle* for Cape Town. Here, with troops hurrying from all quarters of the world, towards South Africa, and the small forces already there being surrounded in three detachments by Boer armies, the British leader must drop out of sight and out of touch with everything for more than two weeks. To-day, he would be talking with both his Capital and the seat of war hourly.

But as it was, the *Dunnottar Castle* lumbered down to Madeira, four days out of England, and paused there to see if any news from the South had been dropped by passing ships. Not a word! Twelve days more they drove on in silence and worry—though the air about them was thronged with unseen forces which would willingly have borne news to them if properly summoned—and when only two days out from Cape Town, a tramp freighter was sighted, obviously coming from that port. The *Dunnottar Castle* signaled her, telling of the Commander's presence on board, and asking for news. The freighter altered her course so as to pass close to the other vessel, and an officer held up a blackboard on which was chalked, "Three battles. Penn Symmonds killed." And on she went, leaving the General to make what he could out of a cryptic message, whose only import to him was that war seemed to have broken out while he was incommunicado on the high seas.

By this time the Wireless Telegraph and Signal Company (later changed to the Marconi Wireless Telegraph Company) had been organized in England to own and promote Marconi's patents. He carried on experiments on both British and Italian warships during their 1899 manœuvers. In the British tests he covered a distance of seventy-four miles. This confirmed a belief which had long been growing upon him, but which others doubted, namely, that the curvature of the earth offers little or no obstruction to the waves. In September and October, his wireless went to America and reported to New York City the International Yacht Races between *Shamrock* and *Columbia* off Sandy Hook.

There has been much dispute as to the date of installation of the first wireless set on a commercial vessel. Karl Barslaag in *SOS to the Rescue* gives the huge North German liner *Kaiser Wilhelm der Grosse* credit as the pioneer and the date as March, 1900. But Marconi says—and it would seem that he ought to know—that there was a set in use on the American liner *St.*

Paul in the previous year; and to prove it, he has a copy of the first newspaper ever issued on shipboard with the aid of wireless, its date being November 15, 1899.

Wireless had not yet become of great aid to shipping because its range was still so small. Signals from land stations faded completely when the vessel was a few miles out; and then the operator had nothing to do but exhibit the apparatus to awed or skeptical passengers until he approached shore on the other side. The *St. Paul* was eastbound that week in November, and many on board were eager to hear the latest news from the South African war, then in its early stages. There was a wireless station at The Needles, a cape on the Isle of Wight, and at sixty-six miles distance, the *St. Paul* picked it up, though very faintly, and upon establishing better communication, asked for news. The resulting items were hastily printed on a leaflet and distributed among those on board before the vessel reached Southampton—just a stunt, but a significant prophecy of things to come. The sheet was christened *Transatlantic Times,* and its first few "Marconigrams," in the order they were received, were as follows:

1.50 P.M.—First signal received; 66 miles from Needles.
2.40.—"Was that you, *St. Paul?*" 50 miles from Needles.
2.50.—"Hurrah! Welcome home! Where are you?"
3.30.—40 miles. Ladysmith, Kimberley and Mafeking holding out well. No big battles. 15,000 men recently landed.
4.00.—Sorry to say the U.S.A. cruiser *Charleston* is lost. All hands saved. . . .

There were several other items.

Coincident with the installation on the *Kaiser Wilhelm der Grosse,* early in 1900, a German lightship and lighthouse were similarly equipped, so that the big liner might talk with the home shores when near enough. In November of that year, the Dover-Ostend mail packet *Princess Clementine* was fitted up with wireless, and soon proved its worth by summoning assistance for a bark which she saw stranded on a shoal. Later she had to call for help for herself in an emergency. The first com-

444

From Radio Corporation of America

MARCONI AND HIS FIRST WIRELESS SET

munication between ships took place in the summer of 1901. The *Lake Champlain,* which ran between England and Canada, began her first voyage with a wireless set late in May. On the return trip, eastbound, as she neared the Irish coast, the operator began trying to pick up a station on shore, when to his astonishment, he was answered from the Cunarder *Lucania,* outbound from England with her bran-new wireless outfit.

In 1900, Marconi had made another long stride forward—he learned how to send powerful trains or successions of waves, and tune his receiver so that it would not be affected by a single vagrant wave, but only by a rapid procession of them, of the proper frequency. With this improvement aiding him, he increased his distance to two hundred miles, and now began to think of bridging the ocean.

Meanwhile, a change had been made in the business method of his company. Up to that time, it had simply made and sold apparatus to whomsoever desired to use it. But other wireless ideas were now blossoming. Inventors in Germany, France, America and elsewhere were obtaining patents. True, the Marconi system had the start of them, but it would not maintain it long merely by the merchandizing of equipment. A better way to tie the world to its cart-tail seemed to be to organize a great telegraph system of its own; to have its own land stations, strategically located on trade routes, to place its own operators on ships, and order them to refuse communication with any upstart who might venture to use the air under other patents. This dog-in-the-manger policy was the first gesture in a wireless war, a precursor of a virtual state of anarchy to which that means of communication came within a decade. To carry out the new plan, the Marconi International Marine Communications Company was created in 1900, and in May, 1901, opened several stations on the shores of England and Ireland. The Italian, Canadian, Belgian and Newfoundland Governments quickly fell into line, later followed by others. Those countries whose own inventors were procuring patents were not won over so easily. In order to push the business in the United States, however, an American Marconi Company was organized.

Within six years from the time of Marconi's first experiments, a new communication had come into full flower, and a huge industry with almost illimitable possibilities had been created. But the quiet young inventor with the tiny smudge of mustache on his upper lip was still just in the early stages of his enthusiasm. He strove tirelessly, with the aid of his chief engineer, Professor James A. Fleming, for greater range. At last, he decided that he was ready to try a signal across the Atlantic. Fleming superintended the building of a tall aërial at Poldhu, on the coast of Cornwall, the western tip of England. There were many setbacks, by the way, in the erecting of those early aërial masts. Usually of wood, they were blown down time and again by wind. The one at Poldhu, in order to have a large area of wire for throwing off the spark, was hung on two tall masts, set far apart, their tops connected by a stout cable. From the little operating building half-way between them a great cluster of wires rose, spraying out into a vast fan shape as they approached the cable which supported them.

On the other shore, near St. Johns, Newfoundland, Marconi did not attempt to build an aërial, but relied upon a big kite to carry his receiving wire into the air. Notifying Fleming by cable when he was ready, Marconi, on December 21, 1901, waited for the signal. It was to be the simplest possible thing that could be sent; just the letter "S"—three dots only in the telegraphic code. And it came!—very, very faintly, it is true, but distinct and undeniable. It was repeated several times; and Marconi, unable to reply by air, rushed joyously to the cable office to notify his company and his fellow-workers of his success.

But the news of this epochal achievement proved an inconvenience to the inventor. The Anglo-American Cable Company, another dog in the manger, evidently had not believed up to that time that Marconi would succeed in the experiment. When he announced his success, they promptly shooed him out of

Newfoundland, claiming to own all rights of transatlantic communication to and from that island. He thereupon set up a station on more friendly soil, at Glace Bay, Cape Breton Island, and experimented there for two or three years.

Thenceforth, progress was as rapid as it had been in the six preceding years; to the lay eye, it might appear even more so. Marconi shortly thereafter journeyed from England to America on the liner *Philadelphia,* and worked with the wireless operator all the way. When they received a message 500 miles out from Ireland, the chief officer rushed to tell his shipmates of it, and was laughed at for a credulous chump. But the next day a gaping crowd packed itself around the door of the wireless room. When Marconi claimed to have received a message from a thousand miles' distance, some of the onlookers believed it, but others muttered "Fake!" The last coherent signal was received from shore when the ship was 1,550 miles distant.

It was on this journey that Marconi learned that the electric waves, like the evil-doers mentioned in the Bible, love darkness rather than light. Clear sky and sunlight acted, as he expressed it, like a blanket of fog upon vision. While night lay over the Atlantic, the waves moved across it regularly and with the mediocre degree of efficiency which was about all that could be expected at that period. As sunrise neared Poldhu, they took a sudden jump upward and became much stronger and clearer for a part of an hour; then, as the sun peeped above the horizon in England, they dropped almost to zero and remained there during the day if it was clear. As the sun set on the American coast, they leaped again to an unusually high efficiency for a brief time, then lapsed to their ordinary nightly level. Had Marconi known all this when he tried his first signal in Newfoundland, he would have done it at night and succeeded much better. Since then, radio apparatus has been greatly improved, and messages are now shot across oceans by day as well as by night. But the night hours are still the best, and when a company must send a message to a great distance, say, half-way around the globe, it prefers to transmit it while darkness lies upon that half of the planet.

Thereafter, ships could easily keep in touch with land on one side or the other of the sea, their wireless sets functioning well for a thousand miles or more. It was not until well along in 1902 that Marconi succeeded in sending a full message across the Atlantic. In 1904, a news service was established on some of the Atlantic liners, the wireless picking up news items from stations in Britain, Canada and the United States, which were first mimeographed, later printed in a ship newspaper.

In 1902, Marconi patented a more efficient form of magnetic detector, which enabled the operator to hear the dots and dashes as musical notes—the familiar whistle or cry of the radio which we still hear in a receiving station. It replaced the Branly coherer type of receiver in use up to that time. With this, the speed of reception was increased to 150 words per minute. For more than ten years the magnetic detector was standard equipment on English and most other European vessels. Americans did not use them, but had two receivers of their own—the electrolytic or chemical type, and the "beertop," which consisted of just two pieces of aluminum and a sewing machine needle. About 1907, the Americans took to the crystal receiver, which slowly crept into use on British ships also; but all British ships had not yet gotten around to using it by 1912-13, when American ships were dropping it in favor of the vacuum valve, now almost universally used. But this is ahead of our story.

As more and more vessels became equipped with wireless, trouble began. To the operators, the thing was a new toy, and they had no end of fun with it. There were no international regulations as to its use, and every operator, though careful to send and receive messages when offered, otherwise did pretty nearly as he pleased. No operator admitted any precedence to another, and those on liners were particularly contemptuous of the rights of those on freighters. There was a thrill in picking up a chap on some other ship, particularly if he happened to be a personal friend, and gossiping with him about nothing of

SENDING UP THE KITE, WITH ANTENNA, IN NEWFOUND-
LAND, WHICH RECEIVED THE FIRST WIRELESS MESSAGE
ACROSS THE ATLANTIC, 1901. MARCONI AT EXTREME LEFT

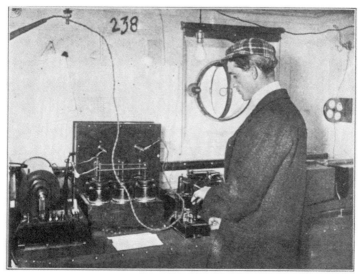

A VERY EARLY SHIP WIRELESS SET, ON THE AMERICAN
LINER, ST. PAUL, ABOUT 1899

consequence. The spark sets of those days—"rock-crushers," they were humorously called because of the deafening noise they made—had so broad a band of action and made so terrific a clamor that two fellows chatting thus practically blanketed any other vessel within fifty miles that might want to use the air.

The only way to choke them off—and it was frequently used by some other operator waiting for a chance to send—was to "drop a book on the key"; that is, lay a book or some other weight on the transmitting key, setting up such a continuous roar of interference that nobody within range could send or hear a word—rendering confusion worse confounded. These and the many other inevitable interferences when everybody was operating at will on the same wave length naturally led to wireless quarrels and feuds, filling the air at times with curses, aspersions and choice obscenities. Luckily, there were no "lady" operators in those early days. Of course, with such conditions. the service was far below the efficiency it should have had.

This condition had by no means reached its worst in 1903 when the first International Wireless Conference was held in Berlin, for comparatively few ships were as yet equipped with sets. But it had begun to be seen that something must be done presently by way of regulation. The art was as yet so new, however, that this first conference did little more than become acquainted with the various questions. Yet the meeting is particularly interesting in that the Italian delegation brought up the matter of distress signals, and suggested a standard call, so that a ship of any nationality would recognize another's cry for help, no matter what tongue the latter's master spoke. However, the only thing agreed upon at this time was a ruling that a distress signal must have precedence over all others.

On the English railways, the letters CQ had long been a general call for the attention of all operators along the line. It announced the time signal at ten in the forenoon and any notice of general importance. The wireless operators employed by the British Marconi Company were nearly all chosen from among these British railway telegraph operators, and they took the CQ call to sea with them. In 1904, the Marconi Company, realizing the necessity for a vigorous and distinctive distress signal, issued an order to its men, saying that while CQ did very well as a general call, it did not express the urgency necessary to appeal for help in emergency, and therefore the letter D, signifying distress, was appended to it. This signal must never be given without the order of the ship's captain or from other vessels or stations re-transmitting it. The public imagination (or perhaps some newspaper writer originated the notion) at once saw in the letters the initials of "Come Quick, Danger!" just as it fancied the later SOS to mean "Save Our Souls"—an appeal which would be futile as sent to human beings, for theoretically, only the Deity can do that.

German ships, on the other hand, had been using as a general call the letters SOE. When the Second Wireless Conference met in Berlin in 1906, a much larger group of conferees representing thirty nations, came together. The matter of a standard distress signal soon came up. The American delegation, headed by Admiral Manning and Ambassador Charlemagne Tower, suggested NC, which was then and still is the distress signal given in the flag code. This made no impression. The Germans countered by insisting upon their call, SOE, and other continental nations were inclined to back them. But it was pointed out that E is not a satisfactory letter with which to end a signal, it being only a single dot in the Morse code, and liable to be lost. Therefore, after much argument, it was decided to replace E with another S, thus making an easily remembered and easily distinguished signal—three dots, three dashes, three dots, sent continuously, and not spaced as if they were S.O.S., as the call is often written and printed; for as will be seen, the letters have no intrinsic meaning at all.

SOS was ratified by most nations by 1908, but the United States Government, slow as usual, did not officially adopt it until 1912, when the *Titanic* disaster called the wandering attention of Congress to the fact that ships and lives were being lost at sea. CQD was still used for several years after 1906 by

British operators; Jack Binns used it in his famous call from the *Republic* in 1909; and when the *Titanic* was sinking, her operators used both SOS and CQD.

Among the other valuable additions to wireless communication of the Marchese Marconi—as the Italian Government designated him in recent years—was the direction finder, by which one vessel could locate the position of another, particularly valuable when the latter was in distress—insurance rates on vessels equipped with it were substantially lowered; the echometer, or depth-sounding device, which gives a vessel by radio the water depths as it approaches shore, and tells whether the bottom there is hard or soft, smooth, irregular or rocky and strewn with great boulders; also the automatic alarm for vessels which did not have continuous wireless service. In the earlier days, most vessels had only one operator, and when he went to his bunk about 10 or 11 o'clock in the evening, the ship became deaf for the rest of the night. Some terrible sea tragedies were the result of this inadequacy. By Marconi's invention, a bell rang in the wireless operating room, in the operator's bedroom and on the bridge of all vessels within a wide range when another ship sent out a distress call.

CHAPTER XXIII

WIRELESS COMES OF AGE

To utter secrets, swiftly sent
From continent to continent
And bring again to mortal ears
The long-lost music of the spheres—
Those early harmonies that rung
When morning stars together sung.

J. B. L. Soule

EUROPE may claim Marconi and the invention of wireless telegraphy, but America may with equal pride boast of having originated the wireless telephone, and of having as citizens the two or three men who did most to develop it; and wireless telephony, be it remembered, means radio broadcasting, a thing which has become so fundamental a part of our lives that the world now would seem chaos to us without it.

While Marconi was experimenting in Italy and England, there was a young student in Yale named Lee de Forest, who, upon hearing for the first time a lecture upon the Hertzian waves by his physics professor, was so excited that he lost a night's sleep; while over at the Western University of Pennsylvania at Allegheny, now the University of Pittsburgh, two other youths, students in electrical engineering, were already making experiments with wireless. They both became prominent engineers, but neither of them made such a stir in wireless as their tawny-bearded professor, whose interest was stimulated by their tinkering. The professor was Reginald Aubrey Fessenden, born in Canada, though of old New England Puritan ancestry. He had for several years been an engineer in the big Westinghouse electrical plant at Pittsburgh.

Fessenden began his experiments between 1897 and 1899

Sarnoff copyrighted by Underwood & Underwood, Washington

LEE DE FOREST   R. A. FESSENDEN

JAMES A. FLEMING   DAVID SARNOFF

and in the latter years he produced his first "detector" or receiver, which had a tiny silver ring mounted with a coil in the circuit of an antenna. Signal currents caused the ring to move slightly, and you could take the message either by eye or by listening to the clicks when the ring was connected with a microphone. About the same time, the inventor learned how to build an aërial for directional reception, which would also tell from which direction the message was coming.

The United States Weather Bureau was interested in wireless, and in 1900 Fessenden became an agent of the Bureau to conduct experiments. He had by this time formed decided opinions as to the future of wireless reception, and his three cardinal principles were all novel at the time—either wholly unknown or but little suspected by others. S. M. Kintner, one of his later co-workers, lists them.[1] First, there must be constant reception instead of reception momentarily broken by the "shaking down" of the coherer—which was heresy at the time, for the coherer was then supposed to be *ne plus ultra* in the matter of sensitiveness. Second, there must be low resistance, so as to take advantage of resonance. Third, there must be response proportional to energy employed.

He was striving towards these ends when he produced his oscillation method for microphone detection, on which he applied for a patent in 1901. His second receiver was a sort of miniature electric lamp bulb with a marvelously thin wire in it, through which a weak current passed. Its sensitiveness was enormously greater than that of the best type of coherer, and it remained the standard type in America until gradually displaced a few years later by de Forest's Audion tube. This detector, when a telephone receiver was hooked up with it, gave through the telephone such excellent reproductions of the different sounds made by each wireless station spark, even when the spark was highly damped, that the listener could, after a

[1] "Pittsburgh's Contributions to Radio," *Proceedings of Institute of Radio Engineers,* Vol. 20, p. 1849.

little experience, identify many of the stations by the sound of their "voices."

Fessenden now said, "If a way can be found to modulate the radiation by the voice, just as the current is changed on a wire telephone line, why may not telephony through the ether be possible?" He tried modulating the current through an aërial by connecting a telephone directly into the circuit, and listening, he heard faintly the voice of his assistant from the sending station. Thus he brought radio telephony into being in the year 1901.

Of course, no wireless stations were sending anything but Morse then, and when you listened through Fessenden's wireless telephone, you heard nothing but the crashes of the spark. He found that a higher spark frequency decreased the noise, but even at several thousand per second, it was very loud. The only solution seemed to be to go still higher in frequency. He had long since become convinced of the necessity for sustained wave transmission to attain his goal as to resonance (for by Marconi's system, there were no waves between sparks). When asked how he could do it, he would reply, "Take a high frequency alternator of 100,000 cycles per second, connect one terminal to antenna and the other to the ground, then tune to resonance."

This sounded naïve to most wireless men, for there was no such alternator in existence then, and most of them did not believe such a machine could be built; or if it could, said Professor Fleming, over in England, in his book on *Electro-Magnetic Waves* in 1906, "it is doubtful if any appreciable radiation would result." But even the wisest may err in speaking of a little-known science, and Fleming's book was scarcely off the press when an alternator built under Fessenden's direction went into service on the Massachusetts coast and astonished the world with its performance.

Two wealthy Pittsburghers, Messrs. Given and Walker, unselfishly backed Fessenden's experiments with their means. In 1903—the year when the inventor had succeeded in throwing his voice over a mile by wireless—they organized the National Electric Signalling Company, to promote his inventions, and put $2,000,000 of their own cash into it first and last, without offering a dollar's worth of stock to the public. Their company built several wireless stations along the Atlantic coast, with ordinary spark-gap oscillation generators, but financially, these were not greatly successful.

Fessenden's heart was set, however, on something newer. For five years he worked on the problem of the high-frequency alternator he desired. A new station was built for him at Brant Rock, on the Massachusetts coast near Duxbury, and there the great 100,000-cycle machine was ready for use in 1906. Another station was set up at Machrihanish, in Scotland. The aërial would look absurd to us to-day—just a big metal tube three feet in diameter and 420 feet tall, stayed with guy wires. Later, an umbrella-shaped contraption of wire was set on top of it, making it look ridiculously like a giant toadstool. But from that antenna Fessenden soon astonished and bewildered many Atlantic seamen.

Fessenden had not only built his high-frequency alternator, but he had patented a high-frequency arc. With this improved apparatus, he succeeded in spanning the Atlantic to his station in Scotland; and on Christmas Eve, 1906, he did another thing for the first time in history. Early that evening, wireless operators on ships within a radius of several hundred miles sprang to attention as they caught the call, "CQ, CQ" in the Morse code. Was it a ship in distress? They listened eagerly, and to their amazement, heard a human voice coming from their instruments—some one speaking! Then a woman's voice rose in song. It was uncanny! Many of them called to officers to come and listen; soon the wireless rooms were crowded. Next some one was heard reading a poem. Then there was a violin solo; then a man made a speech, and they could catch most of the words. Finally, every one who heard the program was asked to write to R. A. Fessenden at Brant Rock, Massachusetts—and many of the operators did. Thus was the first radio broadcast in history put on.

The big aërial in Scotland blew down in a storm in 1907, damaging the station so badly that it was never rebuilt. A large outfit of Fessenden's apparatus was sold to the Government, and installed at Arlington. But in 1906, the same year when he did his first broadcasting, de Forest perfected his Audion tube, and with that, the major features of Fessenden's system were doomed. A pity, too, for as General Squier, a great radio authority, says, "How far we might have gone in that direction cannot now be told." Fessenden devised what is called the heterodyne system, that is, the "beat" or "interference" reception of continuous (undamped) waves, which Armstrong, the Westinghouse engineer, developed a few years later into the "superheterodyne." Fessenden had in all more than one hundred and fifty patents to his credit before he died, many of them not in the field of wireless.

Now let us pick up for a moment the career of the young student at Yale. Lee de Forest, born at Talladega, Alabama, the son of a preacher, was very poor and had a hard scuffle to get through college at all. After graduating, he spent the summer of '98 as a soldier in the war with Spain, and then went back to get his Ph.D. After that, he held various jobs in and around Chicago, with electrical companies and manufacturers, once on the staff of a magazine, teaching three hours a week on the side; but always experimenting in his spare time and some that wasn't spare.

His first development was his "sponder" or "electrolytic anti-coherer," a new type of detector. He tried this out as a telegraph device over the roofs of Chicago, at first with a series of old iron barrel hoops connected by wire as an antenna, and later out in the lake, and attained a range of four to five miles. That was in the summer of 1901, and he was so encouraged that he decided to try reporting the International Yacht Races that fall. He raised enough money to get to New York, but found that the Associated Press had already made a contract with the young Marconi corporation. He turned to a smaller concern, the Publishers' Press Association, and was given a contract. The Association agreed to supply a tug, and de Forest persuaded a friend to put up a thousand dollars to buy parts and equipment, promising him that he should be reimbursed in stock of the American Wireless Telegraph Company—which had not yet begun to be organized. With the aid of two friends who had worked with him in Chicago, and one of whom, Freeman, had invented—or believed that he had—a transmitter, the tug was fitted out and set itself to follow the yachts. Even before the starting gun was fired, the Freeman transmitter burned out, but de Forest had brought a Ruhmkorff coil along for emergency use, and put this into service. The press reporter in the tug's pilot house called out the news to the Morse operator sitting at his table below.

This had been going on for some time as the great white birds tacked to and fro, when both the de Forest and Marconi tugs noticed their stations on shore signaling frantically with flags, "What is the matter? Signals confused. Cannot read." De Forest tried to improve his sending, and as no more wig-wagging was seen, he thought he had succeeded; but when the boat docked, after the race, he was horrified to find that not one intelligible word had been received. The two rough-and-tumble spark sets, with their broad band of interference, had simply jumbled each other into incoherency. The elementary principles of tuning were known, but it had not occurred to either party that it would be necessary in this case. The Marconi boat had learned of the trouble, but had continued through the race as a bluff; and the bluff was kept up by the New York newspaper clients of the two associations, which announced their news as "Received by wireless telegraphy from tug following the yachts."

That was one of the earliest of de Forest's characteristic experiences as an unlucky inventor. With his young Wireless Telegraph Company occupying an old rented machine-shop in Jersey City and himself a hall bedroom, he scraped along for several months, introducing alternating current into wireless as a novelty, but getting nowhere commercially until a breezy promoter, Abraham White, became interested in him and organized a new company, American de Forest Wireless, with an alleged capital of $3,000,000, to take over his puny little corporation and give him some money to work on. Demonstration stations were established on tall buildings in New York, and once the great George Westinghouse was lured in to look at the apparatus, but could see no commercial possibilities in wireless telegraphy. His engineers saw more clearly than he in later years.

In the United States Navy manœuvers off New London in 1902, three systems were tried—Marconi's, de Forest's and Fessenden's. De Forest's apparatus was complimented by General Greely, the Chief Signal Officer, and that inventor was given the job of erecting a wireless station at Fort Mansfield, on the Rhode Island coast, and another at Fort Wadsworth, on New York Bay. The Navy up to that time had been using the Slaby-Arco, a clumsy German system of wireless; the Army was using another European importation, the Braun; the Weather Bureau was using Fessenden's, and the Signal Corps Wildman's, which was a sort of hybrid of all others. A fine jumble! American, European and Japanese armies, by the way, were now all experimenting with wireless in their field manœuvers. They still had to reach high into the air in order to attain any distance at all, and kites were therefore always a part of their equipment.

Wireless men had not yet mastered the problem of tuning, and operators were having nervous prostration at times because of interference. In the British Navy manœuvers of 1903, the signals of the two opposing "sides" so interfered with each other that they were of little account to either. But during the International Yacht Races in the autumn of that year three wireless companies—Marconi, de Forest and Fessenden—succeeded in keeping their signals tolerably well separated, and Sir Thomas Lipton, owner of one of the contesting yachts, was so well pleased with the de Forest set which was installed on his own private yacht for five weeks while he was in American waters that he invited the inventor to England and presented him to British Government officials. Nothing substantial came of that connection, the Marconi Company being too well ingratiated with high authority; but de Forest received a contract from the London *Times* for the supplying of information to its correspondents in Far Eastern waters during the Russo-Japanese war, then just beginning. The New York *Times* joined with the British newspaper in this enterprise.

During that war, through 1904, there were at least six or seven systems of wireless functioning around the North China seas, on the opposing naval vessels, in forts on shore and in newspaper despatch boats and warships of several nations which hovered near, watching the proceedings. The British had more than twenty vessels there, equipped with Marconi service with the Branly coherer. Some Italian vessels used Marconi with the Solari receiver. The Germans used the Slaby-Arco or Braun systems; the French had Braun; the Russians a modification of a German system. Port Arthur had a wireless station on Golden Hill, and when the city was surrounded by the Japanese, it maintained communication with the Russian army at a distance, which appealed to the popular mind as a romantic thing. The Japanese were believed to be using a modified Marconi, but their usual inscrutability prevented any one's learning the truth about it. They asserted, however, that the system was their own—said their army and navy had been experimenting with wireless as far back as 1896.

And finally, there was de Forest Wireless, working for the two big newspapers. It had a station just east of Wei-Hai-Wei, situated on a cliff 150 feet above the water, with a mast reaching 150 feet higher. Its correspondent was the steamer *Haimun,* chartered by the two papers, which cruised about the Yellow Sea. A Russian warship once halted the *Haimun* by a shot across the bows, and notified her that she was to be halted and questioned. The *Haimun* operator at once asked the shore station to notify the British fleet lying at Wei-Hai-Wei. He did so, and reported within a few minutes that John Bull was getting up steam and hoisting anchors. The Russian vessel's wireless was evidently listening to all this, for instead of bullying the despatch boat, it hastily departed in the opposite direction from the British tars.

The Marconi backers had not been neglecting America. An American Marconi Company had been organized, and built a station at Wellfleet, on Cape Cod, intended to communicate with Great Britain on a 1,500-meter wave length. This station succeeded in sending a message in January, 1903, from President Theodore Roosevelt to King Edward VII. But neither the wave-length nor the power of this station proved adequate for regular commercial telegraphy across the Atlantic, and it was used mostly to transmit news and weather reports to ships at sea. A station at Glace Bay, Cape Breton Island, was more successful, however, its correspondent on the other side being on the coast of Ireland. These stations exchanged many messages in 1907, and began regular public service in 1908.

In 1904, de Forest began building five large wireless stations for the United States Navy, the largest in the world at the time, located at Pensacola, Key West, Guantanamo, Cuba, Colon, Canal Zone and San Juan, Puerto Rico. Meanwhile, he was in trouble with Fessenden. A clever assistant named Clifford Babcock had, with de Forest's aid, been responsible for a new form of "electrolytic" detector or receiver (really founded on an earlier discovery by Pupin), and the Navy ordered a large number of them. Fessenden's company now attacked the device, claiming that it was an infringement on his system. The suit thus launched was not ended until 1906, when the Federal courts declared in Fessenden's favor. This was but one of a long series of litigations in American courts, which have constituted a goodly portion of the history of wireless. They are so highly technical in their character, so devoid of the romantic or otherwise peculiar interest attaching to the earlier telegraph and telephone litigation, that it would be tedious to most readers

DR. BELL INAUGURATING NEW YORK–SAN FRANCISCO TELE-
PHONE SERVICE, 1915. IN OVAL, WATSON ANSWERING FROM
SAN FRANCISCO

CABLE AND RADIO OPERATING ROOM, INTERNATIONAL TELE-
PHONE AND TELEGRAPH CORPORATION, NEW YORK

to report them, or even to mention any considerable number of them.

But de Forest's defeat in this suit meant comparatively little to him, for in that same year he perfected a new detector which eventually rendered Fessenden's system practically obsolete. To explain it, we shall have to go back a bit.

Almost from the start, wireless engineers saw that the miniature thunder of the early Marconi spark, with its gaps between, was a nuisance which would some day have to be ameliorated or dispensed with. It certainly could not be used in telephony. The electro-magnetic waves are simply alternating electric and magnetic fluctuations in very high frequency, which induce similar voltages in any wire such as an antenna. The current oscillations may flash up and down the antenna wire at from 500,000 to 1,000,000 frequencies per second. A telephone connected with the antenna could not respond to such rapid vibrations; it would not be physically possible for the diaphragm to move back and forth so rapidly. It occurred to James A. Fleming, Marconi's fellow-worker, that a sort of valve, something that would permit the current to pass in one direction but not in another and thus suppress half the vibrations, might give the telephone a chance to work with wireless.

While pondering this, he recalled the "Edison effect." Twenty years before, Fleming had been a scientific adviser to the Edison Electric Light Company in America, and remembered a thing which Edison once did, which did not at the time appear to have any practical value, but was just one of his experiments. Inside an incandescent light bulb he sealed a little plate of metal, connected with the base of the bulb, and on a separate wire from the filament which made the light. A curious thing was now discovered. Plate and filament stood apart from each other, but when the positive terminal of a battery was connected to the plate and a negative to the filament, current flowed across the space between filament and plate. But send the currents in reverse—positive to the filament and negative to the plate— and no current flowed.

461

OLD WIRES AND NEW WAVES

Neither Edison nor other scientists could explain the phenomenon at the time. But Joseph J. Thomson, after long research, showed in 1889 that the current from filament to plate was but a procession of negative charges or electrons thrown off by the glowing carbon in the vacuum and attracted to the positively charged plate. On the other hand, the plate when negatively charged, would repel those electrons—for unlike charges are the only ones that attract each other under such circumstances. It was found by the German physicist Wehnelt that such a bulb could be used as a rectifier of alternating current, because the negative half of the alternating current would be eliminated by it. He constructed tubes of the sort which were utilized in power rectification.

Now it occurred to Fleming that if the plate of the Edison effect bulb were connected with the antenna, and the filament to the ground, and a telephone placed in the circuit, the frequencies would be so reduced that the receiver might register audibly the effects of the waves. He made improvements, however, by substituting a metal cylinder for the flat plate, and improving the sensitivity of the device by increasing the electronic emissions. This "Fleming valve," so called, was one of the great ideas of wireless communication. It was one of the earliest of the vacuum tubes which have come to be the life and soul of radio.

But unfortunately for the inventor, he did not go far enough. His valve was so quickly overshadowed by an improvement made upon it by de Forest, that Fleming's contribution is inadequately remembered to-day. What de Forest did was to insert in the bulb, *between* Edison's plate and the filament, what he called a "grid"—a tiny gridiron with bars of fine wire. This may not mean much to the initiated, but that miniature gadget was the truest "little giant" in all history, perhaps the nearest approximation to an all-powerful genie that the brain of man ever created. It set unbelievably powerful currents in motion, magnifications of those which flicked up and down the antenna wire, and thus produced voice amplification which made radio telephony a finished product. By adding another tube and another, the amplification was enormously increased—millions, billions of times. Waldemar Kaempffert remarks that the voice of a President speaking in Washington must be amplified 10,000,000,000 times to be heard by an audience sitting in a large hall in New York. To carry it all over the continent, it may be magnified 3,000,000,000,000,000,000,000,000,000 times. In other words, he would have to shout as loud as that to be heard in the far Northwest.

Kaempffert wrote enthusiastically, nearly two decades later:

Signals too feeble even for detection by Fleming's valve could be clearly heard by a de Forest tube or two; the receiving range was increased several hundred times. All the great feats of radio communication, feats that involve telegraphing half way around the world, have been performed with this marvelous device, the master weapon of the radio engineer, it has been called. . . .

Here was a device which made it possible to amplify feeble voice-currents just when they were beginning to vanish altogether. By inserting de Forest's tubes at intervals in the line, it became possible to telephone from New York to San Francisco.

Yet see how one man must lean upon the work of another! De Forest's Audion tube might be called in baseball lingo a quadruple play, if such a thing were possible in baseball— Edison to Wehnelt to Fleming to de Forest. It was Babcock, de Forest's assistant, who suggested the name, Audion, for it; its technical title is the Three-Electrode Thermionic Vacuum Tube—not nearly so euphonious. On December 31, 1906, de Forest projected the first speech across his laboratory with it. He at once patented it, but as a wireless detector and as a telephone repeater or relay. He organized the De Forest Radio Telephone Company in the spring of 1907, but found it difficult to interest people in wireless telephony. He had foreseen radio broadcasting, and talked it assiduously to bankers and capitalists, but they could see no reason whatsoever in his dream. Ah, the lost opportunities of too-wise men!

For a few months between the time of the loss of the Fessenden suit and the perfection of the Audion, the De Forest Wireless Company depended for a receiver upon another recent idea, that of General H. H. C. Dunwoody of the United States Army, and incidentally, one of the De Forest directors. The General discovered that certain crystals such as carborundum, when placed in a receiver, also have the property, like the valve, of suppressing half of the wave frequencies in the antenna. Such crystals are cheap, far cheaper than vacuum tubes, and the crystal receiver became, in after years, standard equipment on low-priced radio sets.

De Forest was doing telephone broadcasting between two New York buildings about three blocks apart that summer of 1907, and two other scientists who were wireless amateurs began picking up his conversations and aiding in the tests. One of these was Peter Cooper Hewitt, the mercury-vapor light inventor, who had a laboratory in the tower of old Madison Square Garden. During the summer a de Forest wireless telephone was installed on a luxurious private yacht in Lake Erie, and its success so impressed the Navy Department that two battleships were equipped. At that, Admiral R. D. Evans urged that his fleet of twenty-four vessels, about to start on a cruise around the globe, be given wireless telephony so that they might talk to each other, and this was done.

In 1908, de Forest went to France and broadcast from the Eiffel Tower, using phonograph records of music, the program being picked up all over western Europe; one engineer who heard it was five hundred miles distant. Early in 1910, after some previous testing with singers, grand opera was broadcast for the first time in history by the De Forest Radio Telephone Company. The first program, on January 20th, was a double bill, *Cavalleria Rusticana* and *Pagliacci,* with Caruso singing in the former. There was one microphone on the stage and another in the wings. It was estimated that this broadcast was heard by perhaps fifty listeners. Wireless amateurs, with their own little sending stations, were now increasing rapidly in number, but the public in general were still deaf to the vast possibilities of radio.

New ideas were blossoming more rapidly than the wireless business could absorb or comprehend them. It was five or six years before the value of the De Forest Audion was generally recognized. He and some of his associates were even arrested, through some sinister influence, in 1912 and tried on a charge of using the mails to defraud by selling stock "in a company incorporated for $2,000,000 whose only assets were de Forest's patents, chiefly directed to a strange device like an incandescent lamp, which he called an Audion, and which had proven to be worthless." Furthermore, as the District Attorney orated, "De Forest has said in many newspapers and over his signature that it would be possible to transmit the human voice across the Atlantic before many years." (Just twenty-three months after this diatribe, Arlington spoke to the Eiffel Tower in Paris, using a development of de Forest's tube.) "Based on these absurd and deliberately misleading statements of de Forest," the commonwealth's doughty champion went on, "the misguided public, Your Honor, had been persuaded to purchase stock in his company, paying as high as ten and twenty dollars a share" —although they didn't buy enough to make the company successful.

It was while in the midst of this trouble that de Forest, driven by the poverty of himself and his company, sold the rights to his Audion amplifier to the American Telephone and Telegraph Company for a small fraction of what it would have brought had he been financially able to stand his ground and fight. By its aid, the telephone company with much ceremony— though without any mention of de Forest's name—inaugurated its long-distance wire service between New York and San Francisco in 1915, and its great engineer, John J. Carty, at once set about developing equipment with which to span the ocean.

In April, 1915, with its aid, Bell engineers talked between Wilmington, Delaware, and Montauk Point, at the outer tip of

Long Island. A month later, Carty from his office in New York, spoke by wire to Montauk, whence his words were tossed through the ether, to St. Simon's Island, near Brunswick, Georgia. Now, with the aid of the Navy station at Arlington, transoceanic telephony was attempted. Three engineers set forth with complete station equipment, one to San Diego, California, one to Darien, Panama, one to Honolulu. Through July and August the engineers in New York and Arlington toiled to perfect connection. Finally, on August 27th, Arlington was heard at Darien. Carty now rushed out to Mare Island Navy Yard in California, and hearing speech clearly there from Arlington, he arranged a demonstration for President Vail. On September 29th, Vail, at his desk in New York, was connected by wire with Arlington, and when he said, "Hello, Mr. Carty! This is Mr. Vail," his words were heard, not only by Carty, but by the listeners in San Diego, Darien and Honolulu. Carty's spoken reply came back to Vail by wire.

The Atlantic was yet to be bridged, but that did not take long. On October 21st, a day when static was at a minimum, the Bell engineers listening at the Eiffel Tower heard a voice from Arlington calling one of their number, "Hello, Shreeve! Hello, Shreeve!" The reception for a few minutes was fairly clear. The French Government, then in a desperate struggle for its life, had courteously given the telephone company every permission and facility possible for the test, undoubtedly realizing that great benefit might result to itself from the new communication. But because of the state of war, the experiment was kept a profound secret. The war interfered with further progress, at the time, and it was not until ten years after that first conversation that telephony across the Atlantic actually became successful and commercially worth while.

During the period between 1903 and 1907, ships and shore stations gradually changed from the old spark-gap to the "quenched" or "damped" spark-gap and the rotary spark-gap developed by Marconi. The coherer faded out and magnetic or crystal detectors took its place. These enabled the operators to

466

hear the sound of the sending clearly, and the stations at Cape Race, Clifden and elsewhere began to be identifiable by their tones, just as Smith and Brown are by their voices. Then came the arc transmitter.

Many of us are old enough to remember the old arc street light, in which two sticks of carbon about the size of bread sticks were placed with their ends slightly apart; and when the current was turned on, an arc of blue-white flame poured across from the one to the other. An Englishman named Duddell said, "The arc is really a continuous spark. Why not use it in wireless transmission?" But he did nothing about it himself. Valdemar Poulsen, a Dane, took the hint and set to work at the beginning of the century to produce a better arc for the purpose. He succeeded by 1903, but a station using his system was not erected in Denmark until 1907. Instead of the loud crackle of the spark, Poulsen's instrument gave off a hissing or frying sound. In 1911, the Federal Telegraph Company of California was organized to control Poulsen's patents in America, and within a year had established communication along the Pacific Coast from Los Angeles to Portland. The Navy, which experimented with many systems, bought Poulsen outfits and installed them at Arlington, San Francisco, in the Panama Canal Zone, Hawaii and the Philippines. But the vacuum tube finally drove the arc out of wireless.

A state of virtual anarchy developed in wireless telegraphy during the first twelve years of the present century. The British Marconi Company, considering itself—as the pioneer in the industry—entitled to a monopoly, and fancying that it could, by a system of non-intercourse and interference, drive competitors out of the business, had placed British operators who would obey orders in all its ships and stations, most of them at extremely low wages. Jack Phillips, for example, chief operator on the *Titanic,* who died with his ship, is said to have drawn only £4 a month, "and found." These men had strict orders to hold no converse with and receive no messages save the distress call from operators employed by other companies. An absurd and ugly situation thus developed, for other companies took the cue and retorted in kind.

Marconi operators would give no news of dangerous derelicts, no storm warnings to alien vessels; if they heard another company sending, they would often "lay a book on the key" and blast out the other fellow's signals. A party of American Government officials and Congressmen on a trip to the Canal Zone were cut off for days from Washington because the nearest stations on shore and that on the ship were competitors. Marconi operators were even ordered to work against their own vessel; to deliver to the captain no messages other than Marconi unless he specifically demanded those from a certain other vessel or correspondent.

In 1913, James Gordon Bennett, always seeking publicity for his New York *Herald,* had a wireless station of his own at the Battery in New York City. At 4:15 every morning it would broadcast for the benefit of ships a digest of the day's news, as well as weather reports and probabilities for Sandy Hook and thereabouts. Ship captains came to depend upon this last feature, and if their Marconi operators did not receive it, gave them orders to do it. This was a point scored for the *Herald.* But when the Woolworth Building was opened during that year, it had a Marconi aërial on top of it. Then one morning, every ship captain in the neighborhood notified the *Herald* that as soon as its broadcast began that morning, another station came in with a loud uproar and drowned all the rest of the signals. During that year and the next, International conferences began to regulate these things; then in 1914 the Great War began, and British Marconi was so busy at home that it had little time to give to the hopeless task of trying to kill competition.

The amateurs in America provided an even worse problem than warring companies. Remember that there was no Federal Radio Commission then, no laws, no rules as to what any station might or might not do. Radio magazines were springing into being everywhere, and they, the popular science magazines and the newspapers were crammed with articles and diagrams

From Drawing by William Herndon Foster in Scribner's Magazine

AN ARMY AEROPLANE WIRELESS SET IN 1910

telling how to build home radio sending and receiving sets, including aërials for both. Clumsy, grotesque towers began thrusting up into the air, the owners began expressing their egos and having no end of fun. There might be dozens of stations, amateur and professional, within a thickly populated area, all using the same or nearly the same wave length, and chaos was but a feeble word for the situation.

The Navy at times found its wireless system completely helpless. In 1906, when President Roosevelt was visiting the fleet off Cape Cod, the Newport Naval Station was unable to get any message to him because of amateur interference, and destroyers had to carry dispatches to and from him. A few years later, when Admiral Evans's fleet was returning from a trip around the world, it was unable to reach Portsmouth Navy Yard because of amateur clamor.

Amateurs would send out fake orders to naval vessels, purporting to come from admirals; they broadcast false distress calls and had Coast Guard and other vessels running wildly about, trying to find the ship in distress. This "joke" was even perpetrated on the other side of the world. In May, 1914, a message was received in Japan, allegedly from the American liner *Siberia,* saying that it was aground and sinking off the coast of Formosa. Vessels at once rushed to her aid, but meanwhile, the *Siberia* arrived at Manila next day, having been nowhere near Formosa and knowing nothing of the distress call.

There being no law to cover most of the amateurs' tricks, few or no police searches were made for them, and the names and locations of the worst offenders were unknown. When remonstrated with by air, these were apt to respond with curses and obscenity. The situation finally became intolerable, and in 1912 a bill was introduced in Congress, placing wireless under regulation by Government. At the news of that bill, amateurs and even some professionals rose up in furious protest all over the land. The old rugged individualism had its back to the wall again. Hearings were held by a Congressional committee; and when the Navy told of the impossibility of getting necessary business done because of amateur interference, certain of the amateur witnesses retorted by reading transcripts of conversation which they had picked out of the air, between naval officers or sometimes between officers and women—cheap gossip, intrigue, assignations, amatory trivia, stuff which caused more red faces in the Navy than it had known in many a day—not to mention reprimands and discipline.

Nevertheless, the amateurs lost. Again, as in the case of movie censorship and Prohibition, unbridled liberty had become license and slain itself. Henceforth, every station must be licensed by Government and be assigned a wave length for sending. But here the Government and the wireless industry played a joke on themselves. They had all along been nursing the delusion that the longer waves were the more valuable. For distance telegraphy, the longer the wave, the better, was the accepted theory. Two German concerns, for example, set up stations in this country in 1912 for telegraphy to Germany, both using a 10,000-meter wave. They were not a great success, and the war eliminated them.

At the time when the radio law was passed, all waves below 200 meters in length were considered practically useless. Lengths above that were therefore reserved for Government and commercial use, and the short waves (with a chuckle) were given to the amateurs to play with. It was as if the powers had handed them the cream and kept the skim milk for themselves. The many amateurs who volunteered and became wireless operators during America's participation in the World War helped to spread the news of the value of short waves. To-day, waves as low as five meters in length are being used!

International regulations for the safety of life at sea were hastened in the year of our radio law by the greatest peacetime disaster in maritime history—the sinking of the giant new liner *Titanic* by an iceberg on her very first voyage across the Atlantic, with a loss of more than fifteen hundred lives. There were some bitter lessons drawn from that disaster. There were ships within radio reach of the *Titanic* which did not know of her trouble because they had no wireless. A smaller passenger vessel, the *Californian,* eastbound, encountered an ice field that evening, and her wireless operator sought to notify the *Titanic,* but the latter's operator, who was exchanging messages with Cape Race, told the other ship to "shut up" and keep out of the conversation. The *Californian's* man listened a few minutes longer to the messages passing between the big liner and the shore and then went to bed, having been on duty for sixteen hours.

Probably he had but just gotten to sleep when, at 11 :40 P.M., an under-water projection of an iceberg ripped open the side of the supposedly unsinkable pride of the White Star fleet, and a few minutes later, Phillips, her chief operator, sent out a CQD call, followed by the newer distress signal, SOS. The *Californian* was then less than twenty miles away—her officers claimed nineteen miles, but *Titanic* seamen swore that her lights were no more than four or five miles distant. Some of her officers stood on deck, watching the rockets shooting up from the unknown vessel and with strange ineptitude, wondering what they were for, though white rockets are inevitably a signal of distress. It never occurred to them to awaken the wireless operator, and not until 4 o'clock in the morning, when he was called, did he learn from his instrument, to his inexpressible anguish, of the awful disaster.

At the same time the Cunarder *Carpathia,* eastbound, was fifty-eight miles from the *Titanic.* Her operator, about to turn in, was just unlacing his shoes, but paused to tell the *Titanic* that there were some messages for her at Cape Cod. Instead, he heard from Phillips, "We have struck an iceberg and are sinking." The gallant forced rush of the slow-footed *Carpathia* to the scene, the amazingly complete preparations of her captain, Arthur Rostron, and the rescue of 712 of the *Titanic's* survivors make a thrilling and beautiful page in ocean history.

As the Army began to adapt aëroplanes to its use, in 1909-10, wireless was tried out on them, the operator, like the pilot, sitting out in the open and taking the wind as it came.

Naturally, the service was pretty crude. It is said that the German military balloon *Condor* was the first aircraft of that type to use wireless. Walter Wellman, who made an ill-equipped effort to cross the Atlantic in the dirigible balloon *America* in October, 1910, carried a wireless outfit, and for the first time, communication was established between an airship, ships at sea and land stations. The venture was sponsored by three newspapers, in New York, Chicago and London, and the wireless operator was to send them news during the journey. But his voltage was so low and his storage batteries gave out so soon that he did not send many messages before his transmission failed, and after that, he could only listen to the talk of other operators. It was particularly vexing to hear stations along the Atlantic coast asking each other if anything had been heard of the *America,* and fears expressed for her safety. The balloon became disabled and fell into the sea after a seventy-two-hour journey, the crew being rescued by a British steamer.

More inventions are yet to be mentioned—de Forest's "cascade amplifier," for example, designed with the aid of his assistants, Logwood and Van Etten, in which three Audions in succession so aided each other that he obtained amplification twenty-sevenfold instead of three. And there was the regenerative or feedback system, which caused so much warfare. It is said that Meissner, in Germany, was first to employ the idea to produce high-frequency oscillations in the vacuum tube. De Forest says that he and Van Etten discovered the oscillatory properties of the Audion in his laboratory in 1912, and they produced their notebooks to prove it. But they did not bring it out just then, and in 1913, Edwin H. Armstrong, a student at Columbia University, with no knowledge of the work of either of the others, conceived the idea of making de Forest's vacuum tube still more efficient by returning or feeding back a part of the current and thus getting still stronger effects—somewhat like piping steam back and using it over again.

Armstrong and de Forest both sought patents, and years of litigation followed, Armstrong being backed by the Westinghouse Company, which had taken over his device. First one then the other won in various courts, and not until 1934 did the Supreme Court decide in de Forest's favor. It was another of those heartbreaking duplications of effort, similar to the case of Bell and Gray. Major Armstrong (he served in the American Expeditionary Force), a professor in Columbia University as this book is being written, has just publicly announced the development of a static-less radio system. As for de Forest, after doing radio broadcasting in New York in 1916 and later—from the Columbia Phonograph laboratory and from his own plant, where he introduced Vaughan de Leath, the first radio singer to receive fan mail—he turned from radio, as it now began to be called, to the development of sound with motion pictures, and later, of radio therapy and other things.

Ernst F. W. Alexanderson, a Swedish-born American engineer who had built some small alternators for Fessenden in earlier years, now improved upon Fessenden's idea and designed alternators which produced smooth, continuous waves—waves that did not quickly die away, and with 50,000 to 100,000 per second frequency. Marconi himself traveled across the ocean to see these alternators demonstrated in the General Electric laboratory at Schenectady, and the British Marconi company soon began negotiating for the machines. No sale resulted immediately, though a 50-kilowatt Alexanderson alternator was installed in the Marconi Company's plant at New Brunswick, New Jersey, in 1917. Then the United States entered the war, the Government seized all wireless stations, and shut down several of them. The alternator had worked so well at New Brunswick, however, that a new 200-kilowatt machine of the same type was installed there by the Navy Department, making that the most powerful station in existence at the time.

At the close of the war, British Marconi renewed its angling for the Alexanderson equipment, offering to place a $5,000,000 order. President Wilson, then in Paris, sent two officers to the General Electric to urge them not to sell or transfer patent rights to foreign concerns; and as the Government still held the radio stations, he was in a position to exert some pressure. The General Electric consented, though it had a heavy investment in the patents and machinery, and no American customer for the wares, there being no company here at the time large enough to use such equipment in quantity. Instead, there were several companies, each controlling one inventor's patents, and all of them needing the other men's devices to complete a perfect wireless system.

In this static situation, Owen D. Young, with the good wishes of the Government, took steps leading towards the organization of the Radio Corporation of America. Fessenden had quarreled with his partners several years before and withdrawn from the National Electric Signalling Company, and they were getting nowhere. They and Westinghouse Electric and Manufacturing Company had just joined hands and organized the International Radio Telegraph Company, but upon sending emissaries abroad, found it difficult to get foreign agreements. Mr. Young, by diplomatic and promotional genius, succeeded in bringing first this company and then the American Marconi Company into the RCA fold. Thus in 1919 was created a corporation which, in power, financial and otherwise, was able to cope with any other in existence. General James G. Harbord, a recently returned war hero, representing Government influence, was elected President, and a young man of twenty-eight named David Sarnoff, whose first job, nearly fifteen years before, had been that of a telegraph messenger boy, was made commercial manager. Eleven years later General Harbord became Chairman of the Board of Directors, and Sarnoff, at the age of thirty-nine, was elected President.

The first message sent across the Atlantic by the new company—immediately after the return to private hands of the stations seized by the Government three years before—was flashed to Europe early on the morning of March 1, 1920. At that time, America had cable communication with England, France, Latin America and eastern Asia, and controlled wireless communication nowhere. To-day, New York is the communication hub of the world. We have wireless communication with practically every country on the globe; the RCA itself sends directly to forty-five countries. As this is written, its principal transmission station, long standing at Rocky Point, Long Island, is installing new equipment which will make it the most powerful in the world. Its forest of towers covers nine square miles!

In 1922, American Telephone and Telegraph engineers buckled down seriously to the job of perfecting transoceanic telephony. With the RCA collaborating (though that company did not go in for wireless telephony), long continued experimenting went on from Rocky Point to Wroughton, England, eastbound, and from the British Broadcasting Company's big station at Rugby westbound to the A. T. & T.'s new station at Houlton, Maine. By the summer of the following year, such slow progress had been made that on an average, only about fifteen out of every hundred words could be distinguished; in winter, transmission was impossible. By the summer of 1925, about sixty out of a hundred words came through. By that time they were beginning to see through the problem, and during the following winter, the average rose to 90 per cent. To-day, what with short waves and other improvements, intercontinental telephony is very nearly as reliable as that by wire.

Just after the close of the great war, Frank Conrad, a so-called wireless "amateur"—though he happened to be one of the Westinghouse Company's best engineers—had a private station in the garage back of his home in Pittsburgh. In the course of his experimenting, he substituted a microphone for the Morse key, and broadcast speaking and music. So many "hams" over a wide area became interested and wrote letters to him that he finally set regular hours in the evening for his broadcasts. Then in 1920, radio receiving sets were put on sale in the furniture and department stores, though their sale at first was slow. H. P. Davis, Vice-President of Westinghouse, noticed this, called Conrad, S. M. Kintner and others together and suggested the opening of a broadcasting station at the company's big plant at East Pittsburgh, to send out a regular program every night. Davis asked if it could be ready by election night, November 2nd, so that the National election returns might be broadcast. It was.

Conrad remained at home that evening, so that a quick shift might be made to his private plant if the other failed in action. But it didn't; and so began (though it had a different name at the start) Station KDKA, which still broadcasts from Pittsburgh. De Forests's and other broadcasts previous to that time had been brief, spasmodic and experimental. KDKA was permanent; it increased its range and its repertoire, and it popularized radio. It is properly regarded as the real pioneer of radio stations.

Within three years, radio had become a fad. New stations sprang up rapidly, new concerns rushed into the manufacture of radio sets. The advertising possibilities of the new craze were discovered. The RCA could not ignore such a lucrative field. Joining forces with Westinghouse, it organized the National Broadcasting Company in 1926 and took over Station WEAF and a large chain, following this with Station WJZ and more auxiliaries. In 1927, the Columbia Broadcasting Company, another big chain, came into existence, with Station WABC.

As this book is a history of communications only, the story of radio broadcasting does not come within its scope. Now that television is, as we are assured, just around the corner—where it has been coyly lurking for several years—it is too soon, anyhow, to attempt a history of broadcasting. By to-morrow, perhaps, or next day at latest, it might be obsolete, because its most important chapter was lacking.

THE LINEMAN

CHAPTER XXIV

HEROIC SERVICE BY WIRE AND WAVE

And rank for her meant duty, various,
Yet equal in its worth, done worthily.
Command was service; humblest service done
By willing and deserving souls was glory.

GEORGE ELIOT

IN 1851, while Taliaferro Shaffner was managing the telegraph office at St. Louis, the new communication medium received wide publicity by achieving the first recorded last-minute rescue of a condemned man from execution. An Indian who had confessed to the murder of a mail-carrier far out on the Santa Fé Trail was in the death house at Jefferson City, when it was discovered that he had confessed to save his aged father, who was the real culprit, and who had been the first to be suspected. This fact was substantiated too late to permit an appeal in the regular way, by document to the President of the United States, so a revolutionary thing was proposed—an appeal by telegraph. On March 13th, the day before that set for the execution, Shaffner was asked to help, and he rushed a telegram to President Fillmore, asking for a thirty-day respite, saying that the proper documents were being prepared and would be forwarded as soon as possible.

This message reached the President that night, but too late to permit a reply, as the telegraph offices were closed. Next morning Mr. Fillmore wrote a dispatch, "The Marshal of the State of Missouri is hereby directed to postpone the execution of the Indian See-see-sah-ma until Friday, the 18th of April." To make sure that the message went through, three copies were prepared. One copy went by the O'Rielly line, via Philadelphia, Pittsburgh, Cincinnati and Louisville, to St. Louis, about 1,100 miles, arriving at 9:50 A.M. Another copy traveled no less than 2,000 miles, via New York, Buffalo and Chicago, arriving at 10:05. The third shot up to Baltimore, then over the Western Telegraph to Wheeling, thence via Louisville, Nashville and Cairo, about sixteen hundred miles, being delivered at 10:08. Each message went over the wires of four different companies, and the last named was ferried across the Ohio at Cairo in a skiff.

The execution had been set for noon. As soon as the first telegram reached Shaffner, he hurried it to the Marshal's office in St. Louis, and that official at 10:20 telegraphed his deputy to halt the execution. Thousands had already gathered about the gallows, and were no doubt bitterly disappointed when the big show was declared off.

Since that time, how many a convicted person has been snatched from death by a Governor's last-minute reprieve, sent by telegraph or telephone! It used to be a favorite climax for a story. A veteran telegrapher told years ago, however, of the possible jeopardy of such unfortunates because of the early faults of the telegraph. The narrator was the operator at Lynchburg, Virginia, during the Civil War. One of the Union sympathizers in eastern Tennessee who burned railroad bridges to hamper Confederate troop movements was tried by a military tribunal at Knoxville and condemned to die next day at 2:00 P.M.

Early next morning, a telegram from the prisoner's daughter to President Davis of the Confederacy came through Lynchburg. She begged clemency for her father, her only support and kinsman, and gave reasons why his sentence was unjust. The Lynchburg operator waited anxiously for the reply, and about noon it came. The kindly Davis had granted a pardon. Eagerly the Lynchburg operator called Knoxville, and the latter had barely answered when suddenly the wire was grounded; a little office between the two cities (later ascertained to be Dublin, Virginia) wanted to gain possession of the wire, so put on his "ground" and cut Lynchburg off—a trick frequently done in those days of single wires. For an hour and a half the interference continued, while the Lynchburg telegrapher sweated and suffered. The execution was set for 2:00 P.M. Not until within twenty minutes of that time did Dublin remove his ground wire. Lynchburg then called Knoxville frantically, and fortunately, reached him without interference. It was feared that the news had come too late, as the execution party had already left the jail for the execution ground; but by hard driving, a messenger in a buggy reached the scene in time.

The story used to be told of a veteran operator in Arizona—many years ago when that sovereign State was a mere Territory and much rougher than it is now—who once saved a man's life by a daring trick. The man had been duly condemned for a murder in a remote county, but on the very eve of his execution, another man confessed to the crime. The sheriff, with no authority to stay the hanging, thundered over many miles on horseback to reach a telegraph station and sent a plea to the Governor for a reprieve until the matter could be legally adjusted. The operator at the State Capital, receiving the message late at night, found that the Governor had been mixing his drinks that evening and had passed out; he "couldn't have been wakened with a cannon." After an uneasy hour of thought, the telegrapher decided to take matters in his own hands, so sent the following message to the sheriff:

Reprieve is granted to (prisoner's name) for ten days. Regular papers go forward in the morning.

―――― ――――, Governor, per ――――
―――― (operator's name), Acting Governor, pro tem.

Well, as usual in such melodramas, the sheriff, after a long and strenuous ride, arrived just in the nick of time. The deputies were proceeding rigidly according to schedule, and the rope was around the man's neck, when they saw the sheriff galloping in the distance, waving his hat. About the same time, the Governor, with a bad headache, was saying angrily to the telegrapher, "This message should have been delivered hours ago. Why wasn't it?"

"You were under the weather," replied the operator, "the Sec-

479

retary of State was out of town, and nobody could attend to your business."

"Then the poor fellow is hung by this time," faltered the Governor, going maudlin, "and I've caused the death of an innocent man."

"That would have been true," admitted the operator, "if I hadn't usurped your place for fifteen minutes."

The Governor was overjoyed when he heard the rest of the story, and gave the operator a worth-while job under the territorial government.

Ah, those Western telegraphers of pioneer days!—what adventures they had, and what opportunities sometimes! There was one nicknamed "Skae" in Virginia City during the boom days on the Comstock Lode, who had an alliance with a San Francisco broker, to whom he wired the contents of telegrams regarding mines and mining stocks half an hour before he sent the telegram itself. This enabled the gambler to make some heavy killings on the stock-market, in all of which Skae received a share. He probably didn't get all that was due him, but he piled up a fortune of several hundred thousand dollars before he was exposed and fled. Then he became a broker and promoter on his own.

There were other operators who had the adventure without the profit; men in little country stations who suddenly found themselves surrounded by squads of rough, bearded fellows with huge pistols, who perhaps bound and gagged the telegrapher or cut the wires or demanded accurate information as to whether a certain train was late or not. The James brothers, Sam Bass, and other brigands of those days not infrequently put the operator out of action thus as their opening move in a train robbery, if they planned to attack the train at the station. On more than one occasion, brave telegraphers were shot to death for not obeying orders strictly enough to suit the outlaws. At other times, in isolated places, the bandits simply remained out of sight until the train drew in, and then rushed upon the crew, ignoring the telegrapher. At Red Rock, Oklahoma, in the summer of 1892,

SIGNAL CORPS TELEPHONE AND TELEGRAPH OFFICE IN AN UNDERGROUND VAULT AT CHÂTEAU-THIERRY

the Dalton gang had robbed a Santa Fé train and were just departing when one of their number, Charley Bryant, saw through the station window the young agent, little more than a boy, with fingers trembling uncertainly towards the telegraph key, eager to notify the Law of the robbery, yet fearful of the consequences if he did it too soon. Bryant had an easy retort to that; his big pistol roared, there was a tinkle of glass from the window and the youth fell forward across his table with a bullet through his brain.

How many, many times telegraph operators (and women are included) have run, stumbling, along a railroad track in darkness and storm with lantern in hand to save a train from disaster by landslide, washout, a broken bridge, a car drifted off a siding or other emergency. They (women included) have swum streams when a bridge was down, to flag a train on the other side. They have stuck to their posts in time of disaster, sometimes until just a moment too late to save themselves from fire or flood.

When (in years before the demon mosquito carrier was discovered) yellow fever ravaged the South, particularly in 1878, when the coast from Norfolk to Texas and the whole lower Mississippi Valley was foul with it, when communities were paralyzed with fear and denizens of the cities were fleeing, leaving them half empty, telegraph operators stayed at their posts, doing the necessary routine business which kept the community alive, calling for aid for the stricken, helping to organize relief, until, sometimes, the operator's own hand faltered and he fell at his table and died from the disease—whereupon there was always a recruit to take his place.

At noon on May 31, 1889, a young engineer named Park galloped down the valley of the South Fork of the Conemaugh in Pennsylvania, shouting, "Run for your lives! The dam is breaking!" Torrential rains had fallen, and he had for hours been watching cracks in the earthen dam which held back a big lake created for sporting purposes by damming the stream. There had been fears for the dam before, and many who heard him were skeptical. Reaching the Pennsylvania Railroad signal tower at South Fork station, Park told the operator, who thereupon began warning Johnstown, Cambria City and other towns down the gorge. After several of these warnings, he took a minute to warn his wife, at their home at Mineral Point, three miles below, telling her to take the children and hurry up the mountain-side. (Incidentally, neighbors convinced her that there was no danger, she remained, was caught by the water and saved only by a miracle.)

The tower man continued his warnings; bulletins were hung up outside the telegraph office in Johnstown, and people stood around, reading them. Many of these, too, were inclined to scoff. "Wolf! Wolf!" had been cried before. But this time the water was to play a trick upon them. At three in the afternoon the dam gave way. The tower man, sticking to the last, saw the wall of water boiling down the gorge, leaped from his upper window and scrambled up the hillside to save himself. Within half an hour that terrible wall had covered the nearly twenty miles to Johnstown; at 4 o'clock the city was well-nigh obliterated.

At that hour, Mrs. Ogle, telegraph operator at Johnstown, was just telling Pittsburgh that she had had to abandon the lower floor and move to an instrument upstairs. "She was sending from the second story and the water was gaining rapidly," said the Western Union superintendent at Pittsburgh. "Our man here said something encouraging to her, and she was talking back as only a cheerful girl operator can, when the receiver's skilled ear caught a sound made by no human hand, which told him that the wires had grounded or that the house had been swept away— no one now knows what. At 4 o'clock the girl was there, and at 4:07 we might as well have asked the grave to answer us."

At Galveston, during the awful disaster of September 8, 1900, when the sea, driven by a hurricane, overwhelmed the city, telegraph and telephone operators stuck to their posts, conveying the repeated warnings of the weather observers and the anxious inquiries of the citizens, calls for help and so on, until the wires went down. Some of them stayed in their offices all through the storm, and some were lost. After the storm, near-by Houston was overwhelmed with wire business. The day after the waters receded, a tug went up to Houston, carrying a group of Galveston newspaper men, each with from twenty to two hundred messages in his pocket which Galveston citizens wished to send to friends, kinsmen or business connections elsewhere. Later in the day another tug came with two thousand more telegrams. Correspondents of outside newspapers were jamming the offices with copy, and at midnight of that day, the Postal Telegraph refused to accept any more until the rush had been broken a bit. The Western Union accepted them "subject to delay."

In the Chicago fire of 1871, in the great Baltimore fire, in the Dayton flood of 1912, in the great floods which have ravaged the eastern states in recent years, the story in both telegraph and telephone has always been the same. At San Francisco in 1906, operators remained on duty when the trembling earth was cracking the walls about them, showering plaster on their heads, and when fire was licking up buildings just across the street or on the same block. Some men and women remained on duty in those downtown semi-ruins from three to five days with almost no rest, separated from their families and knowing, some of them, that their homes were being destroyed. Many remained until there were no wires to operate. The Western Union staff was driven out only when the fire reached their building, and then opened temporary headquarters in the Oakland Ferry house.

A typical picture is that of the bursting of a dam on the Santa Clara River in California in 1928. Telephone operators prevented loss of life by staying at their switchboards and notifying everybody along the valley, so that the news traveled faster than the flood. At each town, the telephone operator was the one who notified the Mayor and the police. One woman remained on duty, knowing that her house and furniture were being washed away, and not assured as to the safety of her husband. Another, off duty, hearing of the disaster, rushed back to her office, leaving her three-months-old baby in the care of a ten-year-old girl. A lineman responded to a call and lost all his belongings, though he could have saved much by staying at home. In every case, the workers stayed on duty until the last minute, though several knew that the office would be swept away. In many cases the lights went out and they had to work by candlelight or none at all.

Among the finest but least known and unsung heroes are the linemen. In time of storm or flood, the lineman's job is to keep the wires working, if possible, for lives and property depend upon them. No matter how dreadful the storm, how great the danger, if the lineman is called from his bed in the middle of the night by an emergency, he goes just as certainly, as unquestioningly, as the old-fashioned country doctor. Some of the most arduous experiences are those of the linemen in western mountains, where there are many miles of telephone wire in wild places, crossing divides and gorges, miles from any house or road. The situation used to be much worse than it is now, for the companies began putting wires underground some thirty years ago; but there are still many miles of wire on poles above the timber line, sometimes reaching 12,000 feet above sea-level, threading cañons or swinging in huge festoons across them, climbing over cliffs and great jumbled rock fields.

In summer the lineman goes as far as he can on horseback, in winter, whenever possible, he uses skis; and remember that he must carry some fifty pounds of wire, a test set and his heavy climbers on his back. Sleet may gather on a wire to a thickness of nine inches, and weigh from ten to twenty pounds to the foot. Electricity causes many breaks in the line—for lightning storms are fearsome things in the big mountains, sometimes bursting glass insulators and burning the cross-arms. Barbed wire is often strung from cross-arms to earth to ground the bolts. When the air is highly charged up there, blue sparks may jump to and from the lineman's spurs as he climbs a pole.

A golden eagle became entangled in a wire up in the Rockies, and died in his struggle with it. The lineman found the great bird hanging there, while his mate sat on a pole nearby. But when the man sought to remove the body, he was attacked by the widow and had a hard battle before he bested her. Which reminds us that the lineman doubtless located the trouble by means of the "Wheatstone Bridge" or induction balance, invented by the great English physicist many decades ago. By its means, a man sitting in an office in New York may discover within a very few miles the location of a leak or "ground" in an ocean cable, so that it may be picked up and repaired. As to a land wire, any trouble can be located within a hundred yards or so. "It's about ninety-two poles west of Big Rock," is the finding, and sure enough, right about there, the lineman finds perhaps a dead crow hanging on the wire or some other interference. If they miss it as much as three poles, they are humiliated; it is almost disgraceful.

President Cleveland closed a telegraph switch to start the machinery at the opening of the World's Columbian Exposition at Chicago in 1893; and since then, Presidents, from Washington or elsewhere have, by pressing a button, opened many other Expositions, set turbines going in huge water-power plants, shot off blasts to begin other projects, and so on. Presidents and diplomats have opened new long-distance wire and wave services; the first Roosevelt's wireless telegram to King Edward VII, for example, already mentioned; while the unemotional Mr. Coolidge inaugurated two new wireless telephone services by sending his homely Vermontese drawl over the air to the President of Mexico and King Alfonso XIII of Spain. Secretary Hull opened the Transpacific telephone service to Japan in December, 1934, and next day the Mayors of New York and Tokio talked to each other.

It is a curious fact that the telegraph was but little used in American diplomacy until John Hay came into the Government as Secretary of State under McKinley. By the time his tenure had extended into Theodore Roosevelt's administration, he was even using a telephone freely among the legations. "Teddy" himself was just the informal sort of person to like that. His historic cablegram to Barbary in behalf of an American citizen kidnapped by a bandit, "Perdiccaris alive or Raisuli dead," may have been a collaboration with his Secretary of State. General Ben Butler might have set the fashion in telegraph diplomacy long before those days had he been elected President, for when he was running for that office in 1884 on three tickets (Anti-Monopoly, National Greenback-Labor and People's Parties), he had a private wire into his headquarters in the Hoffman House in New York, which was considered rather extreme modernism at the time.

Perhaps the only occasion in history when a President was called out of bed at night to answer the telephone occurred early in May, 1898, when a Chicago newspaper staff man rang up the White House and demanded that the night watchman call President McKinley to the phone. The watchman demurred, but he was impressed by the long distance call, and finally he complied. Yawning, Mr. McKinley stumbled to the telephone in his nightshirt, and was rewarded when he heard that Dewey and his men had annihilated the Spanish fleet at Manila.

To-day, the telephone switchboard and telegraph office of the State Department are open and alert day and night. All the great wire, cable and radio companies will give the Secretary of State precedence at any time over all others. Nor does European diplomacy any longer depend upon the dispatch case and the King's messenger. During these troublous times, telephone calls fly back and forth between London and Geneva, Geneva and Paris, Paris and Rome, Rome and Vienna. By air Mussolini directed his legions in Africa, by air the Ethiopian Emperor and Empress attempted to broadcast appeals to the world, but were cut off by some mysterious "static" or "atmospheric conditions."

When war with Spain was threatened in 1898, the United States Signal Corps's annual appropriation was only three thousand dollars. General A. W. Greely, Chief Signal Officer at the breaking out of the war, had neither telegraph nor telephone equipment nor personnel, and only eight hundred dollars in cash with which to equip an army with these and cable service. It will scarcely be believed to-day that even after the lessons of the Civil War, the War Department, fifty and sixty years ago, was not much interested in the telegraph, especially in time of peace. As late as February, 1885, the Department officially declared that electrical communications were not needed by the Army. The Secretary of War wrote to the Senate at that time, "The conveyance of military orders or intelligence by telegraph is not a proper subject for the existence of a bureau of the War Department." One officer, he said, could do all the duty needed. There was even an effort made to abolish the Signal Corps.

It is therefore not surprising that the war of '98 caught the Signal Corps empty-handed. Had not, in response to Greely's pleading, the great communications and electric manufacturing companies come to the rescue, as always in time of war, and loaned men and equipment or charged the latter to the Government, hoping for eventual payment, that little war in which we played so amateurish a part, might have gone very differently with us. Through President Eckert, Greely had a Norwegian vessel, the *Adria,* chartered in the name of the Western Union —which company also bought up all the submarine cable to be found and stored it in the ship's hold. Scrymser of the Mexican Telegraph Company loaned the only cable-laying plant to be had in North America. The American Telephone and Telegraph, General Electric and Western Electric loaned or gave credit for telephone and telegraph instruments, field batteries and an extremely light, insulated field telegraph cable.

As the *Adria* was about to sail from Key West, a number of her crew who were Spanish sympathizers deserted. In their places were hastily assembled a few civilians and a score of artillerymen from the garrison at Key West. Arrived off Santiago, they began to destroy the cables from Cuba to other countries. Says Greely in his autobiography:

They were brave and zealous, but as guileless of war work on cables as a pacifist of the Twentieth Century, and as unfamiliar with the sea as an untraveled denizen of our Western plains.... This untrained, seasick squad, blistered by the tropical sun, their clothing worn to rags, their naked bodies grimed with dirt and wet with sweat, did remarkable work.... Lack of sleep at times caused the feebler men to drop down on deck and fall instantly asleep, but in a few hours they were at it again.... They struggled against a sea at times raging... against appalling physical obstacles.

General Shafter, American commander, was soon put within two hours' reach of the War Department, and after June 29th could reach it within twenty minutes, by insulated land cable (not strung on poles but laid along the ground) and submarine cable. Telephone service between his various army units was also established.

After that lesson, the War Department awoke to the truth; the Signal Corps soon caught up with the times, and thereafter, its telegraph and telephone service kept pace with American commercial progress in those communications, which means, with all modesty, that it was the best in the world. When the United States entered the European war, certain nations over there had some eye-opening lessons in, for example, up-to-date telephony. Before our troops had begun to go across, French military authorities assured the American embassy in Paris that the French communications systems would be ample for the use of the American Army. At that, rush work on telephone and telegraph equipment in our great electrical apparatus plants was halted, and no wire outfits went over with the first American troops. But when an American General at St. Nazaire in the summer of 1917 wished to call General Pershing in Paris, and learned that, what with European methods, plus the war emergency, it would be four hours before he could get a call through, he stormed, "Cancel the call! String four wires on the French poles from here to Paris!" and soon demands came back across the sea that telephone equipment be rushed to France. But it took so long to unwind the red tape at home and find room on ships that months elapsed before the outfits reached French soil.

Even before the Congressional declaration of war, the great wire companies were preparing for the emergency. Vail, Carlton and Mackay offered every assistance, released men for war service and held their jobs open for them. Vail was appointed Chairman of the Committee on Telegraphs and Telephones of the Council of National Defense, and had representatives of all the great wire companies, including the Independent Telephone Association, on the committee with him. When Howard E. Coffin, Chairman of the Committee on Industrial Preparedness, wanted an industrial census made, showing the capacity of every plant in the country to turn out materials necessary for the Nation's needs, Walter S. Gifford, the young statistician of the A. T. & T., was recommended for the job. His survey astonished Coffin by its accuracy and completeness, with the result that he became Economic Director of the Council of National Defense and served on the International Munitions Council in 1918, all of which paved his way towards the Presidency of the A. T. & T., that being attained in 1925.

Enormous work had to be done in the United States in those early months of 1917. Electrical equipment factories doubled, trebled, quadrupled their output. Newly built camps, barracks and munitions factories must be equipped with wire service. Washington's telephone and telegraph needs jumped tenfold overnight. A single cable quickly laid between the Capital and New York contained eighty thousand miles of wire. The Army and Navy were in desperate need of wireless telegraph operators. There was no time to make them out of raw material. An appeal went out to amateurs, and within two months four thousand of them were mustered in, operators whose superiors could not be found anywhere.

Incredibly rapid work was now done to put the American Expeditionary Force's communications on a par for efficiency with what a business man at home might expect and would demand. All this must be done in a foreign country, 3,000 miles across an ocean, when transportation was scarcely to be had, and everything over there had to be done from the ground up. From one factory, 50,000 portable switchboards went forward three weeks and one day after work was begun on them. Men in the experimental laboratories redoubled their efforts at evolving new devices made desirable by the crisis; electric and acoustic detectors through water of the approach of submarines, their direction and distance; direction finders for enemy guns and planes, even in total darkness. Aëroplane wireless telephone sets were now first developed, so that aviators could talk with each other and with the ground. The human voice sounds at a much higher wave frequency per second than the noise of engines, propellers, guns and shells; so those low frequency waves were simply tuned out, and in the receiver, only the aviator's voice was heard coming from the plane.

On August 9, 1917, the first Signal Corps telephone office was opened in Paris, connecting over a French wire with the Signal Corps office in Nevers, a new supply base. It had to be operated with French instruments, for there was as yet no American equipment on that side of the ocean. But on August 30th, an office was opened at Chaumont, to which General Pershing removed his headquarters from Paris on the following day. There the 406th Battalion erected the first American poles on French soil. Two switchboard outfits had already come over, and in five days the battalion had these and one hundred telephones installed, connecting the General with all the near-by army units.

Major Frank H. Fay arrived a little later to upbuild the telegraph service, but with little or no equipment with which to work. Telegraph traffic had so greatly increased, especially between Chaumont and Paris, that the few French wires could not carry it. Fay's first action was to change the French wires from "open" to "closed" circuit; now if he could duplex them, he could double their capacity. But he had no duplex machines, and the French used them almost not at all. Generals were demanding better service, regardless of alibis, so Yankee ingenuity had to go into action. Fay went shopping among the electrical and telegraph supply houses in Paris, picked up a jumble of ill-assorted gadgets, some of which had no affinity whatsoever with telegraphs, pieced them together into four duplex sets, two for Chaumont and two for Paris, and they worked as if made for the purpose.

Everywhere the American telephone and telegraph men, both construction and operative, struck the French dumb with amazement—their speed, their efficiency, ingenuity, resourcefulness, individuality, the new devices which they displayed. Stringing eight or ten wires at once, for example, a sort of crane on a truck holding up all the wires while a lineman attached them to a pole! On the other hand, American telegraph operators could scarcely believe it when they saw French telegraphers still receiving by watching the Morse dots and dashes on a paper strip, instead of by ear.

The French telephone system was far behind the times; and this through no fault of the engineers, but of bureaucracy, which, as we have seen in America in quite recent times, can blight almost everything it touches. Some of the American telephone construction was so clever that the French more than once borrowed our Signal Corps men to do special jobs for them. American Multiplex Printers were introduced to the French Army by the Signal Corps, and men were sent to give the French telegraphers instruction in the use of them. Marshal Foch himself wrote a letter of thanks for the great speeding up of the service. The English also appreciated American methods so profoundly that one Signal Corps captain was asked to come to London to give advice as to a submarine detector. A special destroyer was assigned to take him across the Channel and back, a special train took him to London, and some of the greatest electrical engineers in England sat around him and listened solemnly and respectfully to his advice.

On November 8, 1917, Pershing sent a cable to Washington, requesting the organization of a Women's Telephone Operating Unit. The Chief Signal Officer says in his report:

The use of female telephone operators in France was decided upon for two reasons. The first of these was the unquestioned superiority of women as telephone switchboard operators, and the second was the desire to release for service in the more dangerous telephone centrals at the front the male operators on duty in the larger offices.

The General had asked for only 100 operators, but the first call for volunteers was answered by 7,600 eager applicants. Of course, the ones accepted must be able to speak French, as there would be many French officers using our wires. The first group of 33 girls reached Paris on March 24, 1918. In all, 233 went over, and no man surpassed them in courage or devotion. At a switchboard close to the great St. Mihiel assault and later near Verdun during the Argonne offensive, a group of them sat within sound of the guns, with helmet and gas mask hanging on the back of each chair, and an enemy aëroplane sometimes buzzing overhead. Once when the American troops were locked with the foe in battle and the wires were jammed with calls, division headquarers was almost destroyed by fire, but the girls, because it seemed so necessary, stuck to their board until the roof was burning well-nigh over their heads.

Never before in war had the telephone been so extensively used, and never before did electric communications travel so closely with the troops. As soon as a trench was dug, the telephone went into it, and presently operators and division commanders were calling for "Boston," "Pittsburgh," "Nantucket," "Y-1," "G-7," "X-4" and so on, terms by which the various posts and headquarters were disguised from possibly listening ears. In the very first skirmish in which the Americans took part, that at Seicheprey, the official account says, "During the engagement, the Germans concentrated their artillery fire on American telephone and telegraph wires, which were cut many times. . . . The men of the Signal Corps, many of them smoking cigarettes in the face of a heavy bombardment, restored the wires almost as fast as the enemy disrupted them." When American troops made their first real attack, at Cantigny, within forty-five minutes after they started, a Yankee voice came back over the telephone wire, "Hello! This is Cantigny." Frequently signal men went over the top with a storming party, carrying a

ARTILLERY OBSERVER, IN A RUIN AT MONTFAUÇON, DIRECT-
ING THE FIRE OF HIS BATTERY THROUGH THE OFFICER
WITH THE TELEPHONE IN THE PIT BELOW

telephone and dragging a twisted pair of wires after them, and news was sent back to headquarters during the conflict.

The "twisted pair" was used in America before the war as drop wiring from suburban and country lines to dwellings, filling stations, and so on. Its insulation was so tough that a truck could be driven over it a few times without destroying its usefulness. Hence in hasty construction, such wires were often just laid along the earth, where they were broken now and then by trucks, tanks, shell explosions or careless strokes from picks and spades. Of course poles were preferred, and short ones were used in wooded areas, where they would be concealed from enemy aëroplane vision. The field signalmen at the front nearly always did their wire repairing in the darkness of night, though even then in danger of being revealed by enemy flares or exploding shells.

Troops were occasionally forced back so quickly that a telephone unit was forgotten or necessarily left behind in a dugout or other hiding place. An American force was thus driven back from a village on one occasion, but headquarters was astonished to hear a few minutes later a call from there, given by a voice unmistakably American. A corporal and two privates with the telephone in the cellar of an abandoned house, were unaware that they had been left behind. When informed that the village was now held by Germans, the corporal could not believe it until he had gone up and had a peep outside. The Germans had not discovered them, and the officers told the corporal to hold fast while their artillery blasted the Heinies out of the village, promising to save the building where the squad were in hiding. Two of the doughboys actually went into the upper story of the building and directed the artillery fire by telephone until they were rescued.

A brigade commander said in his report, "During all my years of experience, I have never seen such devotion to duty as that displayed by the Signal Corps detail at ——" it would be unfair to give the name, for, according to the records, they were all like that.

OLD WIRES AND NEW WAVES

A curious development of electrical communication during this war was the listening post. From a dugout, wires would be strung out over the ground, to right, left and front, as near to the enemy lines as possible, each wire ending in a copper mat some two feet square, buried just under the surface of the earth. Of course the planting of these mats had to be done stealthily on a dark night—a man crawling forward on hands and knees with a coil of wire and the mat slung over one shoulder and a digging tool or two in the other hand. Many a man lost his life in such an expedition.

Once planted, the mat picked up from the earth by induction and conveyed back to the listener in the dugout, sitting with a head-set clamped to his ears, electrical impulses from all telegraphs and telephones in the vicinity, and even caught some radio impulses; the operators occasionally heard messages from Berlin or the Eiffel Tower. The operator must know German, of course; and on the German side, the listening-post men must be familiar with English or French, or both. The mats thus picked up not only enemy messages, but those on their own side. The listening-post man was thus able to detect any indiscreet conversation in his own army, which he was expected to report.

Not being a part of any divisional organization, the listening post men were seldom warned of impending attacks or air raids, and were occasionally left behind and captured by the enemy. Loops of wire attached to tree-tops, were sometimes used instead of mats, and caught many messages. Once when the French and German trenches were only fifty yards apart, the French actually tapped the Germans' telephone wires. At another time, when the Germans were stealing too many American messages, a group of our Indian soldiers, all of one tribe, were called upon to man the telephones in a certain area, and ordered to use their ancestral language. That trick must have thrown the Germans on their beam-ends while it lasted.

By January 1, 1918, the Signal Corps had main telephone offices in seventeen cities—London and Southampton in England, and fifteen cities of France. They were sending both telegraph

494

and telephone messages over the same wire, by means of the triple-duplex-multiplex—six messages, three each way, going over each wire, so that a twisted pair carried twelve messages. When Marshal Foch assumed the high command in the spring of 1918, an American signal officer was asked to instal telephone equipment at his headquarters at Senlis. It was noticed that when in the field, Foch would go out of his way to use an American telephone rather than a French one, if one was available. Towards the close, when the Americans turned many of their telephone lines over to the French, the Marshal missed the clear reception to which he had been accustomed, and found that the French had promptly removed the repeating devices. He ordered them restored, and a repeater school was established, with American officers as teachers and the French as pupils.

Twenty-five years and more ago, how deplorably often was it written of a ship that she "left ——— for ——— on a certain date, and was never afterward heard from." That line is seldom written now, and it is growing more infrequent every year. That a ship is now able to send a cry through the air, "Save my people! I am wounded unto death," is worth all the efforts of all the inventors who made it possible, even if wireless meant nothing else.

On a day in January, 1909, the White Star liner *Republic* left New York with 440 passengers, bound for a cruise in the Mediterranean. She ran into fog almost as soon as she left the harbor. At 5:40 next morning, her only wireless operator, Jack Binns, was awakened by blasts from the steamer's siren, followed almost immediately by a terrific crash and shock. A freighter, the *Florida,* had struck her in the fog, killing two of her own seamen and two passengers on the *Republic,* whose side she crushed in. One wall of Binns's radio room was smashed, but his instruments were intact. He had scarcely tested them, however, when the lights went out—the ship's power-plant was flooded. Binns switched to storage batteries, and as the telephone to the bridge was destroyed, he sent out a CQD on his own responsibility. It was picked up at Siasconsett, on Nantucket Island, where the operator, with stronger power, repeated it and Binns's subsequent messages over a larger area.

Binns, saving what little power he had, did little sending until about noon, when he got in touch with the *Baltic,* inbound, and about sixty-four miles distant. But the fog was still so dense, that despite wireless and bombs, the *Baltic* groped for thirteen hours before she found her sister ship, finally sighting her long after midnight. By daybreak next morning there was quite a fleet in the vicinity, drawn by the distress call. The *Baltic* took off the *Republic's* passengers, and most of the crew, leaving the Captain, Binns and a few others on board, while a Coast Guard vessel tried to tow her to shore. This essay was presently found to be vain; the men were taken off her and she sank.

That was the first ship rescue by wireless which attained wide publicity—perhaps because it occurred off the coast of America, where journalists overlook no opportunities. To Americans, a rescue through wireless was a new thrill; and when Binns reached New York, he had been so touted by the press as a super-hero that he was uproariously welcomed and lauded, kissed by silly women, fairly mobbed when he appeared in public—all to his astonishment and annoyance. His deprecatory attitude was regarded as abnormal yet delightful modesty, when as a matter of fact, it was simply intelligent honesty. Other men on the ship had done their duty just as he had. The wireless operator who calls for help when in trouble is not, just for that service, a hero; he is thereby protecting himself as well as others on board. Lest this seem ungracious, let us hasten to say that Binns was of the stuff of which heroes are made; like all other sea operators of whom we have heard, he did his part skilfully, faithfully and fearlessly. There have been instances of operators in more strenuous circumstances than he, who have shown great heroism, fortitude and ingenuity—nursing the feeble power of storage batteries after the ship's power has failed, sending steadily and courageously even to the moment when they said "Good-by!" to the listeners as the ship took her last plunge. Some have died thus at their posts when most of the passengers had escaped in the lifeboats.

There is no more painful picture than that of the wireless operator, forbidden by law to send out the SOS without the Captain's order, compelled to sit passive, secretive, at his instrument while a ship slowly dies, simply because the Captain has been so cowed by the ship-owners' threats of reprisal if he calls for help too soon, is towed to safety, and the owners have to pay salvage charges. Not a few lives have been lost because of this fear. In one of the most sickening sea disasters of recent years—because the loss of life was so unnecessary—that of the *Morro Castle* fire off the New Jersey coast in October, 1934, the three radio operators were unjustly blamed by press and public, called stupid and neglectful for not sending out the distress call sooner, when as a matter of fact, two of them went to the bridge again and again to ask the Acting Captain for permission to do so, but he "seemed dazed" and did not give it until too late to save any more than a hundred lives. Meanwhile Rogers, the chief operator, sitting helpless, had heard another ship, many miles away, which had seen the red glow in the sky, ask the Tuckerton station, on shore, whether there had been any report of a burning vessel. The reply was "No."

When permission was finally given, Rogers was sitting with his feet on his chair rungs, because the floor under him was too hot for comfort. He continued sending until almost suffocated by smoke and acid fumes from below, when he had to be half dragged to safety. Yet the three wireless men remained on board twelve hours longer, and when, after the Captain had cast anchor, a tug essayed to tow the burning vessel ashore, they took their turns at sawing the anchor chain apart with small hack-saw blades.

When the *Vestris,* one day out from New York in 1928, began that slow careening to starboard which finally resulted in her sinking with the loss of more than a hundred lives, her chief operator, O'Loughlin, sat all through an afternoon and night, forbidden to send out a distress call, though by daybreak next morning, the list was so great that walking on her decks was difficult. A Naval operator on shore, who was taking bearings on ships, noticed that she was moving more and more slowly, and became concerned. At 5 o'clock the next morning the *Vestris* was in touch with the northbound *Voltaire* of the same line, and merely exchanged the QRU—"I have nothing for you." At that moment, the passengers were all up and dressed, and nearly everybody on board believed that the ship was doomed. At 8:30, Myers, the operator on shore, noticing that she seemed to have stopped completely, asked if anything was wrong. O'Loughlin evaded the question; and not until nearly 10 A.M. was permission given him to ask for help. Then it was too late for any vessel to reach the *Vestris* until long after she sank. At 1:29 P.M. O'Loughlin said SK (meaning Finis) to listeners— and was among the lost.

On the other hand, books and newspapers are full of thrilling stories of noble sea rescues and emergency aid of one sort and another resulting from radio calls. There was Captain George Fried, for example, headed towards New York with his vessel, asked by another ship to meet her in mid-ocean and take one of her engineers back to America; the poor fellow had just learned by radio of the deaths of all his family by the burning of his home in New Orleans. And the story of the *President Roosevelt,* Captain Fried, standing by the sinking freighter *Antinoe* for four days, trying again and again through mountainous seas to rescue her crew, losing two of the *Roosevelt's* own men in the attempts, but at last succeeding, is an epic which should be read; it makes one think better of one's fellow-men.

To-day, when lifeboats put off from a sinking or burning ship, they need no longer be mere drifting, voiceless specks in the watery waste, likely to be overlooked by all near-by ships, because they have no way of telling of their whereabouts. For now, there is a life-boat radio set which will have a transmission range of a hundred miles—it has reached one hundred and fifty in tests—by which the little boat can call and listen to larger vessels in the vicinity.

HEROIC SERVICE BY WIRE AND WAVE

The latest radio heroes—and heroines—are the once-despised amateurs. They long ago proved themselves among the most valuable of wireless experimenters, and their morals have improved in the past quarter century. Their motto used to be, "Everybody for himself, and the Devil take the hindmost"; now it is "All for one, and one for all." The hams now have at least three organizations in this country—the American Radio Relay League, an Army network and a Navy network; moreover, they have friends and acquaintances, gathered by wave all over the world. They have acquired a moral code and an *esprit de corps;* they are the world's champion Boy Scouts. To-day, if one's radio reception is interfered with by a near-by amateur station, the ham does not invite the sufferer to go to Hell, as his predecessor, twenty-five years ago, might have done, but politely hastens to instal a wave-trap, free of charge.

Finally, the amateurs constitute a highly trained emergency communications service, which has proven its worth again and again in times of disaster. During blizzards and snow blockades in the North, during the floods of recent years in the Middle West and New England, they were invaluable in many places for transmitting news, calls for help, messages to worried friends and kinsmen at a distance, and other necessary services. This was particularly notable in the Vermont floods of 1927, when Montpelier was for a time cut off from all other communication than that supplied by a few radio amateurs.

When the hurricane of 1928 was tearing up through the West Indies, Florida hams, warned by a comrade in the Virgin Islands, notified their communities and made their own emergency arrangements before the storm arrived. Two amateurs in Palm Beach, their own homes wrecked, gathered every dry cell battery in town to supply power for their own station after the city power plant had failed, and for three days they were the only means of communication with the outer world. Again, in the hurricane of 1935, which devastated the Florida Keys, an amateur station down there on the islands was the only voice that could speak to the mainland, to tell what had happened and what was needed.

When an earthquake wrecked Long Beach, California, in 1933, and other communication was broken, a schoolboy's station gave the rest of the country its first news of the disaster. That evening the Mayor asked the Adjutant-General of the State, by amateur wireless, for military protection. Several other hams went into action, and though repeated shocks were still crumbling and threatening the buildings where they worked, they kept the authorities in touch with hospitals, the Red Cross, the Highway Patrol, the relief organizations and distant kinsmen and friends.[1]

[1] For a number of these facts about amateur operators, thanks are due an article by Earl Jerome, "Minute Men of Radio," in the *Reader's Digest* for May, 1936.

OPERATORS SPEAKING MANY TONGUES AT A FOREIGN SWITCHBOARD IN NEW YORK

CHAPTER XXV

THE PALACE OF ALADDIN

He had no sooner begun to rub it, but in an instant a hideous genie of gigantic size appeared before them and said to him in a voice like thunder, "What wouldst thou have? I am ready to obey thee as thy slave, and slave of all those who have that lamp in their hands; I, and the other slaves of the lamp."

Arabian Nights

THIS modern world of ours is a palace of enchantment, and we are all Aladdins. Our great advantage over the first of that name is that each of us has not one djinn only at his beck and call, but thousands, myriads of them; and to summon the most of them, we have not even the troublesome manual labor of rubbing a precious lamp (which must be carefully guarded, lest it be lost), as our predecessor did, but merely touch the tip of a finger to a button. A few of the genii we summon thus may be human in form, but most of them are what we call mechanical—which means that in them we see a natural force put to work by man.

Among these natural forces, the greatest so far revealed to us is electricity; a force which we have learned how to handle and direct, but which we can never conquer—it is capable of turning upon us and striking us dead if we take the slightest liberties with it; a force, the nature of which throughout the ages has remained such a mystery that within the writer's memory the dictionaries were still calling it a fluid—an obviously feeble effort at characterization. When the *Century Dictionary* grappled with the problem of defining the word, it admitted that "the true nature of electricity is as yet not well understood."

Among the greatest of the children of electricity are the

various forms of instantaneous communication. When Morse's crude telegraph began slowly mumbling words over short distances, some men said to each other that the genius of man would find difficulty in going farther; others saw this as only a beginning, and enthusiastically cried that there was no limit to its possibilities. Morse died in 1872, too early to see the practical telephone come into being and so long ago that wireless communication had scarcely been dreamed of by the most imaginative of men, though its consummation came only twenty-five years after his death.

One instance out of thousands which might be cited to show how far we have come in half a century may be found in a Chicago newspaper in 1881 under the heading, "Remarkable Incident of the Telephone." There we read of a downtown Chicago physician who had as patients a family far out on the North Side. Late one winter night they called him by telephone, saying that the baby was ill, feverish and coughing, and they feared it had croup. It was a stormy night, and the doctor disliked the thought of that long journey by street car or buggy. He asked them to hold the baby up to the telephone; he heard its cough and even its breathing. Undoubtedly croup, he said, and "Knowing they had a chest of medicines, I directed them to give aconite and sanguinaria in rapid alternation, and to make certain applications to the throat. 'We have aconite,' they said, 'but we haven't any sanguinaria.'"

"Well, Doctor," said the reporter who was doing the interviewing, "what could you do in such a dilemma?"

"Fortunately, the physician replied, "there is a druggist within a few blocks who, upon inquiry at the central office, I found possesses a telephone. It was not the work of five minutes to call him up and direct him to send to my patients a prescription containing the required sanguinaria. It was put up, delivered and administered inside of half an hour, and the whole transaction, consultation and all, did not extend over that time."

What would that doctor have said if he had been told that a little more than forty years later, to a passenger steamer hurrying up the Atlantic from Rio to New York, a whisper would come through the air from the captain of a freighter, so far away as to be invisible, asking if the liner's surgeon would not please tell him what to do for a seaman, seriously ill. Upon hearing the symptoms, the surgeon, via those same invisible waves in the ether, replies that the man has pleurisy; he gives instructions, among them, to "mobilize the left side." "Thanks, Doctor," the mysterious instrument in the liner's wireless room ticks out, "but please tell us in plain English, what mobilizing a man's side means." The Doctor explains. Next day he asks the freighter, headed in the same direction, but rapidly falling farther behind, how the sick man is. "Much better, thanks," is the report which the obliging genie brings back.

Most of the things done by wire and wave to-day have come to seem commonplace to us. But when one visits, as did this writer, the workshops of the great communications companies and sees the huge, inexpressibly delicate and complex yet smoothly functioning labyrinth of machinery, not to mention the vast human organizations back of these everyday services, he comes to regard these things which are made so simple for us with far more respect. Furthermore, there are numerous tricks and seeming ratiocinations of these almost human, almost intelligent machines of which the average citizen has not the faintest conception until he sees them being accomplished.

Machinery is displacing men and women in the communications arts, yet not as rapidly as some think. They are decreasing in one category, increasing—but less rapidly—in another. A recent cartoon pictured an industrialist showing a visitor over his factory. In a great room filled with machinery, men were rushing about in all directions with wrenches, oil cans and other tools in their hands. At the left sat one calm, spectacled individual at a switchboard. "This man runs the machinery," said the boss. "All the others are repair men." Something like that obtains in communications. Telegraph operators and switchboard girls are undoubtedly decreasing in number. The intricate machinery which displaces them requires many expert men to care for it, but not nearly as many as the numbers it displaces. The situation draws nearer a balance when you learn that the individual expert machinist draws more pay than the switchboard girl. The advantages of automatic telegraph and telephone equipment are not found entirely in the category of wages; the truth is that these machines are quicker and more accurate than men and women.

Attempts at automatic telegraphy began with the very birth of the art. Gauss and Weber's (1833), for example, was automatic in intention. We have long since spoken of House's and Wheatstone's machines; and in that same period, 1845 to 1855, Froment and Brequet in France, Siemens in Germany, Whitehouse in England and Farmer in America worked out systems, all more or less similar. None of these came into extensive use. In fact, even much later inventors toiled with little or no reward of any substantial sort, for automatic telegraphy has come into extensive use only after most of those who developed it are dead.

David Hughes of Kentucky, whose beautiful printing machine we have already mentioned (patented in 1855 and improved by Phelps), contributed the most important improvement upon earlier systems, in most of which the pressure of a letter key caused, with slight delay, the moving of a wheel with type on its rim to the required position. Hughes accelerated the process by achieving constant synchronism between sending and receiving machines. His was one of the only two which knew any success in the nineteenth century. It was widely used in Europe, but the Morse monopoly prevented its ever getting a foothold in the inventor's native country, where it might have made him wealthy.

The next successful printing system, introduced in 1874, was that of Jean Maurice Émile Baudot, an officer of the French telegraph service, who devoted nearly all his life to its development, and to whom automatic telegraphy to-day owes in great part its success. The French Government took over his system in 1877 and made the inventor a Chevalier of the Legion of Honor. "Scarcely any designer to-day," wrote Harrison in 1923, "can avoid embodying some detail which originated with Baudot." Rowland, Murray (1899-1901), Siemens and Halske (1900), Buckingham and Barclay (1900-1902) and others all show his influence.

The English inventor, Donald Murray, sold the American rights for his system to the Western Union in 1912. He was in the United States that year, and found the Western Union using for the most part the Buckingham-Barclay machines. There were no less than eight others being promoted in this country at that time. The Morkrum, invented by Charles L. Krum, a Chicago cold-storage engineer and his son Howard, and backed by Joy Morton, a Chicago capitalist, was being used by the Postal Telegraph, and Murray liked it so much that he purchased the European rights. The Kleinschmidt Telegraph Typewriter was a later invention taken over by the Western Union. In 1923, the Murray Multiplex was further developed by Western Union and Western Electric, and the telegraphers admit that by its use they have saved some millions of dollars.

Thus do the great communications companies improve their systems. In their laboratories, where scientists are given every facility, including all the time they want for tinkering, inventions are frequently developed. But when geniuses outside the organization produce useful devices, they are bought, improved if possible, and they or their best features are welded into the existing system.

Elisha Gray's telautograph, perfected in 1893, by means of which you write with a pen connected with a telegraph wire, and another pen, far away at the other terminus, reproduces your writing in facsimile, was thought by some at the time to be the coming automatic telegraph. But that could not be, for already the typewriter was making inroads on longhand writing in the business world; it was becoming apparent that personal script was soon to be banned, and all communication must be printed.

In the *Journal of Electrical Engineering* in 1925, Don Murray predicted that with the introduction of the teletype or start-stop telegraph printer, provided with a typewriter keyboard and requiring only momentary synchronism:

In the course of years this new development will have a revolutionary effect on telegraph offices, which will become automatic switching exchanges, very like an automatic telephone exchange; and the telegraph operators, like the telephone girls, are doomed to disappear, and their places will be taken by a few engineers and mechanics wandering about in the deserted operating rooms, looking after the telegraph-switching apparatus.

This has not quite been realized, though ominous progress has been made. An Associated Press item on July 26, 1934, announced:

The last of the "brass pounders" has been displaced in the network of news wires of the Associated Press in New York State. To-day, from Niagara Falls to New York City, not a Morse operator is at work, automatic printers having replaced the last Morse circuit.

And yet, when you go into the great Associated or United Press operating rooms in New York City, among a wilderness of teletypes, each machine turning out as many as nine carbon copies of a dispatch, to be flicked out to various regional centers of the organization, your eye soon alights upon a battered table where seven or eight of the old familiar Morse instruments stand in a row, with operators tapping them or lingering near, waiting for a call. They are used, the manager tells you, by small town correspondents whose business does not justify the use of automatic printers. You find the same phenomenon in both of the big telegraph headquarters and even in the Radio Corporation's operating room. "Some of our customers prefer them," says the manager.

And at every one of these tables, in the little reflector, somewhat like the half of a wooden box which holds the sounder or call for each instrument, you will see an empty tobacco tin of the operator's favorite brand wedged against the sounder or dangling from it. It has been a custom almost ever since pipe tobacco began to be sold in tins. Why? Because each tin gives its sounder a different tone, and its operator recognizes its voice, even though he may be a hundred feet away when it calls. It is asserted that this was true, even when there were as many as two hundred and fifty Morse operators working in one big room.

Behind the scenes, among the relay machinery and other mechanisms of a great telephone headquarters, we see men making tests, and always they have a Morse key beside them, on which they click out questions and answers to their fellow-testers. Between the headquarters of the great radio telegraph companies in New York and their sending and receiving stations scattered along the Atlantic coast, there are telegraph wires with men who know how to work the Morse key at either end. Alongside every one of the super-telephone wires which carry our radio broadcasting programs from station to station through a network, there is always a telegraph wire with Morse keys to carry news and give instructions in case the telephone wire goes wrong.

So far, Mr. Murray's dire prediction as to the great, empty operating rooms has not been realized. There are still operators needed for the automatic printers, though now they are women typists instead of "brass pounders." To-day, when you leave a telegram or telephone it in to a city telegraph office, a girl taps it out on a machine with a typewriter keyboard; a receiving machine at destination accepts the message by wire and automatically prints it as it is received on a gummed slip of paper, which a clerk pastes on a message blank to be delivered to the addressee. Thus the telegraph has in its history completed a cycle. The Morse telegraph, you will remember, was a recording system at the beginning, though it recorded the message only in dots and dashes on the fillet. The House and Hughes machines actually printed the message. But the Morse monopoly crowded them out; reception by ear came in, and for decades was the accepted method. Now it is passing out forever, and true recording comes back again.

If you are a large user of the telegraph, you may have a private automatic (or more than one) in your office. On it your own stenographers write telegrams, which are reproduced, letter by letter, as fast as written, in the main telegraph office of your city, thus dispensing even with the messenger boy. In that telegraph office there may be dozens, perhaps scores of Multiplex machines, which also have a type keyboard. Here your message for New York or Los Angeles goes to the operator who handles that particular city, and she retypes it, though now it appears as round holes punched in a tape, the letters of the alphabet and other characters being represented by different groupings—above, below and to right or left—of the holes, sometimes five of them for one letter. As she types, this tape slides through the transmitter, and electric impulses pass through the holes, reproducing them on machines in New York or Los Angeles, which very smartly translate them back into English characters and print them on a tape. The tape is then pasted to a blank and delivered, or goes by private wire into the addressee's own office and is reproduced on his own receiving machine.

Four sending and four receiving machines may be attached to each end of a wire, so that eight messages at once, representing some hundreds of holes in tape, may be passing simultaneously through that single wire.

Now the American Telephone and Telegraph Company is using the teletype over its telephone wires; and in its great city offices, you see long rows of girls sitting in front of a curious hybrid—a typewriter keyboard with a telephone switchboard above it. Here there is no particular operator for each city; any girl, when she receives a message for Boston or New York or Washington, simply plugs in on her switchboard for the required city, and then taps out her message. A teletype message will in many cases convey what you want to say as well as conversation, and it goes more cheaply than the minimum telephone call. The Western Union people are a bit peevish over this; it appears to them that the Bell Telephone is violating its promise of November 10, 1879, to stay out of the telegraph business; but what to do about it?

THE PALACE OF ALADDIN

In the great ocean cable and radio offices, you will see more of those punching machines, creating in paper strips groups of holes which to the layman look like nothing at all. In such offices, you see perfect thickets of those big white rolls of tape sticking in air; the communications people are good patrons of the paper mills. There are all sorts of gadgets there, too, which are mysteries to the uninitiated, even after they are "explained" by a guide. In the cable rooms there, for instance, is Lord Kelvin's siphon recorder, still making its silly-looking continuous, zigzag ink marks on another paper strip. There are nervous belts which, when an operator drops a typed or printed message on them, seize it with demoniac intensity and whisk it away to the other end of the room, or up through a hole in the ceiling or down through the floor or wherever it ought to go.

These cable and radio rooms in New York are at their busiest in the forenoon; pandemonia of clattering machines and strained attention. For then both Europe and America are awake and on the job. Ten A.M. in New York is 3 P.M. on the other side. Stock exchanges, brokers' offices, importers, exporters, are shooting messages back and forth—inquiries, quotations, bids, orders, acceptances, what-not. Of course, all prominent brokers have private wires nowadays, and if there is anybody on earth who expects immediacy in his communications, it is a broker, especially one who deals internationally and sometimes in millions. Know how long it takes a radio wave to cross the Atlantic? About one-fiftieth of a second! Well, the moment that that instantaneous message lands in the New York office, it must be relayed instantaneously over the broker's wire, or he will want to know, Why this unnecessary and inexcusable delay? It is practically always in code, and therefore may often have only three or four words of text; and the companies pride themselves on handling such telegrams in ten or twenty seconds. I stood in the International Telephone and Telegraph operating room in New York and saw message after message delivered in that time; an inexorable time-clock records it on tape and

509

telegram. If it is fumbled for as much as half a minute, the manager's eyebrows are apt to go up in cold inquiry.

In one section of such an operating room stand groups of machines devoted to the great press associations, and these, too, are busiest in the forenoon, when Downing Street and the Ballplatz and Mussolini and Hitler and the latest Spanish Government are hard at it, and making news, as always. By afternoon in Gotham, the day is over in Europe; stock exchanges, brokers' and business offices and chancelleries are closed, and nearly everybody is either resting at home, or is at his favorite evening's amusement. Then the cable and radio offices here become comparatively placid; many operators are off, some others sitting about with intervals of little to do. A cosmopolitan group they are, too. You can actually guess by looking at the faces and heads of some—not all—of them what country they send to; this man to Italy, of course; that one to Germany, another to one of the Scandinavian countries; those dark-eyed fellows over there to Latin America. . . .

One of the enormously important messages which leap the ocean during the first half of the day comes from London every week-day about noon. At late afternoon tea-time over there, 4:15 P.M., to be exact, four "just men," representatives of the four leading British bullion houses specializing in spot silver, meet around a table at Throgmorton and Old Broad Street, within shouting distance of the Bank of England, to set the price for silver, which governs or affects the price the world over. Bids and offers are compared, and the price is determined, all within about thirty minutes. Copies of the figure are quickly made and flash in code by cable and radio around the globe— to the Bund of Shanghai, to Bombay and Berlin and Buenos Aires, to Montreal and Mexico, Lima and La Paz and Washington, and among the rest, to an office at the corner of Fulton and Gold Streets, down in that little area of lower Manhattan still called "The Swamp," (because that was what it was in New Amsterdam days), where the United States price for silver is fixed for the next twenty-four hours.

THE PALACE OF ALADDIN

"Would you like to hear what's going on in Europe this evening?" asks a very human-looking wizard in the RCA operating building, on Broad Street in New York. (The A. T. & T., by the way, brings some of the foreign broadcasts across the ocean, but practically 90 per cent of them come by RCA.)

"This evening?" We glance up at the clock; twelve minutes after three. Why, of course! The evening programs are just beginning over in western Europe. There is no foreign broadcast scheduled for America to-day, but this obliging wizard will let us listen in on European broadcasting stations. He turns to a telegraph key near by (old reliable Morse again!) and jiggles it with his finger—dot, dot, dash, dash, dot—he is calling the receiving station at Riverhead, Long Island, asking it to open the window, so that we may hear the shouts and murmurs of Europe. A few answering clicks, and our magician turns to the control board.

"Let's try Brussels," he says. He turns a knob, and instantly we are at home—an old friend is speaking. What a gloriously universal language is music! For as we reach Brussels, a great symphony orchestra, the grandest of all man's musical developments, is just swinging into the lilting waltz movement of Beethoven's *Pastoral* symphony. We can stay only a few moments; we are sorry to leave, for when our friend touches his magic lamp again and says, "London," we hear only American jazz; the British Broadcasting Company is giving its patrons some froth at the moment.

"Rome," says the magician. "It's later there," and in an instant the magic carpet transports us nine hundred miles as the crow flies. Familiar orchestral strains again and a baritone voice thundering, "Rhadames! Rhadames! Rhadames!" By a curious coincidence, Romans are diverting their minds from the worries of the Ethiop War and world sanctions by listening to another great African story, *Aïda*.

And so we are whisked about Europe. Next we go down into the big telegraph room and listen to the world's voices through another medium—Morse wireless. As our guide throws one switch after another, we hear messages chirping to and from stations thousands of miles away, some of them in cities which are but names and dreams to us; each station with its own peculiar voice uttering those weird, whistling dots and dashes in many tones, varying from deep contralto to high soprano, but always—to at least one pair of ears—with a strange, unearthly sound. "San Francisco," says our companion; "London. . . . Stockholm. . . . Berlin. . . . Moscow. . . . Warsaw. . . . Madrid. . . . Rio. . . . Buenos Aires. . . . Colon. . . . We almost cover the world in three or four minutes.

"This one will be bad," he warns as he touches another switch. "It's Chile." The voice is rough, husky, stuttering. "Having to come lengthwise through those Andes is what does it," is the explanation.

The huge foreign switchboard in the American Telephone and Telegraph's Long Lines Building in New York, with those exotic names printed over each girl's head, gives the lay visitor another thrill. Here every operator speaks from two to four languages. Our mentor offers to let us hear some one speak from the uttermost quarter of South America by the ether waves. One feels apologetic at having these monster forces set in motion just for a visitor's entertainment and instruction, although it seems as easy and simple as turning one's hand over. At a vacant spot on the switchboard we seat ourselves and place receivers to our ears. A young woman a few feet away thrusts a plug into a socket, and instantly great steel towers over in New Jersey begin hurling darts of warning towards the South Pole.

"Hello, Buenos Aires," our operator is saying, mildly, into the little cornucopia at her lips. "Hello, Buenos Aires! Hello, Buenos Aires!"

Even as witches of old called three times to summon demons and familiars, so our third call is scarce uttered when a voice from the debonair capital of Argentina, sounding as clear and strong as that of the girl at our elbow, replies, "Hello, New York!"

A TELETYPE SWITCHBOARD

THE PALACE OF ALADDIN

"We have some visitors here," says Miss New York, "and they want to hear us talk." Miss Buenos Aires replies in cultured English with just a dainty Spanish touch here and there; they discuss—of course—the weather, and another item or so. The black-haired Señorita (she *must* have been black-haired; we pictured her so, and we won't have her any other way) told us that it was a lovely Spring day there, though still a bit chilly; it was October with us. I did not time the call, but I am sure the connection was completed in a few seconds, perhaps not more than a quarter of a minute.

What a difference middle-aged folk notice, by the way, in the ease of putting through long distance calls by land wire, now and twenty years or more ago. No more do we ring off and wait, sometimes half an hour, for the girl to get the call through; connection is completed now while we wait. The telephone people tell us in modern jargon that the average time of completing a call now is "two-point-four" (in good English, two and four-tenths) minutes.

Suppose we should want to call some one in Sydney or Melbourne, on the other side of the globe. The A. T. & T. does not send directly to Australia, but through the British Broadcasting Company's transmission station at Rugby, which, with its 820-foot towers a quarter-mile apart, has been the world's most powerful station up to the present time (RCA is just about to surpass it at Rocky Point). By directing its beam, the Rugby station can send the message either way, southeastward or southwestward around the globe to kangaroo land, making its choice according to atmospheric conditions. Darkness is preferred; if it is night and not too stormy in the Eastern Hemisphere, the waves shoot down across Europe and southwestern Asia, some 10,600 miles, to Sydney. But if darkness covers the Western Hemisphere, our words may rebound from Rugby, right back across the American continent and the vast reaches of the southern Pacific, a leap of more than 13,000 miles.

The RCA publicity man showed me a good photograph of a

ship wireless operator at his instrument, and I remarked that I should like to have it to use on the jacket of my book.

"Glad to let you have it," was the reply, "but this operator himself controls the photograph. We'll have to ask his permission."

He turned to his telephone, called the operating room on Broad Street and dictated a message to the operator, giving his name and ship, and adding, "Please make this a special rush."

We talked perhaps half an hour longer, and as I rose to go, the telephone rang; it was the reply from the operator, granting the desired permission. Somewhere in the Atlantic waste between here and South America, the searching waves had found his ship, spoken to him and dashed back again.

Still more remarkable is the wireless telephone's ship-to-shore service. Fancy a switchboard with—instead of names of cities or individual telephone numbers—names such as *Aquitania, Normandie, Bremen, Columbus, Conte di Savoia, Empress of Britain, Queen of Bermuda, Ile de France, Europa* and so on— all the great greyhounds of the sea. You may lift the receiver in your home and call any of them anywhere. A Chicago woman who had suffered a nervous breakdown was ordered by her physician to take a trip around the world. But in order that she might be frequently assured that husband and children were in good health and everything all right at home, her husband arranged with the A. T. & T. to call her once a week while she was on the ship; and so for three minutes each week, no matter whether she was on the Indian Ocean or where else, she heard the voices of home, and was saved from worry.

Back in the very beginning of their experiments with trans-oceanic wireless telephony, the Bell engineers saw that the great fault of such service would be its lack of secrecy; all the world might listen in. Who would want to use the air telephone under such conditions? Even then, the idea of somehow scrambling or overlapping the waves so that words tossed into the air might not be understood, occurred to them. But if it could be done,

THE PALACE OF ALADDIN

how unscramble them again? Suffice it to say that after long labor, they succeeded, and to-day you may telephone the most profound secret to your wife or business associate in Europe, and any one tuning in on either side of the Atlantic will hear nothing but gibberish; but your *vis-à-vis,* with receiver at ear on the other side hears your voice pronounce the words as clearly, provided there isn't too much static, as though you were only a block distant.

Another queer yet perfectly logical thing is that you listen in as much as your please, yet you are never likely to solve the mystery, because everybody's voice scrambles just a bit differently; slight variations in enunciation, in tone and quality of voice vary the scrambled words a bit as they come from you or from me. Let us listen in on the scrambling process in the Long Lines Building, one of the A. T. & T.'s three great wonderlands in New York, the other two being the Bell Telephone Laboratories and the New York Telephone Company. (More than 4,000 persons, by the way, work in each of those buildings, and the private switchboard of each is that of a considerable city.)

We are not permitted to hear actual messages crossing the ocean—for the reassurance of telephone users, that is against the rules. But you may hear the gibberish which the strange machine makes of words spoken by your companion on the other side of the same room. And you may meet there a quiet, modest magician named Joseph L. Richey, who has worked with it so long that he can talk and write the scrambled language! "Your names, Mr. and Mrs. Alvin F. Harlow," he says, "as I speak them, will sound approximately like this," and he writes it down. Then he speaks our names into a receiver, and sure enough, he has translated them correctly into the djinn language. "Now I'll send it the other way," he says, and speaks "Scrambled" into the receiver, whereupon our names come back to us very clearly, though with just a slight "foreign" accent, as if an educated "Rooshian, Turk or Prooshian" of long residence in this country were speaking them; for there are twists in this unearthly language with which the human tongue cannot quite cope.

That seemingly immortal stanza,

> Mary had a little lamb,
> Its fleece was white as snow;
> And everywhere that Mary went
> The lamb was sure to go,

when spoken by Mr. Richey, comes out like this:

> Noyl hob oh ylippey ylond,
> Heezz fludz yez yout oz smay
> Umb adjew yahrr thop noyl yump
> Thoo ylond yez theer pee gay.

And speaking of scrambling, here is a believe-it-or-not story for the reader to chew upon. During the recent war, the A.E.F. wanted a more baffling telegraph cipher code than any yet devised. Whereupon an obliging Bell Telephone engineer named Vernam produced an enciphering machine which, when English is typed into it, turns it into what is declared to be an undecipherable cipher, written on a tape. Only the sister machine at the other terminus can turn it back into real language. But this isn't all. A. Lincoln Lavine, in his book, *Circuits of Victory*, assures us that Vernam even trained this robot to translate from one language to another. At Paris, you typed "Do you speak French?" into it, and if desired, it came out at Chaumont, "Parlez vous Français?" "I would not have believed this," says Mr. Lavine, "if I had not seen it done." Which reminds us of a remark of Greville, the diarist, three-quarters of a century ago. Lord Derby had just told him, one day in 1859, that a signal had been sent by telegraph from London to Corfu and back in six seconds. "I would not have believed this on any other authority," wrote Greville. Thus do those uncanny partners, Science and Nature, astound each generation with feats which in a few years have, to thoughtless Society, become commonplaces. Just the other day, President Gifford of the A. T. & T. lifted his receiver and spoke in an ordinary tone to another official in a neighboring room; but to reach the other man, his voice had traveled by wire and wave around the globe!

Of course, you may ask in vain at Washington and the telephone laboratories about that cipher machine. There might be another war!

In this 26-story Long Lines Building in New York, there are seven floors of switchboards! Fifty thousand long-distance calls come into New York City daily, and thirty thousand go out of it. Another of the interesting features of the building is the department which takes care of the radio broadcasting business for the whole country. Every program which is distributed over a network of stations, whether National, Columbia, Mutual or other system, is carried to each station by a telephone wire. Any important speech or event in no matter what remote part of the country may be clearly heard by every citizen because these clever chaps here in this building arrange a nation-wide "hook-up" for it, eliminating as nearly as possible all interfering noises, and because there are repeater stations in between, modestly doing their bit to amplify the sound. You find these men seated before mazes of switches, each with a clock, a Morse telegraph key, a head-set, a loud-speaker and a map of the network in which he is particularly interested. Their eyes, frequently glancing at the clock, become particularly alert as the quarter-hour approaches, when programs change. They are carefully testing the wires, listening for induction noises and other troubles. Already they know that there is sleet on the line at one place, a break at another, making detours, sometimes of two hundred miles or more, necessary. Trouble may conceivably arise in the very last minute or so before a program begins, making another hasty re-routing necessary.

Our guide turns on a musical program, coming from a New York studio. "Now I'll send it to Chicago and back by wire," he says. "See if you can detect any deterioration."

We would not have noticed any difference if we had not been expecting it. The impulse which had traveled nearly two thousand miles is what we would ordinarily call perfectly satisfactory reproduction.

"Now let's hear it directly from the studio and via Chicago simultaneously." Another touch, and now we hear the music slightly stuttering, as if an echo were quickly following it; for the sound shot over to Chicago and back is inevitably falling just a little behind that which must come only a few blocks. How much behind? About one-seventh of a second!

Seven-eighths of a century ago—in 1850, to be exact—when *Godey's Lady's Book* was the fashion leader of America, there was arising such a babble of imitators and competitors, such announcing of "anticipated styles" and "forecast styles" that Mr. Godey in his Arm-Chair page, remarked, in what he conceived to be the ultimate of satirical language, that he was hourly "expecting our contemporaries to advertise their fashions as received by *telegraph!*" How impossible for him to foresee that a few decades later, fashions, yea, even the photographs and drawings, would be traveling, not only by wire, but through the air. Had he been more familiar with science, he would have known that even as he wrote, pen and ink drawings or written page facsimiles could be sent by telegraph by Alexander Bain and one or two other men.

And even those first crude machines were built upon a principle which is a fundamental of the picture telegraph of to-day —a revolving cylinder which simultaneously moves slowly endwise. Around the cylinder of the modern machine your photograph is wrapped, face outward, and the drum begins to spin, turning a hundred times while it is moving an inch axially or endwise. Close alongside the end of it as it begins moving is a little black box, with a mere pinhole in it on the side next the drum, and through that hole you see a tiny spot of light falling on the photograph. There is another of those marvelous modern genii in that box—a photo-electric cell. As the drum revolves, the point of light covers a little square on the picture just one one-hundredth of an inch across. The drum, revolving and moving endwise, prolongs that spot into a spiral strip which covers the whole picture from end to end. The photo-electric eye "sees" the picture thoroughly and reports by wire or wave to a similar cell at the other terminus just what it sees—blacks, whites and all the delicate shadings in between; and that sister cell busily and faithfully reproduces upon a piece of unexposed photographic film—wrapped around a drum running in perfect synchronism with the first—just what it is told. Of course, the two cylinders must move in precise synchronism, and the receiving one must be enclosed in a light-proof case. When the resulting film is developed and printed, the result, if it comes by wire, is a photograph practically as good as the original. By air across the ocean, this is as yet a bit more difficult to accomplish, and an air photograph of a riot in Spain or the finish of the Grand National at Aintree still looks a bit fuzzy.

Nowadays, you may have telegrams sent in facsimile by this process if you wish to be certain that your message reaches the addressee without the slightest change, or desire a telegram that will go on the witness stand and testify that you sent it just as you claimed you did.

As this book goes to press, the Radio Corporation of America is just launching a new facsimile service between New York and Philadelphia, with a three-meter wave, the shortest and in some respects the most miraculous wave yet used. It reproduces a picture, letter, drawing or document at the rate of eight and one-half square inches per minute, therefore requiring six minutes to send a letter or picture six by eight inches in size. Two pictures can be sent simultaneously on the same wave, and two automatic typewriter channels and a telegraph channel for operation in both directions at the same time can be added. As the range of these extraordinarily short waves is limited to line-of-vision, two automatic relay stations are necessary to help or bend the waves around the earth's curvature. The first of these is thirty miles, the second sixty-six miles from New York, the latter being twenty-five miles from Philadelphia. Because of this line-of-sight limitation, new circuits can later be set up to and between other cities without any overlapping of the waves. Because of its enormous capacity, the cost of operation will be so reasonable that the RCA is actually expecting to take a great many letters away from the mails.

And how may one express one's wonder at the new co-axial cable which the American Telephone and Telegraph Company is at present bringing towards practicality—really a tube through which electro-magnetic waves are directed, instead of scattering them on the air. Hundreds of messages will pass through it simultaneously—two hundred and eighty-five is the present maximum estimate, though some engineers believe that it will eventually be set much higher!

Now that the machine is on the defensive, being charged with causing unemployment, the telephone magnates show no little sensitiveness over the dial telephone, and say that switchboard operators in large numbers are still needed. True, but not as many as formerly. They point to the fact that even in New York, large areas of the city are still on old-fashioned switchboard operation; and there are communities, they say, where the dial telephone may never be used—though one might warn them that this making of predictions has proven rather a futile business.

However, there is another aspect to the situation, the improvement in service brought about by the dial. Most people, this deponent included, were very unhappy when first compelled to use the dial telephone; it was so much easier just to lift the receiver and tell a genial young lady your wants. But we are becoming accustomed to steady increase in the complications of life; we soon learned that dialing is not such a chore, after all, and even though most of us may not have discovered it, the service is faster and less subject to error than when so much of it was done by human agency.

The story of the growth of the dial telephone is an amusing one, as well as being one of the wonder tales of invention. The Bell Telephone Company was scarcely started when two or three fellows began toying with the idea of automatic switching, but never got very far with it. Then, along in the 1880's, Almon

B. Strowger, an undertaker or, as we now say more elegantly, a mortician, in Kansas City, comes on the stage. Strowger had so much trouble with "busy" wires that he conceived the notion that a competitor had bribed the exchange operators to ruin his business by preventing his using the telephone. Why not, mused he, eliminate the fallible and corruptible telephone girl?

Perhaps he had heard of the slight gestures of other men towards automatic switching, perhaps he hadn't. Anyhow, he set to work seriously, and just had his first attempt assembled when Joe Harris, a "drummer" traveling out of Chicago, came in, hoping to make some sales to Strowger. In the course of the conversation, Strowger narrated his woes with the telephone, and showed Harris his first experimental machine, which, as we are solemnly assured, was made from a collar box, some pins and a lead pencil. "Others laughed at the 'crazy undertaker,'" said Harris, "but his fool contraption didn't seem funny to me."

So he kept in touch with Strowger as the latter's experiments progressed, until at last, in 1891, Strowger sold his business and went to Chicago, where, with Harris and others, he organized the Strowger Automatic Telephone Exchange. Fortunately, they brought in A. E. Keith, a young electrical engineer, lately with the Brush Electrical Company, and largely to his genius is due the modern automatic central or machine switching. Thirty years later, the Strowger factory covered ten acres of floor space and employed three thousand people.

The dial instrument of to-day seems to this writer to be the most nearly human robot that has yet been developed in electrical communication. Its workings cannot be adequately described in print without becoming depressingly technical. To be properly awed by its enormous complexity and by the speed and sureness with which so tangled a mechanism works, one should go behind the scenes in a great telephone exchange like one of the two hundred and fifty or thereabouts in New York City, each of which may have as high as 5,000 to 10,500 subscribers, all wanting at some time or other to talk to the million and a half other telephones in the city, not to mention suburbs and elsewhere.

An illustration herewith shows a selector frame, where your robot picks out trunk lines or numbers. Your call in New York City may have to go through six or eight frames like this before it is completed; and yet it is all done more quickly than a human operator could, as a general rule, connect you. As you look at the row upon row of these huge mechanisms, it is pretty difficult for you to imagine any process of evolution which could develop these from Strowger's collar box, pins and pencil. Notice in the picture the close-set rows of long rods with what appear to be knobs on them, running from the top of the frame to the bottom. Hundreds, thousands of wires run crosswise through the frame back of the rods. Those "knobs" hold little strips of metal called brushes; and when a call comes through a certain wire, the rod shoots upward until a brush finds and touches that wire. The knobs which you see in the picture dotted irregularly here and there indicate telephones which are in use at the moment.

Immediately when you take down your receiver, a brush in the line-finder frame leaps up to your wire, and you at once get the "dial tone"—a pleasant little humming sound by which the genie says, "I am ready for you." You begin dialing. Suppose you are calling my number in the Wadsworth exchange, WA3-1592. By the time you have finished dialing the WA3—perhaps ten miles uptown from where you are calling—the impulse has reached the Wadsworth exchange and picked out the 3 frame, and is waiting for the last four figures. A device actually had to be installed to restrain its impatience, because it acts faster than the human brain and finger. To describe the various selectors frames through which the impulse must go would involve too much technology for this book to attempt.

But this robot doesn't merely connect you with a number correctly dialed. It can deal with emergencies. Suppose you call a big concern which has three trunk lines, numbered 1200, 1201, and 1202. If you call 1200 and that is busy, the sagacious brush creeps up to 1201, and if that, too, is busy, it tries 1202. When

JUST A SMALL PORTION OF THE MACHINERY THAT IS RE-
QUIRED TO OPERATE YOUR DIAL TELEPHONE

a subscriber changes telephone numbers, the old number is left blank for a few months; and when people call it, as of course they invariably do, the dial robot turns them directly over to a group of switchboard girls who have little books before them with records of all these changes. If you make a mistake in your dialing and call a number which doesn't exist, the robot says, "Here, this is beyond me," and turns you over to a girl whose duty it is to take care of thoughtless persons like yourself.

In New York there is a peculiar problem, in that a portion of the city is still on the old manual system—that is, the sort with a switchboard and human operators. Calls are passing continually from exchanges of one sort to the other. How do they manage it? Well, from manual to dial switching, it is easy. In every dial exchange, there is a switchboard for that particular purpose. The girls there receive by ear the calls from the manual exchanges and press buttons in the table before them with the required letters and figures on them—which operates the selectors just as if the number had been dialed.

But to transmit back from dial to manual—ah, that was a proposition which caused many corrugated brows. But the telephone engineers worked it out; they always do. They found a girl with a fine voice and well-nigh perfect enunciation, and caused her to speak the names of the ten digits into a sort of phonograph wherein a needle recorded the sounds on strips of celluloid. A strip of each digit was then mounted on a different cylinder in a machine. One cylinder says nothing but "One," another "Two" and so on. Now when you dial, say, Murray Hill 2-4618, the automatic switch connects you instantly with a girl at the Murray Hill 2 switchboard, and commands Cylinders 4, 6, 1, and 8 to speak to her. At the same speed at which another operator would pronounce the figures, she hears "4, 6, 1, 8," as naturally as if it came from another operator; in fact, the girls have frequently said that they cannot tell whether the call is coming from a dial or a manual exchange.

The dial telephone, as every one has discovered, knows when you have talked your three-minute quota from a public call box, and summons an operator, who demands another nickel from you. It also registers every call from your private telephone in the office "ledger," which is a huge bank of automatic counting machines, one machine for every subscriber. But some calls, even in New York City, cost ten cents and some fifteen. For example, if I call far-away Flushing—still inside the city limits—from my home in Manhattan, the charge is fifteen cents, and the knowing machine clicks my counter three times instead of one. So far, it cannot count higher than three, but give it time; it will learn.

And so the big city switchboard, with its 2,000,000 parts, upon which toiling inventors through half a century past have been granted more than a thousand patents, is slowly losing ground. It will continue to be used for many years yet in smaller communities, but in New York City (and others) as the boards now in use deteriorate, they will be replaced by dial switching.

The handset, or as we have been calling it, the French telephone, is another newcomer of recent years, about which an amusing story may be told. It's a joke on us, for this isn't a French device at all, but an American one which we tossed away. Away back in the latter '70's, when the telephone was in its infancy, there was a young technician named Robert G. Brown working for the Gold and Stock Telegraph Company in New York. The G. and S. was then using the Edison transmitter and a receiver invented by George Phelps. As was the necessary custom then, you held the transmitter in one hand and the receiver in the other. Brown, wearied with this labor, conceived the idea of fastening them together with a short, curved rod, so that the user could have one hand free.

Just as the Western Union was about to succumb to the Bell Company in the Dowd suit in 1879, Brown was invited to France to be chief engineer for the French Government system of telephones, just being installed, and he took his handset with him. If the Bell Company ever heard of it, they were not interested in any silly gadget that a Western Union man might have produced. So the handset was introduced first in France, then

THE PALACE OF ALADDIN

spread to England and other European countries. Independent telephone companies in America began using a handset years before the A. T. & T. adopted it. The latter's engineers were laboring for a smaller magnet and a more rugged construction, which could endure the frequent rough banging of the instrument back on its stand, and they had these before they brought the handset into their own system.

Morse and Wheatstone, Bell and Gray, Hertz and Fleming and Fessenden have passed away; but what miracles have Marconi and de Forest and Alexanderson and dozens of other still living scientists who have contributed to wire and wave communication seen come to pass in their own lifetimes, none of them as yet overlong! Never has a new science developed and grown to giant size in so brief a span of time as wireless communication. It and its older sisters are still developing so rapidly that it would be presumptuous to say that one has completed a history of them, a story which may be out of date almost before the ink upon its pages is dry.

As the writer closes this book, he is impressed and depressed by the conviction that in a single volume of five hundred pages or thereabouts, one can draw only a charcoal sketch of the triple-headed subject. It is so vast that a fair picture of it, drawn with the detail which Alma-Tadema loved, would occupy several volumes—and then nobody would read it. Merely to call the roll of the hundreds of inventors who, by their genius and toil, have contributed to the art and name all their achievements would fill a not-inconsiderable volume. Only a few of the more noted ones have been mentioned herein, as well as a scant selection from the list of promoters, capitalists, executives and other functionaries who have helped to make our communication system what it is. To all the others, an inclusive tribute of admiration and gratitude is hereby given.

BIBLIOGRAPHY

Anything resembling a full bibliography on the subject of wire and wave communication would fill a whole volume such as this. There have been thousands of pamphlets written on these subjects; magazine and newspaper articles, technical and non-technical, are as the sands of the sea; the lawsuits over patents are too numerous to consider; every cla·s of literature on the subject is voluminous, and many titles must necessarily be omitted. First are quoted the leading books, pamphlets and magazine articles.

Account of the Experiments Made by some Gentlemen of the Royal Society, An... (London, 1748).

Addresses at the Unveiling of the Joseph Henry Statue at Washington, April 19, 1883, by Chief Justice Waite, Chancellor of the Smithsonian Institution, and Noah Porter, President of Yale College (Washington, 1884).

Age of Humbug, The (Chicago, 1869).

ALBERT, ARTHUR LEMUEL.—*Electrical Communication* (New York, and London, 1934).

AMERICAN TELEGRAPH CONVENTION.—*Proceedings* (Philadelphia, 1853).

ANGLO-AMERICAN TELEGRAPH COMPANY (LIMITED).—*Agreements* (London, 1867).

Atlantic Cable Mismanagement; Correspondence between J. W. Simonton, Cyrus W. Field and Others (New York, 1871).

BAARSLAG, KARL.—*SOS to the Rescue* (New York, 1935).

BAKEWELL, F. C.—*Electric Science* (London, 1853).

BANCROFT, HUBERT HOWE.—*Chronicles of the Builders* (San Francisco, 1890-92).

Banquet to Elisha Gray, Inventor of the Telephone, at Highland Park, Illinois, November 15, 1878 (Chicago, 1878).

BATES, DAVID HOMER.—*Lincoln in the Telegraph Office* (New York, 1907).

——— *Lincoln Stories* (New York, 1926).

BEESLEY, LAWRENCE.—*The Loss of the Steamship Titanic, its Story and its Lessons* (Boston, 1912).

BELL, ALEXANDER GRAHAM.—*The Bell Telephone* (Deposition in suit brought by United States) (Boston, 1908).

BELL, ALEXANDER GRAHAM.—*The Telephone; a Lecture* (London and New York, 1878).

Bell Patents, The Decisions of the Patent Office and the Courts Sustaining the Patents and Defining their Scope (Boston, 1885).

BOCOCK, JOHN PAUL.—"The Romance of the Telephone," *Munsey's Magazine*, November, 1900.

BRIGGS, CHARLES F. and MAVERICK, AUGUSTUS.—*The Story of the Telegraph and a History of the Great Atlantic Cable* (New York, 1858).

BRIGHT, CHARLES.—*The Evolution of the Submarine Telegraph* (London, 1904).

BRIGHT, EDWARD BRAILSFORD.—*The Life Story of the Late Sir Charles Tilston Bright* (Westminster, England, 1899).

British Telegraph Monopoly, The (n.p., 1858).

BRYAN, GEORGE S.—*Edison, the Man and His Work* (New York, 1926).

BUREAU OF FRANCHISES, BOARD OF ESTIMATE AND APPOINTMENT, NEW YORK CITY.—*Result of Investigation of the Operation of a Dual System of Telephones in Various Cities* (New York, 1906).

BYRN, E. W.—*Progress of Invention in the Nineteenth Century* (New York, 1900).

CARNEAL, GEORGETTE.—*Conqueror of Space: Life of Lee de Forest* (New York, 1930).

CARNEGIE, ANDREW.—*Autobiography* (Boston and New York, 1920).

CARTY, JOHN J.—*Telephone Service in America* (New York, 1910).

CASSON, HERBERT N.—*History of the Telephone* (Chicago, 1910).

CAVALLO, TIBERIUS.—*A Complete Treatise on Electricity*, 3 volumes (London, 1795).

CHIEF SIGNAL OFFICER.—*Report of, to Secretary of War* (Washington, 1919).

CLAMPITT, JOHN W.—*Echoes from the Rocky Mountains* (New York and San Francisco, 1889).

COLLINS, FRANCIS A.—*The Wireless Man* (New York, 1914).

COOKE, T. FOTHERGILL.—*Invention of the Electric Telegraph. The Charge Against Sir Charles Wheatstone of Tampering with the Press* (London and Bath, 1869).

―――― *The Electric Telegraph; was it Invented by Professor Wheatstone?* (London, 1854).

CORNELL, ALONZO B.—*History of the Electro-Magnetic Telegraph* (Schenectady, 1894).

BIBLIOGRAPHY

(————) *True and Firm. Biography of Ezra Cornell* (New York, 1884).

COUTANT, C. G.—*History of Wyoming and the Far West* (Laramie, Wyoming, 1899).

COVINGTON, S. F.—*The Postal Telegraph* (n.p., 1875).

CRAIG, DANIEL H.—*Answer of ... to the United States Commission on Education and Labor* (New York, 1883).

———— *A Review of "An Exposition of the Differences Existing between Different Presses and Different Lines of Telegraph Respecting the Transmission of Foreign News," etc.* (Halifax, Nova Scotia, 1850).

CRAWLEY, CHETWODE G.—*From Telegraphy to Television* (London, 1931).

DANA, CHARLES A.—*Recollections of the Civil War* (New York, 1899).

DESPECHER, JULES.—*Projet de Télégraphe Transatlantique* (Paris, 1863).

DICKERSON, E. N.—*Argument of, for Complainants, in American Bell Telephone Company, against People's Telephone Company, et al.* (Boston, 1884).

———— *Joseph Henry and the Magnetic Telegraph* (New York, 1885).

DICKSON, W. K. L. and DICKSON, A.—*Life and Inventions of Thomas Alva Edison* (New York, 1892).

DOLBEAR, A. E.—*The Telephone* (Boston and New York, 1877).

DRESSLER, ALBERT, Editor.—*California Chinese Chatter* (San Francisco, 1927).

DU MONCEL, THEODORE A. L.—*The Telephone, the Microphone and the Phonograph* (New York, 1879).

DYER, FRANK LEWIS, and MARTIN, THOMAS COMMERFORD.—*Edison, His Life and Inventions,* 2 volumes (New York and London, 1910).

ECKERT, THOMAS T.—*Memorandum Concerning the Petitions of Typographical Unions, Printers and Others for a Government Telegraph* (New York, 1894).

EDGEWORTH, RICHARD LOVELL.—*Letter to Lord Charlemont on the Tellograph and the Defense of Ireland* (Dublin, 1797).

———— *Memoirs of, begun by himself and concluded by his Daughter, Maria Edgeworth* (London, 3rd edition, 1844).

EXECUTIVE COMMITTEE, NATIONAL TELEGRAPH COMPANY.—*Report ... on Little's Automatic System of Fast Telegraphy* (New York, 1869).

Exposure of the Schemes for Nullifying the O'Rielly Contract (St. Louis, 1848).

FAHIE, J. J.—*A History of Electric Telegraphy to the Year 1837* (London, 1884).

────── *History of Wireless Telegraphy* (Edinburgh and London, 1900).

FERGUSON, R. M.—*Electricity* (London and Edinburgh, 1867).

FIELD, HENRY M.—*The Story of the Atlantic Telegraph* (New York, 1866).

FLOOD, JOHN P.—*History of Company C., 304th Field Signal Battalion, United States Army* (Philadelphia, 1920).

FOREMAN, EDWARD R.—"The Henry O'Rielly Documents in the Archives of the Rochester Historical Society," *Rochester Historical Society Publication Fund Series,* Vol. IX, 1930.

GIFFORD, WALTER S.—*Addresses, Papers and Interviews* (New York, 1928).

GOODE, GEORGE B.—*An Account of the Smithsonian Institution* (Washington, 1895).

GRACIE, ARCHIBALD.—*The Truth about the Titanic* (New York, 1913).

GRAY, THOMAS.—*The Inventors of the Telegraph and Telephone* (*in Smithsonian Institution Report for 1892*) (Washington, 1893).

GREELY, MAJOR-GENERAL A. W.—*Reminiscences of Adventure and Service* (New York and London, 1927).

HARBORD, GENERAL JAMES G.—*World Wireless* (Princeton, 1936).

HARRISON, H. H.—*Printing Telegraph Systems and Mechanisms* (London, 1923).

HAUPT, GENERAL HERMAN.—*Reminiscences* (Milwaukee, 1901).

HAYES, JEFF W.—*Autographs and Memories of the Telegraph* (Adrian, Michigan, 1916).

HERBERT, THOMAS E.—*Telegraphy; a Detailed Exposition of the Telegraph System of the British Post Office* (London, 1906).

HIGHTON, E.—*The Electric Telegraph; its History and Progress* (London, 1852).

HILL, LYSANDER.—*Argument of, in support of the Drawbaugh Defense, before United States Circuit Court, Philadelphia, January 23, 1884* (New York, 1884).

History Getting Right on the Invention of the Telegraph (Washington, 1872).

HOUSTON, EDWIN J.—Articles on Philipp Reis and his telegraph, *Journal of the Franklin Institute,* January, October, 1887.

BIBLIOGRAPHY

HUBBARD, GARDINER G.—*The Proposed Changes in the Telegraphic System* (Boston, 1873).

Intercontinental Telegraph, Papers Relating to the (Washington, 1864).

International Wireless Telegraph Convention concluded between Germany, the United States of America, France, Great Britain (and twenty-three other nations) (Washington, 1907).

JOHNSTON, W. J.—*Telegraphic Tales and Telegraphic History* (New York, 1882).

JONES, ALEXANDER.—*Historical Sketch of the Electric Telegraph* (New York, 1852).

JONES, FRANCIS ARTHUR.—*Life Story of Thomas Alva Edison* (New York, 1908).

JUDSON, ISABELLA FIELD.—*Cyrus W. Field, his Life and Work* (New York, 1896).

KAEMPFFERT, WALDEMAR.—*A Popular History of American Invention* (New York, 1924).

KENDALL, AMOS.—*Morse's Patent; Full Exposure of Dr. Charles T. Jackson's Pretensions to the Invention of the American Electro-Magnetic Telegraph . . .* (New York, 1850).

KINGSBURY, J. E.—*The Telephone, and Telephone Exchanges* (London and New York, 1915).

KINTNER, S. M.—"Pittsburgh's Contributions to Radio," *Proceedings of Institute of Radio Engineers*, Vol. 20, p. 1849.

LAVINE, A. LINCOLN.—*Circuits of Victory* (Garden City, New York, 1921).

LEFFERTS, MARSHALL.—"The Electric Telegraph," *Bulletin of American Geographic and Statistical Survey*, 1856.

McCALLUM, DAVID.—*The Globotype Telegraph* (London, 1856).

MACKAY, CLARENCE H.—*Extracts from Testimony given before a Committee of the Legislature of the State of New York, January 21, 1910* (New York, 1910).

MACKENZIE, CATHERINE.—*Alexander Graham Bell* (Boston and New York, 1928).

MANNERING, MITCHELL.—"Government Ownership of Telephones," *National Magazine*, Boston, July, 1904.

MARCONI, G.—*The Progress of Wireless Telegraphy* (New York, 1912).

—— *Wireless Telegraphy* (*Smithsonian Institution Report for 1901*) (Washington, 1902).

Memorial of Samuel Finley Breese Morse, A, Published by Order of Congress (Washington, 1875).

531

Memorial of Samuel F. B. Morse, A, from the City of Boston
(Boston, 1872).

MENDENHALL, T. C.—*A Century of Electricity* (Boston, 1892).

MERRIAM, AUGUSTUS C.—"Telegraphing Among the Ancients,"
Papers of the Archaeological Institute of America, Classical
Series III, Cambridge, 1890.

MERWIN, H. C.—"The Telephone Case" and "Dan Drawbaugh,"
Atlantic Monthly, July and September, 1888.

MICHAUD, L.—*Histoire Complète des Télégraphes* (Geneva and
Paris, 1855).

MILLS, JOHN.—Pamphlets: *The Magic of Communication, The
Last Word in Telephotography, Some Universal Principles of
Communication, Through Electrical Eyes, etc.,* various dates.

MINISTER OF MINES.—*Report of, for the year 1905 ... of the
Province of British Columbia* (Victoria, B. C., 1906).

MOIGNO, L'ABBÉ.—*Traité de Télégraphie Electrique,* Second Edition (Paris, 1852).

*Monopoly of the Electric Telegraph. Remarks on the Decision of
Judge Kane in the Case of French against Rogers and others*
(New York, 1851).

MORSE, EDWARD LIND.—*Samuel F. B. Morse, his Letters and Journals,* 2 volumes (Boston and New York, 1914).

MORSE, SAMUEL F. B.—*Examination of the Telegraphic Apparatus
and the Processes in Telegraphy* (Washington, 1869).

—— *Modern Telegraphy* (Paris, 1867).

MOTT, EDWARD HAROLD.—*Between the Ocean and the Lakes; the
Story of Erie* (New York, 1899).

MULLALY, JOHN.—*The First Atlantic Telegraph Cable* (Philadelphia, 1907).

—— *The Laying of the Cable; or the Ocean Telegraph* (New
York, 1858).

NATIONAL IMPROVED TELEPHONE COMPANY.—*A Concise Statement
of Facts, with Admissions by Alexander Graham Bell, Showing that he did not Invent the Telephone, etc.* (New Orleans,
1886 ?).

NERNEY, MARY CHILDS.—*Thomas A. Edison, a Modern Olympian*
(New York, 1934).

NICOLAY, JOHN G. and HAY, JOHN.—*Abraham Lincoln; a History*
(New York, 1890).

*Ocean Telegraphy; the Twenty-fifth Anniversary of the Organiza-
tion of the First Company ever formed to lay an Ocean Cable,*
(New York, March 10, 1879).

BIBLIOGRAPHY

O'RIELLY, HENRY.—*Christopher Colles and the First Proposal of a Telegraph System in the United States* (Morrisania, New York, 1869).

—— "Materials for a Telegraphic History," *Historical Magazine and Notes and Queries,* Series 2, vol. 5, Morrisania, N. Y., January-June, 1869.

—— *Telegraph material; letters, documents, pamphlets, circulars, newspaper clippings, etc.,* 51 volumes, 31 boxes, New York Historical Society, 1845-1860.

PAINE, ALBERT BIGELOW.—*In One Man's Life* (New York and London, 1921).

PARIS, COMTE DE.—*History of the Civil War in America* (Philadelphia, 1875-1888).

PARKER, JANE MARSH.—"How Men of Rochester Saved the Telegraph," *Rochester Historical Society Publication Fund Series,* vol. 5, Rochester, 1926.

PARSONS, FRANK.—*The Telegraph Monopoly* (Philadelphia, 1899).

PHILLIPS, WALTER P.—*Sketches Old and New* (New York, 1897).

PLUM, WILLIAM R.—*The Military Telegraph during the Civil War in the United States,* 2 volumes (Chicago, 1882).

POPE, FRANKLIN LEONARD.—"The American Inventors of the Telegraph," *Century Magazine,* April, 1888.

—— *Modern Practice of the Electric Telegraph* (New York, 1870).

POPHAM, SIR HOME.—*Telegraphic Signals or Marine Vocabulary* (London, 1803).

POUND, ARTHUR.—*The Telephone Idea; Fifty Years After* (New York, 1926).

PRESCOTT, GEORGE BARTLETT.—*Bell's Electric Speaking Telephone* (New York, 1884).

—— *The Electric Telephone* (New York, 1890).

—— *Electricity and the Electric Telegraph* (New York, 8th edition, 1892).

—— *History, Theory and Practice of the Electric Telegraph* (Boston, 1860).

PRIME, SAMUEL IRENAEUS.—*Life of Samuel F. B. Morse, LL.D.* (New York, 1875).

Prospectus of a Company for the Introduction of the Electric Telegraph across the Isthmus from Aspinwall to Panama, New Granada (Baltimore, 1852).

READ, FREDERICK BRENT.—*Up to the Heights of Fame and Fortune* (Cincinnati, 1873).

REID, JAMES D.—*The Telegraph in America* (New York, 1886).

REIS, PHILIPP.—"Telephoning by means of the Electric Current" (From *Annual Report of the Physical Society of Frankfort-on-the-Main, 1860-61*) (Frankfort, 1862).

Remonstrance against the Petition of Peter Cooper and others Respecting Exclusive Privileges in Relation to a Sub-Marine Telegraph Cable between Europe and America, A (Boston, 1857).

Report of the Committee Appointed by the Citizens of Louisville to Examine the Subject of the Telegraph, and the Responses of the Chairman of the Committee to the Hon. Amos Kendall's Attack upon the Committee (n.p., 1847).

RHODES, FREDERICK LELAND.—*The Beginnings of Telephony* (New York and London, 1929).

——— *John J. Carty; an Appreciation* (New York, 1932).

RICH, JOSEPH S.—*Some Notes on the Telegraph Companies of the United States; their Stamps and Franks* (New York, 1900).

RONALDS, FRANCIS.—*Descriptions of an Electrical Telegraph; and some other Electrical Apparatus* (London, 1823).

ROOT, FRANK A., and CONNELLY, WILLIAM ELSEY.—*The Overland Stage to California* (Topeka, 1901).

ROSTRON, SIR ARTHUR H.—*Home from the Sea* (New York, 1931).

RUSSELL, R. W.—*History of the Invention of the Electric Telegraph* (New York, 1853).

RUSSELL, WILLIAM H.—*The Atlantic Telegraph* (London, 1866).

SABINE, R.—*History and Progress of the Electric Telegraph* (New York, 1869).

SCHAUBLE, PETER LAMBERT.—*The First Battalion; the Story of the 406th Telegraph Battalion, Signal Corps* (Philadelphia, 1921).

SCHELLEN, H. D.—*Der Electromagnetische Telegraph* (Brunswick, Germany, 1867).

SHAFFNER, TALIAFERRO P.—*The Telegraph Manual* (New York, 1859).

SIBLEY, HIRAM W.—"Memoirs of Hiram Sibley," *Rochester Historical Society Publication Fund Series,* Vol. 2 (Rochester, 1923).

SMITH, JOSEPH M.—*History of the 412th Battalion, United States Signal Corps* (n.p., 1929).

SMITHSONIAN INSTITUTION.—*Extract from the Proceedings of the Board of Regents of the, in Reference to the Electro-magnetic Telegraph* (Washington, 1857).

——— *Report for 1857* (Washington, 1858).

SPRING, AGNES WRIGHT.—*Casper Collins; the Life and Exploits of an Indian Fighter of the Sixties* (New York, 1927).

BIBLIOGRAPHY

SQUIER, GEORGE O., MAJOR.—*Multiplex Telephony and Telegraphy* (Washington, 1911).
—— *Telling the World* (Baltimore, 1933).
STONE, EDITH W.—"Joseph Henry," *Scientific Monthly*, September, 1931.
STONE, MELVILLE E.—*Fifty Years a Journalist* (Garden City, New York, and Toronto, 1921).
STRANGER, RALPH.—*Wireless, the Modern Magic Carpet* (London, 1928).
SUMNER, CHARLES A.—*The Postal Telegraph* (San Francisco, 1879).
SWAN, WILLIAM UPHAM.—"Early Visual Telegraphs in Massachusetts," *Proceedings of the Bostonian Society for 1933* (Boston, 1933).
TAYLOR, WILLIAM B.—*An Historical Sketch of Henry's Contribution to the Electro-Magnetic Telegraph* (Washington, 1879).
—— *A Memoir of Joseph Henry* (Philadelphia, 1879).
TEGG, WILLIAM.—*Posts and Telegraphs, Past and Present* (London, 1878).
THOMPSON, SILVANUS P.—*Philipp Reis, Inventor of the Telephone* (London and New York, 1883).
TOWERS, WALTER KELLOGG.—*Masters of Space* (New York and London, 1917).
TUCK, LIEUTENANT OSWALD T.—"The Old Telegraph," *Fighting Forces*, London, 1924.
TURNBULL, LAWRENCE.—*The Electro-Magnetic Telegraph* (Philadelphia, 1852).
UNITED STATES DEPARTMENT OF COMMERCE AND LABOR.—*Investigation of Western Union and Postal Telegraph Cable Companies* (Washington, 1909).
UNITED STATES PATENT OFFICE.—*The Speaking Telephone Interferences* (Washington, 1880).
UNITED STATES REPORTS, SUPREME COURT.—October term, 1887, Vol. 126, *The Telephone Cases* (New York and Albany, 1888).
USHER, ELLIS B.—"The Telegraph in Wisconsin," *Proceedings State Historical Society of Wisconsin for 1913* (Madison, 1914).
VAIL, ALFRED.—*Description of the American Electro-Magnetic Telegraph* (Washington, 1845).
VAIL, J. CUMMINGS.—*The American Electro-Magnetic Telegraph; its Early History as Shown by Extracts from the Records of Alfred Vail; Arranged by his son, J. Cummings Vail* (New York, 1914).

VAIL, DR. WILLIAM P.—"The First Week of the Telegraph," *Hours at Home* (Scribner), September, 1869.

VAN RENSSELAER, CORTLANDT.—*Signals from the Atlantic Cable* (Philadelphia, 1858).

WATSON, THOMAS A.—*The Birth and Babyhood of the Telephone* (New York, 1913).

—— *Exploring Life* (New York and London, 1926).

WHEATSTONE, SIR CHARLES.—*A Reply to Mr. Cooke's Pamphlet, "The Electric Telegraph; was it invented by Professor Wheatstone?"* (London, 1855).

WILE, FREDERICK WILLIAM.—*Emile Berliner, Maker of the Microphone* (Indianapolis, 1926).

WILLIAMS, ARCHIBALD.—*Telegraphy and Telephony* (London, 1928).

WILSON, BEN HUR.—"Telegraph Pioneering," *Palimpsest* (State Historical Society of Iowa Publication), November, 1925.

WILSON, WILLIAM BENDER.—*A Few Acts and Actors in the Tragedy of the Civil War in the United States* (Philadelphia, 1892).

—— *A Glimpse of the United States Military Telegraph Corps and of Abraham Lincoln* (Holmesburg, Pennsylvania, 1889).

Wireless and Shipping; a Record of Progress (London, 1932).

WOODBURY, C. J. H.—*The Telephone System of Today* (New York, 1903).

PERIODICALS

American Telegraph Magazine, 1852-1853
American Telephone Journal, 1900-1908
Annales Télégraphiques, Paris, 1855-1899
Bell System Technical Journal, 1922-1935
Bell Telephone Quarterly, 1922-1936
Institute of Radio Engineers, Proceedings, 1913-1936
International System News, 1929-1933
Journal of the Telegraph, 1868-1914
Journal Telegraphique, Berlin, 1869-1933
Long Lines Magazine, 1921-1936
Marconi Review, London, 1932-1936
Marconigraph, 1911-1913
National Radio News, 1928-1931
National Telegraph Review and Operator's Companion, 1853-1854

BIBLIOGRAPHY

Old Time Telegraphers' and Historical Association, Annual Reunion, 1904, 1910, 1916
Radio, 1920-1936
Radio Age, 1922-1928
Radio News and the Short Wave, 1919-1935
RCA News, 1921-1932
Shaffner's Telegraph Companion, 1854-1855
Telegrapher, The, 1864-1877
Telephone Engineer, 1909-1935
Telephone Magazine, 1893-1905
Telephone Review, 1910-1935
Telephony, 1907-1935
Wireless Age, 1913-1925

Also frequent articles in the following:

American Institute of Electrical Engineers Proceedings, 1901-1935
American Journal of Science (Silliman), 1837-1935
Annales de Chimie et de Physique, Paris, 1790-1913
Annals of Electricity (Sturgeon), London, 1837-1843
Annals of Philosophy (T. Thomson), London, 1813-1826
Electrical Age, 1891-1910
Electrical Engineer, London, 1888-1912
Electrical Engineering, 1903-1919
Electrical Review, 1883-1933
Electrical World, 1883-1935
Journal für Chemie und Physik (J. S. C. Schweigger), Nurenberg, 1806-1833
Journal of the Franklin Institute, 1826-1835
Journal de Physique, de Chimie, d'histoire naturelle et des Arts, Paris, 1773-1819
London, Edinburgh and Dublin Philosophical Magazine and Journal of Science, 1800-1935
Popular Science Monthly, 1872-1936
Quarterly Journal of Science and the Arts, Royal Institute of Great Britain, London, 1816-1850
Scientific American, 1851-1936
Scientific Monthly, 1915-1935
Technical World Magazine, 1904-1915

OLD WIRES AND NEW WAVES

Likewise numerous articles not so technical in such magazines as the *Arena, Independent, Nation, Literary Digest, Current Opinion, Harper's Weekly, Leslie's Weekly,* etc.

MISCELLANEOUS

Congressional Committee Reports on Government Telegraph, 1845, 1869, 1870, 1872, 1874, 1875, 1881, 1883, 1884, 1890, 1896.
Congressional Globe and Record, 1844-1936
Postmaster-General's Reports, 1845-1895
United States Census Reports, 1860-1930
United States Statistics Bureau. Commerce and Labor Department, Reports—Monthly Summaries of Commerce and Finance.
Telegraph Suits.—Samuel F. B. Morse and Alfred Vail *vs.* Francis O. J. Smith; Benjamin B. French *et al. vs.* Henry J. Rogers *et al.;* Henry O'Rielly *et al. vs.* S. F. B. Morse *et al.;* Alexander Bain *vs.* Samuel F. B. Morse; Samuel F. B. Morse, Alfred Vail and Francis O. J. Smith *vs.* Henry O'Rielly, Eugene L. Whitman and W. F. Hastings; Francis O. J. Smith *vs.* Hugh Downing and many others.
Telephone Suits.—Bell Telephone Company *vs.* Peter A. Dowd; Bell Telephone Company *vs.* Albert Spencer *et al.;* Amos E. Dolbear *vs.* American Bell Telephone Company; Molecular Telephone Company *vs.* American Bell Telephone Company; American Bell Telephone Company *vs.* Molecular Telephone Company; Overland Telephone Company *vs.* American Bell Telephone Company; American Bell Telephone Company *vs.* People's Telephone Company; Clay Commercial Telephone Company *vs.* American Bell Telephone Company; United States *vs.* American Bell Telephone Company; United States *vs.* American Bell Telephone Company and Emil Berliner; and nearly 600 others regarding the Bell patents.
Wireless Suits.—National Electric Signalling Company *vs.* De Forest Wireless Telegraph Company; Marconi Wireless Telegraph Company *vs.* De Forest Wireless Telegraph Company; Westinghouse Electric and Manufacturing Company *vs.* De Forest Wireless Telegraph Company; de Forest *vs.* Westinghouse and Armstrong, and many more.

INDEX

539

INDEX

541

INDEX

INDEX

545

(1)

HISTORY OF BROADCASTING:
Radio To Television
An Arno Press/New York Times Collection

Archer, Gleason L.
Big Business and Radio. 1939.

Archer, Gleason L.
History of Radio to 1926. 1938.

Arnheim, Rudolf.
Radio. 1936.

Blacklisting: Two Key Documents. 1952–1956.

Cantril, Hadley and Gordon W. Allport.
The Psychology of Radio. 1935.

Codel, Martin, editor.
Radio and Its Future. 1930.

Cooper, Isabella M.
Bibliography on Educational Broadcasting. 1942.

Dinsdale, Alfred.
First Principles of Television. 1932.

Dunlap, Orrin E., Jr.
Marconi: The Man and His Wireless. 1938.

Dunlap, Orrin E., Jr.
The Outlook for Television. 1932.

Fahie, J. J.
A History of Wireless Telegraphy. 1901.

Federal Communications Commission.
Annual Reports of the Federal Communications Commission.
1934/1935–1955.

Federal Radio Commission.
Annual Reports of the Federal Radio Commission. 1927–1933.

Frost, S. E., Jr.
Education's Own Stations. 1937.

Grandin, Thomas.
The Political Use of the Radio. 1939.

Harlow, Alvin.
Old Wires and New Waves. 1936.

Hettinger, Herman S.
A Decade of Radio Advertising. 1933.

Huth, Arno.
Radio Today: The Present State of Broadcasting. 1942.

Jome, Hiram L.
Economics of the Radio Industry. 1925.

Lazarsfeld, Paul F.
Radio and the Printed Page. 1940.

Lumley, Frederick H.
Measurement in Radio. 1934.

Maclaurin, W. Rupert.
Invention and Innovation in the Radio Industry. 1949.

Radio: Selected A.A.P.S.S. Surveys. 1929–1941.

Rose, Cornelia B., Jr.
National Policy for Radio Broadcasting. 1940.

Rothafel, Samuel L. and Raymond Francis Yates.
Broadcasting: Its New Day. 1925.

Schubert, Paul.
The Electric Word: The Rise of Radio. 1928.

Studies in the Control of Radio: Nos. 1–6. 1940–1948.

Summers, Harrison B., editor.
Radio Censorship. 1939.

Summers, Harrison B., editor.
**A Thirty-Year History of Programs Carried on
National Radio Networks in the United States, 1926–1956.** 1958.

Waldrop, Frank C. and Joseph Borkin.
Television: A Struggle for Power. 1938.

White, Llewellyn.
The American Radio. 1947.

World Broadcast Advertising: Four Reports. 1930–1932.